THE GOLDEN LYRE

THE GOLDEN LYRE

The Themes of the Greek Lyric Poets

DAVID A. CAMPBELL

DUCKWORTH

First published in 1983 by
Gerald Duckworth & Co. Ltd
The Old Piano Factory
43 Gloucester Crescent, London NW1

© 1983 by David A. Campbell

ISBN 0 7156 1563 7 (cased)

British Library Cataloguing in Publication Data

Campbell, D. A.
    The golden lyre.
    1. Greek poetry—Translations into Englısn
    2. English poetry—Translations in Greek
    I. Title
    884'.01'08   PA3622

    ISBN 0-7156-1563-7

Filmset in Monophoto Baskerville by
Latimer Trend & Company Ltd, Plymouth
Printed in Great Britain by
Ebenezer Baylis and Son Ltd
The Trinity Press, Worcester and London

Contents

For Alison, Helen and Fiona

εὐπλοκάμοις θυγατράσι

Preface

Most books on Greek lyric poetry begin at the beginning and work through to the end. This one differs in that I begin at the beginning several times over in order to examine how the most important lyric themes were handled by successive poets. I have also cast a backward glance to Homer and Hesiod when it seemed helpful to show what the predecessors of the lyric poets had done. I put the lower boundary in the mid-fifth century B.C.: Ion and Euenus are included but not Critias and Timotheus.

My book is intended for various groups of readers: students of Greek Lyric in Translation; students of the Greek language coming to Lyric for the first time; and poetry-lovers who want to know what the Greek lyric poets wrote about. All the Greek has been rendered in a deliberately graceless translation in the hope that this will give more assistance to those who have little or no knowledge of the Greek language.

I should like to acknowledge most gratefully the assistance of Rosemary Harriott, who has given wise advice at all stages of the work, Niall Rudd and Sam Scully, who made helpful comments on Chapters 1 and 5 respectively, and Nancy Nasser, who typed the manuscript with unfailing patience and great skill. I am grateful also for the award of a Leave Fellowship by the Social Sciences and Humanities Research Council of Canada which enabled me to enjoy six months of Study Leave in 1979, and for a number of Faculty Research Grants awarded by the University of Victoria.

D.A.C.

Introductory Note

The study of Greek lyric poetry is a frustrating business. We have to deal with mere fragments of poems except for the works of Theognis and the victory-odes of Pindar, which have been transmitted by a regular manuscript tradition. Although Alexandrian scholars of the third century B.C. and later gathered the works of Sappho, Anacreon, Bacchylides and others and arranged them in books, those books were not continuously copied in later ages and do not survive.

The fragments have reached us haphazardly by two routes: (1) they are quoted in the works of other writers who were interested in their content, dialect, syntax, grammar or metre: for example, the opening lines of some of Sappho's poems are in Hephaestion's manual (2nd c. A.D.) to illustrate various metres, and lines of Anacreon (398) are quoted by a Homeric scholar in his enquiry into the gender of the word for 'dice'; in these circumstances we are lucky if we are given a complete sentence, very lucky if we have a complete poem: Sappho 1 is quoted in its entirety by the critic Dionysius (1st c. B.C.) as an example of a certain style of composition; (2) they have turned up on scraps of papyrus found in the sands of Egypt; usually the papyrus is severely damaged, and the poems are things of shreds and patches. Editors have displayed the greatest skill and ingenuity in their decipherment; their supplements of defective texts are conventionally shown in square brackets.

CHAPTER ONE

Love

The Homeric gods and heroes made love, and Homer has formulaic expressions to describe the activity. The commonest belongs to the type *philotēti migēmenai*, a colourless phrase meaning 'to be united in love': colourless since the noun *philotēs* may just as readily be used of friendship as of lovemaking. Slightly less pallid is a formula of the kind *eunēi d'ou pot' emikto* 'he had never been united with her in bed'; and the two nouns may be used together: *migē philotēti kai eunēi*, 'she was united with him in love and bed', or, for metrical convenience, *eunēi kai philotēti*, 'in bed and love'. Homer has a few variations on these: *paralexomai en philotēti*, 'I shall lie with her in love', or *katheudeton en philotēti*, 'the pair of them are bedded together in love'.

Only rarely does Homer speak of sexual desire. One example is the passage in the *Odyssey* where Penelope, adorned by Athena, appears before the suitors:

τῶν δ' αὐτοῦ λύτο γούνατ', ἔρῳ δ' ἄρα θυμὸν ἔθελχθεν,
πάντες δ' ἠρήσαντο παραὶ λεχέεσσι κλιθῆναι (18.212-13).

'And thereupon their knees were loosened'—Homer's phrase for a wounded warrior whose legs can no longer carry him—'and their hearts were enchanted with love (eros), and they all prayed to lie in bed with her.' The most strongly erotic passage forms an interlude in the battle-scenes of *Iliad* 14. Hera, eager as always to help the Greek army, decides to divert the attention of her husband, Zeus, from the fighting by a display of her most alluring charms,

εἴ πως ἱμείραιτο παραδραθέειν φιλότητι
ᾗ χροιῇ (163-4),

'in the hope that he would desire to lie beside her in love, beside her flesh'. Washed, perfumed and suitably dressed, she applies for help to Aphrodite—a delicate matter, since Aphrodite supported the Trojans in the war, so that Hera had to resort to deception. She asks for love and desire, the means by which Aphrodite subdues gods and men alike:

δὸς νῦν μοι φιλότητα καὶ ἵμερον, ᾧ τε σὺ πάντας
δαμνᾷ ἀθανάτους ἠδὲ θνητοὺς ἀνθρώπους (198-9).

And by way of explanation she pretends that she needs them to restore the love of her estranged foster-parents, Ocean and Tethys. Aphrodite complies and gives Hera a magic girdle:

> ἔνθ' ἔνι μὲν φιλότης, ἐν δ' ἵμερος, ἐν δ' ὀαριστὺς
> πάρφασις, ἥ τ' ἔκλεψε νόον πύκα περ φρονεόντων (216-17).

'In it is love, in it is desire, in it is the persuasive talk which robs even wise men of their wits.' Thus equipped, Hera confronts her husband, who is overwhelmed:

> ὡς δ' ἴδεν, ὥς μιν ἔρος πυκινὰς φρένας ἀμφεκάλυψεν,
> οἷον ὅτε πρῶτόν περ ἐμισγέσθην φιλότητι,
> εἰς εὐνὴν φοιτῶντε φίλους λήθοντε τοκῆας (294-6).

'The moment he saw her, love enwrapped his wise heart, just as when the pair of them were first united in love, going to bed together without the knowledge of their parents.' Zeus will hear nothing of her visit to Ocean and Tethys:

> νῶι δ' ἄγ' ἐν φιλότητι τραπείομεν εὐνηθέντε·
> οὐ γὰρ πώ ποτέ μ' ὧδε θεᾶς ἔρος οὐδὲ γυναικὸς
> θυμὸν ἐνὶ στήθεσσι περιπροχυθεὶς ἐδάμασσεν,
> οὐδ' ὁπότ' ἠρασάμην Ἰξιονίης ἀλόχοιο . . .
> ὡς σέο νῦν ἔραμαι καί με γλυκὺς ἵμερος αἱρεῖ (314-28).

'Come, let us go to bed and enjoy ourselves in love-making. For never has desire for goddess or woman so flooded my heart and subdued it in my breast, not even when I fell in love with Ixion's wife [Homer continues with a brief catalogue of great moments in the love-life of Zeus] . . . as I now desire you, seized by sweet longing.' Much of this language is formular and is used for example to describe the love-making of Paris and Helen at the end of Book 3 (441ff.); but for his description of the divine mating Homer uses a heightened lyricism that led the Victorian editors, Leaf and Bayfield, to label the passage the most 'romantic' in Homer:

> τοῖσι δ' ὑπὸ χθὼν δῖα φύεν νεοθηλέα ποίην,
> λωτόν θ' ἑρσήεντα ἰδὲ κρόκον ἠδ' ὑάκινθον
> πυκνὸν καὶ μαλακόν, ὃς ἀπὸ χθονὸς ὑψόσ' ἔεργε.
> τῷ ἔνι λεξάσθην, ἐπὶ δὲ νεφέλην ἕσσαντο
> καλὴν χρυσείην· στιλπναὶ δ' ἀνέπιπτον ἔερσαι (347-51).

'Under them the divine earth made fresh grass grow, dewy lotus and crocus and a soft clump of hyacinth, which kept them high off the ground. In this they lay, and they wrapped themselves in a fair gold cloud, from which shining drops fell.' The sensuous quality combined with the air of unreality has no parallel till we come to fragments 2 and 96 of Sappho's lyrics; but we should note that the language of the earlier parts of the passage is adventurous enough to prepare us for this climax: 'love enwrapped (*amphekalupsen*) his wise heart', 'desire . . . flooded my heart' (the impressive participle *periprokhutheis* occurs here only), 'sweet longing seizes me'. It was imagery of this kind that the lyric poets seized on and extended when they set about describing their own emotions.

The theme of the *Iliad* did not allow much eroticism: the Greeks had slave-women to satisfy their sexual needs, and the only Trojan on whose love life Homer dwells for a moment is naturally enough Paris, whom Aphrodite rescues from certain death in single combat against Menelaus and restores to Helen's arms (*Il.* 3.441ff.). The *Odyssey* tells in Homer's customary decent language of the relations between Odysseus and the divine Calypso and Circe; the only erotic poetry of any length and detail is Demodocus' tale of the adultery of Ares and golden Aphrodite (*Od.* 8.267–366). The last five lines exemplify the lyrical quality noted also in the account of Zeus and Hera in *Iliad* 14: when Hephaestus releases the guilty couple, Ares makes for Thrace:

> ἡ δ' ἄρα Κύπρον ἵκανε φιλομμειδὴς Ἀφροδίτη
> ἐς Πάφον, ἔνθα τέ οἱ τέμενος βωμός τε θυήεις.
> ἔνθα δέ μιν Χάριτες λοῦσαν καὶ χρῖσαν ἐλαίῳ
> ἀμβρότῳ, οἷα θεοὺς ἐπενήνοθεν αἰὲν ἐόντας,
> ἀμφὶ δὲ εἵματα ἕσσαν ἐπήρατα, θαῦμα ἰδέσθαι (362-6).

'Aphrodite, lover of smiles, went to Paphos in Cyprus, where her precinct and fragrant altar are. There the Graces washed her and anointed her with ambrosial oil such as covers the immortal gods, and about her they put her lovely clothes, a marvel to behold.'

Homer, then, generally avoids the erotic and uses only the most reticent terms for sexual union when he does mention it. Although he has language to express desire, he nowhere describes the feelings, the unhappiness or torment, of someone in love. The same is true of Hesiod, who uses such expressions as 'came to the couch of' in his list of divine couplings in the *Theogony*. But he too provided language that writers of love poetry took over: Eros in his account is one of the four original gods—in Homer he does not appear at all—and is described as

> κάλλιστος ἐν ἀθανάτοισι θεοῖσι,
> λυσιμελής, πάντων τε θεῶν πάντων τ' ἀνθρώπων
> δάμναται ἐν στήθεσσι νόον καὶ ἐπίφρονα βουλήν (120-2).

'Most beautiful among the immortal gods, loosener of limbs, he subdues the mind and wise counsels of all gods and all men in their breasts.' Aphrodite emerges from the sea on Cyprus,

αἰδοίη καλὴ θεός, ἀμφὶ δὲ ποίη
ποσσὶν ὕπο ῥαδινοῖσιν ἀέξετο (194-5),

'a reverend beautiful goddess, and grass grew around her and under her slender feet'. The association of grass and flowers with Aphrodite, already noted in *Iliad* 14, was regularly observed by the lyric poets. Hesiod adds that her companions from the beginning were Eros and Himerus, Love and Desire, and that her province is

παρθενίους τ᾽ ὀάρους μειδήματά τ᾽ ἐξαπάτας τε
τέρψιν τε γλυκερὴν φιλότητά τε μειλιχίην τε (205-6),

'maidens' talk and smiles and deceits and sweet pleasure and love-making and tenderness'. The birth of the Graces is also described with rich imagery:

τῶν καὶ ἀπὸ βλεφάρων ἔρος εἴβετο δερκομενάων
λυσιμελής· καλὸν δέ θ᾽ ὑπ᾽ ὀφρύσι δερκιόωνται (910-11).

'From their eyes as they glanced love dripped down, loosener of limbs, and beautifully they glance from under their brows.' When he describes the creation of woman in *Works and Days* he recounts the specifications of Zeus:

καὶ χάριν ἀμφιχέαι κεφαλῇ χρυσῆν Ἀφροδίτην
καὶ πόθον ἀργαλέον καὶ γυιοβόρους μελεδώνας (65-6).

'He told golden Aphrodite to pour attractiveness over her head and cruel longing for her and cares that devour the limbs.' It was from this longing and these cares that the lyric poets made their songs.

The Homeric Hymn to Aphrodite, not necessarily earlier than the first lyric poetry, uses language similar to Homer's and Hesiod's for the story of Aphrodite's love for Anchises: Zeus fills her with 'sweet desire' for the mortal, and 'violent desire' (57 *ekpaglos . . . himeros*) seized her heart. There is a strongly erotic tone in the description of her toilet preparations, her arrival on mount Ida, where wild beasts couple under her influence, and Anchises' removal of her jewellery and clothes when she has reached his couch. It was left for the lyric poets to use this language to record their own love. The use of the first person singular pronoun is the crucial step forward.

*   *   *

The new approach to the art of poetry is to be found in Archilochus; if earlier poets composed in this manner, their work is lost. He composed short poems, some perhaps no longer than a single couplet; he used a wide variety of metres; and he drew on his own experiences for the material of his poetry. All this is in marked contrast to the work of Homer and other predecessors, whose poems were long and exclusively in dactylic hexameters and whose subject-matter was drawn mainly from history and mythology. At times Archilochus seems to be flaunting a set of values which is in direct contrast to the heroic code of Homer: for example, he writes in flippant tone of the shield which he abandoned by a bush—'but I saved my life. What do I care about that shield? It can go to hell. I'll get another just as good some day' (5). Small wonder that the Spartans were said to have banned his poetry. He begins another short poem with *ou phileō megan stratēgon* . . .: 'I do not like a tall general with straddling legs, proud of his curls, shaven under the chin: give me a short one, bandy-legged, walking firmly on his two feet and full of courage.' Archilochus is concerned and expects his listeners to be concerned with his own likes and dislikes.

A few fragments of Archilochus attempt for the first time to express how it feels to be the victim of erotic desire. In the absence of a context we cannot say for certain that he is speaking of his own experience, but this does not greatly matter. Here he uses the Homeric hexameter alternately with a short iambic line:

δύστηνος ἔγκειμαι πόθῳ
ἄψυχος, χαλεπῇσι θεῶν ὀδύνῃσιν ἕκητι
πεπαρμένος δι' ὀστέων (193).

'Wretched I lie in desire, lifeless, pierced through the bones by grievous pains, thanks to the gods.' The imagery is from the battle-field: the lover is a dead warrior, pierced as if by a spear. The colourless verb *enkeimai* ('I lie in') is given force by the startling adjective *apsukhos*, so that it suggests 'I lie dead—with desire'. The language comes in part from epic: the use of *khalepēisi*, 'grievous', to qualify *oduneisin*, 'pains', and the expression 'pierced by pains' are in Homer; but Archilochus' theme is love, not war. Elsewhere he uses similar metaphors to describe the death of friends in shipwreck: their loss is 'a bloody wound'; endurance is the only 'remedy' for 'incurable' evils.

In another scrap of amatory poetry the imagery again suggests warfare:

ἀλλά μ' ὁ λυσιμελής, ὦ 'ταῖρε, δάμναται πόθος (196).

'But, my friend, desire that loosens man's limbs subdues me.' Homer had used the adjective *lusimelēs*, 'limb-loosening', of the relaxing effect of sleep; Hesiod first applied it to love, but Homer had shown the way in his description of Penelope's effect on her suitors: 'their limbs were loosened.' The verb *damnatai*, 'subdues', and its cognates are at home on the battlefield, but were applied by Homer and Hesiod to the power of love.

The most remarkable fragment of Archilochus' love poetry is usually taken to refer to Archilochus himself, but there can be no certainty:

τοῖος γὰρ φιλότητος ἔρως ὑπὸ καρδίην ἐλυσθεὶς

πολλὴν κατ' ἀχλὺν ὀμμάτων ἔχευεν
κλέψας ἐκ στηθέων ἁπαλὰς φρένας (191).

'Such was the passion for love that curled up under (my) heart and shed a great mist over (my) eyes, robbing (my) breast of its tender wits.' Archilochus describes this eros in a phrase which recalls Homer's description of Odysseus escaping from the Cyclops' cave 'curled up under the shaggy belly' of a ram, *lasiēn hupo gaster' elustheis*, and there may be quiet humour in the reminiscence. The mist over the lover's eyes recalls Homer's formula for the death of a warrior, *kata d' ophthalmōn kekhut' akhlus*, 'and a mist was shed over his eyes'. On more than one occasion Homer used a similar expression to describe the effect of love: *erōs phrenas amphekalupsen* (e.g. *Il.* 3.442), 'love enwrapped my wits', but the 'mist' of Archilochus is more pictorial. Two of his phrases are difficult to interpret: *philotētos erōs* may mean simply 'sexual desire', but the expression can carry several interpretations—desire 'caused by love', desire 'for love', desire 'that *is* love'; and in the third line the translation of *hapalas* perhaps depends on the context, now lost: if the passage is about a girl in love, the word may have been chosen as applicable to the weaker sex—her 'tender' wits; if it is about Archilochus or another male, the word may have the derogatory sense of 'feeble' or, more probably, it may denote the youth and inexperience of the lover.

It is unfortunate that we have no complete love poem of Archilochus, since his influence on later writers, Sappho among them, was strong. There is a delicate line on the girl to whom he was engaged to be married:

εἰ γὰρ ὣς ἐμοὶ γένοιτο χεῖρα Νεοβούλης θιγεῖν (118),

'if only I might touch thus the hand of Neobule'. She may be the girl who is charmingly described in the iambic lines,

ἔχουσα θαλλὸν μυρσίνης ἐτέρπετο
ῥοδῆς τε καλὸν ἄνθος,
ἡ δέ οἱ κόμη
ὤμους κατεσκίαζε καὶ μετάφρενα (30, 31).

'She was enjoying herself, holding a branch of myrtle and the fair flower of the rosebush', 'and her hair shadowed her shoulders and back.' Elsewhere he speaks of 'perfumed hair and breast: even an old man would have fallen in love' (48.5–6). His trochaic lines can be less delicate:

καὶ πεσεῖν δρήστην ἐπ' ἀσκὸν κἀπὶ γαστρὶ γαστέρα
προσβαλεῖν μηρούς τε μηροῖς (119),

'and to fall upon her busy paunch and thrust belly against belly, thighs against thighs'. The unhomeric coarseness, admissible in trochaics, has its comic side, since the language seems to parody a Homeric description of close fighting, and the use of *askos*, 'wineskin', for 'paunch' is humorous.

A recently discovered papyrus fragment likewise deals with sex rather than love; according to one interpretation it belongs in the company of poetry of blame rather than with love-poetry. Not all the supplements are certain:

εἰ δ' ὦν ἐπείγεαι καί σε θυμὸς ἰθύει,
    ἔστιν ἐν ἡμετέρου ἣ νῦν μέγ' ἰμείρε[ι γάμου
καλὴ τέρεινα παρθένος· δοκέω δέ μι[ν
    εἶδος ἄμωμον ἔχειν· τὴν δὴ σὺ ποίη[σαι φίλην.'   5
τοσαῦτ' ἐφώνει· τὴν δ' ἐγὼ ἀνταμει[6όμην·
    ''Ἀμφιμεδοῦς θύγατερ, ἐσθλῆς τε καὶ [μακαρτάτης
γυναικός, ἣν νῦν γῆ κατ' εὐρώεσσ' ἔ[χει,
    τ]έρψιές εἰσι θεῆς πολλαὶ νέοισιν ἀνδ[ράσιν
παρὲξ τὸ θεῖον χρῆμα· τῶν τις ἀρκέσε[ι.   10
    τ]αῦτα δ' ἐπ' ἡσυχίης εὖτ' ἂν μελανθῆ[ι μοι γένυς
ἐ]γώ τε καὶ σὺ σὺν θεῷ 6ουλεύσομεν·
    π]είσομαι ὥς με κέλεαι· πολλόν μ' [ἐποτρύνει πόθος.
θρ]ιγκοῦ δ' ἔνερθε καὶ πυλέων ὑποφ[θάνειν
    μ]ή τι μέγαιρε, φίλη· σχήσω γὰρ ἐς ποη[φόρους   15
κ]ήπους. τὸ δὴ νῦν γνῶθι· Νεοβούλη[ν μὲν ὦν
    ἄλλος ἀνὴρ ἐχέτω· αἰαῖ, πέπειρα δ[ὴ πέλει,
ἄν]θος δ' ἀπερρύηκε παρθενήϊον
    κ]αὶ χάρις ἣ πρὶν ἐπῆν· κόρον γὰρ οὐ κ[ατέσχε πω,
ἥ6]ης δὲ μέτρ' ἔφηνε μαινόλις γυνή·   20
    ἐς] κόρακας ἄπεχε· μὴ τοῦτ' ἐφοῖτ' ἄν[αξ θεῶν
ὅ]πως ἐγὼ γυναῖκα τοιαύτην ἔχων
    γεί]τοσι χάρμ' ἔσομαι· πολλὸν σὲ 6ούλο[μαι πάρος.
σὺ] μὲν γὰρ οὔτ' ἄπιστος οὔτε διπλόη,
    ἣ δ]ὲ μάλ' ὀξυτέρη, πολλοὺς δὲ ποιεῖτα[ι φίλους·   25
δέ]δοιχ' ὅπως μὴ τυφλὰ κἀλιτήμερα
    σπ]ουδῇ ἐπειγόμενος τὼς ὥσπερ ἡ κ[ύων τέκω.'
τοσ]αῦτ' ἐφώνεον· παρθένον δ' ἐν ἄνθε[σιν
    τηλ]εθάεσσι λαβὼν ἔκλινα· μαλθακῇ δ[έ μιν
χλαί]νῃ καλύψας, αὐχέν' ἀγκάλης ἔχω[ν,   30
    δεί]ματι † παυ[σ]αμένην † τὼς ὥστε νέ6ρ[ον εἱλόμην
μαζ]ῶν τε χερσὶν ἠπίως ἐφηψάμην
    ἧπε]ρ ἔφηνε νέον ἥ6ης ἐπήλυσιν χρόα·
ἅπαν τ]ε σῶμα καλὸν ἀμφαφώμενος
    λευκ]ὸν ἀφῆκα μένος, ξανθῆς ἐπιψαύ[ων τριχός   (196A).   35

The missing part of the seducer's tale may have run as follows: Speaker (presumably Archilochus himself): 'Let's make love.' Girl: 'My mother said not before marriage.' The papyrus begins in the middle of her speech and ends with the end of the poem. ' ". . . If then you are in a hurry and your spirit urges you, there is in our house a beautiful tender girl who greatly desires (marriage?) now. I think she has faultless beauty. Make *her* your friend." These were her words, and I answered her: "Daughter of Amphimedo, that good and blessed lady, whom the mouldy earth now covers, there are many delights of the goddess for young men apart from that divine business. One of them will be enough. God willing, you and I shall discuss these other matters at leisure when (my cheek?) turns black. I shall obey your instructions. (Desire urges?) me strongly. Do not grudge, my dear, (that I should be the first?) under the fence and gateway; for I shall put ashore in grassy meadows. Now let me tell you this: another man can have Neobule: alas, she is over-ripe, and her maiden bloom is shed together with the grace that was on her once; for she has never checked her excessive lust, and, a crazed woman, has revealed the limits of her youth. To the crows with her! May the king of the gods not instruct that I have a woman like that and provide glee for the neighbours. I greatly want you rather; for you are neither faithless nor double-dealing, whereas she is far too impetuous and makes many men her friends. I am scared that if I rush on in haste I may father blind premature young like the bitch in the proverb." These were my words, and I took the girl and made her lie down among the blossoming flowers; I covered her with a soft cloak, and holding her neck in my arm (held her trembling in fear?) like a fawn, gently touched her breasts with my hands where she showed her young skin, the onset of her youth, and feeling all her beautiful body released my (white?) strength, touching her yellow hair.'

The poem, the content of which has no close parallel in Greek literature, presents many problems. Other scraps of Archilochus offer clues to the interpretation: one line has the words, 'the younger daughter of Lycambes alone', where it is tempting to supply the verb 'I found' (38), and a badly damaged fragment of papyrus has been interpreted as meaning, 'I have already had the elder daughter of Lycambes, now it is the turn of the younger one' (54). Dioscorides, a poet of the third century B.C., makes Lycambes' daughters say in effect, 'We never saw Archilochus either in the streets or in Hera's great precinct; despite what he said, we never disgraced our maidenhood or our parents or the island of Paros' (*AP* 7.351). Perhaps Hera's precinct provided the flowery setting for the seduction in the new poem. But what is the poem's purpose, and for what audience was it intended? Is it no more than the lively narrative of a conquest, composed to amuse friends? Or was its purpose to shame Lycambes and his family? There is a tenderness in the last eight lines which makes that interpretation improbable. The imagery is often interesting —the fence (or coping-stone), gates and grassy meadows, all with sexual connotation, and the over-ripeness of Neobule. There are colloquialisms ('to the crows' and the proverbial bitch of line 27), but despite the subject-matter there is no coarse language such as Archilochus used in his iambics. The dactylic element of the rhythmical structure, iambic trimeter alternating with dactylic hemiepes plus iambic dimeter, may have exerted a pull in the direction of Homeric reticence.

*   *   *

Alcman, a writer of choral poetry, left a few fragments of personal lyric.

ἔρως με δηὖτε Κύπριδος *Ϝέκατι*
γλυκὺς κατείβων καρδίαν ἰαίνει (59a).

'Once again, thanks to the Cyprian, love pours sweetly down and warms my heart.' Eros was usually regarded as the child of Aphrodite, but it is uncertain whether he is personified here: the mention of Aphrodite, the Cyprian, might suggest it, but the image of a flood makes it unlikely. The force of the verb *iainei* is perhaps not so strong as 'warms' might suggest, since Homer had used it of things which 'cheer' the heart. Alcman uses the expression *dēute*, which became almost a catchword of Greek love poetry. It comprises the two words *dē aute*, 'look, again' or 'why, again'; Sappho and, above all, Anacreon used it of the renewed onset of love. Its force is in part humorous, in part pathetic.

Aphrodite and Eros, this time clearly personified, appear in another poem:

Ἀφροδίτα μὲν οὐκ ἔστι, μάργος δ' Ἔρως οἶα <παῖς> παίσδει
ἄκρ' ἐπ' ἄνθη καβαίνων, ἃ μή μοι θίγῃς, τῶ κυπαιρίσκω (58).

'It is not Aphrodite, but mad Eros playing like the boy he is, coming down over the topmost flowers—do not touch them, please—of the galingale.' Alcman seems to be contrasting Aphrodite with Eros, depicted here for the first time as the irresponsible player of games; the adjective *margos*, 'mad', may carry the meaning of 'lustful', which it has in later writers. The wild boy is pictured as coming down from heaven to the sedges of the Spartan plain, so roughly that he seems likely to damage them.

It seems probable enough that Alcman is speaking of his own emotions in these pieces; at any rate the compiler of the *Suda* describes him as *erōtikos panu*, 'very amorous', doubtless arguing from the content of his poetry to his character. But some of his erotic poetry is less straightforward: he was famous for his 'partheneia', choral poetry performed in Sparta by girls' choirs, and in these poems the choir speaks collectively of its leader in the language of love. This fragmentary piece provides a good example:

λυσιμελεῖ τε πόσῳ, τακερώτερα
δ' ὕπνω καὶ σανάτω ποτιδέρκεται (3.61-2),

'. . . with limb-loosening desire; and her glances are more melting than sleep or death'. 'Limb-loosening desire' repeats the words of Archilochus, but the 'melting' looks do not occur in earlier writers: the imagery is close to Alcman's own *erōs . . . kardian iainei*, 'love . . . warms, melts, the heart'. The mention of sleep and death may be due to the associations of the adjective *lusimelei*, 'limb-loosening', in the previous line.

Shortly after Alcman composed his 'maiden-songs', Sappho and Alcaeus were delighting their friends on the island of Lesbos with personal lyrics which have no match in Greek literature—or in Latin—for the way in which intensity of passion is expressed in perfectly controlled, meticulously planned poetry. The love songs of Alcaeus are lost, but Horace tells us (*Carm.* 1.32.9–12) that among the themes of his poetry were 'Venus and the boy who ever clings to her, and Lycus, handsome with his black eyes and his black hair'. A scrap of a poem requests that 'charming' or 'graceful' Menon (*ton kharienta Menōna*) be invited to a symposium if Alcaeus is to enjoy it (368). A tantalising fragment formed the opening of a poem in which the speaker is a girl or a woman:

ἔμε δείλαν, ἔμε παίσαν κακοτάτων πεδέχοισαν (10B),

'Wretched me, with a share in every misery': Horace's poem in the same rare ionic rhythm (*Carm.* 3.12 miserarum est neque amori dare ludum . . .) may have been based on Alcaeus' poem; if it was, the girl's miseries were the tortures of love.

Sappho's love poetry has suffered almost the same obliteration. Indeed it is hard to realise that her high reputation rests with one certain and one possible exception on mere fragments. The certain exception is the prayer to Aphrodite, which was preserved in the text of the critic Dionysius of Halicarnassus.

> ποικιλόθρον’ ἀθανάτ’ Ἀφρόδιτα,
> παῖ Δίος δολόπλοκε, λίσσομαί σε,
> μή μ’ ἄσαισι μηδ’ ὀνίαισι δάμνα,
> πότνια, θῦμον,
>
> ἀλλὰ τυίδ’ ἔλθ’, αἴ ποτα κἀτέρωτα   5
> τάς ἔμας αὔδας ἀίοισα πήλοι
> ἔκλυες, πάτρος δὲ δόμον λίποισα
> χρύσιον ἦλθες
>
> ἄρμ’ ὑπασδεύξαισα· κάλοι δέ σ’ ἄγον
> ὤκεες στροῦθοι περὶ γᾶς μελαίνας   10
> πύκνα δίννεντες πτέρ’ ἀπ’ ὡράνω αἴθε-
> ρος διὰ μέσσω,
>
> αἶψα δ’ ἐξίκοντο· σὺ δ’, ὦ μάκαιρα,
> μειδιαίσαισ’ ἀθανάτῳ προσώπῳ
> ἤρε’ ὄττι δηὖτε πέπονθα κὤττι   15
> δηὖτε κάλημμι,

κὤττι μοι μάλιστα θέλω γένεσθαι
μαινόλᾳ θύμῳ· τίνα δηὖτε πείθω
ἄψ σ' ἄγην ἐς Fὰν φιλότατα; τίς σ', ὦ
Ψάπφ', ἀδικήσι;   20

καὶ γὰρ αἰ φεύγει, ταχέως διώξει·
αἰ δὲ δῶρα μὴ δέκετ', ἀλλὰ δώσει·
αἰ δὲ μὴ φίλει, ταχέως φιλήσει
κωὐκ ἐθέλοισα.

ἔλθε μοι καὶ νῦν, χαλέπαν δὲ λῦσον   25
ἐκ μερίμναν, ὅσσα δέ μοι τέλεσσαι
θῦμος ἱμέρρει, τέλεσον· σὺ δ' αὖτα
σύμμαχος ἔσσο (1).

'Ornate-throned immortal Aphrodite, wile-weaving daughter of Zeus, I entreat you: do not overpower my heart, mistress, with ache and anguish, but come here, if ever in the past you heard my voice from afar and acquiesced and came, leaving your father's golden house, with chariot yoked: beautiful swift sparrows whirring fast-beating wings brought you above the dark earth down from heaven through the mid-air, and soon they arrived; and you, blessed one, with a smile on your immortal face asked what was the matter with me this time and why I was calling this time and what is my maddened heart I most wished to happen for myself: "Whom am I to persuade this time to lead you back to her love? Who wrongs you, Sappho? If she runs away, soon she shall pursue; if she does not accept gifts, why, she shall give them instead; if she does not love, soon she shall love even against her will." Come to me now again and deliver me from oppressive anxieties; fulfil all that my heart longs to fulfil, and you yourself be my fellow-fighter.'

Dionysius chose the poem to illustrate what he called *glaphura kai anthēra sunthesis*, 'polished and exuberant composition'. His remarks are confined to the first of these qualities: the composition is polished and smooth, not harsh and jolting. 'The verbal beauty,' he says, 'and the charm of the writing lie in the cohesion and smoothness of the joinery. Word follows word inwoven according to certain natural affinities and groupings of the letters.' Dionysius does not spell out what he means, but we note Sappho's marked preference for the liquids *l*, *m*, *n*, and her complete avoidance of the hard consonant *b*, all the more surprising in the Lesbian dialect, in which the consonant is commoner than in other dialects, since all words beginning with *rh* have initial *b*: *broda*, 'roses', *bradios*, 'easy', and so on. If Sappho deliberately said to herself, 'I shall compose my poem without introducing the letter *b*', she deprived herself of the use of several of her favourite words, among them *broda*, 'roses', *bōmoi*, 'altars', *libanōtos*, 'frankincense', *abros*, 'delicate'. It is noteworthy that Alcaeus has no *b* in the three surviving stanzas of his hymn to Castor and Pollux (34a); and we know that Lasus of Hermione, composing some fifty years after Sappho, wrote an 'asigmatic' ode, a hymn in which he avoided the sibilant *s*.

The least we can say is that Sappho chose her consonants carefully, and that the same care was lavished on the vowels: note the a and o sounds of the first stanza, for example. Alliteration plays an important part: it is frequent but not usually obtrusive: line 2, *pai Dios doloploke*, is typical; in line 22, where it is obtrusive, *ai de dōra mē deket' alla dōsei*, it underlines the antithesis of refusing and giving gifts and emphasises the finality of Aphrodite's answer. Assonance and rhyme are important too: note 1–3 *Aphrodita . . . damna*, 5–7 *katerōta . . . lipoisa*, 15–16 *kōtti . . . kalēmmi*, 18–19 *peithō . . . tis s', ō*, and especially 21–23 *diōxei . . . dōsei . . . philēsei*, where the rhyme reinforces the words of Aphrodite; and the poem ends with the assonances of *telessai, teleson* and *esso*.

Sappho chose for her poem the stanza-form which carries her name and seems to have been her favourite: when her poetry was collected, all the poems in the sapphic stanza were placed in Book 1, which had 1320 lines in all or the equivalent of about 50 poems of the length of our present one. The pattern of the stanza is particularly satisfying to the ear: the three eleven-syllable lines are rounded off by the five-syllable line, which provides a pleasing cadence, similar to the ending of the longer lines but sufficiently different to be interesting. In this poem Sappho has a light pause in sense at the end of the first four stanzas, a pause which deserves a comma but no more; stanza 5 ends with the end of Aphrodite's questions, and the strong stops in stanza 6 give an almost hieratic tone to her promises. Stanza 6 is the first to be self-contained, and the last stanza is necessarily self-contained in consequence. This contrast between the earlier stanzas, where the sense runs over, and the last stanzas, where the sense is enclosed, helps to mark the finality of Aphrodite's answer: all is now clear-cut; it is as though a problem had been stated and solved. The shape of the stanza is cleverly used in stanza 6, where the three identical lines contain the three parallel statements,

> She runs away? She shall pursue.
> She rejects gifts? She shall give.
> She does not love? She shall love,

and the short final line contains the crushing *kōuk etheloisa*, 'even against her will', which extends its sense to all three verbs, 'pursue', 'give', 'love'. Sappho exploits the structure of the stanza also in lines 11–12, where the close connection between the third and fourth lines is used to illustrate the swoop of the chariot 'from heaven through the air between', *ap' ōranō aithe-ros dia messō*.

Sappho's poem is a prayer; not of course a prayer which might be used in public worship, but a personal prayer; and she realised that the form of an invocation, as Homer, for example, had composed it, gave an acceptably tight structure to a poem. The framework begins, 'I beseech you, come to me, if ever you came before': Sappho describes the previous coming, and finishes in line 25, 'Come again now', one of the clearer examples of ring composition. The poem is held together by *alla tuid' elth'* (5), *ēlthes* (8), *elthe moi kai nun* (25): 'come hither . . . if ever you came . . . Come to me now too'. Sappho's prayer, however, takes some interesting turns: the mention of the previous epiphany of the goddess leads into a narrative section which occupies almost all of the central five stanzas of the poem; and the leisurely narrative with its chariot and sparrows gives way to the words of Aphrodite, moving from indirect to direct question at line 18 and to bluntly direct statement at line 21.

In what tone did Sappho compose her prayer? The poem has been seen as an expression of 'the vanity and impermanence of her passion', composed in a spirit of self-mockery: Aphrodite on her earlier visit teased Sappho with the inconstancy of her passion and indicated that her suffering would soon pass. But this is not the most obvious interpretation of the poem; in particular, it does not explain the emphasis which is laid on the divinity and power of Aphrodite. Prayers generally began with complimentary epithets: here the opening word of the poem refers to Aphrodite's elaborate throne and sets her on the heights of Olympus among Olympian gods; Homer had used *euthronos Ēōs*, 'Dawn of the fair throne', in the same way. Aphrodite is *athanata*, 'immortal'; *pai Dios*, 'child of Zeus', no less; *potnia* (4) may be translated as 'august'; her father, Zeus, reappears in line 7, and the mention of his 'golden house' serves the same purpose as the reference to Aphrodite's throne. In line 13 she is *makaira*, 'blessed one', and in the next line she smiles on her 'immortal' face: here the unusual use of *athanatos* to describe a *part* of a god is easily explained if Sappho is at pains to emphasise the divinity and power of Aphrodite. Everything leads up to the goddess' final words *kōuk etheloisa*: she *is* a goddess, and she will have her way. Aphrodite, then, gave real help before: she did not come to laugh and preach on the mutability of love—she smilingly proved her divinity, and that is why Sappho summons her again.

It is just possible that we have a second complete poem by Sappho: the writer of the *Peri hupsous*, 'On the Sublime', quotes four stanzas which form a satisfactory whole; but they are followed by six puzzling words which are almost certainly the beginning of a fifth stanza—although why the author or a scribe broke off near the beginning of the stanza and in the middle of a sentence has not been explained.

φαίνεταί μοι κῆνος ἴσος θέοισιν
ἔμμεν' ὤνηρ, ὄττις ἐνάντιός τοι
ἰσδάνει καὶ πλάσιον ἆδυ φωνεί-
σας ὐπακούει

καὶ γελαίσας ἰμέροεν, τό μ' ἦ μὰν   5
καρδίαν ἐν στήθεσιν ἐπτόαισεν·
ὡς γὰρ ἔς σ' ἴδω βρόχε', ὤς με φώνη-
σ' οὐδὲν ἔτ' εἴκει,

The Golden Lyre

ἀλλά † καμ † μὲν γλῶσσα † ἔαγε †, λέπτον
δ' αὔτικα χρῷ πῦρ ὑπαδεδρόμακεν,   10
ὀππάτεσσι δ' οὐδὲν ὄρημμ', ἐπιβρό-
μεισι δ' ἄκουαι,

† ἔκαδε † μ' ἴδρως κακχέεται, τρόμος δὲ
παῖσαν ἄγρει, χλωροτέρα δὲ ποίας
ἔμμι, τεθνάκην δ'ὀλίγω 'πιδεύης   15
φαίνομ' ἔμ' αὔτᾳ.

ἀλλὰ πὰν τόλματον, ἐπεὶ † καὶ πένητα † (31).

'That man seems to me to be the equal of the gods who sits opposite you and close by hears your sweet words and lovely laughter: this, I swear, makes my heart pound within my breast; for when I glance at you for a moment, I can no longer speak, my tongue (is fixed in silence?), a thin flame at once runs under my skin, I see nothing with my eyes, my ears hum, sweat flows down me, trembling seizes me all over, I am paler than grass and I seem to be not far short of death. But all can be endured, since . . .'

A girl whom Sappho loves is in the company of a man, and this situation overwhelms Sappho with jealousy, since the merest glance at the girl produces violent physical reactions. The directness of the third and fourth stanzas contrasts with the greater syntactical complexity of the first two stanzas. Enjambment is used throughout and there are scarcely any strong stops in the poem, so that the climax of lines 15–16 is carefully prepared. Also noteworthy is the way in which Sappho moves from *kēnos* ('that man') of line 1 via 'you' of lines 2–7 to the first person which dominates the poem from 7 to 16. Sappho relies on blunt statement rather than on imagery, though the 'thin fire' of 9–10 and the comparison, 'paler (more greeny-yellow) than grass' are striking.

The first and last stanzas of an incomplete poem provide some of the finest lines of all Greek poetry:

ο]ἰ μὲν ἰππήων στρότον, οἰ δὲ πέσδων,
οἰ δὲ νάων φαῖσ' ἐπ[ὶ] γᾶν μέλαι[ν]αν
ἔ]μμεναι κάλλιστον, ἔγω δὲ κῆν ὅτ-
τω τις ἔραται·

πά]γχυ δ' εὔμαρες σύνετον πόησαι   5
π]άντι τ[ο]ῦτ', ἀ γὰρ πόλυ περσκέθοισα
κάλλος [ἀνθ]ρώπων Ἐλένα [τὸ]ν ἄνδρα
τὸν [πανάρ]ιστον

καλλ[ίποι]σ' ἔβα 'ς Τροΐαν πλέοι[σα
κωὐδ[ὲ πα]ῖδος οὐδὲ φίλων το[κ]ήων   10

πά[μπαν] ἐμνάσθη, ἀλλὰ παράγαγ' αὔταν
  ]σαν

  ]αμπτον γὰρ [
  ]. . . κούφως τ[   ]οησ[.]ν
. .]με νῦν 'Ανακτορί[ας ὀ]νέμναι-   15
σ' οὐ] παρεοίσας·

τᾶ]ς κε βολλοίμαν ἔρατόν τε βᾶμα
κἀμάρυχμα λάμπρον ἴδην προσώπω
ἢ τὰ Λύδων ἄρματα κἀν ὄπλοισι
πεσδομ]άχεντας (16).   20

'Some say that a host of cavalrymen is the fairest thing on the black earth, some a host of infantry, others of ships: I say it is what one loves. It is quite easy to make this intelligible to all: Helen, who far surpassed all mortals in beauty, abandoned her excellent husband and went sailing off to Troy without a single thought for her daughter or her dear parents—(the Cyprian) led her astray (the moment she set eyes on him?); for easily swayed is . . . (She) has now reminded me of the absent Anactoria: *her* lovely walk and the bright sparkle of *her* face I would rather see than those chariots of the Lydians and infantry in armour.'

Sappho begins with the device known as 'priamel', a preamble in which she lists the views of others, only to reject them for her own. In the space of one sapphic stanza she sets up the contrast between three other views and her own, establishes also a latent contrast between male values and hers, finds room for a Homeric echo in the expression 'the black earth', and unerringly positions the crucial word *eratai*, 'loves', at the end. After the bravado of this opening Sappho reduces the intensity with the playful, leisurely introduction of her proof; and the proof itself is hardly rigorous: Helen, says Sappho, was the most beautiful of women, but she left husband, daughter and parents for Paris. The intensity returns when Sappho speaks of the absent Anactoria, of whom she has been reminded by the story of lovely Helen: the contrasts of the first stanza are repeated, but Sappho is no longer generalising: she would rather see Anactoria's walk and the sparkle of her face than the Lydian chariots and fully armed infantrymen. This time Sappho sets the contrasted objects in the first two and the last two lines of the stanza: the chariots and foot-soldiers clearly recall the soldiery of the opening stanza; and the description of the girl is remarkable for the adjective *eraton*, 'lovely' (the Greek word has much stronger erotic significance than the English: Homer had used it only of the gifts of Aphrodite, and Hesiod applied it to *philotēs*, 'love-making'), and the noun *amarukhma*, a rare, melodious word used of flashing eyes.

Two poems are concerned with absent friends. In one (94) Sappho uses the device of 'reminding' the departed girl of their happy times together: she recalls garlands of violets and roses, perfume, shrines and groves, and—in a unique reference to physical contact—soft beds on which the girl satisfied her desire. In the other (96) she uses the Homeric technique of expanded simile: she writes to comfort Atthis by assuring her that her departed friend, now in Lydia, still longs for her.

-σε θέᾳ σ᾽ ἰκέλαν ἀρι-
γνώτᾳ, σᾷ δὲ μάλιστ᾽ ἔχαιρε μόλπᾳ.   5

νῦν δὲ Λύδαισιν ἐμπρέπεται γυναί-
κεσσιν ὥς ποτ᾽ ἀελίω
δύντος ἀ βροδοδάκτυλος σελάννα

πάντα περρέχοισ᾽ ἄστρα· φάος δ᾽ ἐπί-
σχει θάλασσαν ἐπ᾽ ἀλμύραν   10
ἴσως καὶ πολυανθέμοις ἀρούραις·

ἀ δ᾽ ἐέρσα κάλα κέχυται, τεθά-
λαισι δὲ βρόδα κἄπαλ᾽ ἄν-
θρυσκα καὶ μελίλωτος ἀνθεμώδης·

πόλλα δὲ ζαφοίταισ᾽, ἀγάνας ἐπι-   15
μνάσθεισ᾽ Ἄτθιδος ἰμέρῳ
λέπταν ποι φρένα κ[ᾶ]ρ[ι σᾷ] βόρηται (96. 4-17).

'. . . (she thought) you like a goddess manifest, and in your song she took most pleasure. Now she shines among Lydian women, as the rosy-fingered moon surpassing all the stars when the sun has set: it extends its light over salt sea and flowery fields alike, the dew is spread in beauty, the roses flourish and delicate chervil and blossoming clover. Often as she goes to and fro, remembering gentle Atthis with longing, her tender heart is consumed (because of your fate) . . .' We cannot say what proportion of the poem is occupied by the simile, but it is clear that once the point of comparison has been made—a girl pre-eminent among her companions as the moon among the stars—Sappho feels free to concentrate on the moon and elaborates the picture for its own sake.

Another substantial fragment takes the form of an invitation to Aphrodite to visit a shrine:

δεῦρύ μ᾽ ἐκ Κρήτας ἐπ[ὶ τόνδ]ε ναῦον
ἄγνον, ὄππ[ᾳ τοι] χάριεν μὲν ἄλσος
μαλί[αν], βῶμοι δὲ τεθυμιάμε-
νοι [λι]βανώτῳ.

ἐν δ᾽ ὔδωρ ψῦχρον κελάδει δι᾽ ὔσδων   5
μαλίνων, βρόδοισι δὲ παῖς ὁ χῶρος

ἐσκίαστ᾿, αἰθυσσομένων δὲ φύλλων
κῶμα καταίρει·

ἐν δὲ λείμων ἱππόβοτος τέθαλεν
ἠρίνοισιν ἄνθεσιν, αἰ δ᾿ ἄηται   10
μέλλιχα πνέοισιν [
[   ]

ἔνθα δὴ σὺ . . . . ἔλοισα Κύπρι
χρυσίαισιν ἐν κυλίκεσσιν ἄβρως
ὀμμεμείχμενον θαλίαισι νέκταρ   15
οἰνοχόαισον (2).

'. . . Come hither, I pray, from Crete to this holy temple, where your lovely apple orchard is and altars smoking with frankincense. In it cold water gurgles through the apple branches, the place is all shadowy with roses, and from the quivering leaves sleep comes down. In it a meadow where horses graze blossoms with spring flowers, and the breezes blow sweetly . . . There, Cyprian goddess, take . . . and in gold cups gracefully pour nectar that mingles with our festivity.'

In this poem too Sappho lingers over detail, and in some of her most melodious lines creates a dream-like picture of an earthly paradise. The imagery of apples, flowers, gardens and horses has a strong erotic element, and we notice that all the senses are involved—sight, smell, touch, hearing, even taste in the mention of nectar. Sappho uses the stanza as the unit (so far as we can see), but none of the lines is end-stopped; this serves to avoid monotony in a catalogue which is held together by the loosest parataxis, the *men*-clause with the following *de*-clauses corresponding roughly to the repetition of 'and' in English.

In two poems, only scraps of which survive, Sappho uses remarkable language to describe the impact of love:

Ἔρος δ᾿ ἐτίναξέ μοι
φρένας, ὡς ἄνεμος κὰτ ὄρος δρύσιν ἐμπέτων (47).

'Love shook my heart, like the wind falling on oaks on a mountain'; and

Ἔρος δηὖτέ μ᾿ ὁ λυσιμέλης δόνει,
γλυκύπικρον ἀμάχανον ὄρπετον (130).

'Once again Love, the loosener of limbs, shakes me, that sweet-bitter, irresistible creature.' Hesiod composed a fine description of Boreas falling on oaks and pines in the mountain glens (*Op.* 507ff.), and Homer compared two stout warriors to oaks resisting wind and rain on the mountains (*Il.* 12.131ff.). Sappho effectively applies the simile to her own situation. The images in the second passage are bold: the verb *donei* is used by Homer of the battering of the wind; *lusimelēs*, 'limb-loosening', was used of love by Archilochus and Hesiod, and may be regarded as a traditional epithet, but the verb *donei* gives it fresh life; *glukupikros*, 'sweet-bitter', is an extraordinary compound, the more remarkable in that it is applied to *orpeton*, a 'creature' or even a 'monster'. That love can be both bitter and sweet became commonplace in poetry, but as far as we know the idea is expressed first here; Homer more straight-forwardly spoke of *glukus himeros*, 'sweet longing'. Sappho stresses her point by the second long epithet, *amakhanon*, used of something with which one cannot cope. She sees love's assault as both physical and mental.

Two lines resemble folk-song in their content:

> γλύκηα μᾶτερ, οὔτοι δύναμαι κρέκην τὸν ἴστον,
> πόθῳ δάμεισα παῖδος βραδίναν δι' ᾿Αφροδίταν (102).

'Sweet mother, I cannot weave my web; thanks to slender Aphrodite I am overcome by desire for a boy.' It is impossible to say whether Sappho is speaking of herself or not; she does not usually cast herself in the role of love-sick young girl distracted from her loom. The language of *pothōi dameisa*, 'overcome by desire', is traditional by her time, but the adjective *bradinan*, 'slender', is a distinctive touch.

One other short piece deserves mention here, since it may well be the work of Sappho although proof is impossible; the feminine adjective *mona*, 'alone', shows that the speaker is a woman:

> δέδυκε μὲν ἀ σελάννα
> καὶ Πληΐαδες, μέσαι δὲ
> νύκτες, παρὰ δ' ἔρχετ' ὤρα,
> ἔγω δὲ μόνα κατεύδω (fr. adesp. 976 *PMG*).

'The moon has set and the Pleiads; it is midnight; time passes by; and I sleep alone'; four enchanting lines, which rely for their effect on their graceful rhythm, their simple paratactic structure, similar to that of the first stanza of fr. 16, the enjambment at the end of the second line, and above all the direct-ness of the statement.

*   *   *

Solon, the famous Athenian statesman, lawgiver and moraliser, deserves a passing glance here as author of a couplet which surprised later generations:

> ἔσθ' ἥβης ἐρατοῖσιν ἐπ' ἄνθεσι παιδοφιλήσῃ,
> μηρῶν ἱμείρων καὶ γλυκεροῦ στόματος (25),

'while in the delightful flower of his youth he loves a boy, desiring thighs and sweet mouth'. Solon composed his poem at the period when homosexual scenes first appear on Attic vases. The language of the first line is partly traditional, 'the flower of youth' being Homeric (*Il.* 13.484) and *eratos*, 'lovely, delightful' (but more erotic) a regular epithet in this context; but no poet, so far as we know, had used the verb *paidophilein*, 'love a boy', or spoken so frankly as in the second line, where *mērōn himeirōn* may be a deliberate pun.

Two poems written some fifty years after Sappho by the western Greek poet Ibycus have the intensity of some of her work. The first may be regarded as a more elaborate version of Sappho's comparison of love to a gale-force wind:

> ἦρι μὲν αἵ τε Κυδώνιαι
> μαλίδες ἀρδόμεναι ῥοᾶν
> ἐκ ποταμῶν, ἵνα Παρθένων
> κᾶπος ἀκήρατος, αἵ τ' οἰνανθίδες
> αὐξόμεναι σκιεροῖσιν ὑφ' ἔρνεσιν   5
> οἰναρέοις θαλέθοισιν, ἐμοὶ δ' ἔρος
>   οὐδεμίαν κατάκοιτος ὥραν·
> ἀλλ' ἄθ' ὑπὸ στεροπᾶς φλέγων
> Θρηίκιος βορέας ἀίσ-
> σων παρὰ Κύπριδος ἀζαλέαις μανί-   10
> αισιν ἐρεμνὸς ἀθαμβὴς
>   ἐγκρατέως πεδόθεν τινάσσει
> ἀμετέρας φρένας (286).

'In the spring flourish Cydonian quince-trees, watered from flowing rivers where stands the inviolate garden of the Maidens, and vine-blossoms growing under the shady vine-branches; but for me Love rests at no season: like the Thracian north wind blazing with lightning rushing from the Cyprian with parching fits of madness, dark and shameless, it powerfully shakes my heart from the roots.'

Ibycus contrasts the seasonal regularity of nature with his ever-present love which knows no seasons, and makes a further contrast between the tranquillity of nature and the harshness of love's attack, a contrast underlined by the repeated vowel-sounds of the first six lines (*Kudōniai . . . ardomenai . . . oinanthides auxomenai skieroisin . . . oinareois thalethoisin*). The image of *katakoitos* is apt enough: Love 'goes to bed' at no season. Then comes the description of the wind of love, in which as in Sappho the physical assault is linked with a mental battering (*maniaisin*, 'fits of madness'). There is a picturesque interweaving of epithets: *eremnos*, 'dark', suggests the clouds carried by the wind, whereas *athambēs*, 'shameless', belongs rather to a personified Love.

Another splendid poem depends equally on its imagery:

> Ἔρος αὖτέ με κυανέοισιν ὑπὸ

βλεφάροις τακέρ' ὄμμασι δερκόμενος
κηλήμασι παντοδαποῖς ἐς ἄπει-
ρα δίκτυα Κύπριδος ἐσβάλλει·
ἦ μὰν τρομέω νιν ἐπερχόμενον,
ὥστε φερέζυγος ἵππος ἀεθλοφόρος ποτὶ γήρᾳ
ἀέκων σὺν ὄχεσφι θοοῖς ἐς ἄμιλλαν ἔβα (287).

'Again Love, looking at me meltingly from under his dark eyelids, hurls me with his manifold enchantments into the boundless nets of the Cyprian. How I fear his onset, as a prize-winning horse still bearing the yoke in his old age goes unwillingly with swift chariot to the race.'

Eros here is a handsome youth, the accomplice of his mother, the Cyprian, and doubtless his dark eyelids are the mark of the boy whose charms now enchant and disturb the poet. The metaphor of the hunt, in which young Eros drives the prey into Aphrodite's nets, is smoothly succeeded by the imagery of the chariot-race. There is humour as well as pathos in the picture of the old horse, successful in earlier days but now reluctant to compete. Ibycus makes cunning use of metre in line 4, where the long syllables of *esballei* slow the pace effectively at the end of the hunt, and in line 6, where the dactyls and the plosive sounds suggest the pounding hooves of the racecourse.

In another fragment he addresses a youth called Euryalus in equally rich language, reminiscent of choral lyric poetry rather than of the solo song of Sappho and others:

Εὐρύαλε γλαυκέων Χαρίτων θάλος, <῾Ωρᾶν>
καλλικόμων μελέδημα, σὲ μὲν Κύπρις
ἅ τ' ἀγανοβλέφαρος Πει-
θὼ ῥοδέοισιν ἐν ἄνθεσι θρέψαν (288).

'Euryalus, offshoot of the blue-eyed Graces, darling of the lovely-haired Seasons, the Cyprian and soft-lidded Persuasion nursed you among rose-blossoms.' No other early Greek poet expressed his love with this hymnal elaboration. One can detect a new fashion, and it seems likely that it was due to the tastes of the court of Polycrates, the prosperous ruler who attracted Ibycus and Anacreon to Samos. These poets had to write to please a patron, and a new style was created.

*   *   *

Anacreon relied less on a rich, sensuous style than on careful craftsmanship, elegance and wit. One of the finest examples of his meticulous composition is an address to a young girl, written in lilting trochaics:

πῶλε Θρηκίη, τί δή με λοξὸν ὄμμασι βλέπουσα
νηλέως φεύγεις, δοκεῖς δέ μ' οὐδὲν εἰδέναι σοφόν;

ἴσθι τοι, καλῶς μὲν ἄν τοι τὸν χαλινὸν ἐμβάλοιμι,
ἡνίας δ' ἔχων στρέφοιμί σ' ἀμφὶ τέρματα δρόμου ·
νῦν δὲ λειμῶνάς τε βόσκεαι κοῦφά τε σκιρτῶσα παίζεις · 5
δεξιὸν γὰρ ἱπποπείρην οὐκ ἔχεις ἐπεμβάτην (417).

'Thracian filly, why do you look at me out of the corner of your eye and run pitilessly from me, and suppose that I have no skill? Let me tell you, I could neatly put a bridle on you and holding the reins wheel you round the turning-post of the course; as it is, you graze the meadows and play, skipping lightly, for you have no clever horseman to ride you.' Anacreon relies for his effect on his risqué imagery, common in Greek poetry and used sometimes coarsely, as by Aristophanes, sometimes delicately, as here and in Alcman's maiden-songs. Thracian horses were famous, and if the poem was addressed to a Thracian girl, this might explain the choice of the imagery. The manner is gay and lively with its questions and mock-solemn statement of the speaker's abilities. There is a pleasant touch in the adverb *nēleōs*, 'pitilessly', which belongs to the language of epic and is used here with mock-heroic effect: the girl has an epic stubbornness.

Another encounter with a girl forms the material for one of Anacreon's wittiest poems, in which much is stated and much suggested in very short space:

σφαίρῃ δηὖτέ με πορφυρῇ
βάλλων χρυσοκόμης Ἔρως
νήνι ποικιλοσαμβάλῳ
   συμπαίζειν προκαλεῖται ·
ἡ δ', ἐστὶν γὰρ ἀπ' εὐκτίτου
Λέσβου, τὴν μὲν ἐμὴν κόμην,
λευκὴ γάρ, καταμέμφεται,
   πρὸς δ' ἄλλην τινὰ χάσκει (358).

'Once again golden-haired Eros hits me with a purple ball and challenges me to play with the girl with the fancy shoes; but she, coming as she does from Lesbos with its proud cities, finds fault with my hair, since it is white, and gawps after another—a girl!' Anacreon uses his first stanza to set the scene of this miniature drama: stripped of their imagery the lines say simply that 'once again' (by now a catchword of love poetry) the poet has fallen in love, this time with a girl distinguished by her elaborate footwear. The description no doubt served to identify the girl for Anacreon's listeners, like 'the Thracian filly' of the last poem. The pictorial quality of the stanza is remarkable: each noun is distinguished by a colour-epithet: purple ball, golden-haired Eros, motley sandalled girl; the second stanza has only the white of Anacreon's hair; and of course the imagery is all-important: it is Eros who by aiming his ball sets the drama in motion. In the second stanza he stands aside and the drama unfolds: Anacreon misleads his listeners more than once before revealing the truth of the matter: Lesbos is dignified by an epic-type adjective *euktitou* which draws attention to its fine ancient cities, and the suggestion is that a girl from such a background might consider Anacreon's social status too mean for her; but the reason she actually gives is Anacreon's age: 'Your hair—it's white!' The sad truth is reserved for the last line of the poem: the proclivities of Sappho and her friends were not forgotten, and this girl like them comes from Lesbos. She has eyes only for some other girl—no noun is needed in the Greek, so that the point is the more concisely made—and she concentrates, open-mouthed in her single-mindedness, on her. The poem, which began with bright colours and gay imagery, finishes with mutual fault-finding and the harsh hiss of the verb *khaskei*, 'gapes'.

Love, the ball-player here, has other roles in Anacreon's poetry: we find him as boxer:

φέρ' ὕδωρ, φέρ' οἶνον, ὦ παῖ, φέρε <δ'> ἀνθεμόεντας ἡμὶν
στεφάνους· ἔνεικον, ὡς δὴ πρὸς Ἔρωτα πυκταλίζω (396).

'Bring water and bring wine, boy; bring us flowery garlands: fetch them, so that I may box against Eros'; or as dice-player:

ἀστραγάλαι δ' Ἔρωτός εἰσιν
μανίαι τε καὶ κυδοιμοί (398).

'The dice of Eros are fits of madness and turmoils.' Here *maniai*, 'madness', is commonplace, but not so the epic noun *kudoimoi*, which Homer uses of the uproar of battle. In all these cases Eros plays games of a competitive nature such as a young boy might play; but in another poem Anacreon makes him a blacksmith:

μεγάλῳ δηὖτέ μ' Ἔρως ἔκοψεν ὥστε χαλκεὺς
πελέκει, χειμερίη δ' ἔλουσεν ἐν χαράδρῃ (413).

'Once again Eros hit me with a great hammer like a blacksmith, and soused me in the wintry stream.' Anacreon may have had a Homeric simile in mind: 'as when a blacksmith dips a great hammer or an adze in cold water' (*Od.* 9.391f.); but his imagery is none the less vivid for the Homeric reminiscence.

In another poem it is not Eros but the beloved boy himself who is a charioteer:

ὦ παῖ παρθένιον βλέπων
δίζημαί σε, σὺ δ' οὐ κοεῖς,
οὐκ εἰδὼς ὅτι τῆς ἐμῆς
ψυχῆς ἡνιοχεύεις (360).

'Boy with the virgin glance, I pursue you, but you pay no attention, not realising that you hold the reins of my soul.' This short stanza is a fine example of Anacreon's skilful technique: the first line is notable for the alliteration, and the rhymes and near-rhymes of the other three help to tighten the structure of the stanza. Even in such short lines Anacreon can create a neat antithesis: 'I pursue *you*, but *you* pay no attention'; the pronouns are placed side-by-side for maximum effect. The stanza moves quietly to the impressive epic verb *hēniokheueis* with its unexpected metaphor. Everything is carefully contrived, but the whole reads smoothly and naturally.

Yet another metaphor appears in this fragment:

> ἀρθεὶς δηὖτ' ἀπὸ Λευκάδος
> πέτρης ἐς πολιὸν κῦμα κολυμβῶ μεθύων ἔρωτι (376).

'Once again I take off from the Leucadian rock and dive into the white wave, drunk with love.' To leap from the high cliffs at the southern tip of the island of Leucas was regarded as a cure for love, and there was a story that Sappho ended her life in this way because of her unrequited love for the handsome Phaon. Anacreon's 'drunk with love' may bear some relation to the leap from the cliff if frustrated lovers bolstered their courage with wine before taking the plunge; in any case this imagery, like so much more of Anacreon's, became common usage in later Greek poetry, where the lover 'drinks a draught of love' or is 'drunk on love'.

An ancient authority, who must have known more of Anacreon's poetry than we do, tells us that he was for ever singing of Cleobulus' eyes. This boy is the subject of two surviving pieces: the first depends for its effect on the witty changes of case when his name is given, genitive, then dative, then accusative:

> Κλεοβούλου μὲν ἔγωγ' ἐρέω,
> Κλεοβούλῳ δ' ἐπιμαίνομαι,
> Κλεόβουλον δὲ διοσκέω (359).

'I love Cleobulus, I am mad about Cleobulus, I can't take my eyes off Cleobulus.' The point all but disappears in translation. The other poem takes the form of a prayer to Dionysus and distantly recalls Sappho's prayer to Aphrodite:

> ὦναξ, ᾧ δαμάλης Ἔρως
> καὶ Νύμφαι κυανώπιδες
> πορφυρῆ τ' Ἀφροδίτη
> συμπαίζουσιν, ἐπιστρέφεαι
> δ' ὑψηλὰς ὀρέων κορυφάς·
> γουνοῦμαί σε, σὺ δ' εὐμενὴς
> ἔλθ' ἡμίν, κεχαρισμένης
> δ' εὐχωλῆς ἐπακούειν·
> Κλεοβούλῳ δ' ἀγαθὸς γένεο
> σύμβουλος, τὸν ἐμόν γ' ἔρω-
> τ', ὦ Δεόνυσε, δέχεσθαι (357).

'Lord, with whom Love the subduer and the blue-eyed Nymphs and radiant Aphrodite play, you who haunt the high peaks of the mountains, I beseech you, and do you come graciously at my request. May my prayer be acceptable: I beg you, hear it, and give good advice to Cleobulus, that he accept my love, Dionysus.' Dionysus was not the obvious addressee for a prayer of this nature; but Anacreon, like Alcaeus, may have sung his song with a wine-cup in front of him; in any case the god keeps suitable company—not only his nurses, the Nymphs, but Eros and Aphrodite as well. There is the same deft choice of words as in the other poems: in lines 1–3 the deities each have their own epithet, and the arrangement is chiastic, so that we find the sequence adjective-noun, noun-adjective, adjective-noun. In the sixth line there is the same neat juxta-position of pronouns as in fr. 360, and Anacreon ends with a pun on the boy's name, *Kleoboulōi . . . sumboulos*: the metre reinforces the point.

* * *

Love-poetry of a different kind was composed by Theognis, a contemporary of Anacreon. Some two hundred short poems in elegiac couplets are attributed to him, many of them addressed to a youth called Cyrnus. Much of the content is political, but several of the poems are amatory.

ὦ παῖ, μέχρι τίνος με προφεύξεαι; ὥς σε διώκων
    δίζημ᾿· ἀλλά τί μοι τέρμα γένοιτο κιχεῖν
σῆς ὀργῆς. σὺ δὲ μάργον ἔχων καὶ ἀγήνορα θυμὸν
    φεύγεις, ἰκτίνου σχέτλιον ἦθος ἔχων.
ἀλλ᾿ ἐπίμεινον, ἐμοὶ δὲ δίδου χάριν· οὐκέτι δηρὸν
    ἕξεις Κυπρογενοῦς δῶρον ἰοστεφάνου (1299-1304).

'Boy, how long will you flee from me? How I pursue and seek you! May I be granted some end to your anger. But you have a greedy, proud heart, and you flee with the cruel nature of a kite. Come, stay and grant me your favour: not for long will you have the gift of the violet-crowned Cyprus-born.' This is typical of Theognis in several ways: the bitter, complaining tone, the one sharp image of the kite, the final blunt statement that the boy will not be young for ever. Some of the language is traditional: youthful charms are the 'gift' of Aphrodite, and the goddess is 'violet-crowned', as in Solon and elsewhere, and 'Cyprus-born'; but the poem makes a strong effect and has the stamp of individuality.

Another poem makes a forceful plea for true love, and shows the appropriate-ness of the elegiac couplet for reflective and moralising poetry.

μή μ᾿ ἔπεσιν μὲν στέργε, νόον δ᾿ ἔχε καὶ φρένας ἄλλῃ,
    εἴ με φιλεῖς καί σοι πιστὸς ἔνεστι νόος.
ἤ με φίλει καθαρὸν θέμενος νόον, ἤ μ᾿ ἀποειπὼν

ἔχθαιρ᾿ ἀμφαδίην νεῖκος ἀειράμενος.
ὃς δὲ μιῇ γλώσσῃ δίχ᾿ ἔχει νόον, οὗτος ἑταῖρος
δεινός, Κύρν᾿, ἐχθρὸς βέλτερος ἢ φίλος ὤν (87-92).

'Do not love me in word alone, keeping your mind and heart elsewhere, if you love me and have a loyal mind. Either love me with a pure mind, or refuse and hate me, stirring up an open quarrel. The man who with one tongue thinks double thoughts is a grim companion, Cyrnus, better an enemy than a friend.' Theognis is sometimes slipshod in his expression—a more meticulous writer might not have used the noun *noos*, 'mind', so often, and might have made a neater point than the contrast between the 'one tongue' and 'two minds'; but the poem has great strength, derived partly from the large number of verbs and from the anomalies of 'grim companion', 'better enemy'.

By the end of the sixth century personal lyrics along with elegiac and iambic poetry were less frequently composed than choral lyric poetry, the themes of which did not readily allow an erotic element. Yet Pindar's victory-odes occasionally speak of a successful young athlete as inspiring love: the closing lines of the tenth *Olympian* are a good example:

παῖδ᾿ ἐρατὸν <δ᾿> Ἀρχεστράτου
αἴνησα, τὸν εἶδον κρατέοντα χερὸς ἀλκᾷ
βωμὸν παρ᾿ Ὀλύμπιον
κεῖνον κατὰ χρόνον
ἰδέᾳ τε καλὸν
ὥρᾳ τε κεκραμένον, ἅ ποτε
ἀναιδέα Γανυμήδει θάνατον
ἆλκε σὺν Κυπρογενεῖ (99-105).

'And I have praised the lovely son of Archestratus, whom I saw on that occasion winning with the might of his hands by the Olympic altar, beautiful in appearance and touched by the youthfulness which once kept shameless death away from Ganymede, with the help of the Cyprus-born.' The use of *eratos*, 'lovely', the comparison with Ganymede, Zeus' favourite boy, and the final reference to Aphrodite all contribute to the erotic atmosphere, and Pindar adds a typical touch in the untranslatable *hōrāi . . . kekramenon*, 'mixed with youthful beauty'. The sixth *Pythian* ends with extended praise of Thrasybulus, son of the victor: the closing words are

γλυκεῖα δὲ φρὴν καὶ συμπόταισιν ὁμιλεῖν
μελισσᾶν ἀμείβεται τρητὸν πόνον (52-4),

'Sweet is his temper and as a companion in the symposium he surpasses the perforated labour of the bees.' A drinking-song addressed by Pindar to this young friend, sweeter than the honeycomb, is quoted in the chapter which follows.

If we possessed more of Pindar's verse we should almost certainly have other examples of compliments of this kind. As it is, we have the beginning of an encomium of Theoxenus in whose arms Pindar is said to have died:

χρῆν μὲν κατὰ καιρὸν ἐρώ-
    των δρέπεσθαι, θυμέ, σὺν ἁλικίᾳ·
τὰς δὲ Θεοξένου ἀκτῖνας πρὸς ὄσσων
μαρμαρυζοίσας δρακεὶς
ὃς μὴ πόθῳ κυμαίνεται, ἐξ ἀδάμαντος
ἢ σιδάρου κεχάλκευται μέλαιναν καρδίαν   5

ψυχρᾷ φλογί, πρὸς δ᾽ Ἀφροδί-
    τας ἀτιμασθεὶς ἑλικογλεφάρου
ἢ περὶ χρήμασι μοχθίζει βιαίως
ἢ γυναικείῳ θράσει
ψυχὰν φορεῖται πᾶσαν ὁδὸν θεραπεύων.
ἀλλ᾽ ἐγὼ τᾶς ἕκατι κηρὸς ὣς δαχθεὶς ἕλᾳ   10

ἱρᾶν μελισσᾶν τάκομαι, εὖτ᾽ ἂν ἴδω
παίδων νεόγυιον ἐς ἥβαν·
ἐν δ᾽ ἄρα καὶ Τενέδῳ
Πειθώ τ᾽ ἔναιεν καὶ Χάρις
υἱὸν Ἀγησίλα (fr. 123).   15

'One should pick love's flowers in due season, my heart, in one's youth; but if any man sees the rays flashing from Theoxenus' eyes and is not tossed on a sea of desire, his black heart has been forged from adamant or iron in a cold flame. Dishonoured by Aphrodite of the sparkling eyes he either toils under compulsion for money or (rushes the length of life's path tending his existence?) with womanish courage. But I, stung thanks to her, melt like the wax of holy bees in the sun's heat, whenever I look at the fresh-limbed youth of boys; and it seems that in Tenedos Persuasion and Grace dwell in the son of Hagesilas.' The textual difficulties and with them the uncertainty of interpretation of the passage are notorious, but the richness and variety of the imagery are evident. One is reminded of Mimnermus' picking of the flowers or fruit of love (see p. 215 below), the flashing eyes of Sappho's Anactoria, the melting glances of Alcman's chorus-leader, Persuasion and the Graces in Hesiod and Sappho, but it is only in the choral lyric of Pindar that one would find them in so bold and happy a combination.

The reader might be forgiven for asking if 'Love' is the appropriate title for this chapter. If he approaches the subject from popular fiction or cinema or from 'Romeo and Juliet' or 'Antony and Cleopatra' or from the Troubadours or even from Catullus and Propertius, he will look in vain for anything resembling his idea of love. The theme of the Greek lyric poets is sexual, usually homosexual, desire, a temporary admixture of admiration and lust caused by Eros or his mother Aphrodite.

Notions of love arise from the conditions of society as well as from literary and religious traditions. Greek societies differed from ours principally in the matter of the inferior status of women and the importance of the family unit; but the responses of the poets were not uniform in their treatment of love and differed from one period to another. Homer had emphasised the family bond in his picture of Odysseus, pining for his wife as part of his lost home and estate, or of Penelope, longing for her absent husband and praising him staunchly, or of Nausicaa, so ready to fall for the handsome stranger, who responds by wishing her the greatest gift of the gods, marital harmony. In none of these cases is there explicit mention of Aphrodite or Eros, of love as opposed to love-making, only of suitors, marriage-gifts and the shared bed. The tragic poets were to concentrate on the destructiveness of Eros, 'invincible in battle' and 'inescapable': the chorus of the *Medea* or *Hippolytus* prays for divine protection against the onset of the young god when they see his effect on Medea or Phaedra.

The focus of Greek lyric is narrower. It concentrates on a love that comes to nothing, a leisure pursuit, basically pleasurable, even if the poets sometimes talk in terms of pain and madness. The condition is not seen as permanent: 'once again, Eros . . .' is a catchword of their poetry, and they note that the beloved will age—the girl becoming 'over-ripe', the boy bearded—and be undesirable. Friendship rarely has anything to do with this love. Theognis is the main exception: his alliance with the young man Cyrnus is a friendship based on politics, although it also has an erotic element.

CHAPTER TWO

Wine

The pleasure of wine-drinking was celebrated by Greek poets from Homer onwards. Odysseus puts the matter in a nutshell when he says to his host Alcinous, king of the Phaeacians, 'I say that the summit of delight is when festivity reigns throughout the whole realm, and banqueters seated in their places in the hall listen to a minstrel, and the tables beside them are laden with bread and meat, and a steward ladles wine from the mixing-bowl and pours it in their cups. This to my mind is the finest thing of all' (*Od.* 9.5–11). When Odysseus goes on to tell how he incapacitated the Cyclops by making him drunk, we are given an enthusiastic description of the remarkable wine that he used: it was one of several splendid gifts given to him by the priest of Apollo at Ismarus on the Thracian coast when he called there on his homeward journey from Troy.

> δῶκε δέ μοι κρητῆρα πανάργυρον, αὐτὰρ ἔπειτα
> οἶνον ἐν ἀμφιφορεῦσι δυώδεκα πᾶσιν ἀφύσσας
> ἡδὺν ἀκηράσιον, θεῖον ποτόν· οὐδέ τις αὐτὸν
> ἠείδη δμώων οὐδ' ἀμφιπόλων ἐνὶ οἴκῳ,
> ἀλλ' αὐτὸς ἄλοχος τε φίλη ταμίη τε μί' οἴη.
> τὸν δ' ὅτε πίνοιεν μελιηδέα οἶνον ἐρυθρόν,
> ἓν δέπας ἐμπλήσας ὕδατος ἀνὰ εἴκοσι μέτρα
> χεῦ', ὀδμὴ δ' ἡδεῖα ἀπὸ κρητῆρος ὀδώδει,
> θεσπεσίη· τότ' ἂν οὔ τοι ἀποσχέσθαι φίλον ἦεν (*Od.* 9.203-11).

'And he gave me a mixing-bowl of solid silver, together with a wine which he drew off, twelve jars in all, a sweet unmixed wine, a drink for the gods. None of his servants or attendants in the house knew of it—only he himself, his dear wife and one stewardess. When they drank this red honey-sweet wine, he would take one cupful and pour it over twenty measures of water, and its sweet bouquet rose from the mixing-bowl, a divine bouquet. On those occasions abstinence would give no pleasure.'

One sees why Horace spoke of 'vinosus Homerus'; this is Homer at his most lyrical, the Homer who described Hera's seduction of Zeus with such lively imagination. But he expressed elsewhere the hazards of drinking: Odysseus, hoping to borrow a cloak from Eumaeus, begins:

εὐξάμενός τι ἔπος ἐρέω· οἶνος γὰρ ἀνώγει
ἠλεός, ὅς τ' ἐφέηκε πολύφρονά περ μάλ' ἀεῖσαι
καί θ' ἁπαλὸν γελάσαι, καί τ' ὀρχήσασθαι ἀνῆκε,
καί τι ἔπος προέηκεν ὅ πέρ τ' ἄρρητον ἄμεινον (*Od.* 14.463-6).

'I have formed a wish and shall speak: the wine prompts me—crazy wine, which sets even a wise man singing and laughing like a young girl and makes him dance and utter words which would be better unspoken.'

The *Iliad* has more references to wine-drinking than one might expect: Nestor offers Pramnian wine to his guests in a remarkable golden cup (11.632ff.); Hecuba gives her son Hector wine so that he may pour libation to the gods and then refresh himself; and the gods drink their nectar with the same gusto as men their wine.

These few excerpts show that in Homer's time the conventions of wine-drinking were much as in later Greece. Wine was regarded not as a luxury but as a daily necessity which regularly brought much pleasure and occasionally led to unseemly behaviour. It was seldom drunk neat, except for medicinal purposes and by barbarians; and of course libations to the gods were of un-mixed wine. The practice was to mix the wine with water in proportions which varied according to the strength of the wine or the intentions of the drinkers. The *kratēr*, a large mixing-bowl, was an essential piece of equipment; according to Xenophanes (fr. 4) the water was poured in first and the wine on top, as in Homer's account of the Ismaric wine.

Hesiod in one of his most lyrical passages recommends a mixture of three parts water to one part wine for drinking out-of-doors in summer:

ἐπὶ δ' αἴθοπα πινέμεν οἶνον,
ἐν σκιῇ ἑζόμενον, κεκορημένον ἦτορ ἐδωδῆς,
ἀντίον ἀκραέος Ζεφύρου τρέψαντα πρόσωπα·
κρήνης δ' αἰενάου καὶ ἀπορρύτου, ἥ τ' ἀθόλωτος,
τρὶς ὕδατος προχέειν, τὸ δὲ τέτρατον ἱέμεν οἴνου (*Op.* 592-6).

'Then drink the glowing wine, as you sit in the shade, satisfied with a good meal, turning your face towards the brisk West wind: pour three measures of water from a constant running spring, unpolluted, and add the fourth part of wine.' We shall see that Anacreon recommends 2 : 1 for restrained drinking and that the more boisterous Alcaeus prescribes 1 : 2. The practice of diluting the wine was obviously regarded as a means for prolonging a party; only abandoned men, loose women and barbarians drank unmixed wine. The corollary was that drunkenness was reprehensible: *oinobarēs*, 'heavy with wine', is used as an opprobrious epithet in *Iliad* 1.225.

*   *   *

Wine was a favourite theme of the lyric poets, and it is likely that the symposium, the evening drinking-party, was the occasion for the performance of much of their poetry. We can reconstruct its conventions from the poetry of Alcaeus, Anacreon, Theognis and others, and for the late fifth century from Aristophanes' comedies and Plato's and Xenophon's accounts of symposia at which Socrates was present. It was an all-male gathering: if women or girls were present, they were musicians, dancers or prostitutes hired for their services. Libations were poured in honour of the gods, a hymn was sung or prayer made, and the drinking began with the election of a symposiarch or master of ceremonies, one of whose duties was to decide the proportion of wine and water; the phrase 'beside the mixing-bowl' signifies 'at the symposium'. Garlands were worn and perfume was often used. There might be earnest conversation or riddles or games; scolia might be sung, one performer capping the song of another; and in the late fifth century well-known lines of Alcaeus or Anacreon or Simonides might be sung.

The symposiasts were often linked by a social or political bond: Alcaeus sings for those who oppose the various tyrants in Mytilene, Theognis for his fellow-aristocrats in Megara; some of the scolia belong to Athenian democratic circles, others to the nobles and oligarchs. In such groups or *hetaireiai* loyalty and secrecy were important, so the songs emphasise the theme that wine shows a man in his true colours and loosens his tongue when taken in excess. For the young aristocrat the symposium was an important formative influence outside his home: Theognis is the best example of an older man giving his younger friend instruction in politics, morality and social relationships.

Alcaeus stands out as the toper among the lyric poets; Athenaeus, to whom we owe many of the surviving drinking-songs, comments that Alcaeus is found drinking in all seasons and circumstances. One scrap of his poetry mentions springtime:

> ἦρος ἀνθεμόεντος ἐπάιον ἐρχομένοιο . . .
> ἐν δὲ κέρνατε τὼ μελιάδεος ὄττι τάχιστα
> κράτηρα (367).

'I heard the flowery spring coming . . . mix a bowl of the honey-sweet wine as fast as you can.' The midsummer heat of the dogdays is mentioned more than once:

> πώνωμεν, τὸ γὰρ ἄστρον περιτέλλεται . . . (352),

'Let us drink: the dogstar is coming round . . .'; and, more colourfully,

> τέγγε πλεύμονας οἴνῳ, τὸ γὰρ ἄστρον περιτέλλεται,
> ἀ δ' ὤρα χαλέπα, πάντα δὲ δίψαισ' ὐπὰ καύματος,
> ἄχει δ' ἐκ πετάλων ἄδεα τέττιξ, πτερύγων δ' ὐπα
> κακχέει λιγύραν <πύκνον> ἀοίδαν, <θέρος> ὄπποτα
> φλόγιον † καθέταν ἐπιπτάμενον καταυδείη † . . .   5

ἄνθει δὲ σκόλυμος· νῦν δὲ γύναικες μιαρώταται,
λέπτοι δ' ἄνδρες, ἐπεὶ <δὴ> κεφάλαν καὶ γόνα Σείριος
ἄσδει . . . (347).

'Wet your lungs with wine: the dogstar is coming round, the season is harsh, everything thirsts under the heat, the cicada chirps sweetly from the leaves, pouring incessantly its clear song from under its wings, when flaming summer . . . The artichoke is in flower. Now are women at their most pestilential, but men are feeble, since Sirius parches their heads and knees . . .' This lively piece is a recasting of lines of Hesiod (*Op.* 582–8) in lyric metre and Lesbian dialect, and the detail is his except for the opening flourish which bears the stamp of Alcaeus, with its verb in the first place and what is either a popular turn of phrase or a colourful invention, 'wet your lungs'. Winter offers an equally valid excuse for drinking:

ὔει μὲν ὁ Ζεῦς, ἐκ δ' ὀράνω μέγας
χείμων, πεπάγαισιν δ' ὐδάτων ῥόαι . . .

κάββαλλε τὸν χείμων', ἐπὶ μὲν τίθεις   5
πῦρ, ἐν δὲ κέρναις οἶνον ἀφειδέως
μέλιχρον, αὐτὰρ ἀμφὶ κόρσα
μόλθακον ἀμφι<βάλων> γνόφαλλον (338).

'Zeus is raining, a great storm comes from the heavens, flowing streams are frozen solid . . . Down with the storm! Stoke up the fire, mix the sweet wine without sparing it, and put a soft pillow about your head.' This is vigorous writing: the clauses and phrases are remarkably short, and they are linked by the simplest connectives: *men . . . de . . . de . . .*; *men . . . de . . . autar . . . .* The verbs come emphatically at the beginnings of the clauses and give an air of briskness and busy activity. The whole is made orderly and precise by the use of the four-line alcaic stanza: this metrical scheme, the commonest in the fragments of Alcaeus, manages to combine tightness of structure with remarkable variations in pace, and is one of the finest creations of the lyric poets.

Equally vigorous is this exhortation in the asclepiad metre:

πώνωμεν· τί τὰ λύχν' ὀμμένομεν; δάκτυλος ἀμέρα·
κὰδ δάερρε κυλίχναις μεγάλαις, ἄϊτα, ποικίλαις·
οἶνον γὰρ Σεμέλας καὶ Δίος υἶος λαθικάδεον
ἀνθρώποισιν ἔδωκ'. ἔγχεε κέρναις ἔνα καὶ δύο
πλήαις κὰκ κεφάλας, <ἀ> δ' ἀτέρα τὰν ἀτέραν κύλιξ   5
ὠθήτω . . . (346).

'Let's drink! Why do we wait for the lamps? A finger's breadth of daylight is all that remains. Take down the great decorated cups, my friend; for the

32 *The Golden Lyre*

son of Zeus and Semele gave men wine to make them forget their worries. Pour it in brimful, mixing one part of water to two of wine, and let one cup elbow the next. . . .' Alcaeus shows here the same tendency to begin his sentences with verbs, and the same preference for short units of expression: notice how much he packs into his first line. We cannot say whether the striking *daktulos amera*, 'a finger's breadth of daylight', was a commonplace or an invention of Alcaeus; it certainly was proverbial after his time. The jostling of the cups is another happy idea, and Alcaeus exploits the metre for an amusing effect in *a d' atera tan ateran*.

The idea that one should drown one's sorrows is stated more elaborately in the following alcaic stanza:

οὐ χρῆ κάκοισι θῦμον ἐπιτρέπην·
προκόψομεν γὰρ οὐδὲν ἀσάμενοι,
ὦ Βύκχι, φαρμάκων δ' ἄριστον
οἶνον ἐνεικαμένοις μεθύσθην (335).

'We should not surrender our hearts to our troubles, for we shall make no headway by distressing ourselves, Bycchis. The best cure is to bring wine and get drunk.' The language is lively: the verb *prokoptein*, 'to make headway', is not attested for any writer before Alcaeus, but we cannot say whether it was bold metaphor (presumably from roadbuilding) or common usage. The medical term *pharmakon*, 'remedy', 'cure', was used figuratively by Hesiod and Archilochus before Alcaeus; the participle *asamenoi*, 'distressing ourselves', may form part of the same imagery as *pharmakon*, since the noun *asē* and its derived adjectives belong above all to medical writers and denote physical distress, perhaps nausea. We cannot say who Bycchis was; he is mentioned elsewhere by Alcaeus, once in a context of revelry, but we know nothing of their relationship. The use of the personal name gives added vividness to the poem, and reminds us that much early Greek lyric was didactic in tone.

Alcaeus was deeply involved in the politics of Mytilene, and one famous song, inspired by the death of a politician, began

νῦν χρῆ μεθύσθην καί τινα πὲρ βίαν
πώνην, ἐπεὶ δὴ κάτθανε Μύρσιλος . . . (332).

'Now is the time to get drunk, now everyone should drink with all his might: Myrsilus is dead . . .' Horace, who based several of his odes on poems by Alcaeus, echoed the opening phrase of this forthright piece in his ode on the death of Cleopatra: *nunc est bibendum* (*Carm.* 1.37.1).

Another drinking-song is a sombre reminder that we have only one life to enjoy, and makes its point by allusion to the myth of Sisyphus, the trickster who cheated Death into letting him return from the underworld. The text comes from a tattered piece of papyrus, and my translation gives what I take to be the general sense:

πῶνε [καὶ μέθυ' ὦ] Μελάνιππ' ἄμ' ἔμοι· τί [φαῖς
† ὄταμε [. . . .] διννάεντ' † 'Αχέροντα μεγ[
ζάβαι[ς ἀ]ελίω κόθαρον φάος [ἄψερον
ὄψεσθ'; ἀλλ' ἄγι μὴ μεγάλων ἐπ[ιβάλλεο·
καὶ γὰρ Σίσυφος Αἰολίδαις βασίλευς [ἔφα   5
ἀνδρῶν πλεῖστα νοησάμενος [θανάτω κρέτην·
ἀλλὰ καὶ πολύιδρις ἔων ὑπὰ κᾶρι [δὶς
διννάεντ' 'Αχέροντ' ἐπέραισε, μ[
αὔτω μόχθον ἔχην Κρονίδαις βα[σίλευς κάτω
μελαίνας χθόνος· ἀλλ' ἄγι μὴ τά[δ' ἐπέλπεο·   10
θᾶς] τ' ἀβάσομεν αἴ ποτα κἄλλοτα. [
. . .] ην ὄττινα τῶνδε πάθην τά[χα δῶ θέος (38A).

'Drink and get drunk with me, Melanippus. Why do you suppose that when you have crossed eddying Acheron you will see the sun's pure light again? Come on, do not set your heart on great exploits: why, king Sisyphus, son of Aeolus, supposed that he, cleverest of men, was victorious over death: but despite his cunning he crossed eddying Acheron twice at fate's command, and king Zeus, son of Cronus, ordained great toil for him under the black earth. Come on, do not hope for such exploits. Now if ever, while we are young, we should take whatever enjoyment of these things God may chance to give us.' It is not certain that the poem ended at this point, but it is interesting in any case to find Alcaeus using a mythological example as the text for his brief sermon. The story of Sisyphus, told allusively on the assumption that his hearers knew the detail, occupies the central position, and is flanked by the exhortations to drink and be merry. Even although the text is so gappy, we can sense the vigour and appreciate the conciseness and economy which distinguish Alcaeus' composition.

A few other striking phrases have been recorded from his poems:

οἶνος, ὦ φίλε παῖ, καὶ ἀλάθεα (366),

'Wine, dear boy, and truth', has generally been taken to make the same point as the Latin tag, *in vino veritas*. The vocative case, *ō phile pai*, 'dear boy', displays the didactic tone which we have already noted, but the context in which Theocritus used the line in one of his idylls (29.1) shows that the poem was amatory. A similar point is made by the line

οἶνος γὰρ ἀνθρώπω δίοπτρον (333),

'wine is a peephole into a man'. The noun *dioptron* is found here only; Aeschylus later used the common word *katoptron* when he wrote that wine is the 'mirror' of the mind. Theognis put it less adventurously:

ἀνδϱὸς δ' οἶνος ἔδειξε νόον (500),

'wine shows up a man's mind'. Another line of Alcaeus refers to the *kōmos*, the drunken procession of revellers through the streets, a favourite subject of vase-paintings:

δέξαι με κωμάσδοντα δέξαι, λίσσομαί σε λίσσομαι (374),

'welcome me the reveller, welcome me, I beg you, I beg you'. The insistence of the repeated verbs is lively, and the unusual iambic line moves rapidly. Lastly, a line, perhaps a take-off of Hesiod's precepts, which captured Horace's imagination and forms the beginning of his drinking-song *nullam, Vare, sacra vite prius severis arborem* (*Carm.* 1.18):

μηδὲν ἄλλο φυτεύσῃς πϱότεϱον δένδϱεον ἀμπέλω (342),

'plant no tree sooner than the vine'.

*   *   *

Alcaeus has pride of place in this chapter, but Archilochus had provided a precedent for drinking-songs written in boisterous tone. One pair of couplets speaks of drinking while on guard-duty on board ship:

ἀλλ' ἄγε σὺν κώθωνι θοῆς διὰ σέλματα νηὸς
φοίτα καὶ κοίλων πώματ' ἄφελκε κάδων,
ἄγϱει δ' οἶνον ἐϱυθϱὸν ἀπὸ τϱυγός· οὐδὲ γὰϱ ἡμεῖς
νηφέμεν ἐν φυλακῇ τῇδε δυνησόμεθα (4.6-9).

'Come on, go up and down the benches of the swift ship with your jug and remove the covers from the hollow casks: draw off the red wine right down to the lees: for not even we shall be able to stay sober on this watch.' There is doubt about the detail: *phoita* may mean 'keep going up and down', *aphelke* may be 'wrench the covers from the casks', *agrei* may be 'seize the red wine'; and if these interpretations are accepted, the carousal becomes still more hectic. Archilochus is writing in elegiac couplets, a dactylic framework in which Homeric formulae are at home, so that he uses the conventional epithets, 'swift ship', 'hollow casks', 'red wine'. As Alcaeus did later, he gives prominence to his verbs; and Alcaeus may have recollected the introductory *all' age* (38A). A papyrus scrap provides the beginnings of the four lines which precede this fragment, and the couplet immediately before our four lines seems to run, 'There is no dinner ready for you or for me.'

Archilochus speaks of wine in the context of warfare in his famous couplet,

ἐν δορὶ μέν μοι μᾶζα μεμαγμένη, ἐν δορὶ δ' οἶνος
Ἰσμαρικός, πίνω δ' ἐν δορὶ κεκλιμένος (2).

'In my spear is my kneaded bread, in my spear is my Ismaric wine, and I drink it leaning on my spear.' He seems to be saying that his spear earns him his food and drink; the Ismaric wine reminds us of the Cyclops story in *Odyssey* 9, but since Archilochus fought against Thracian tribes, Ismaric wine may have been no more than the *vin du pays* for him. The couplet is neatly constructed with its anaphora of *en dori*; there is unusually prominent alliteration of *m* in the opening phrase.

Another two lines of Archilochus, this time in trochaic metre, are important for the history of the dithyramb or hymn to Dionysus and relevant here for the imaginative language:

ὡς Διωνύσοι' ἄνακτος καλὸν ἐξάρξαι μέλος
οἶδα διθύραμβον οἴνῳ συγκεραυνωθεὶς φρένας (120).

'Since I know how to start off the fair song of lord Dionysus, the dithyramb, when my brain is blitzed with wine.' Later poets, Simonides and Pindar among them, composed elaborate choral dithyrambs in honour of Dionysus, but the song sung by the wine-crazed Archilochus was perhaps no more than an artless formula of praise. *Oinōi sunkeraunōtheis phrenas*, 'my brain struck by wine as if by a thunderbolt', is an impressive phrase, original so far as we can say. Another description of revelry, quoted out of context, is

ἔξωθεν ἕκαστος
ἔπινεν, ἐν δὲ βαχχίη (194),

'each man drank outside, and within there was Bacchic revelry'; and we have a reprimand to a friend, Pericles by name, for gate-crashing parties:

πολλὸν δὲ πίνων καὶ χαλίκρητον μέθυ,
οὔτε τῖμον εἰσενείκας . . .
οὐδὲ μὲν κληθεὶς . . . . ἦλθες οἷα δὴ φίλος,
ἀλλά σεο γαστὴρ νόον τε καὶ φρένας παρήγαγεν
εἰς ἀναιδείην . . . (124b).

'You drank unmixed wine in great quantities but did not pay your share . . . You did not come invited as a friend: your belly misled your wits and brain into shamelessness.' Archilochus' tone is lofty, as in his other complaints about injuries done him by friends; and we note that the depraved Pericles went so far as to drink his host's wine unmixed.

Other early poets have less to say on the subject. The choral poet Alcman, who spoke of himself as a glutton, praised the wines of half-a-dozen cities in a passage the text of which is corrupt, and described certain wine as *apuros*, 'unfired, unboiled', and *antheos osdōn*, 'smelling of flowers' (92). There is no mention of wine in the surviving fragments of Mimnermus, although one might have expected him to list it as one of the blessings of our fleeting life. Solon was altogether too sober to write drinking songs, but he does mention Dionysus among the givers of joy:

> ἔργα δὲ Κυπρογενοῦς νῦν μοι φίλα καὶ Διονύσου
> καὶ Μουσέων, ἃ τίθησ' ἀνδράσιν εὐφροσύνας (20).

'Now are the works of Cyprian Aphrodite dear to me, and of Dionysus and the Muses—the things which give joys to men.' Sappho was presumably debarred by her sex from taking part in the symposia which her contemporary Alcaeus enjoyed; she can only request Aphrodite to appear and pour out the divine equivalent of wine:

> χρυσίαισιν ἐν κυλίκεσσιν ἄβρως
> ὀμμεμείχμενον θαλίαισι νέκταρ
> οἰνοχόαισον . . . (2).

'In gold cups pour gracefully the nectar that is mingled with our festivities.'

* * *

From the second half of the sixth century onwards poets display two attitudes towards wine-drinking. There is still the straightforward exhortation to drink and drown one's sorrows; but a cautionary note is also heard: one should drink with moderation and decorum, only certain topics are suited to the drinking-song, and so on.

Anacreon writes in both moods. Posterity regarded him as a drunkard, and there was a story that he died by choking on a grape-pip. Here is the lover's cry for wine and water which was quoted in the last chapter:

> φέρ' ὕδωρ, φέρ' οἶνον, ὦ παῖ, φέρε <δ'> ἀνθεμόεντας ἡμὶν
> στεφάνους· ἔνεικον, ὡς δὴ πρὸς Ἔρωτα πυκταλίζω (396).

'Bring water, bring wine, boy! Come, bring us garlands of flowers: fetch them, so that I may box against Eros.' The jollity of tone is unrestrained, and the anacreontic metre adds to the pace of the poem. An elegiac scrap, quoted out of context, suggests a spirit of revelry:

> οἰνοπότης δὲ πεποίημαι (eleg. 4),

'I have been made into a wine-drinker'. He describes parties in two surviving fragments:

οἰνοχόει δ᾽ ἀμφίπολος μελιχρὸν
οἶνον τρικύαθον κελέβην ἔχουσα (383).

'The serving-girl pours out the sweet wine, holding a bowl that takes three ladlesful';

and   ἐπὶ δ᾽ ὀφρύσιν σελίνων στεφανίσκους
                       θέμενοι θάλειαν ἑορτὴν ἀγάγωμεν
                       Διονύσῳ (410).

'Let us put garlands of celery on our brows and celebrate a vigorous festival in honour of Dionysus.' In one of his love-poems, mentioned in the last chapter, he requests the wine-god to help him in his love-affair (357): that poem must have been intended for performance at a drinking-party. The exaggeration in the next piece suggests an abandoned carousal:

ἠρίστησα μὲν ἰτρίου λεπτοῦ μικρὸν ἀποκλάς,
οἴνου δ᾽ ἐξέπιον κάδον· νῦν δ᾽ ἁβρῶς ἐρόεσσαν
ψάλλω πηκτίδα τῇ φίλῃ κωμάζων <παρὰ> παιδί (373).

'I lunched on a small piece I broke off a thin honeycake, but I drained a cask of wine. Now I delicately pluck my lovely lyre as I sing a serenade by the side of my dear girl.' The text and interpretation are doubtful at certain points. Ancient scholars thought that Anacreon must have used *kados*, 'cask', in the sense of 'cup', but the verb *exepion*, 'I drained', and the associations of *habrōs* with luxurious living and of *kōmazōn* with drunken revelry suggest that their interpretation was wrong. I take it that Anacreon was contrasting his frugal eating with his hearty drinking. 'Lovely' is a pale translation of *eroessan*; 'my amorous lyre' is perhaps too colourful, but it at least conveys the erotic tone. The last two words of the fragment are uncertain; Anacreon may have given the name of his dear girl—Poliarche perhaps, or Poliagre or Iambe.

Against these poems we must set a small group in which Anacreon preaches moderation: first, two sections of a drinking-song in anacreontic rhythm:

(a)   ἄγε δὴ φέρ᾽ ἡμὶν ὦ παῖ
                       κελέβην, ὅκως ἄμυστιν
                       προπίω, τὰ μὲν δέκ᾽ ἐγχέας
                       ὕδατος, τὰ πέντε δ᾽ οἴνου
                       κυάθους ὡς ἀνυβριστὶ
                       ἀνὰ δηὖτε βασσαρήσω.
(b)   ἄγε δηὖτε μηκέτ᾽ οὕτω
                       πατάγῳ τε κἀλαλητῷ
                       Σκυθικὴν πόσιν παρ᾽ οἴνῳ
                       μελετῶμεν, ἀλλὰ καλοῖς
                       ὑποπίνοντες ἐν ὕμνοις (356).

'Come, boy, bring us a bowl, so that I may drink without stopping for breath. Pour in ten ladles of water and five of wine, so that I may decorously play the Bacchant yet again.' 'Come on, let us no longer practise Scythian-style drinking like this with clatter and shouting over our wine: let's drink in moderation amid lovely hymns.' The second excerpt is unambiguous: Anacreon in the role of master of ceremonies gives warning that the party is getting out of control. 'Hymns' is somewhat misleading as a translation of *humnoi*, since these could be cult-songs for heroes as well as gods, but it is clear that Anacreon is prescribing dignified performances. The Scythians were notorious as drinkers of neat wine. The tone of the first excerpt is less clear: the words *amustin propiō*, 'drink without stopping for breath', suggest undisciplined drinking, but *amustis* may have meant only a large drinking-cup. The proportion of water to wine is high: Alcaeus' prescription was for a mixture four times as strong. The text is corrupt at the end of the fifth line, but the proposed reading *anubristi*, 'decorously, without outrage', fits the idea of moderation which is inherent in the weak mixture. The verb *bassarēsō* is an unusual word: *bassara* was said to be a Cyrenaic term for 'fox', and *Bassareus* was a cult title of Dionysus, so that *ana-bassareō* denotes the behaviour of a devotee of Dionysus; it is not certain whether it would have suggested simply drinking or excessive drinking. On balance I think that Anacreon calls for moderation in the first excerpt as he does in the second. Another fragment prescribes a clean bowl and a weak mixture:

καθαρῇ δ' ἐν κελέβῃ πέντε <τε> καὶ τρεῖς ἀναχείσθω (409).

'In a clean bowl let him pour five of water and three of wine.' And another scrap tells a woman to watch her tongue while she is drinking:

μηδ' ὥστε κῦμα πόντιον
λάλαζε, τῇ πολυκρότῃ
σὺν Γαστροδώρῃ καταχύδην
πίνουσα τὴν ἐπίστιον (427).

'And don't babble like a wave of the sea, swilling down the hearth-cup along with that battered Gastrodora.' There is a plainly satirical element in these lively iambic lines, and the name 'Gastro-dora' reads like a comic version of 'Metrodora' or something similar. Anacreon uses one striking device after another: the comparison of the talkative woman to the sea-wave, the onomatopoeic verb *lalaze*, 'babble', the ambiguous epithet *polukrotēi*, probably 'battered' with allusion to a busy sex life, but capable of meaning 'wily' or 'noisy', the adverb *katakhudēn*, attested only here, 'like someone pouring it down', and lastly the unusual word *epistion*, 'the hearth-cup', said to mean the same as *anisōma*, 'the equalisation-cup'—which is to explain the obscure by the obscure. The lines are a fine example of the wit, economy and neatness of Anacreon.

For his most forthright statement on the correct conduct of a symposium Anacreon used the elegiac couplet, the metre commonly used both for reflective poetry and for prescriptive writing:

> οὐ φιλέω ὃς κρητῆρι παρὰ πλέῳ οἰνοποτάζων
> νείκεα καὶ πόλεμον δακρυόεντα λέγει,
> ἀλλ' ὅστις Μουσέων τε καὶ ἀγλαὰ δῶρ' Ἀφροδίτης
> συμμίσγων ἐρατῆς μνήσκεται εὐφροσύνης (eleg. 2).

'I don't love the man who while drinking his wine beside the full mixing-bowl talks of quarrels and tearful war: give me the man who by mixing the splendid gifts of the Muses and Aphrodite keeps lovely festivity in mind.' Love-song, then, the poetry for which Anacreon himself was most renowned, is what the civilised drinker should sing; and, as we have noticed before, 'lovely' is an inadequate translation of *eratēs*, which has a more erotic flavour, especially when Aphrodite is in the offing. The participle *summisgōn*, 'mixing', is apt in the context of a symposium, where the mixing of water and wine was of such importance. When Anacreon rejects 'quarrels and tearful war', he may be thinking of his predecessor Alcaeus, whose drinking-songs were often concerned with the violent politics of Lesbos, or contrasting lyric with epic.

*   *   *

Xenophanes, a contemporary of Anacreon, gives the most detailed account of a well-ordered party:

> νῦν γὰρ δὴ ζάπεδον καθαρὸν καὶ χεῖρες ἁπάντων
> καὶ κύλικες· πλεκτοὺς δ' ἀμφιτιθεῖ στεφάνους,
> ἄλλος δ' εὐῶδες μύρον ἐν φιάλῃ παρατείνει·
> κρητὴρ δ' ἔστηκεν μεστὸς εὐφροσύνης·
> ἄλλος δ' οἶνος ἑτοῖμος, ὃς οὔποτέ φησι προδώσειν   5
> μείλιχος ἐν κεράμοις ἄνθεος ὀζόμενος.
> ἐν δὲ μέσοις ἁγνὴν ὀδμὴν λιβανωτὸς ἵησι,
> ψυχρὸν δ' ἐστὶν ὕδωρ καὶ γλυκὺ καὶ καθαρόν·
> παρκέαται δ' ἄρτοι ξανθοὶ γεραρή τε τράπεζα
> τυροῦ καὶ μέλιτος πίονος ἀχθομένη·   10
> βωμὸς δ' ἄνθεσιν ἂν τὸ μέσον πάντη πεπύκασται,
> μολπὴ δ' ἀμφὶς ἔχει δώματα καὶ θαλίη.
> χρὴ δὲ πρῶτον μὲν θεὸν ὑμνεῖν εὔφρονας ἄνδρας
> εὐφήμοις μύθοις καὶ καθαροῖσι λόγοις·
> σπείσαντάς τε καὶ εὐξαμένους τὰ δίκαια δύνασθαι   15
> πρήσσειν – ταῦτα γὰρ ὦν ἐστι προχειρότερον –
> οὐχ ὕβρις πίνειν ὁπόσον κεν ἔχων ἀφίκοιο
> οἴκαδ' ἄνευ προπόλου μὴ πάνυ γηραλέος.

ἀνδρῶν δ' αἰνεῖν τοῦτον ὃς ἐσθλὰ πιὼν ἀναφαίνει,
ὡς οἱ μνημοσύνη καὶ τόνος ἀμφ' ἀρετῆς.   20
οὔ τι μάχας διέπει Τιτήνων οὐδὲ Γιγάντων
    οὐδέ <τι> Κενταύρων, πλάσματα τῶν προτέρων,
ἢ στάσιας σφεδανάς· τοῖς οὐδὲν χρηστὸν ἔνεστι·
    θεῶν <δὲ> προμηθείην αἰὲν ἔχειν ἀγαθόν (1).

'For now the floor is clean and everyone's hands and the cups. One attendant puts woven garlands about our heads, another offers sweet-scented perfume in a dish. The mixing-bowl stands full of merriment, and another wine is ready, a wine which says it will never betray us, gentle and smelling of flowers in its jars. In our midst frankincense gives forth its pure scent, and there is cold water, sweet and clean. Yellow loaves lie beside us and a venerable table, laden with cheese and rich honey. The altar in the middle is decked with flowers on all sides, and singing and festivity fill the house. Festive men ought first of all to hymn God with reverent tales and clean words. When they have made libation and prayed for power to act justly—for indeed this is the obvious prayer to make—it is no outrage to drink as much as will allow you to reach home without the help of an attendant—unless you are very old. Commend that man who after drinking gives an honourable performance, as his memory and his enthusiasm for virtue enable him. He does not deal with the battles of Titans or Giants or of Centaurs either, the creations of our predecessors, nor with violent factions: there is no good in them. To give consideration to the gods at all times is a good thing.'

The poet's insistence on cleanliness and godliness sets this exhortation in a class of its own. The word *katharos*, 'clean', is used of the floor, the guests' hands and the cups (1), of the water (8), and in the second part of the poem of the words that are to be used in the hymns (14). This repetition contributes to the pleasing balance between the two twelve-line sections of our poem: the preparations for the symposium are to be matched in beauty and order by the song and story. The moral tone is strong: *hubris*, outrage, is to be avoided in the drinking, goodness and excellence (*esthla, aretēs, khrēston*) are of crucial importance in the singing and story-telling. A remarkable feature of the composition is the personification of the wine, which declares its loyalty, and of the table, which is 'venerable' or 'reverend': it is impossible to say whether this is an affectation of the poet or a reflection of mystical beliefs. The repeated adjective *katharos*, 'clean', may refer to ritual purity, and it makes sense to view the poem as written for a ritual meal of a philosophic club, dining together in the manner of the Pythagoreans, although there are no strong grounds for the belief that Xenophanes was president of such a school. In another fragment he prescribes the topics of a more intimate conversation.

πὰρ πυρὶ χρὴ τοιαῦτα λέγειν χειμῶνος ἐν ὥρῃ

ἐν κλίνῃ μαλακῇ κατακείμενον, ἔμπλεον ὄντα,
πίνοντα γλυκὺν οἶνον, ὑποτρώγοντ᾽ ἐρεβίνθους·
'τίς πόθεν εἰς ἀνδρῶν; πόσα τοι ἔτε᾽ ἐστί, φέριστε;
πηλίκος ἦσθ᾽, ὅθ᾽ ὁ Μῆδος ἀφίκετο;' . . . (18D.).

'This is what one ought to say, when one is reclining by the fireside in winter-time on a soft couch, with a full stomach, drinking sweet wine and nibbling chick-peas: "Who are you, and where do you come from? How many years since you were born, my friend? How old were you when the Medes came?" . . .' The passage, written in hexameters, has a strongly Homeric flavour, notably in the string of questions; it is curiously moving, partly because of the detail of the first three lines, partly because of the idea of a bond established by a common catastrophe, the Median attack on the Ionian cities.

One of our few fragments of another contemporary, Phocylides, consists of two hexameters written in the same genre:

χρὴ δ᾽ ἐν συμποσίῳ κυλίκων περινισομενάων
ἡδέα κωτίλλοντα καθήμενον οἰνοποτάζειν (14D.).

'At the symposium while the cups pass round one ought to chat pleasantly as one sits drinking the wine.' Phocylides uses long rolling words to make the point that quarrels and unpleasantness are to be avoided. An isolated iambic line of Hipponax runs

ὀλίγα φρονέουσιν οἱ χάλιν πεπωκότες (67).

'Those who have drunk unmixed wine have little sense.'

*   *   *

The theme of wine-drinking is treated more fully by yet another contemporary, Theognis, much of whose poetry must have been recited, perhaps sung, at Megarian parties. One short poem makes the point that wine is both a blessing and a curse:

οἶνε, τὰ μέν σ᾽ αἰνῶ, τὰ δὲ μέμφομαι· οὐδέ σε πάμπαν
οὔτε ποτ᾽ ἐχθαίρειν οὔτε φιλεῖν δύναμαι.
ἐσθλὸν καὶ κακόν ἐσσι. τίς ἂν σέ γε μωμήσαιτο,
τίς δ᾽ ἂν ἐπαινήσαι μέτρον ἔχων σοφίης; (873-6).

'Wine, I both praise you and blame you; I cannot ever hate you or love you completely. You are blessing and curse. What man with due measure of wisdom could find fault with you, what man commend you?' The other poems of Theognis neatly illustrate this antithesis. There is unqualified praise of wine:

ἄφρονες ἄνθρωποι καὶ νήπιοι, οἵτινες οἶνον
μὴ πίνουσ' ἄστρου καὶ κυνὸς ἀρχομένου (1039-40).

'They are fools and simpletons who do not drink wine when the Dogstar begins.' The sentiment goes back to Alcaeus and beyond him to Hesiod: the expression is vigorous and pithy, in Theognis' best manner. In the following piece he lingers over the origin of a wine:

πῖν' οἶνον, τὸν ἐμοὶ κορυφῆς ὕπο Τηϋγέτοιο
ἄμπελοι ἤνεγκαν τὰς ἐφύτευσ' ὁ γέρων   880
οὔρεος ἐν βήσσῃσι θεοῖσι φίλος Θεότιμος,
ἐκ Πλατανιστοῦντος ψυχρὸν ὕδωρ ἐπάγων.
τοῦ πίνων ἀπὸ μὲν χαλεπὰς σκεδάσεις μελεδώνας,
θωρηχθεὶς δ' ἔσεαι πολλὸν ἐλαφρότερος (879-84).

'Drink a wine which vines bore for me under the peaks of Taygetus; old Theotimus, beloved by the gods, planted them in the mountain valleys, bringing in cold water from Platanistus. Drink from it, and you will scatter your troublesome cares; when you are drunk, you will be more light-hearted by far.' The opening has a fine flourish and again recalls Alcaeus' songs; the description of the Spartan vineyard on the foothills of Mount Taygetus is leisurely; note how Theognis plays on the name of Theotimus, 'God-honoured'; the final couplet resumes the vigorous tone of the opening, and introduces a favourite word of Theognis, *thōrēkhtheis*, 'breastplated' or 'drunk': wine like a breastplate keeps the heart warm and protected from external attacks; there may be a paradox in the assertion that the wearer of the breast-plate will be 'lighter, nimbler'. The couplet which precedes these lines in our manuscripts may well be part of the poem:

ἥβα μοι, φίλε θυμέ· τάχ' αὖ τινες ἄλλοι ἔσονται
ἄνδρες, ἐγὼ δὲ θανὼν γαῖα μέλαιν' ἔσομαι (877-8).

'Be youthful, my heart! Soon others will be men, and I shall die and be black earth.' If Theognis wrote the lines as a single poem, the brevity of life is offered as the reason for enjoying it, and the message is the same as in 973–8:

οὐδεὶς ἀνθρώπων, ὃν πρῶτ' ἐπὶ γαῖα καλύψῃ
εἴς τ' Ἔρεβος καταβῇ, δώματα Περσεφόνης,
τέρπεται οὔτε λύρης οὔτ' αὐλητῆρος ἀκούων   975
οὔτε Διωνύσου δῶρ' ἐσαειράμενος.
ταῦτ' ἐσορῶν κραδίην εὖ πείσομαι, ὄφρα τ' ἐλαφρὰ
γούνατα καὶ κεφαλὴν ἀτρεμέως προφέρω.

'No man, when once the earth covers him and he goes down to Erebos, the dwelling of Persephone, takes pleasure in hearing either lyre or piper or in raising to his lips the gifts of Dionysus. I see this, and so I shall make my heart merry while my knees are still nimble and I carry an unshaking head.' The picturesque details are attractive: 'Erebos, home of Persephone'; the music that the poet will miss; the nimble knees and steady head. Another couplet unites the theme of an unknown future with present decorum:

νῦν μὲν πίνοντες τερπώμεθα, καλὰ λέγοντες·
ἄσσα δ' ἔπειτ' ἔσται, ταῦτα θέοισι μέλει (1047-8).

'Now let us take pleasure in drinking, speaking honourable words. What will be hereafter is the concern of the gods.'

But a cautionary tone is more commonly heard in Theognis' poetry. He counsels moderation again and again, notably in a thirty-line poem addressed to one Simonides (467ff.), part of which runs as follows:

τῷ πίνειν δ' ἐθέλοντι παρασταδὸν οἰνοχοείτω·
οὐ πάσας νύκτας γίνεται ἁβρὰ παθεῖν.
αὐτὰρ ἐγώ, μέτρον γὰρ ἔχω μελιηδέος οἴνου,   475
ὕπνου λυσικάκου μνήσομαι οἴκαδ' ἰών.
ἥξω δ' ὡς οἶνος χαριέστατος ἀνδρὶ πεπόσθαι·
οὔτε τι γὰρ νήφω οὔτε λίην μεθύω.
ὃς δ' ἂν ὑπερβάλλῃ πόσιος μέτρον, οὐκέτι κεῖνος
τῆς αὐτοῦ γλώσσης καρτερὸς οὐδὲ νόου,   480
μυθεῖται δ' ἀπάλαμνα, τὰ νήφοσι γίνεται αἰσχρά,
αἰδεῖται δ' ἔρδων οὐδὲν ὅταν μεθύῃ,
τὸ πρὶν ἐὼν σώφρων, τότε νήπιος. ἀλλὰ σὺ ταῦτα
γινώσκων μὴ πῖν' οἶνον ὑπερβολάδην,
ἀλλ' ἢ πρὶν μεθύειν ὑπανίστασο – μή σε βιάσθω   485
γαστὴρ ὥστε κακὸν λάτριν ἐφημέριον –
ἢ παρεὼν μὴ πῖνε. σὺ δ' 'ἔγχεε'· τοῦτο μάταιον
κωτίλλεις αἰεί· τούνεκά τοι μεθύεις·
ἡ μὲν γὰρ φέρεται φιλοτήσιος, ἡ δὲ πρόκειται,
τὴν δὲ θεοῖς σπένδεις, τὴν δ' ἐπὶ χειρὸς ἔχεις,   490
ἀρνεῖσθαι δ' οὐκ οἶδας. ἀνίκητος δέ τοι οὗτος,
ὃς πολλὰς πίνων μή τι μάταιον ἐρεῖ (473-92)

Theognis begins by telling Simonides not to use compulsion on any of the guests: he must not make them stay or go home, wake up or sleep, against their will. 'And if any man wants to drink, let the servant stand beside him and pour the wine: we cannot live a life of luxury every night. But I have drunk my measure of honey-sweet wine, and so I shall think about care-dispelling sleep as I make my way home. I shall arrive in the pleasantest condition for the wine-drinker: I am neither sober nor too drunk. The man who goes beyond due measure in drinking is no longer master of his tongue or his wits; his speech is foolish, a disgrace to sober men, and there is nothing that he is ashamed to do when he is drunk: he was sensible once, now he is a simpleton. Realise this, and don't drink wine to excess: either get up and go before you are drunk and don't let your belly force you as though you were a wretched day-labourer, or stay put and don't drink. But you—"Fill it up" is your constant stupid refrain; and so you are drunk: one cup is brought to be a loving-cup, another is a prize, another is your libation to the gods, another is in your hand: you can't say no! The champion is the man who drinks many cups without saying anything stupid.' Theognis ends with an admonition to the guests to watch their speech and avoid quarrels: this, he says, is the prescription for a pleasant symposium. Moderation is emphasised by the repeated noun, *metron*, 'due measure', and the verb *huperballein*, echoed by the impressive adverb *huperboladēn*, 'excessively'; the pleasantest state is to be neither sober nor too drunk. Moderation is the point of several shorter poems:

> ἄφρονος ἀνδρὸς ὁμῶς καὶ σώφρονος οἶνος ὅταν δὴ
> πίνῃ ὑπὲρ μέτρον κοῦφον ἔθηκε νόον (497-8).

'It is true of wise man and fool alike that wine drunk beyond due measure enfeebles the wits.' And, more elaborately,

> ἐν πυρὶ μὲν χρυσόν τε καὶ ἄργυρον ἴδριες ἄνδρες
> γινώσκουσ', ἀνδρὸς δ' οἶνος ἔδειξε νόον,
> καὶ μάλα περ πινυτοῦ, τὸν ὑπὲρ μέτρον ἤρατο πίνων,
> ὥστε καταισχῦναι καὶ πρὶν ἐόντα σοφόν (499-502).

'Skilled craftsmen recognise gold and silver by means of fire; but it is wine that shows up the mind of a man, even a very shrewd man—the wine which he raises to his lips and drinks beyond due measure, so that it disgraces him, even though he was once a wise man.' Theognis' fine opening line is reminiscent of Homer's language and imagery, and the commonplace that wine is the test of a man's wisdom is enriched by this introduction. Another piece depends similarly on Homer for its effect:

> δισσαί τοι πόσιος κῆρες δειλοῖσι βροτοῖσιν,
> δίψα τε λυσιμελὴς καὶ μέθυσις χαλεπή·
> τούτων δ' ἂν τὸ μέσον στρωφήσομαι, οὐδέ με πείσεις
> οὔτε τι μὴ πίνειν οὔτε λίην μεθύειν (837-40).

'Wretched mortals have two fates in drinking, thirst that loosens a man's limbs and drunkenness which is disagreeable. I shall range in the middle of these two, and you will not persuade me either not to drink at all or to get too drunk.' The two *kēres*, 'fates', of Achilles are well-known from *Iliad* 9.410–16:

the first was to die young and glorious at Troy, the second to return home and live a long but inglorious life. Mimnermus had used the image in an elegiac poem in which he spoke of the two black Fates which stand in wait for a young man, grim old age and death. Theognis followed Mimnermus' usage in 767–8; here the fates, which the poets normally connected with death, appear in new surroundings, although the Homeric *deiloisi brotoisin*, 'wretched mortals', reminds us of their usual associations. *Lusimelēs* was, as we have seen, used by the lyric poets to describe the effect of love, but it too reminds us of Homeric warriors whose limbs were loosened by a deathblow, and Theognis is exploiting these associations too for comic effect. This time *to metron*, 'due measure', is replaced by *to meson*, 'the middle' or 'the mean', and Theognis gives a twist to the expression by his use of another Homeric word, *strōphēsomai*: 'I shall move to and fro in the space between thirst and drunkenness.'

In the poem addressed to Simonides Theognis mentioned a cup of wine offered as a prize (489): the interpretation is somewhat uncertain there, but he certainly knew of drinking contests and disapproved of them:

> τίς δ' ἀρετὴ πίνοντ' ἐπιοίνιον ἄθλον ἑλέσθαι;
> πολλάκι τοι νικᾷ καὶ κακὸς ἄνδρ' ἀγαθόν (971-2).

'What virtue is it to win the wine-drinker's prize? Often a bad man defeats a good one.' Theognis' answer to his indignant question is to be understood in political and social terms: he saw the aristocratic families of Megara as 'the good men', the *nouveaux riches* and political upstarts as 'the bad'; and his implication may be that drinking-bouts are better left to the riff-raff.

A personal note distinguishes the following poem:

> οἰνοβαρέω κεφαλήν, Ὀνομάκριτε, καί με βιᾶται
> οἶνος, ἀτὰρ γνώμης οὐκέτ' ἐγὼ ταμίης
> ἡμετέρης, τὸ δὲ δῶμα περιτρέχει. ἀλλ' ἄγ' ἀναστὰς
> πειρηθῶ μή πως καὶ πόδας οἶνος ἔχει
> καὶ νόον ἐν στήθεσσι· δέδοικα δὲ μή τι μάταιον
> ἔρξω θωρηχθεὶς καὶ μέγ' ὄνειδος ἔχω.
> οἶνος πινόμενος πουλὺς κακόν· ἢν δέ τις αὐτὸν
> πίνῃ ἐπισταμένως, οὐ κακόν, ἀλλ' ἀγαθόν (503-10).

'My head is heavy with wine, Onomacritus; the wine is treating me roughly: I am no longer master of my wits, and the room is revolving. Come, I must stand up and test to see whether the wine has hold of my legs as it has of the wits within my breast. I am afraid that I may do something foolish in my drunken state and be severely reproached for it. Wine drunk in great quantity is an evil; but if one drinks it knowledgeably, it is not an evil but a blessing.' It is not certain whether the last couplet belongs here or is an independent poem, but it is tempting to attach it: the humour of the first six lines is then capped by the humour of the sound advice so belatedly recollected by the poet.

The reason for caution in drinking is occasionally made explicit: here the context may well be amatory:

> πίνων δ' οὐχ οὕτως θωρήξομαι, οὐδέ με οἶνος
> ἐξάγει, ὥστ' εἰπεῖν δεινὸν ἔπος περὶ σοῦ (413-14).

'In my drinking I shall not become so drunk nor will the wine so mislead me that I speak ill of you.' The following lines remind us of Theognis' obsession with his 'enemies':

> οἶνος ἐμοὶ τὰ μὲν ἄλλα χαρίζεται, ἐν δ' ἀχάριστος,
> εὖτ' ἂν θωρήξας μ' ἄνδρα πρὸς ἐχθρὸν ἄγῃ.
> ἀλλ' ὁπόταν καθύπερθεν ἐόνθ' ὑπένερθε γένηται,
> τουτάκις οἴκαδ' ἴμεν παυσάμενοι πόσιος (841-4).

'Wine grants me kind favours in all else, but in one thing it is unkind—when it makes me drunk and leads me against my enemy. No, when what was below turns up above, it is time for men to finish drinking and go home.' Here again it is doubtful whether the couplets should be joined to form a single poem; there is certainly humour in both, since *thōrēxas* can mean both 'arming me with a breastplate' and 'making me drunk'. The third line presumably describes the hallucinations of the drunk man: the floor has changed places with the ceiling.

The politics of Megara made Theognis, an aristocrat dispossessed of his property, bitter towards his enemies and suspicious of his friends. 'Be like the octopus,' he advises (213–18), 'and suit your colour to your surroundings'; he complains of friends' disloyalty in time of trouble, grumbles about unrequited affection, protests his own trustworthiness, and bemoans the lot of mortals. Even the symposium has its dangers:

> μή μοι ἀνὴρ εἴη γλώσσῃ φίλος, ἀλλὰ καὶ ἔργῳ·
> χερσίν τε σπεύδοι χρήμασί τ', ἀμφότερα·
> μηδὲ παρὰ κρητῆρι λόγοισιν ἐμὴν φρένα θέλγοι,
> ἀλλ' ἔρδων φαίνοιτ' εἴ τι δύναιτ' ἀγαθόν (979-82).

'May a man be my friend not simply in word but in deed also. May he help in earnest, both with his hands and his money. May he not cast a spell over my mind with his talk beside the mixing-bowl: may he visibly do some good if he can.' He makes this point elsewhere:

> πολλοὶ πὰρ κρητῆρι φίλοι γίνονται ἑταῖροι,
> ἐν δὲ σπουδαίῳ πρήγματι παυρότεροι (643-4).

'Many men turn into dear comrades beside the mixing-bowl, fewer in serious business.' The theme that one should accommodate one's mood to one's neighbours' mood appears also in sympotic surroundings:

αἰσχρόν τοι μεθύοντα παρ' ἀνδράσι νήφοσιν εἶναι,
αἰσχρὸν δ' εἰ νήφων πὰρ μεθύουσι μένει (627-8).

'It is disgraceful to be drunk among sober men, disgraceful too to remain sober among drunk men'; and, with a different conclusion,

πῖν' ὁπόταν πίνωσιν· ὅταν δέ τι θυμὸν ἀσηθῇς,
μηδεὶς ἀνθρώπων γνῷ σε βαρυνόμενον (989-90).

'Drink when they drink; but when you are sick at heart, let no man realise that you are distressed.' Malice is foremost in one terse couplet:

δεῦρο σὺν αὐλητῆρι· παρὰ κλαίοντι γελῶντες
πίνωμεν, κείνου κήδεσι τερπόμενοι (1041-2).

'Come here with the piper. Let's laugh and drink beside our weeping companion, taking pleasure in his pains.'

*   *   *

The sixth century and the early years of the fifth were the heyday of these festive couplets, but the genre did not quite die out then. Ion of Chios wrote both elegiacs and lyric poetry of a sympotic nature. His elegiacs show a tendency towards cleverness and allusiveness which make him more akin to Hellenistic poets than to his predecessors. In this example the opening is badly preserved, but Ion is saying that Dionysus has been the theme of stories at gatherings of Greeks and feasts of kings,

ἐξ οὗ βοτρυόεσσ' οἰνὰς ὑποχθόνιον
πτόρθον ἀνασχομένη θαλερῷ ἐπορέξατο πήχει   5
αἰθέρος, ὀφθαλμῶν δ' ἐξέθορον πυκινοὶ
παῖδες φωνήεντες, ὅταν πέσῃ ἄλλος ἐπ' ἄλλῳ·
πρὶν δὲ σιωπῶσιν· παυσάμενοι δὲ βοῆς
νέκταρ ἀμέλγονται, πόνον ὄλβιον ἀνθρώποισιν,
ξυνὸν τοῦ χαίρειν φάρμακον αὐτοφυές.   10
τοῦ θαλίαι φίλα τέκνα φιλοφροσύναι τε χοροί τε·
τῶν <δ'> ἀγαθῶν βασιλεὺς οἶνος ἔδειξε φύσιν.
τῷ σύ, πάτερ Διόνυσε, φιλοστεφάνοισιν ἀρέσκων
ἀνδράσιν, εὐθύμων συμποσίων πρύτανι,
χαῖρε· δίδου δ' αἰῶνα, καλῶν ἐπιήρανε ἔργων,   15
πίνειν καὶ παίζειν καὶ τὰ δίκαια φρονεῖν (26.4-16).

'. . . ever since the vine with her clusters lifted her rooted stem and stretched

out for the sky with her luxuriant arm; and from her eyes there jumped a
crowd of children, noisy when they fall on top of each other, but silent till then.
When they stop their shouting, they are milked of their nectar, a blessed toil for
mankind, a self-grown remedy, common to all men, for the bringing of joy. Its
dear children are feasts and jollities and dancing choirs. King wine shows up
the nature of good men. And so, father Dionysus, you who give pleasure to
garlanded banqueters and preside over cheerful feasts, my greetings to you!
Helper in noble works, grant me a lifetime of drinking, sporting, and thinking
just thoughts.' This remarkable poem is a mixture of conventional ideas and
expressions and what seems wholly original. *Oinos edeixe phusin* (12) is a clear
echo of Theognis 500 *oinos edeixe noon*, 'wine shows up the mind of a man';
wine is a *pharmakon* in Alcaeus 335, and wine as a blessing for men and a
bringer of joy is not new. The personification of the vine is the most startling
feature of the poem: the opening is exciting, but it gives way to a riddling style.
The term *ophthalmoi*, the 'eyes' of the vine, is less remarkable in Greek than in
English, since it was used also for the 'buds' of a tree. The picture of the grapes
popping in the winepress is delightful, but Ion spoils the effect by introducing
the metaphor of *amelgontai*, 'they are milked'. The direct appeal to Dionysus
does not, oddly enough, play an important part in earlier sympotic verse, but
it is lively, and the unexpected twist in the last half-line of the prayer makes a
fine ending.

In a lyric fragment Ion strings together a list of epithets for Dionysus or wine:

> ἄδαμον
> παῖδα ταυρωπόν, νέον οὐ νέον,
> ἥδιστον πρόπολον βαρυ-
> γδούπων ἐρώτων,
> οἶνον ἀερσίνοον
> ἀνθρώπων πρύτανιν (744).

'untamed child, bull-faced, young but not young, sweetest attendant of noisy
loves, wine that exhilarates, ruler of mankind'. We cannot say to what genre
this fragment belongs; it has the excitement of the choral songs of the *Bacchae*
of Euripides, and it might possibly come from one of Ion's tragedies.

Another fifth-century writer, Euenus of Paros, is credited in the Palatine
Anthology with a short elegiac poem which treats the traditional topic with an
individual touch:

> Βάκχου μέτρον ἄριστον ὃ μὴ πολὺ μηδ' ἐλάχιστον·
> ἔστι γὰρ ἢ λύπης αἴτιος ἢ μανίης.
> χαίρει κιρνάμενος τρισὶ Νύμφαις τέτρατος αὐτός·
> τῆμος καὶ θαλάμοις ἐστὶν ἑτοιμότατος.
> εἰ δὲ πολὺς πνεύσειεν, ἀπέστραπται μὲν ἔρωτας,   5
> βαπτίζει δ' ὕπνῳ, γείτονι τοῦ θανάτου (2).

'The best measure of Bacchus is not much nor yet very little; for he is the cause of either grief or madness. He enjoys mixing with three water-nymphs to make a fourth: then he is most suited to the bedroom. If his breath is strong, he turns his back on love and plunges us in sleep, death's neighbour.' Euenus personifies the wine and water as Bacchus and the Nymphs; *erōtas*, 'loves', may also be regarded as a personification; and he concludes with a variation on Homer's 'Sleep, brother of Death'. Euenus prescribes the same weak mixture as Hesiod, three parts water to one of wine, as the best 'measure'; *metron* seems to carry both its literal sense and the idea of moderation.

* * *

Another type of drinking-song, the *skolion* or 'crooked' song, became popular in the fifth-century democracy at Athens. Our twenty-five surviving examples are quoted by Athenaeus, who tells us that they might be sung in chorus by all the guests at a party, or in succession round the table, or by the best singers present: this last practice explains their name as due to the crooked course of the song among the guests. Most of our examples have the same four-line metrical pattern, and it seems that the tunes were traditional and that new scolia were fitted, calypso-like, to the existing musical and metrical frameworks.

Athenaeus noted the predominance of moral and practical content in these songs, and it is remarkable that only one speaks of the symposium:

ἔγχει καὶ Κήδωνι, διάκονε, μηδ' ἐπιλήθου
εἰ χρὴ τοῖς ἀγαθοῖς ἀνδράσιν οἰνοχοεῖν (906).

'Fill Cedon's cup too, attendant, and do not forget him, since you must pour out wine for good men.' This couplet reminds us of Theognis in its directness and in its political reference; in this Athenian poem, however, the 'good men' are the democrats: Cedon was celebrated for his attack on the tyrants of Athens at the close of the sixth century. Another scolion, in asclepiad rhythm, is also reminiscent of Theognis:

σύν μοι πῖνε συνήβα συνέρα συστεφανηφόρει,
σύν μοι μαινομένῳ μαίνεο, σὺν σώφρονι σωφρόνει (902).

'Drink with me, be youthful with me, love with me, wear garlands with me, be mad with me when I am mad, sober with me when I am sober.'

* * *

It remains to consider the convivial poetry of the three great writers of choral lyric, Simonides, Pindar and Bacchylides. An ancient commentator on Pindar said that the Pindaric sentence

αἴνει δὲ παλαιὸν μὲν οἶνον, ἄνθεα δ' ὕμνων
νεωτέρων (*Ol.* 9.48-9),

'Praise an old wine but the flowers of new songs', was written to contradict
some lines of Simonides, the text of which is corrupt:

ἐξελέγχει νέος οἶνος οὔπω
<τὸ> πέρυσι δῶρον ἀμπέλου·
† ὁ δὲ μῦθος· ὁ δὲ κενεόφρων· κούρων δὲ † (602).

Simonides seems to quote a saying and then comment on it: ' "New wine does
not yet bring to the test last year's gift of the vine": that is an empty-headed
saying of children'; in other words, a one-year-old wine does indicate the
quality of the vintage. Pindar's remark is part of a victory-ode, and it is likely
that Simonides' lines too belong to something other than a drinking-song, since
that is almost the only genre of poetry which is not attributed to him. It would
be interesting to know the context and the precise meaning of another line of
Simonides in which he said that wine and music have the same beginning
(647). Two scraps of his elegiacs may have been sympotic in origin:

. . . οἶνον ἀμύντορα δυσφροσυνάων (eleg. 4),

'wine, the repeller of worries', and

οὐδὲν ἀπόβλητον Διονύσιον, οὐδὲ γίγαρτον (eleg. 5).

'Nothing that belongs to Dionysus should be thrown away, not even a grape-
pip.' Athenaeus, who quotes these phrases, says also that he spoke of 'a cup
with ears', presumably a two-handled cup. There is always doubt about the
authenticity of elegiacs ascribed to Simonides, but these quotations show
that Athenaeus at least regarded him as a writer of drinking-songs.

Pindar's victory-odes often refer to celebratory banquets. He ends the ninth
Nemean with a call to revelry:

ἡσυχία δὲ φιλεῖ μὲν συμπόσιον· νεοθαλὴς δ' αὔξεται
μαλθακᾷ νικαφορία σὺν ἀοιδᾷ·
        θαρσαλέα δὲ παρὰ κρατῆρα φωνὰ γίνεται.
ἐγκιρνάτω τίς νιν, γλυκὺν κώμου προφάταν,
ἀργυρέαισι δὲ νωμάτω φιάλαισι βιατὰν
ἀμπέλου παῖδ' . . .   (48-52).

'But peace loves the banquet, and new-born victory grows strong with the help
of gentle song; and the voice becomes bold beside the mixing-bowl. Let someone mix the wine, that sweet prophet of revelry, and serve in the silver cups
the forceful child of the vine. . . .' Pindar's exhortation to a carousal is
prompted by the silver cups, which were the prize for the chariot race on this

occasion. He colours the invitation by his bold, shifting imagery in his usual manner: victory is a newly-born child, fostered by the poet's song; wine is 'sweet prophet of revelry' and 'forceful child of the vine'. In fragmentary lines, less restrained in tone, he speaks of a drunken party at which he will throw the cottabus (128): he refers to a game often portrayed on vases, in which revellers with a flick of the wrist aimed the drops in the bottom of their cups at a metal bowl. He spoke of the drunkenness of the Centaurs in vivid terms in an unknown context:

ἀνδροδάμαντα δ' ἐπεὶ Φῆρες δάεν
ῥιπὰν μελιαδέος οἴνου,
ἐσσυμένως ἀπὸ μὲν λευκὸν γάλα χερσὶ τραπεζᾶν
ὤθεον, αὐτόματοι δ' ἐξ ἀργυρέων κεράτων
πίνοντες ἐπλάζοντο . . . (166).

'And when the Beasts sensed the deadly gust of the honeysweet wine, they hastily pushed their white milk from the tables and drank uninvited from the silver horns and went astray. . . .' The occasion is the wedding of Pirithous, king of the Lapiths, at which the Centaurs, fuddled by their wine, fought against the Lapiths. *Androdamanta . . . rhipan*, 'the deadly gust', is a comically impressive description of the bouquet of the wine, difficult to translate, since the words can equally well mean 'the man-slaying onslaught'.

The best-preserved example of Pindar's treatment of a sympotic theme is a fragment of an 'encomium' written for a young Sicilian noble, Thrasybulus of Acragas, and intended to be sung by a choir. The term 'encomium' was used by the Alexandrian scholars to denote a eulogy of a distinguished figure, but it meant in origin a song sung *en kōmōi*, 'at a revel', and the best-known examples, by Pindar and Bacchylides, have a strongly sympotic tone. Pindar's begins

ὦ Θρασύβουλ', ἐρατᾶν ὄχημ' ἀοιδᾶν
τοῦτό <τοι> πέμπω μεταδόρπιον. ἐν ξυνῷ κεν εἴη
συμπόταισίν τε γλυκερὸν καὶ Διωνύσοιο καρπῷ

καὶ κυλίκεσσιν Ἀθαναίαισι κέντρον·
ἁνίκ' ἀνθρώπων καματώδεες οἴχονται μέριμναι
στηθέων ἔξω· πελάγει δ' ἐν πολυχρύσοιο πλούτου

πάντες ἴσα νέομεν ψευδῆ πρὸς ἀκτάν·
ὃς μὲν ἀχρήμων, ἀφνεὸς τότε, τοὶ δ' αὖ πλουτέοντες
. . .
. . . ἀέξονται φρένας ἀμπελίνοις τόξοις δαμέντες (124a, b).

'Thrasybulus, I send you this chariot of lovely songs to follow your supper. When the company meets may it be a sweet goad to your fellow-drinkers, to the harvest of Dionysus, and to the Athenian cups, when the men's toilsome worries have departed from their breasts, and we all sail alike on a sea of golden wealth to a false shore; then the poor man is rich, and the wealthy . . . their hearts expand when they are struck by the arrows of the vine.' This is a fine example of Pindar's opulent language used on a frivolous theme; and, as it happens, we have a poem by Pindar's contemporary and rival, Bacchylides, in which he treats the same topic for the same purpose, the eulogy of Alexander, ruler of Macedon from 498 to 454:

> ὦ βάρβιτε, μηκέτι πάσσαλον φυλάσ[σων
> ἑπτάτονον λιγυρὰν κάππαυε γᾶρυν·
> δεῦρ' ἐς ἐμὰς χέρας· ὁρμαίνω τι πέμπ[ειν
> χρύσεον Μουσᾶν Ἀλεξάνδρῳ πτερόν
>
> καὶ συμποσ[ίαι]σιν ἄγαλμ' [ἐν] εἰκάδεσ[σιν,   5
> εὖτε νέων ἁ[παλὸν] γλυκεῖ' ἀνάγκα
> σευομενᾶν κυλίκων θάλπησι θυμόν,
> Κυπριδός τ' ἐλπὶς διαιθύσσῃ φρένας,
>
> ἀμμειγνυμένα Διονυσίοισι δώροις·
> ἀνδράσι δ' ὑψοτάτω πέμπει μερίμνας·   10
> αὐτίκα μὲν πολίων κράδεμνα λύει,
> πᾶσι δ' ἀνθρώποις μοναρχήσειν δοκεῖ·
>
> χρυσῷ δ' ἐλέφαντί τε μαρμαίρουσιν οἶκοι
> πυροφόροι δὲ κατ' αἰγλάεντα πόντον
> νᾶες ἄγουσιν ἀπ' Αἰγύπτου μέγιστον   15
> πλοῦτον· ὡς πίνοντος ὁρμαίνει κέαρ (20B).

'My lyre, cling no longer to your peg, silencing your clear voice with its seven notes. Come to my hands! I am eager to send Alexander a golden wing of the Muses, an adornment for banquets at the month's end, when the sweet compulsion of the speeding cups warms the tender hearts of the young men, and hope of Aphrodite, mingling with the gifts of Dionysus, makes their hearts flutter. The wine sends a man's thoughts soaring on high: immediately he is destroying the battlements of cities, and he expects to be monarch over all the world; his house gleams with gold and ivory, and wheat-bearing ships bring great wealth from Egypt over a dazzling sea. Such are the musings of the drinker's heart.' The text of the following stanzas is badly damaged, but Bacchylides advises Alexander to enjoy himself since prosperity is fleeting. Comparison of the poem with Pindar's encomium to Thrasybulus is inevitable and was doubtless expected by the later poet; but which in this instance was the later? The two were almost exact contemporaries; Pindar's poem can be dated approximately to 490 B.C., but we cannot date Bacchylides', unless we deduce from the subject-matter that Alexander was a young man, in which case it is Pindar who is the debtor. The poets both use the dactylo-epitrite metre, but Bacchylides' pattern is somewhat lighter and gayer. As usual, he excels in the clarity of his images; he takes only one risk, when he refers to his poem as 'a golden wing of the Muses'; Pindar takes risks in almost every sentence he composes, and when the subject demands a light touch, as here, he comes off second-best. Finally, another short example of Bacchylides' style: he is inviting the Dioscuri, Castor and Polydeuces, to a feast:

οὐ βοῶν πάρεστι σώματ᾽, οὔτε χρυσός,
οὔτε πορφύρεοι τάπητες,
ἀλλὰ θυμὸς εὐμενής,
Μοῦσα τε γλυκεῖα, καὶ Βοιωτίοισιν
ἐν σκύφοισιν οἶνος ἡδύς (21).

'There are no whole oxen here, no gold, no crimson rugs; but there is a friendly heart, the pleasant Muse, and sweet wine in Boeotian cups.' The trochaic rhythm moves rapidly, the units are short, and the detail of the crimson rugs and the plain Boeotian ware catches our attention.

CHAPTER THREE

Athletics

Homer devoted most of what we know as Book 23 of the *Iliad* to an account of the Funeral Games held in honour of the dead warrior, Patroclus. The Games form an interlude between two high-points of the narrative, the physical clash of Book 22, where the finest Greek hero, Achilles, kills the finest Trojan hero, Hector, and the emotional climax of Book 24, where the aged king Priam confronts the young Achilles and succeeds in ransoming Hector's body for burial. Book 23 provides contrast and relaxation; and Homer is fired by his subject to compose some of his finest passages, notably the description of the chariot-race. We perhaps tend to remember it most for the vivid and often humorous character-drawing: the garrulity of old Nestor, the generosity of Achilles, the impetuousness of Antilochus, the quarrel between the heated spectators, Idomeneus and Ajax; but the race itself is wonderfully exciting: the five two-horse chariots set off over the plain of Troy,

> ὑπὸ δὲ στέρνοισι κονίη
> ἵστατ' ἀειρομένη ὥς τε νέφος ἠὲ θύελλα,
> χαῖται δ' ἐρρώοντο μετὰ πνοιῆς ἀνέμοιο.
> ἅρματα δ' ἄλλοτε μὲν χθονὶ πίλνατο πουλυβοτείρῃ,
> ἄλλοτε δ' ἀίξασκε μετήορα· τοὶ δ' ἐλατῆρες
> ἕστασαν ἐν δίφροισι, πάτασσε δὲ θυμὸς ἑκάστου
> νίκης ἱεμένων . . . (*Il.* 23.365-71).

'From under the horses' chests the dust stood up, rising like a mist or a storm-cloud, and their manes streamed behind in the blast of the wind. At one moment the chariots were close to the fruitful earth, at the next they leapt high in the air; and the drivers stood in their chariots, each man's heart pounding as they strained for victory.' Homer conveys admirably the excitement of the spectator and the tenseness of the competitor; the exhilaration which the Greeks felt at athletic contests, their obsessive fondness for competition and their acknowledgment of divine assistance are all here.

But although Homer's games foreshadow in these ways the great festivals at Olympia, Delphi and elsewhere, they differ from them in several important ways. Homer tells us of no regular festival such as the four-yearly Olympic games; what he describes is an impromptu celebration, organised by Achilles for the sole purpose of honouring his dead friend, Patroclus. Funeral games for Pelias had been held in the time of the Argonauts, and Homer's Nestor speaks of his youthful prowess in games held by the sons of an Epean king Amarynceus in honour of their dead father. The Olympic games themselves were held on the site of Pelops' tomb and are likely to have originated as funeral games. Again, Homer's competitors are all noblemen, the commanders of the Greek army; it was unthinkable that common soldiers might line up side by side with their superiors. There were prizes for all the competitors, even for Nestor whose athletic achievements were many years behind him; Achilles' generosity in prize-giving was the measure of his devotion to Patroclus. The events were, of course, such as would mark off the successful warrior: skill in chariot-driving, running, throwing and shooting were essential on the battlefield, and boxing and wrestling techniques were needed in close combat. Other early festivals included musical events: Hesiod tells us that he carried off a tripod as first prize in a song-contest at games held at Chalcis by the sons of Amphidamas in honour of their father (*Op.* 654-9), and the Homeric hymn to Apollo refers to the Ionian festival at Delos with its boxing, dancing and singing (147ff.).

In the *Odyssey* the Phaeacians show their paces in athletic games, and their prince Laodamas challenges Odysseus to take part:

οὐ μὲν γὰρ μεῖζον κλέος ἀνέρος ὄφρα κεν ᾖσιν
ἢ ὅ τι ποσσίν τε ῥέξῃ καὶ χερσὶν ἐῇσιν (8.147-8).

'For a man has no greater glory while he lives than what he achieves with his feet and his hands.' This was to be a refrain of Pindar's victory-songs; and we notice another anticipation of the lyric poets in Homer's description of the champion Euryclus as *brotoloigōi isos Arēi* (115), 'a match for Ares, the destroyer of mortals', and in Odysseus' proud but cautious boast that with the sole exception of Philoctetes he is the finest archer alive:

ἀνδράσι δὲ προτέροισιν ἐρίζεμεν οὐκ ἐθελήσω,
οὔθ᾽ Ἡρακλῆϊ οὔτ᾽ Εὐρύτῳ Οἰχαλιῆϊ (223-4).

'But I should not wish to compete with men of previous generations, either with Heracles or with Eurytus of Oechalia.' The lyric poets were fond of comparing living athletes with the great heroes of the past, and we shall find that in Simonides' eulogy of the boxer Glaucus of Carystus the heroes come off second best.

* * *

The festival at Olympia was reorganised, we are told, in 776 B.C.: the list of winners dates from that year, and from the fourth century B.C. years were reckoned in relation to that first Olympiad. There are indications of a festival

before that time, and Pindar attributes its origin to Heracles: after cleansing
the stables of Augeas and killing him, the story runs, Heracles used the spoils of
his victory to found the Olympian games 'by the ancient tomb of Pelops' (*Ol.*
10.24ff.) ; and Pelops' chariot-race against Oenomaus, which Pindar describes
in the first *Olympian*, could be regarded as a prototype of later contests. For
the first century of its recorded history it remained a festival of only local
importance; the victors come from the western Peloponnese, and there is no
mention of it in Homer. In the seventh and sixth centuries the story is one of
constant growth in the prestige of Olympia, and by the mid-sixth century
winners from Thessaly, Asia Minor, Sicily and Italy are recorded. From then
onwards the contests are pan-Hellenic and attract great numbers of spectators.

In the second half of the seventh century the elegiac poet Tyrtaeus of
Sparta drew an unfavourable comparison between the athlete and the warrior:

> οὔτ' ἂν μνησαίμην οὔτ' ἐν λόγῳ ἄνδρα τιθείην
> οὔτε ποδῶν ἀρετῆς οὔτε παλαιμοσύνης,
> οὐδ' εἰ Κυκλώπων μὲν ἔχοι μέγεθός τε βίην τε,
> νικῴη δὲ θέων Θρήϊκιον Βορέην . . .
> οὐδ' εἰ πᾶσαν ἔχοι δόξαν πλὴν θούριδος ἀλκῆς·
> οὐ γὰρ ἀνὴρ ἀγαθὸς γίνεται ἐν πολέμῳ
> εἰ μὴ τετλαίη μὲν ὁρῶν φόνον αἱματόεντα
> καὶ δήων ὀρέγοιτ' ἐγγύθεν ἱστάμενος.
> ἥδ' ἀρετή, τόδ' ἄεθλον ἐν ἀνθρώποισιν ἄριστον
> κάλλιστόν τε φέρειν γίνεται ἀνδρὶ νέῳ (12.1-4, 9-14).

'I would not make mention of a man nor take any account of him either for his
excellence in running or in wrestling, or if he had the size and strength of the
Cyclopes or could outrun the Thracian North-wind (or if he had the looks of
Tithonus, the wealth of Midas or Cinyras, the kingly power of Pelops, or the
eloquence of Adrastus), or if he had a reputation for everything except fierce
courage. For a man does not prove himself good in war, unless he could bear
to see bloody slaughter and take aim at the enemy, standing close by them.
This excellence, this prize is the best among men and the finest for a youth to
win.' Tyrtaeus, composing at the time of the long grim war in which the
Spartans for the second time asserted their supremacy over the Messenians,
uses the needs of wartime as his criterion of excellence. He lists various forms of
excellence (*aretē*), giving prominence to athletic skill, only to reject them all
in favour of 'fierce courage': this excellence, this prize—the word *aethlon* would
make his hearers think again of athletic games—is the finest. Tyrtaeus is not
attacking athletics and its prizes as an abstraction, any more than he is
attacking wealth or eloquence: what he emphasises is that those are not the
qualities which count in war. It is interesting to note that these lines belong to
the period in which Spartan athletes held a marked dominance in the Olympic
games. A few decades after Tyrtaeus' time Sparta stopped competing and

became a grim, xenophobic military state. The poet's point was taken.

In the sixth century athletic festivals prospered. At Delphi the Pythian festival in honour of Apollo was finally reorganised in 582 along the lines of the Olympic games, and perhaps in the same year the Isthmian games of Poseidon were refounded by the Corinthians. The Nemean festival, the last of the four 'sacred festivals' or 'garland festivals', followed soon after, in 573; its site was near Cleonae, south-west of Corinth, and like the Olympic festival it was held in honour of Zeus. At Olympia too there was further reorganisation and rebuilding. By the year 570, then, there were four major festivals; three were in the Peloponnese, and the fourth, the Pythia, owed its foundation and development in part at least to a Peloponnesian, Cleisthenes, tyrant of Sicyon. Since the Isthmia and Nemea were biennial, an athlete could now compete in six major festivals within four years, and in addition there were many local games which never acquired the prestige of the others. It is a popular belief that the glory and the garland were the only rewards won by Greek athletes, but this is far from the case. It is true that at the great games the prize awarded was a garland, of wild olive at Olympia, bay at Delphi, celery leaves at the Isthmian and Nemean games; but there were valuable prizes at the other festivals: at the Panathenaea, for example, the Athenians gave 140 jars of Attic olive oil to the winner of the chariot-race. Moreover, the fellow-citizens of the victorious athlete gave him monetary rewards and various privileges on his homecoming; his praises were sung at the festival itself and again, often in more elaboration, in his home-town, and if he was an Olympic victor it was common for his statue to be erected at Olympia. Ambitious politicians found that success in the games did much to promote their interests.

The Athenian statesman Solon, probably at some date between 582 and 560, made two pronouncements about the prizes awarded to athletes: Plutarch's life (23.3) records that 'he arranged that 100 drachmas be given to an Isthmian victor, 500 to an Olympic victor': this has been seen as an attempt to encourage Athenian athletes, and the amounts offered are certainly large for that period; but it seems better to regard these sums as a limit, imposed to prevent extravagant awards: Diogenes Laertius (1.55–6) and Diodorus (9.2.3ff.) both interpreted the award in this way, and they may have been paraphrasing an elegiac poem of Solon when they report his view that it was boorish to increase their rewards: only those who died in battle should have their rewards increased, and their sons should be fed and educated at state expense; 'boxers, sprinters and other athletes make no worthwhile contribution to the safety of their cities: only those who excel in wisdom and prowess can protect their countries in time of danger.'

Solon's protest has a Tyrtaean ring, and it was itself echoed by Xenophanes in the most famous and most detailed complaint about the prizes given to Olympic victors. Xenophanes had a long life, from c. 570 to c. 478 or even later, and we cannot say whether his poem belongs to the first few decades after

The Golden Lyre

Solon or was written as a reaction to the victory-songs of Simonides, Pindar and Bacchylides. Bowra pointed out that Xenophanes does not mention the race in armour, which was introduced at Olympia in 520, but his reference to 'swiftness of foot' covers races of every type, and the conclusion that Xenophanes was writing before 520 is untenable. On the other hand we should observe that Xenophanes refers neither to victory-odes nor to statues but only to civic awards:

> ἀλλ' εἰ μὲν ταχυτῆτι ποδῶν νίκην τις ἄροιτο
> ἢ πενταθλεύων, ἔνθα Διὸς τέμενος
> πὰρ Πίσαο ῥοῆς ἐν Ὀλυμπίῃ, εἴτε παλαίων
> ἢ καὶ πυκτοσύνην ἀλγινόεσσαν ἔχων,
> εἴτε τὸ δεινὸν ἄεθλον ὃ παγκράτιον καλέουσιν,   5
> ἀστοῖσίν κ' εἴη κυδρότερος προσορᾶν,
> καί κε προεδρίην φανερὴν ἐν ἀγῶσιν ἄροιτο,
> καί κεν σῖτ' εἴη δημοσίων κτεάνων
> ἐκ πόλιος καὶ δῶρον, ὅ οἱ κειμήλιον εἴη·
> εἴτε καὶ ἵπποισιν· ταῦτά κε πάντα λάχοι   10
> οὐκ ἐὼν ἄξιος ὥσπερ ἐγώ· ῥώμης γὰρ ἀμείνων
> ἀνδρῶν ἠδ' ἵππων ἡμετέρη σοφίη.
> ἀλλ' εἰκῆ μάλα τοῦτο νομίζεται, οὐδὲ δίκαιον
> προκρίνειν ῥώμην τῆς ἀγαθῆς σοφίης.
> οὔτε γὰρ εἰ πύκτης ἀγαθὸς λαοῖσι μετείη   15
> οὔτ' εἰ πενταθλεῖν οὔτε παλαισμοσύνην
> οὐδὲ μὲν εἰ ταχυτῆτι ποδῶν, τόπερ ἐστὶ πρότιμον
> ῥώμης ὅσσ' ἀνδρῶν ἔργ' ἐν ἀγῶνι πέλει,
> τούνεκεν ἂν δὴ μᾶλλον ἐν εὐνομίῃ πόλις εἴη·
> σμικρὸν δ' ἄν τι πόλει χάρμα γένοιτ' ἐπὶ τῷ,   20
> εἴ τις ἀεθλεύων νικῷ Πίσαο παρ' ὄχθας·
> οὐ γὰρ πιαίνει ταῦτα μυχοὺς πόλιος (2).

'But if a man were to win a victory by the swiftness of his feet or in the pentathlon, where the precinct of Zeus stands in Olympia by the waters of Pises, or in wrestling or the painful boxing-match or that grim contest they call the pankration, he would be more glorious for the citizens to look upon, and he would win a conspicuous front seat at festivals; he would get his meals from his city at public expense and a gift for him to treasure; or if he won with his horses, he would get all these, although not deserving them as I do: better than the strength of men or of horses is our skill. No, this practice is completely haphazard, and it is not just to judge strength ahead of my good skill. For if a good boxer lived among the populace or a good pentathlete or wrestler or a good runner—and swiftness of foot is most honoured of all man's deeds of strength at a festival—the city would not be any the better governed: small would be the joy of a city, if a man won an athletic contest by the banks of Pises: that does not enrich a city's chambers.'

Xenophanes is said to have lived in Zancle and Catana in Sicily, and he may also have visited Elea in south Italy, and we know that the Greek cities of Sicily and Italy enjoyed a dominance in the Olympic games during his lifetime. He maintains that the civic honours awarded to successful Olympic athletes ought rather to be given to him because of the contribution which his *sophiē*, 'skill', 'wisdom', makes to the well-being of the city. By *sophiē* he probably refers to his poetic skill: Solon had used the word in this sense, and Pindar, Xenophanes' much younger contemporary, was fond of the usage; but of course it was the poet's 'wisdom', 'philosophy' even, expressed in his poems, that he regarded as advantageous to the city, and the word may carry the double sense. The proper condition for the city is referred to as *eunomiē* (19), a term which here seems to denote both the existence of good laws and the readiness of the citizens to obey them. The closing protest that the athlete does nothing to enrich the city's chambers is no doubt a hit at the cost of the athletes' awards, but it must also derive its meaning in part from the mention of *eunomiē*: the poet by his wise advice enriches the city as the athlete cannot. The passage is well-constructed, the length of the preamble of 1–10 giving tremendous force to the half-line *ouk eōn axios hōsper egō*, 'not deserving them as I do'; the sentence which follows is similarly designed to throw the emphasis on *hēmeterē sophiē*, 'our skill', and in the following couplet he deftly substitutes *tēs agathēs sophiēs*, 'good skill'. There is a pleasing sarcasm in the Homeric echoes, *ho pankration kaleousin*, 'which they call the pankration', and *dōran, ho hoi keimēlion eiē*, 'a gift for him to treasure', and in the contemptuous repetition of *par Pisao rhoēis* (3) in *Pisao par' okhthas* (21). Xenophanes may not be the most melodious of early Greek poets, but he makes his points vigorously.

*   *   *

The sixth century saw artists and sculptors begin to play a major role in the glorification of athletes. The statues of victors were set up at Olympia, and vase-painters portrayed athletic events and heroes such as Heracles and Theseus, whose exploits were often triumphs of athleticism. By the end of the century the poets too were playing their part: Simonides' earliest victory-odes probably belong to the last two decades of the century, and the master-pieces of Pindar and Bacchylides belong to the first half of the fifth century. The great victory over the Persians gave the impetus for a growth in the spirit of pan-hellenism, and the festival of 476, the first after the wars, was an occasion for unprecedented national rejoicing. Three of Pindar's finest poems and one of Bacchylides' celebrated the victories of Sicilian princes in those games. The temple of Zeus, which was to be the architectural glory of Olympia, was begun in the seventies but not completed till 457, and the famous statue of Zeus by Pheidias was not in its place for another twenty years. It is hard to remember that only one of Pindar's *Olympians*, the short fourth, belongs to the period after the temple's completion.

Simonides seems to have been the first poet to write victory-odes ('epinicians': *epinikia* or *epinikoi humnoi*), and we know of poems for winners in sprinting, wrestling, the pentathlon, boxing, riding, chariot-racing and mule-racing. Unfortunately hardly anything of them survives, and we can say little about his methods of composition. In the poem for a prize wrestler he wrote

ἐπέξαθ' ὁ Κριὸς οὐκ ἀεικέως
ἐλθὼν ἐς εὔδενδρον ἀγλαὸν Διὸς
τέμενος (507).

'Crius got a good shearing when he came to the glorious wooded precinct of Zeus.' He plays on the name Crius, 'Ram', and the poem was presumably composed to honour the wrestler who defeated Crius. We know from Aristophanes that the song was popular among the older generation of his day, and there is a lightness of touch seldom present in later victory-songs. The same lightness takes the form of exaggeration in the ode for the famous boxer, Glaucus of Carystus:

οὐδὲ Πολυδεύκεος βία
χεῖρας ἀντείναιτό κ' ἐναντίον αὐτῷ,
οὐδὲ σιδάρεον 'Αλκμάνας τέκος (509).

'Not even the mighty Polydeuces would raise his hands to fight him, nor Alcmene's iron son.' Ancient moralists seem to have been disturbed over the supposed impiety of declaring a human boxer superior to Polydeuces and Heracles, but, as Lucian, who quotes the fragment, pointed out, the gods did not punish either the poet or the boxer. Indeed the gods seem rather to have kept a protective eye on Simonides: it was said of one of his poems on victorious boxers (510) that he had so much to say of the Dioscuri (the heroes, Castor and Polydeuces) that Scopas, the Thessalian ruler who commissioned the poem, cut the poet's fee by half, declaring that Castor and Polydeuces would pay the rest; these rash words proved true when Scopas' banquet-hall collapsed, killing the entire household, and Simonides was miraculously saved by the agency of the Dioscuri. Cicero and Quintilian tell the story with amusing elaboration (*De Oratore* 2.86; *Inst. Orat.* 11.2.11); it gives valuable proof that Simonides devoted much of at least one of his victory-odes to mythological material. The mule-race was introduced at Olympia in 500 B.C., and Simonides, it is said, was reluctant to demean himself by singing of mules, until his fee was raised; thereupon he composed a poem with the comically magnificent opening,

χαίρετ' ἀελλοπόδων θύγατρες ἵππων (515),

'Greetings, daughters of storm-footed horses!' His avarice was the subject of many anecdotes, doubtless because he was the first poet to charge fees for his services. A strong lyrical impulse may be seen in a fragment of a poem written for a pentathlon winner:

ὡς ὁπόταν
χειμέριον κατὰ μῆνα πινύσκῃ
Ζεὺς ἤματα τέσσαρα καὶ δέκα,
λαθάνεμον δέ μιν ὥραν
καλέουσιν ἐπιχθόνιοι
ἱερὰν παιδοτρόφον ποικίλας
ἀλκυόνος (508).

'As when in the winter month Zeus admonishes fourteen days (makes them calm?), and mortals call it the holy season which forgets the winds, the season of child-rearing for the dappled halcyon.' Unfortunately we can only guess at the relevance of the simile of the halcyon days; perhaps Simonides was speaking of the time of calm relaxation which followed the pentathlete's victory.

*   *   *

We can form a clear picture of the victory-ode from about forty-five surviving examples of Pindar and some fourteen fragmentary poems of Bacchylides; indeed our evidence for this genre is far more complete than for any other type of Greek lyric poetry. The two poets were almost exact contemporaries, and they belong to the generation after Simonides, who was Bacchylides' uncle. That they were also rivals and on bad terms has been deduced from Pindar's allusion in *Olympian* 2.86–8 to the pair of chattering crows:

σοφὸς ὁ πολλὰ εἰδὼς φυᾷ·
μαθόντες δὲ λάβροι
παγγλωσσίᾳ κόρακες ὣς ἄκραντα γαρύετον
Διὸς πρὸς ὄρνιχα θεῖον.

'The wise man is he who knows many things by the gift of nature: those who learned, boisterous in their garrulity, utter (the pair of them) idle words like crows against the holy bird of Zeus.' Pindar has reached the close of his poem, and mentions his 'arrows' which speak to the intelligent but must be interpreted to the common man. In this context the word *sophos*, 'wise', indicates the skill of the poet, which, as we have seen, was often referred to as *sophia*. Pindar claims that the true poet owes his skill to Nature: those who have had to learn are undisciplined chatterboxes, ineffective in competition with the Pindaric eagle. The dual voice of *garueton*, which denotes a pair of birds, is usually thought to point to the uncle and nephew who were his rivals. It may be, however, that Pindar talks of two crows simply from his observation of a pair of birds fending off an eagle in the nesting season, and that it is mistaken to look for a reference to a pair of rival poets. Ancient scholars with a quick eye for slander saw uncomplimentary reference to Bacchylides in other passages also, notably

κραγέται δὲ κολοιοὶ ταπεινὰ νέμονται (*Nem.* 3.82),

'shrieking jackdaws inhabit low levels'. What is certain is that the poets were accepting commissions from the same patrons at the same period: Bacchylides' fifth ode and Pindar's first *Olympian* both celebrate the 476 horse-race victory of Hieron, tyrant of Syracuse; in 470 Bacchylides wrote the short ode 4 for Hieron's Pythian victory in the chariot-race, Pindar his splendid first *Pythian*. Two years later Bacchylides celebrated Hieron's victory in the chariot-race at Olympia in ode 3, but Pindar for some reason wrote no work for this, the most splendid of Hieron's triumphs, unless the second *Pythian* celebrates it. We shall first note some of the attitudes of the two poets towards athletics, then look at one ode of each poet.

The excitement of the games is well expressed by Bacchylides: it is he who speaks of the hot breath of the runner and tells how he drenches the spectators with the oil from his body as he falls among them at the end of the race (10.22–4), or of the cheers of the excited spectators at the pentathlon:

πενταέθλοισιν γὰρ ἐνέπρεπεν ὡς
    ἄστρων διακρίνει φάη
νυκτὸς διχομηνίδος εὐφεγγὴς σελάνα·
τοῖος Ἑλλάνων δι' ἀπείρονα κύκλον   30
φαῖνε θαυμαστὸν δέμας
δίσκον τροχοειδέα ῥίπτων,
καὶ μελαμφύλλου κλάδον
ἀκτέας ἐς αἰπεινὰν προπέμπων
αἰθέρ' ἐκ χειρὸς βοὰν ὤτρυνε λαῶν   35
ἢ τελευτάσας ἀμάρυγμα πάλας (9.27-36).

'For he was conspicuous among the pentathletes as the bright moon outshines the light of the stars on the night when it is full: even so among the immense circle of the Greeks did he display his wonderful form as he threw the round discus, and hurling from his hand the branch of the black-leaved elder into the lofty heaven aroused the shout of the people, or completing the flashing movement of the wrestling.' Bacchylides borrows the simile of the moon and stars from Sappho, who used it of a girl who outshone her companions in beauty (96.5ff.; cf. 34); and the rare word *amarugma*, 'flashing movement', is also an echo of her poetry (16.18), whether deliberate or accidental. When Bacchylides turns from simile to actual description, he still uses words applicable to the full moon, *kuklon*, the 'circle' of spectators, *phaine*, 'displayed' or 'shone', *trokhoeidea*, 'round, wheelshaped'. The passage is a good example of the clarity and liveliness of his composition; so is his description of Hieron's victorious horse:

οὔπω νιν ὑπὸ προτέρων
ἵππων ἐν ἀγῶνι κατέχρανεν κόνις
πρὸς τέλος ὀρνύμενον·   45
ῥιπᾷ γὰρ ἴσος βορέα
ὃν κυβερνήταν φυλάσσων
ἵεται νεόκροτον
νίκαν Ἱέρωνι φιλοξείνῳ τιτύσκων (5.43-9).

'Never yet has dust from horses ahead of him dirtied him at a festival as he raced to the finish: like the blast of the north wind he rushes, keeping his rider safe, winning for hospitable Hieron a victory greeted by fresh applause.' His methods are simple and successful: the picture of the dust-cloud, always behind the horse and never in front, is economical and vivid, and the comparison to the north-wind, a commonplace among the poets, is briefly made and takes slight emphasis from the following phrase: the horse is not destructive like the north-wind, but 'keeps his rider safe'.

Pindar has far less to say about the actual performances of the victors and the excitement of the festival crowd; his comments are rather on matters of deeper significance, the importance to the victor of rich natural gifts, of hard work and of the co-operation of the gods; the glories and the pitfalls of his victory; the divine origin and ambience of the games; and, not least, the inspired authority with which the poet can speak of these things. His praise of the Olympic games is well-known:

ἄριστον μὲν ὕδωρ, ὁ δὲ χρυσὸς αἰθόμενον πῦρ
ἄτε διαπρέπει νυκτὶ μεγάνορος ἔξοχα πλούτου·
εἰ δ' ἄεθλα γαρύεν
ἔλδεαι, φίλον ἦτορ,
μηκέτ' ἀελίου σκόπει   5
ἄλλο θαλπνότερον ἐν ἁμέρα φαεν-
    νὸν ἄστρον ἐρήμας δι' αἰθέρος,
μηδ' Ὀλυμπίας ἀγῶνα φέρτερον αὐδάσομεν (*Ol.* 1.1-7).

'The best thing is water, and gold, like blazing fire at night, shines out beyond other noble wealth; but if it is games that you wish to speak of, my dear heart, look for no warmer shining star than the sun by day in the lonely heavens, and let us not speak of any festival as greater than Olympia.' Pindar's approach is devious and exciting: he sings of water and gold, supreme among the elements and precious metals, and the mention of Olympia, supreme among festivals, is delayed so that he may introduce another image: as the sun is the warmest body in the day sky, so is Olympia the finest festival. His stark statements are given life by the personal touches, his Homeric communing with his 'dear heart' and the closing exhortation, 'let us not speak . . .'.

In a passage in the first *Isthmian* Pindar expresses many of his central beliefs:

εἰ δ' ἀρετᾷ κατάκειται πᾶσαν ὀργάν,
ἀμφότερον δαπάναις τε καὶ πόνοις,
χρή νιν εὑρόντεσσιν ἀγάνορα κόμπον
μὴ φθονεραῖσι φέρειν
γνώμαις. ἐπεὶ κούφα δόσις ἀνδρὶ σοφῷ   45
ἀντὶ μόχθων παντοδαπῶν ἔπος εἰ-
          πόντ' ἀγαθὸν ξυνὸν ὀρθῶσαι καλόν.

μισθὸς γὰρ ἄλλοις ἄλλος ἔπ' ἔργμασιν ἀνθρώποις γλυκύς,
μηλοβότᾳ τ' ἀρότᾳ τ' ὀρ-
          νιχολόχῳ τε καὶ ὃν πόντος τράφει.
γαστρὶ δὲ πᾶς τις ἀμύνων λιμὸν αἰανῆ τέταται ·
ὃς δ' ἀμφ' ἀέθλοις ἢ πολεμίζων ἄρηται κῦδος ἁβρόν,   50
εὐαγορηθεὶς κέρδος ὕψιστον δέκεται, πολια-
          τᾶν καὶ ξένων γλώσσας ἄωτον (*Isthm.* 1.41-52).

'If a man devotes his every impulse to excellence, sparing neither expense nor hard work, it is right to bring noble praise with heart that feels no envy to those who find that excellence; for it is an easy gift for a wise poet to speak good words in return for the man's various hardships and so to extol his splendour for the community to share. Different are the rewards which men find sweet for different deeds, the shepherd, the ploughman, the birdcatcher, the man whom the sea nourishes: everyone strains to ward off nagging hunger from his belly; but he who wins splendid glory in games or in war is well spoken of and so receives the highest reward, the choicest praises of fellow-citizens and strangers.'

Pindar emphasises the hard physical effort and expense needed for victory; the reward, greater than the gain of shepherd, ploughman, fowler or fisherman, is the praise the victor wins from his fellows and from the poet: *aganora kompon* is a typically bold phrase, difficult to render: 'praise for his manliness' or 'praise which ennobles a man' are possible interpretations. The envy (*phthonos*) to which the victor is exposed is a common theme of Pindar, and the 'goodness' of the words which the poet speaks may lie in the absence of envy. The imagery at the end of line 46 is difficult to grasp: 'to raise a shared beauty' suggests the erecting of a statue or the raising to his feet of a man who has undergone all kinds of hardship; the beauty is shared in that the victor's city shares the praise he wins. The adjective *habron*, applied to glory in line 50, is startling: it denotes splendour or delicacy with overtones of luxury and effeminacy; perhaps Pindar refers to the comfortable relaxation which follows the victor's hard training. The closing word is a favourite expression of Pindar for the peak of excellence; originally used of the best wool, it came to be used for anything of choice quality, the cream or flower or prime.

A famous sentence in the sixth *Olympian*, composed for a winner in the mule race, emphasises the hardship and indeed danger which precede victory:

ἀκίνδυνοι δ' ἀρεταὶ
οὔτε παρ' ἀνδράσιν οὔτ' ἐν ναυσὶ κοίλαις
τίμιαι· πολλοὶ δὲ μέμνανται, καλὸν εἴ τι ποναθῇ (9-11).

'Excellences that involve no danger are honoured neither among men nor on
hollow ships, but many men remember a glory that is won by hardship.' But
even hard work will not produce a victor if his natural gifts are poor:

τὸ δὲ φυᾷ κράτιστον ἅπαν· πολλοὶ δὲ διδακταῖς
ἀνθρώπων ἀρεταῖς κλέος
ὤρουσαν ἀρέσθαι·
ἄνευ δὲ θεοῦ σεσιγαμένον
οὐ σκαιότερον χρῆμ' ἕκαστον (*Ol.* 9.100-4).

'Everything that comes from nature is best: many men have striven to win
glory by means of taught excellence, but anything that is without God is no
worse-omened for being suppressed in silence.' This is very similar to the
contrast made in the second *Olympian* between the wise man who knows many
things *phuāi*, 'by nature', and the unfortunates who have had to learn
(*mathontes*). If nature and God have been unkind, there is no hope of success.
So in the fifth *Nemean*:

πότμος δὲ κρίνει συγγενὴς ἔργων πέρι
πάντων (40-1).

'The destiny that is born in a man is the judge of every deed', and in the third
Nemean, where the same adjective *sungenēs*, 'inborn', is used:

συγγενεῖ δέ τις εὐδοξίᾳ μέγα βρίθει·
ὃς δὲ διδάκτ' ἔχει, ψεφεννὸς ἀνὴρ
ἄλλοτ' ἄλλα πνέων οὔ ποτ' ἀτρεκεῖ
κατέβα ποδί, μυριᾶν δ' ἀρετᾶν ἀτελεῖ νόῳ γεύεται (40-2).

'He whose glory is inborn prevails; the man who has been taught is obscure,
blowing now this way, now that, never walking with steady foot, tasting a
thousand excellences with ineffectual mind.' The 'inborn' glory or destiny
is sometimes, although not always, to be explained by victories won by the
athlete's ancestors:

τὸ δὲ συγγενὲς ἐμβέβακεν ἴχνεσιν πατρὸς
Ὀλυμπιονίκα δίς (*Pyth.* 10.12-13),

'his inborn quality has trodden in the steps of his father, who was twice an
Olympic victor'. Such quality alone is not enough, however: the lines which
immediately precede these words are

Ἄπολλον, γλυκὺ δ' ἀνθρώπων τέλος ἀρχά
τε δαίμονος ὀρνύντος αὔξεται·
ὁ μέν που τεοῖς τε μήδεσι τοῦτ' ἔπραξεν (10-11).

'Apollo, the end and the beginning of man's endeavours are sweet and prosperous when god sets them in motion; and he must have achieved this by your devising.' The *daimōn* or 'god' in this case is Apollo himself, presiding god of the Pythian games, but it is sometimes an unspecified *daimōn* or *theos* whose hand guides the victor. Occasionally the mention of the god is linked with warnings:

εἴ τις ἀνδρῶν εὐτυχήσαις ἢ σὺν εὐδόξοις ἀέθλοις
ἢ σθένει πλούτου κατέχει φρασὶν αἰανῆ κόρον,
ἄξιος εὐλογίαις ἀστῶν μεμίχθαι.
Ζεῦ, μεγάλαι δ' ἀρεταὶ θνατοῖς ἕπονται
ἐκ σέθεν· ζώει δὲ μάσσων
ὄλβος ὀπιζομένων, πλαγίαις δὲ φρένεσσιν
οὐχ ὁμῶς πάντα χρόνον θάλλων ὁμιλεῖ (*Isthm.* 3.1-6).

'If a man prospers either in glorious games or in might of wealth and still checks in his heart nagging ambition, then he deserves to be mingled with the praises of the citizens. From you, Zeus, do great excellences come the way of mortals. Prosperity lives longer when men are reverent; if their thoughts are crooked, it does not thrive in their company for all time alike.' Pindar, in pontifical vein despite the festive occasion, warns against *koros*, the excess or ambitious desire which comes from great prosperity and which is often linked by the poets with *hubris* and infatuation. The same warning appears in its most succinct form in

μὴ μάτευε Ζεὺς γενέσθαι (*Isthm.* 5.14),

'Do not seek to become Zeus'. It is this combination of the grand style and lofty moralising that distinguishes Pindar from Bacchylides and indeed from almost all Greek poets with the exception of his other contemporary, Aeschylus.

*   *   *

Bacchylides' ode 3 was composed for Hieron, tyrant of Syracuse, on the occasion of his greatest athletic triumph, victory in the chariot-race at the Olympic games of 468 B.C. The poem was Bacchylides' most important commission and is the finest display of his talent, a vivid, exciting work, only half as long as his epinician for Hieron's victory in the Olympic horse-race of 476 (ode 5), but no less impressive for its briefer compass. The poem, like almost all the victory-odes of Bacchylides and Pindar, is in triadic structure: here a strophe of four lines in iambic and aeolic rhythm is answered by an antistrophe in the same rhythm and followed by a six-line epode in dactylo-epitrites, the fourteen-line pattern aab occurring seven times in all.

The poem begins with commemoration of Hieron's victory and description of the rejoicing in Syracuse:

> ἀριστοκάρπου Σικελίας κρέουσαν
> Δάματρα ἰοστέφανόν τε Κούραν
> ὕμνει, γλυκύδωρε Κλεοῖ, θοάς τ' Ὀ-
>   λυμπιοδρόμους Ἱέρωνος ἵππους·
>
> σεύον]το γὰρ σὺν ὑπερόχῳ τε Νίκᾳ   5
> σὺν Ἀγ]λαΐᾳ τε παρ' εὐρυδίναν
> Ἀλφεόν, τόθι] Δεινομένεος ἔθηκαν
>   ὄλβιον τ[έκος στεφάνω]ν κυρῆσαι·
>
> θρόησε δὲ λ[αὸς ἀπείρων,
>   ἃ τρισευδαίμ]ων ἀνήρ,   10
> ὃς παρὰ Ζηνὸς λαχὼν
>   πλείσταρχον Ἑλλάνων γέρας
> οἶδε πυργωθέντα πλοῦτον μὴ μελαμ-
>   φαρέϊ κρύπτειν σκότῳ.
>
> βρύει μὲν ἱερὰ βουθύτοις ἑορταῖς,   15
> βρύουσι φιλοξενίας ἀγυιαί·
> λάμπει δ' ὑπὸ μαρμαρυγαῖς ὁ χρυσός,
>   ὑψιδαιδάλτων τριπόδων σταθέντων
>
> πάροιθε ναοῦ, τόθι μέγιστον ἄλσος
> Φοίβου παρὰ Κασταλίας ῥεέθροις   20
> Δελφοὶ διέπουσι. θεὸν θ[εό]ν τις
>   ἀγλαϊζέθω· γὰρ ἄριστος ὄλβων (1-22).

'Of Demeter, the queen of Sicily with its rich cornlands, and of the violet-crowned Maid, sing, Clio, giver of sweetness; and of the swift horses of Hieron that ran at Olympia. They sped alongside distinguished Victory and Glory at the banks of wide-eddying Alpheus, where they made Deinomenes' prosperous son the winner of garlands; and the immense crowd shouted, "Ah, thrice-blessed man: he got from Zeus the privilege of ruling over the greatest number of Greeks, and he knows how to avoid hiding his towering wealth in black-cloaked darkness." The temples abound in rich feasts at which oxen are slaughtered, the streets abound in rich hospitality; and gold shines with flashing light from the high elaborate tripods set before the temple where the people of Delphi tend the great sanctuary of Phoebus by the waters of Castalia. Let God, God, be glorified; for that is the best of prosperities.'

Bacchylides begins impressively with Demeter and Persephone, the two goddesses closely associated with Sicily; Hieron was their hereditary priest, and his brother Gelon had built them temples in Syracuse. There is an epic richness in the prelude, due largely to the compound adjectives which Bacchylides creates so generously: Sicily is 'best in crops' (the poem opens with *aristo-* as Pindar's first *Olympian* had begun with *ariston*), Persephone is 'violet-crowned', Clio 'giver of sweetness', the swift horses 'Olympic runners'. Clio, one of Bacchylides' favourite Muses, is asked to sing of Demeter, Persephone, and—with a sudden shift to the secular—of Hieron's horses. The personified Victory and Glory maintain the elevated tone, as the scene moves from Sicily to Olympia. It is uncertain whether the exclamation of lines 10–14, 'Ah, thrice-blessed man . . .', should be regarded as the cry of the spectators or of Bacchylides himself; in either case it is exciting, and its theme, that great glory or great wealth should be proclaimed abroad and not kept hidden is common in epinician poetry, although it may be accompanied by warnings against presumptuous behaviour. Bacchylides moves on to such a pro-clamation: the repeated verb *bruein* is applicable to swelling plants (cf. 'bryony') or teeming resources; and in this passage too there is a sudden shift, from the rich celebrations at Syracuse to the wealth displayed at Delphi, the tripods dedicated there by Hieron and his brother before him. With this movement to Delphi Bacchylides has prepared the way for the next section of the poem; but he completes his introductory material with the generalisation that God should be glorified—honoured, that is, by the giving of gifts: the expression *ho gar aristos olbōn* is perhaps too compressed to be easily intelligible, but I take it that Bacchylides is commending the prosperity of the man who like Hieron gives generously to God. The echoes in this line (6 *Aglaia . . . aglaizetō*, 1 *aristo- . . . aristos*, 8 *olbion . . . olbos*) round off the first section of the poem, and the repetition 'God, God' maintains the atmosphere of religious excitement.

Bacchylides now begins the narrative section, and introduces Croesus of Lydia as an example of a prosperous ruler who gave rich gifts to God and was himself richly repaid. Pindar in his first *Pythian*, written for Hieron two years earlier, took Croesus as an illustration of piety rewarded:

οὐ φθίνει Κροίσου φιλόφρων ἀρετά (*Pyth.* 1.94),

'the excellent generosity of Croesus does not perish'. Bacchylides is likely to have found there the idea of telling the story in detail.

ἐπεί ποτε καὶ δαμασίππου
    Λυδίας ἀρχαγέταν,
εὖτε τὰν πεπ[ρωμέναν   25
    Ζηνὸς τελέ[σσαντος κρί]σιν
Σάρδιες Περσᾶ[ν ἁλίσκοντο στρ]ατῷ,
    Κροῖσον ὁ χρυσά[ορος

φύλαξ' Ἀπόλλων. [ὁ δ' ἐς] ἄελπτον ἆμαρ
μ[ο]λὼν πολυδ[άκρυο]ν οὐκ ἔμελλε   30
μίμνειν ἔτι δ[ουλοσύ]ναν, πυ[ρ]ὰν δὲ
   χαλκ[ο]τειχέος π[ροπάροι]θεν αὐ[λᾶς

ναήσατ', ἔνθα σὺ[ν ἀλόχῳ] τε κεδ[νᾷ
σὺν εὐπλοκάμοι[ς τ'] ἐπέβαιν' ἄλα[στον
θυ[γ]ατράσι δυρομέναις· χέρας δ' [ἐς   35
   αἰ]πὺν αἰθέρα σφετέρας ἀείρας

γέγω]νεν· ὑπέρ[βι]ε δαῖμον,
   πο]ῦ θεῶν ἐστιν χάρις;
πο]ῦ δὲ Λατοίδας ἄναξ;
   ἔρρουσ]ιν Ἀλυά[τ]τα δόμοι   40
        ] μυρίων
        ]ν.

        ] ἄστυ,
ἐρεύθεται αἵματι χρυσο]δίνας
Πακτωλός, ἀεικελίως γυναῖκες   45
   ἐξ ἐϋκτίτων μεγάρων ἄγονται·

τὰ πρόσθεν [ἐχ]θρὰ φίλα· θανεῖν γλύκιστον.'
τόσ' εἶπε, καὶ ἁβ[ρο]βάταν κ[έλε]υσεν
ἅπτειν ξύλινον δόμον. ἐκ[λα]γον δὲ
   παρθένοι, φίλας τ' ἀνὰ ματρὶ χεῖρας   50

ἔβαλλον· ὁ γὰρ προφανὴς θνατοῖσιν ἔχθιστος φόνων·
ἀλλ' ἐπεὶ δεινοῦ πυρὸς
   λαμπρὸν διάϊ[σσεν μέ]νος,
Ζεὺς ἐπιστάσας [μελαγκευ]θὲς νέφος   55
   σβέννυεν ξανθὰ[ν φλόγα.

ἄπιστον οὐδέν, ὅ τι θ[εῶν μέ]ριμνα
τεύχει· τότε Δαλογενὴ[ς Ἀπό]λλων
φέρων ἐς Ὑπερβορέο[υς γ]έροντα
   σὺν τανισφύροις κατ[έν]ασσε κούραις   60

δι' εὐσέβειαν, ὅτι μέ[γιστα] θνατῶν
ἐς ἀγαθέαν <ἀν>έπεμψε Π[υθ]ώ (23-62).

'Since once upon a time the commander of horse-taming Lydia, when Zeus had brought about the fated issue and Sardis was captured by the Persian army, was protected by Apollo of the golden sword: Croesus, having reached the day he had hoped to avoid, had no intention of waiting for tearful slavery; he had a pyre built in front of his bronze-walled palace, and mounted it together with his beloved wife and beautiful-haired daughters, who wailed inconsolably. Raising his hands to the sheer heavens above he shouted, "Almighty Spirit, where is the gratitude of the gods? Where is lord Apollo, Leto's son? The house of Alyattes is falling. (Apollo shows no gratitude for my) countless (gifts: the Persians are sacking my) city. The Pactolus, that carries gold in its eddying waters, is reddened with blood, the women are being shamefully carried off from the fine halls. What once was hateful is welcome: to die is sweetest." Such were his words, and he ordered his soft-stepping attendant to light the wooden building. The girls shrieked and threw up their hands to their mother: the death that is foreseen is most hateful to mankind. But when the shining strength of the grim fire was darting through the pyre, Zeus placed a dark enveloping cloud overhead and quenched the yellow flame. Nothing that the devising of the gods achieves is past belief: Delos-born Apollo carried the old man then to the Hyperboreans and settled him there with his slender-ankled daughters, all for his piety, since he had sent to holy Pytho greater gifts than any other mortal.'

Bacchylides moves briskly into the myth by presenting it as a reason for the generalisation he has just made, and he maintains the pace in his narrative, using short clauses linked by the simplest connectives, and introducing direct speech and brief comment for variation. In this section of the poem, moreover, he prefers conventional epithets, 'beautiful-haired', 'slender-ankled', with the result that the listener's attention is not distracted from the story. The last two lines (61–2) establish the relevance of the myth beyond question: it was Croesus' generosity to Apollo in Delphi that led to his miraculous preservation.

This account of Croesus' fortunes differs from that given later by Herodotus (1.86ff.): there Croesus is put on the pyre by Cyrus' orders, and after his rescue he lives on at Cyrus' court (3.36). Bacchylides, however, did not invent the story of Croesus' self-immolation: a red-figured amphora dated *c.* 500 B.C. shows Croesus seated on the pyre and calmly making libation, while a 'kindly' attendant, labelled *Euthumos*, busies himself with the pyre. It is remarkable that Croesus should have joined the ranks of mythological figures within eighty years of his death: the Hyperboreans belong to legend, a happy, musical race living in the far north, favourites of Apollo.

Bacchylides now links the story of Croesus with his patron Hieron:

ὅσο[ι] <γε> μὲν Ἑλλάδ' ἔχουσιν, [ο]ὔτι[ς,
ὦ μεγαίνητε Ἱέρων, θελήσει

φάμ]εν σέο πλείονα χρυσὸν   65
Λοξί]ᾳ πέμψαι βροτῶν.
εὖ λέ]γειν πάρεστιν, ὅσ-
τις μ]ὴ φθόνῳ πιαίνεται

θεοφι]λῆ φίλιππον ἄνδρ' ἀρήϊον
  ξειν]ίου σκᾶπτρον Διός   70

ἰοπλό]κων τε μέρο[ς ἔχοντ]α Μουσᾶν
. . . .]μαλέα ποτ[ὲ . . . . . .]΄.ιων
. . . .]νος ἐφάμερον α]. . . . . .].
    . . . .]α σκοπεῖς· βραχ[ύς ἐστιν αἰών·

πτερ]όεσσα δ' ἐλπὶς ὑπ[ολύει ν]όημα   75
ἐφαμ]ερίων· ὁ δ' ἄναξ ['Απόλλων
. . . . .]΄.λος εἶπε Φέρη[τος υἷι·
    'θνατὸν εὖντα χρὴ διδύμους ἀέξειν

γνώμας, ὅτι τ' αὔριον ὄψεαι
    μοῦνον ἁλίου φάος,   80
χὤτι πεντήκοντ' ἔτεα
    ζωὰν βαθύπλουτον τελεῖς.
ὅσια δρῶν εὔφραινε θυμόν· τοῦτο γὰρ
    κερδέων ὑπέρτατον.'

φρονέοντι συνετὰ γαρύω· βαθὺς μὲν   85
αἰθὴρ ἀμίαντος· ὕδωρ δὲ πόντου
οὐ σάπεται· εὐφροσύνα δ' ὁ χρυσός·
    ἀνδρὶ δ' οὐ θέμις, πολιὸν π[αρ]έντα

γῆρας, θάλ[εια]ν αὖτις ἀγκομίσσαι
ἥβαν. ἀρετᾶ[ς γε μ]ὲν οὐ μινύθει   90
βροτῶν ἅμα σ[ώμ]ατι φέγγος, ἀλλὰ
    Μοῦσά νιν τρ[έφει.] 'Ιέρων, σὺ δ' ὄλβου

κάλλιστ' ἐπεδ[είξ]αο θνατοῖς
    ἄνθεα· πράξα[ντι] δ' εὖ
οὐ φέρει κόσμ[ον σι]ω-   95
    πά. σὺν δ' ἀλαθ[είᾳ] καλῶν
καὶ μελιγλώσσου τις ὑμνήσει χάριν
    Κηΐας ἀηδόνος (63-98).

'Of all mortals who dwell in Greece none, illustrious Hieron, will be ready to claim that he sent more gold to Loxias than you. Anyone who does not fatten himself on envy may sing the praises of this god-loved, horse-loving warrior, who holds the sceptre of Zeus, god of hospitality, and has his share in the violet-haired Muses: once (you raged in battle with terrible hand, now) you look (in peace on the pleasure) of the day. Life is brief, and winged hope undoes the thoughts of mortals. Lord Apollo (the far-shooter) said to the son of Pheres, "If you are mortal, you must foster two thoughts: first, that tomorrow will be the only day on which you look upon the sun's light; secondly, that you will live for fifty years a life of ample wealth. Gladden your heart by doing holy deeds: this is the highest of gains." I speak words which the wise may understand: the deep heavens are unsoiled, and the water of the sea does not decay; gold is a joy; but a man may not pass grey old age and then win back again his flourishing youth. The light of man's excellence does not diminish with his body: no, the Muse fosters it. Hieron, you have displayed to mortals the loveliest flowers of wealth, and when a man has prospered, silence does not bring him his proper adornment: together with your true glories men will praise also the grace of the melodious Cean nightingale.'

The gold sent by Hieron to Apollo at Delphi is again the link by which Bacchylides ties the myth to its context, and the description of Hieron as *philippon*, 'horse-loving', reminds us of Croesus, ruler of a 'horse-taming' people (23). The tyrant's praises are sung, not merely as Olympic victor but on wider grounds, his wealth, his power and his literary interests. Then Bacchylides offers advice to his patron, citing Apollo's words to the son of Pheres, Admetus, the mortal king whom the god had served as a menial: mortals should live their lives on the assumption that they may die tomorrow, and should make the most of their time; and equally on the assumption that they have fifty years to live, and should plan for the future. The two consequences are compressed into the four words *hosia drōn euphraine thumon*: 'do holy deeds', thus showing forethought, and 'gladden your heart', thus enjoying the present moment.

In his closing passage Bacchylides draws heavily on Pindaric material: 'I speak words which the wise may understand' is a less bold version of Pindar's 'arrows that speak to the wise' (*Ol.* 2.83–5); and in the following lines Bacchylides uses the opening lines of the first *Olympian*, which Pindar had written eight years before for Hieron; Pindar's splendid lines moved from the images of water, gold and the sun to the Olympic games; Bacchylides, copying the abrupt, paratactic style, moves from air, sea and gold to the irretrievability of man's youth, and then from bodily decay to immortality conferred by the Muse; but his grip on the Pindaric manner is insecure; Horace said centuries later that anyone who tries to imitate Pindar crashes to earth like Icarus, and it seems true of Bacchylides here.

Self-advertisement was frequent in poets who accepted commissions: Pindar ended his first *Olympian* with a prayer for Hieron's prosperity and his own success, and so here Bacchylides' last words are of himself, the nightingale from the island of Ceos; since his talent is linked with the 'true glories' of Hieron, he too can hope for immortality.

*   *   *

Pindar's seventh *Olympian* was written in 464 B.C. for the boxer Diagoras of Rhodes, one of the most distinguished athletes of the Greek world. It is one of his finest odes, and was said to have been inscribed in gold letters in the temple of Athena at Lindus. It is written in the dactylo-epitrite rhythm, which Pindar uses for about half of his odes, and it consists of five triads, the second, third and fourth of which deal with the mythology of Rhodes.

φιάλαν ὡς εἴ τις ἀφνειᾶς ἀπὸ χειρὸς ἑλὼν
ἔνδον ἀμπέλου καχλάζοισαν δρόσῳ
δωρήσεται
νεανίᾳ γαμβρῷ προπίνων
    οἴκοθεν οἴκαδε, πάγχρυσον, κορυφὰν κτεάνων,
συμποσίου τε χάριν κᾶ-
    δός τε τιμάσαις νέον, ἐν δὲ φίλων   5
παρεόντων θῆκέ νιν ζαλωτὸν ὁμόφρονος εὐνᾶς·

καὶ ἐγὼ νέκταρ χυτόν, Μοισᾶν δόσιν, ἀεθλοφόροις
ἀνδράσιν πέμπων, γλυκὺν καρπὸν φρενός,
ἱλάσκομαι,
Ὀλυμπίᾳ Πυθοῖ τε νικών-
τεσσιν· ὁ δ' ὄλβιος, ὃν φᾶμαι κατέχωντ' ἀγαθαί·   10
ἄλλοτε δ' ἄλλον ἐποπτεύ-
    ει Χάρις ζωθάλμιος ἁδυμελεῖ
θαμὰ μὲν φόρμιγγι παμφώνοισί τ' ἐν ἔντεσιν αὐλῶν.

καί νυν ὑπ' ἀμφοτέρων σὺν
    Διαγόρᾳ κατέβαν, τὰν ποντίαν
ὑμνέων, παῖδ' Ἀφροδίτας
    Ἀελίοιό τε νύμφαν, Ῥόδον,
εὐθυμάχαν ὄφρα πελώριον ἄνδρα παρ' Ἀλ-
    φειῷ στεφανωσάμενον   15
αἰνέσω πυγμᾶς ἄποινα
καὶ παρὰ Κασταλίᾳ, πα-
    τέρα τε Δαμάγητον ἁδόντα Δίκᾳ,
Ἀσίας εὐρυχόρου τρίπολιν νᾶσον πέλας
ἐμβόλῳ ναίοντας Ἀργείᾳ σὺν αἰχμᾷ (1-19).

'As when a man takes in his wealthy hand a bowl bubbling with the vine's moisture it holds and presents it to his young son-in-law, drinking his health from one house to another, a bowl of solid gold, crowning glory of his possessions, grace of the banquet, honouring the new member of his family, and in the presence of his friends makes him envied thereby for his harmonious marriage, so I send a draught of nectar, the gift of the Muses, sweet harvest of my mind, to the prize-winning man, victorious at Olympia and Pytho, and pay my homage. That man is blessed whom good reports surround; but the Grace who makes life flourish looks favourably now upon this man, now upon that, often with the sweet song of the lyre and the many notes of the pipes.

And so now I have come ashore with Diagoras to the sound of both, singing of the sea-child, the daughter of Aphrodite and bride of the Sun, Rhodes, so that I may praise in reward for his boxing the gigantic man, the honest fighter, who won the garland by the banks of the Alpheus, yes, and by Castalia too; and his father also, Damagetus, who pleased Justice; men who dwell in the island of the three cities close to the promontory of broad Asia with the help of their Argive spear.'

The simile with which Pindar opens the poem has been much admired and with good reason: the scene is a family celebration, at which a valuable cup, elaborately described, is presented to a bridegroom; comparable with this splendid cup is the poem which Pindar sends to victors in the games: he describes it as 'nectar', the drink of the gods which made them immortal, an apt image for an epinician ode which was designed to make the victor immortal; as 'the gift of the Muses', a more conventional expression, although it gains some colour here from the idea of generous giving which dominates the first six lines; and as the 'sweet harvest of my mind', another striking image: Pindar describes his poetry with the same elaboration as the cup. His point is clearly made because his Homeric-type simile is underlined by the metrical parallelism of lines 1ff. and 7ff. His aphorism in line 10, 'That man is blessed whom good reports surround', refers to glory given to the victor by the poet; but it leads to another aphorism, an unexpectedly gloomy reference to the vicissitudes of fortune in the games: the Grace, *Kharis*, is for Pindar the deity who grants success in games, and his short fourteenth *Olympian* takes the form of a hymn to the Graces. Here he applies to her a unique epithet, *zōthalmios*, compounded from *zēn*, 'to live', and *thallein*, 'to flourish', and alludes to the name of Thalia, one of the Three. Vicissitude will be a recurrent theme in this poem; but here Pindar moves on rapidly from the general to the particular. It is Diagoras' turn for victory, and Pindar has come to Rhodes—or at least has sent his poem—in order to sing his praises. In this section (13–19) Pindar mentions several themes which he will treat more fully later in the poem: Diagoras of course, Rhodes and the Sun-god, the three cities of Rhodes, and the link between Rhodes and Argos.

Pindar uses the name *Rhodos* for both the island itself and the nymph of the island. At this first mention Rhodes is the nymph, a sea-creature, child of Aphrodite, no less, and bride of the Sun: the epithets come first, and *Rhodon* gains emphasis from the postponement. We must remember too that *rhodon* is the Greek word for 'the rose', and that the Rhodians themselves used the rose as an emblem on their coins. The description of the island as 'close to the jutting promontory of wide Asia' suggests that Pindar had been there: the long mountain ranges of Asia Minor are clearly visible from the island.

The first triad is a complete unit, and the metrical break, unusually for Pindar, marks the point of transition to the mythological material.

ἐθελήσω τοῖσιν ἐξ ἀρχᾶς ἀπὸ Τλαπολέμου   20
ξυνὸν ἀγγέλλων διορθῶσαι λόγον,
Ἡρακλέος
εὐρυσθενεῖ γέννα. τὸ μὲν γὰρ
        πατρόθεν ἐκ Διὸς εὔχονται· τὸ δ' Ἀμυντορίδαι
ματρόθεν Ἀστυδαμείας.
        ἀμφὶ δ' ἀνθρώπων φρασὶν ἀμπλακίαι
ἀναρίθμητοι κρέμανται· τοῦτο δ' ἀμάχανον εὑρεῖν,   25

ὅτι νῦν ἐν καὶ τελευτᾷ φέρτατον ἀνδρὶ τυχεῖν.
καὶ γὰρ Ἀλκμήνας κασίγνητον νόθον
σκάπτῳ θενὼν
σκληρᾶς ἐλαίας ἔκτανεν Τί-
        ρυνθι Λικύμνιον ἐλθόντ' ἐκ θαλάμων Μιδέας
τᾶσδέ ποτε χθονὸς οἰκι-
        στὴρ χολωθείς. αἱ δὲ φρενῶν ταραχαὶ   30
παρέπλαγξαν καὶ σοφόν. μαντεύσατο δ' ἐς θεὸν ἐλθών.

τῷ μὲν ὁ χρυσοκόμας εὐ-
        ώδεος ἐξ ἀδύτου ναῶν πλόον
εἶπε Λερναίας ἀπ' ἀκτᾶς
        εὐθὺν ἐς ἀμφιθάλασσον νομόν (20-33).

'I shall tell correctly the story of their community from its beginning with Tlepolemus. They are of the mighty race of Heracles: on the father's side they claim descent from Zeus, on the mother's side from Astydamia, so that they are of the family of Amyntor. Now, about the minds of men countless failings hang, and it is impossible to discover what is best both now and in the end for a man to get. Why, Alcmena's bastard brother, Licymnius, was killed at Tiryns, struck with a staff of hard olive as he came from Midea's room, by the founder of this land [Tlepolemus] in a fit of anger once: confusions of the mind send even a wise man wandering. So he [Tlepolemus] went to the god and consulted the oracle: golden-haired Apollo from the fragrant shrine of the temple prescribed for him a voyage from the shore of Lerna [near Argos and Tiryns] straight to the island pasture [Rhodes] . . . .'.

Most of the story of Tlepolemus is to be found in *Iliad* 2.653ff., where Homer tells in his Catalogue of the nine ships he took from Rhodes to Troy. The details in Pindar—the fit of anger in which Tlepolemus killed his great-uncle, and the room of Midea, mother of Licymnius—may have come from Hesiod, who also told their story (fr. 232 M–W); Midea's room, at least, seems irrelevant and may simply echo an earlier telling of the story, but the fit of anger does something to exonerate the founder of Rhodes. The family tree is as follows:

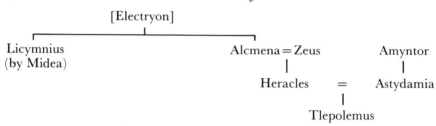

Pindar's gloomy aphorism at 24ff. is appropriate to the story: Tlepolemus killed a relative and had to consult the oracle at Delphi; and Apollo's advice was to leave Argos for Rhodes. This might have been regarded by Tlepolemus as calamitous, but 'the minds of men' cannot see ahead. Pindar will show later in the poem that what Tlepolemus got was best in the end.

We are now given a still earlier episode in the history of Rhodes. Pindar moves to it easily in mid-sentence:

ἔνθα ποτὲ βρέχε θεῶν βασιλεὺς ὁ μέγας
    χρυσέαις νιφάδεσσι πόλιν,
ἁνίχ' Ἀφαίστου τέχναισιν   35
χαλκελάτῳ πελέκει πα-
    τέρος Ἀθαναία κορυφὰν κατ' ἄκραν
ἀνορούσαισ' ἀλάλαξεν ὑπερμάκει βοᾷ.
Οὐρανὸς δ' ἔφριξέ νιν καὶ Γαῖα μάτηρ.

τότε καὶ φαυσίμβροτος δαίμων Ὑπεριονίδας
μέλλον ἔντειλεν φυλάξασθαι χρέος   40
παισίν φίλοις,
ὡς ἂν θεᾷ πρῶτοι κτίσαιεν
    βωμὸν ἐναργέα, καὶ σεμνὰν θυσίαν θέμενοι
πατρί τε θυμὸν ἰάναι-
    εν κόρᾳ τ' ἐγχειβρόμῳ. ἐν δ' ἀρετὰν
ἔβαλεν καὶ χάρματ' ἀνθρώποισι Προμαθέος Αἰδώς.

ἐπὶ μὰν βαίνει τι καὶ λάθας ἀτέκμαρτα νέφος,   45
καὶ παρέλκει πραγμάτων ὀρθὰν ὁδὸν
ἔξω φρενῶν.
καὶ τοὶ γὰρ αἰθοίσας ἔχοντες
    σπέρμ' ἀνέβαν φλογὸς οὔ. τεῦξαν δ' ἀπύροις ἱεροῖς
ἄλσος ἐν ἀκροπόλει. κεί-
    νοισι μὲν ξανθὰν ἀγαγὼν νεφέλαν
πολὺν ὗσε χρυσόν· αὐτὰ δέ σφισιν ὤπασε τέχναν   50

πᾶσαν ἐπιχθονίων Γλαυκ-
    ῶπις ἀριστοπόνοις χερσὶ κρατεῖν.

ἔργα δὲ ζωοῖσιν ἑρπόν-
τεσσί θ' ὁμοῖα κέλευθοι φέρον.
ἦν δὲ κλέος βαθύ. δαέντι δὲ καὶ σοφία
μείζων ἄδολος τελέθει (34-53).

'. . . where once the great king of the gods showered the city with golden snow-flakes, at the time when through the craft of Hephaestus Athena sprang at the blow of a bronze axe from the crown of her father's head and shouted a tremendous battle-cry, and Heaven and mother Earth shuddered at her. Then the Sun-god, Hyperion's child, who gives light to mortals, commanded his dear children [the Rhodians] to pay heed to a future obligation: they should be the first to found a conspicuous altar for the goddess and by making holy sacrifice should gladden the heart of the father [Zeus] and of the maiden who thunders with her spear [Athena]: Respect, daughter of Forethought, sets among mankind excellence and joy. However, a cloud of forgetfulness comes bafflingly over men and tugs the straight course of events from out of their minds: why, they went up [to worship her on their acropolis] without the seed of blazing flame, and they founded a sanctuary on their acropolis for offerings made without fire. He [Zeus] brought a yellow cloud and rained a torrent of gold on them, while she, the grey-eyed goddess [Athena], gave them every skill, so that they surpassed all mortals in the cunning of their craftsmen's hands. Their roads carried works of art that looked like living and moving things; and their glory was deep. In the eyes of the wise man skill is greater if it is free of guile.' Pindar frequently introduces his myth or a new part of a myth by using a relative clause as here: 'to the island pasture, where once . . .' Subordination of clauses is not a feature of Pindar's style any more than of his predecessors'; he commonly strings his main clauses together with a repeated *de*, as for example in lines 52–3, and indeed part of the interpreter's difficulty is to decide whether the appropriate English conjunction is 'and', 'and so', 'but' or 'for'. By using the relative clause as in 34 Pindar makes a smooth transition to new material. The use of *pote*, 'once', takes us back to a far earlier period in the history of Rhodes, the moment of Athena's birth, when Zeus snowed or rained gold on the city. The image is likely to be Pindar's fanciful elaboration of Homer's closing line on the Rhodians:

καί σφιν θεσπέσιον πλοῦτον κατέχευε Κρονίων (*Il.* 2.670),

'and Zeus poured down on them untold riches': 'a metaphor turned into a myth' by Pindar, as the commentator Gildersleeve puts it.

As in the Tlepolemus episode Pindar recounts a near-disaster. The forgetful Rhodians, advised to be the first to honour Athena, ahead even of the Athenians, went up to their acropolis without fire. Here, as in the Tlepolemus story, Pindar prefaces an aphorism to his account of the mistake: the 'cloud of forgetfulness' serves to excuse their folly, and there is a touch of humour in the extraordinary positioning of the negative *ou* at the end of its sentence: did they have fire when they went up? No! But all was well: the sacrifice was acceptable, Zeus gave them wealth, Athena gave them artistic skill: their roads carried works of art of astonishing realism. These roads are usually taken literally: the streets of the Rhodian cities 'carried' masterpieces of statuary; but it may be better to regard the roads as metaphorical paths of experiment or development.

Two generalisations in the passage still need to be explained, and are difficult even in Pindar. In 43–4 I translate, 'Respect, daughter of Fore-thought, sets among mankind excellence and joy.' *Aidōs* and *Promatheus* I regard as personified, like *Dikē*, Justice, in 17, and take them to refer to the qualities shown by the early Rhodians: respect or reverence for the gods and for Athena in particular, and forethought in that their 'future obligation' of worshipping Athena was likely to be rewarded by a grateful goddess. The other aphorism, with which Pindar closes this section, is even more troublesome: I translate it, with little confidence, 'In the eyes of the wise man skill is greater if it is free of guile', and take *sophia* as alluding to the technical skill of the Rhodians which Pindar has just described. The difficulty is *adolos*, 'free of guile': can Pindar be contrasting the skill of Rhodian craftsmen with the magical art of the Telchines, a semi-divine race said to have inhabited Rhodes in its earliest times? Such an allusion is unlikely when Pindar nowhere mentions the Telchines in his poem, but without such an allusion the reference to the absence of guile seems pointless. D. C. Young takes the sentence to mean, 'If a man has learned knowledge, his native wisdom becomes greater, also', but this gives an improbable sense to *adolos* ('native') and goes against the usual Pindaric view that native wisdom is altogether superior to knowledge that has been taught and learned. Another version, 'Is not the poet/Who's informed the greater for his truth?' (Ruck and Matheson) sees in *sophia* a reference to the poet's skill and finds a contrast between Pindar's telling of the history of Rhodes and the account in *Iliad* 2: 'the centre of the poem is the correction of the Homeric tradition.' But, as I see it, Pindar is not so much correcting Homer as expanding his lines as a lyric poet might and laying the emphasis on different points.

Pindar now moves to his third Rhodian story, this time drawing explicitly on popular tradition:

> φαντὶ δ᾽ ἀνθρώπων παλαιαὶ
> ῥήσιες, οὔπω, ὅτε χθό-
> να δατέοντο Ζεύς τε καὶ ἀθάνατοι,   55
> φανερὰν ἐν πελάγει Ῥόδον ἔμμεν ποντίῳ,
> ἁλμυροῖς δ᾽ ἐν βένθεσιν νᾶσον κεκρύφθαι.
>
> ἀπεόντος δ᾽ οὔτις ἔνδειξεν λάχος Ἀελίου·

καί ϱά νιν χώρας ἀκλάρωτον λίπον,
ἁγνὸν θεόν.   60
μνασθέντι δὲ Ζεὺς ἄμπαλον μέλ-
    λεν θέμεν. ἀλλά νιν οὐκ εἴασεν· ἐπεὶ πολιᾶς
εἶπέ τιν' αὐτὸς ὁρᾶν ἔν-
    δον θαλάσσας αὐξομέναν πεδόθεν
πολύβοσκον γαῖαν ἀνθρώποισι καὶ εὔφρονα μήλοις.

ἐκέλευσεν δ' αὐτίκα χρυσάμπυκα μὲν Λάχεσιν
χεῖρας ἀντεῖναι, θεῶν δ' ὅρκον μέγαν   65
μὴ παρφάμεν,
    ἀλλὰ Κρόνου σὺν παιδὶ νεῦσαι,
    φαεννὸν ἐς αἰθέρα μιν πεμφθεῖσαν ἑᾷ κεφαλᾷ
ἐξοπίσω γέρας ἔσσε-
    σθαι. τελεύταθεν δὲ λόγων κορυφαὶ
ἐν ἀλαθείᾳ πετοῖσαι· βλάστε μὲν ἐξ ἁλὸς ὑγρᾶς

νᾶσος, ἔχει τέ μιν ὀξει-
    ᾶν ὁ γενέθλιος ἀκτίνων πατήρ,   70
πῦρ πνεόντων ἀρχὸς ἵππων·
    ἔνθα Ῥόδῳ ποτὲ μιχθεὶς τέκεν
ἑπτὰ σοφώτατα νοήματ' ἐπὶ προτέρων
    ἀνδρῶν παραδεξαμένους
παῖδας, ὧν εἷς μὲν Κάμιρον
πρεσβύτατόν τε Ἰάλυ-
    σον ἔτεκεν Λίνδον τ'· ἀπάτερθε δ' ἔχον
διὰ γαῖαν τρίχα δασσάμενοι πατρωΐαν   75
ἀστέων μοίρας, κέκληνται δέ σφιν ἕδραι (54-76).

'Ancient stories of mankind tell that when Zeus and the other immortals shared out the earth, Rhodes was not yet visible on the sea's wide surface: the island was hidden in the salty depths. And since the Sun was absent, no one pointed out a portion as his; and they left him with no share in the land, that holy god. When he mentioned it, Zeus was for holding a second drawing of lots, but he did not allow it; for he said that he could himself distinguish within the grey sea a land growing from its foundations, providing nourishment for men and kindly to flocks. At once he ordered Lachesis of the golden headband [one of the Fates] to raise her hands and to avoid taking in vain the gods' mighty oath, but to consent together with Cronus' son [Zeus] that when it rose into the bright air it would thenceforth be a perquisite for himself alone. The high points of these words were accomplished, falling out truthfully. There grew from the salt sea-water an island, and the life-giving father of the piercing shafts of sunlight, lord of the firebreathing horses, possesses it. There he once lay with Rhodes and fathered seven sons who inherited the wisest minds in time past; and one of them begot Camirus and Ialysus, his eldest, and Lindus; and dividing their ancestral land into three shares, they kept their appointed cities apart, and the settlements are called by their names.'

The narrative moves with great rapidity in this section. There is no comment from the poet, no explanation of the Sun's absence; there is much picturesque detail and clever exploitation of the metre: 'that holy god', at the end of the sentence, is emphasised since it forms a complete metrical unit in itself; and the emergence of the island of Rhodes is delightfully pictured by the positioning of the solitary word *nasos*, 'island', at the beginning of the epode. The typically Pindaric *logōn koruphai*, the 'peaks' or 'high points' of the Sun's words, may also suggest the emergence, peaks first, of the island. The language of 74–6 is closely reminiscent of Homer:

> οἳ Ῥόδον ἀμφενέμοντο διὰ τρίχα κοσμηθέντες,
> Λίνδον Ἰηλυσόν τε καὶ ἀργινόεντα Κάμειρον (*Il.* 2.655-6),

'who dwelt in Rhodes, organised in three cities, Lindus, Ialysus and gleaming Camirus.'

It remains to round off the story of Tlepolemus and move to the praises of the victor, Diagoras:

> τόθι λύτρον συμφορᾶς οἰκτρᾶς γλυκὺ Τλαπολέμῳ
> ἵσταται Τιρυνθίων ἀρχαγέτᾳ,
> ὥσπερ θεῷ,
> μήλων τε κνισάεσσα πομπὰ
>   καὶ κρίσις ἀμφ᾽ ἀέθλοις. τῶν ἄνθεσι Διαγόρας   80
> ἐστεφανώσατο δίς, κλει-
>   νᾷ τ᾽ ἐν Ἰσθμῷ τετράκις εὐτυχέων,
> Νεμέᾳ τ᾽ ἄλλαν ἐπ᾽ ἄλλᾳ, καὶ κρανααῖς ἐν Ἀθάναις.
>
> ὅ τ᾽ ἐν Ἄργει χαλκὸς ἔγνω νιν, τά τ᾽ ἐν Ἀρκαδίᾳ
> ἔργα καὶ Θήβαις, ἀγῶνές τ᾽ ἔννομοι
> Βοιωτίων,   85
> Πέλλανά τ᾽· Αἰγίνᾳ τε νικῶνθ᾽
>   ἑξάκις· ἐν Μεγάροισίν τ᾽ οὐχ ἕτερον λιθίνα
> ψᾶφος ἔχει λόγον. ἀλλ᾽ ὦ
>   Ζεῦ πάτερ, νώτοισιν Ἀταβυρίου
> μεδέων, τίμα μὲν ὕμνου τεθμὸν Ὀλυμπιονίκαν,
>
> ἄνδρα τε πὺξ ἀρετὰν εὑ-
>   ρόντα. δίδοι τέ οἱ αἰδοίαν χάριν
> καὶ ποτ᾽ ἀστῶν καὶ ποτὶ ξεί-
>   νων. ἐπεὶ ὕβριος ἐχθρὰν ὁδὸν   90
> εὐθυπορεῖ, σάφα δαεὶς ἅ τέ οἱ πατέρων
>   ὀρθαὶ φρένες ἐξ ἀγαθῶν

ἔχρεον. μὴ κρύπτε κοινὸν
σπέρμ' ἀπὸ Καλλιάνακτος·
Ἐρατιδᾶν τοι σὺν χαρίτεσσιν ἔχει
θαλίας καὶ πόλις· ἐν δὲ μιᾷ μοίρᾳ χρόνου
ἄλλοτ' ἀλλοῖαι διαιθύσσοισιν αὖραι (77-95).

'There a sweet recompense for pitiable misfortune is established for Tlepolemus, commander of Tiryns, as if for a god: a procession of beasts for rich-smelling sacrifice and a contest in games.

With the flowers of these games Diagoras garlanded himself twice, and at the famous Isthmus four times in his success: at Nemea one garland followed another, and in rocky Athens too. The bronze shield at Argos learned his name, and the works of art [the prizes] in Arcadia and Thebes, and the regular contests of the Boeotians, and Pellene; in Aegina he conquered six times, in Megara the stone column tells the same tale. Come, father Zeus, ruler of the broad back of mount Atabyrium [on Rhodes], honour my hymn ordained for an Olympic victor, honour too the man who attained excellence with his fists, and grant him the pleasure of being respected by both citizens and strangers; for he travels unswervingly along a path that is hostile to presumptuousness, taught clearly what the upright minds of his fathers furnished from their store of goodness. Do not hide the lineage he shares with Callianax [an ancestor of Diagoras]: in the grateful honours paid him by the Eratid clan the city too holds festivity. But in one single portion of time the breezes shift their quivering breath from this quarter to that.'

Mention of the Rhodian games for Tlepolemus allows Pindar to turn to the catalogue of Diagoras' victories, which he lists with great brevity and the imagination needed to make poetry from prosaic material. His prayer to Zeus is not only for Diagoras but for his own poem, described in august terms as *humnou tethmon*, 'the ordinance of the hymn'. For Diagoras he asks *aidoian kharin*, a difficult phrase to translate: we have seen *Kharis* already as the goddess to whom athletic success is due: here the word seems to denote gratitude, requital, joy too, and its epithet *aidoia*, 'reverend', marks out the correct attitude to be shown to the victor—not neglect or envy, but respect and reverence, since, Pindar goes on, he avoids *hubris*, 'outrage' or 'presumptuousness'. Here we have a clearly metaphorical 'path' and once more the personification of an abstract quality in 'a path that is hostile to presumptuousness'. In line 93 Pindar uses for the fourth time in the poem a form of the word *kharis*, this time with reference to the athletic successes of the Eratidae, the clan of Diagoras, and perhaps to the gratitude shown to him and the pleasure taken in his victory. The chilly aphorism with which Pindar ends his poem recalls line 11 (note *allote d' allon . . . allot' alloiai*): in each case the context is athletic success, but here the words *en de miāi moirāi khronou*, which seems to refer to a man's life-span, give the expression wider significance. Diagoras may be happy now, but he should bear in mind that happiness is not permanent.

Much has been written about the unity of the poem and in particular about such unity as is given by the imagery. As I see it, Pindar has used various threads which are at one moment hidden behind his fabric but at the next appear on the surface: for example, the picture of marriage festivity with which Pindar opens the poem so happily is not irrelevant or forgotten: the union of the Sun and Rhodes, mentioned in line 14, forms a climax in the poem at 71, and the festivity of the Eratidae is its penultimate theme; festive rites also mark the birth of Athena and the honour done to Tlepolemus. Again, the word *thalias*, which Pindar uses for festivity in 94, recalls the unique epithet *zōthalmios* (11) and the goddess Thalia, a *Kharis* who herself makes several appearances, whether personified or not. Gold is mentioned four times in the first three triads; the 'peak' of possessions (4) is echoed by the 'peaks' of his words (68). The connection between Rhodes and the rose is not so important in the poem as is sometimes claimed: it is at its clearest in 62, *auxomenan pedothen*, 'growing from its foundations', and in 69–70, 'there grew from the salt sea-water an island'; but the ideas of birth, growth and flourishing are recurrent and important: note 'the seed of fire' (48) and 'the seed from Callianax' (93). Imagery from the weather is allied to this: the golden snowflakes (34), the cloud of forgetfulness (45), the yellow cloud and golden rain (49–50) and the fickle breezes with which the poem ends are all appropriate in a context in which the Sun-god is so important. Perhaps most striking of all is Pindar's insistence on the mutability of fortune: Tlepolemus killed a relative and had to leave Tiryns but found honour in Rhodes; the children of the Sun forgot fire when they went up to sacrifice to Athena, but Athena and her father were generous to them; the Sun was neglected in his absence, but got Rhodes in the end; even Diagoras' victory-ode is described as *pugmas apoina* (16), 'reward for his boxing', a phrase which is recalled by *lutron sumphoras* (77), the 'recompense for misfortune' of Tlepolemus: Diagoras' victory followed the rigours of training and the battering of the match. And it is the theme of vicissitude that Pindar leaves with his hearers at the close of his poem.

*   *   *

The genre of the victory-ode all but disappears after Pindar and Bacchylides. A more sceptical outlook towards the gods and a professionalism in athletics are both conspicuous by the end of the fifth century, and the patronage of poets by wealthy noblemen declined. We have fragments of Euripides' ode written to mark the astonishing performance of Alcibiades in the chariot-race at Olympia in 416 B.C., when he won first, second and third prizes (*PMG* 755, 756; Thucydides 6.16.2 says he won first, second and fourth prizes), but that is our last isolated example; against it we must set Euripides' denunciation of athletic idols:

κακῶν γὰρ ὄντων μυρίων καθ' Ἑλλάδα
οὐδὲν κάκιόν ἐστιν ἀθλητῶν γένους κτλ. (fr. 282N²),

'There are a thousand evils in Greece, but none is worse than the tribe of athletes.' In this long speech from the lost satyr-play *Autolycus* athletes are denounced for their evil lives, their improvidence, their moral and psychological softness; glorious in their heyday, they finish as threadbare cloaks. In words strongly reminiscent of Xenophanes' complaint Euripides decries the honours paid to athletes, who contribute so little to the community: better to honour the wise and the good, the just politician and the peacemaker.

CHAPTER FOUR

Politics

Once the events of the poet's own life were regarded as material for his poetry, it was natural that political and social themes should be prominent. The early lyric poets were actively involved in the politics of their day. Except in Sparta, hereditary kingship had disappeared, giving way to tyranny, and in Alcaeus' lyrics we read the reactions of a man who took part in the struggle for power in Mytilene about 600 B.C. His contemporary, Solon, used verse to set out the aims of his legislation and to answer his critics shortly before tyranny was established in Athens. Theognis of Megara appears from his poems as a disgruntled aristocrat outraged at the invasion of the city by boorish peasants, and he cries out against the new rich. It was a time of political ferment: on the island of Chios democratic institutions had appeared for the first time in the Greek world by the middle of the sixth century. Verse was a forceful medium for the diffusion of political beliefs, whether it was sung at the symposium among one's own associates like Alcaeus' songs or recited to a wider audience like some of Solon's poetry.

Organised emigration was another feature of the period. For two centuries from about 750 B.C. groups of citizens left their mother-cities and established 'colonies' on the western Mediterranean, the north Aegean and the Black Sea shores. The poet Semonides is said to have led the Samians who colonised Amorgos, and several fragments of Archilochus deal with the emigration from Paros to Thasos. A trochaic line implicitly contrasts the dreary poverty of Paros with better prospects elsewhere:

ἔα Πάρον καὶ σῦκα κεῖνα καὶ θαλάσσιον βίον (116),

'let Paros be and those figs and the life of the sea', a vivid line in which the harsh alliteration strengthens the derisive tone. But other poems show that life on the frontier was grim in various ways. Even the appearance of Thasos was disappointing:

ἥδε δ' ὥστ' ὄνου ῥάχις
ἔστηκεν ὕλης ἀγρίης ἐπιστεφής (21),

'but this island stands up like the backbone of an ass, covered with savage forest'. The comparison with the ass's spine is lively and, so far as we can say, original, although later writers could use the noun for the 'ridge' of a mountain. The last three words are sometimes taken to mean 'wreathed with savage forest', but Homer and Alcman use the adjective and its cognates simply to denote fulness, as in Homer's *krētēras epistepheas oinoio*, 'bowls full of wine'; in any case the idea of a wreath scarcely suits the high island, wooded except for its bare summit. Thasos had none of the attractions of the gulf of Tarentum in South Italy, a favourite place for colonisation:

οὐ γάρ τι καλὸς χῶρος οὐδ' ἐφίμερος
οὐδ' ἐρατός, οἷος ἀμφὶ Σίριος ῥοάς (22),

'For it is by no means a beautiful place or desirable or lovely like the district by the waters of the Siris.' Archilochus' adjectives *ephimeros* and *eratos* are stronger than they appear in translation, since, as has been noted above, both have erotic association only faintly felt in 'desirable' and 'lovely'. The place was *trisoizuros* (228), 'thrice-wretched', and the settlers were the wretches of the Greek world:

Πανελλήνων ὀϊζὺς ἐς Θάσον συνέδραμεν (102),

'the misery of all Greece converged on Thasos.'

The Thasians fought the Thracians on the mainland opposite the island, probably for control of their gold-mines. Fighting is mentioned in various fragments of Archilochus, two of which have already been quoted in Chapter Two. One famous poem mentions the Saians, a Thracian tribe:

ἀσπίδι μὲν Σαΐων τις ἀγάλλεται, ἣν παρὰ θάμνῳ,
ἔντος ἀμώμητον, κάλλιπον οὐκ ἐθέλων·
αὐτὸν δ' ἐξεσάωσα. τί μοι μέλει ἀσπὶς ἐκείνη;
ἐρρέτω· ἐξαῦτις κτήσομαι οὐ κακίω (5).

'One of the Saians exults in the shield which I abandoned unwillingly by a bush, a blameless piece of equipment; but I saved myself. What do I care about that shield? It can go to hell! Some day I shall get another no worse.' Archilochus packs a great amount into two superbly constructed couplets: a long sentence for the contrast between the shield, which he lost, and himself, whom he preserved, and then the lively question, the single verb of imprecation, and the final statement. There is humour in the epic ring of *agalletai*, 'exults', and the 'blameless piece of equipment' in a poem of markedly unheroic content. As in many of these early poems alliteration is conspicuous, this time in the last sentence, and there may also be a pun in *Saiōn* and *exesaōsa*, words which occur at the same position in the hexameters.

Of the settlers' plight in general Archilochus writes,

κλαίω τὰ Θασίων, οὐ τὰ Μαγνήτων κακά (20),

'I weep for the misfortunes of the Thasians, not the Magnesians', alluding to the recent destruction of Magnesia by the Cimmerian hordes. Elsewhere he prays that the stone of Tantalus be not poised over 'this island' (91.14f.), although we cannot be certain that Thasos rather than Paros is meant; and according to Heraclitus, the investigator of Homeric allegory, he compared the Thracian war to the billows of the sea in the following passage:

Γλαῦχ', ὅρα· βαθὺς γὰρ ἤδη κύμασιν ταράσσεται
πόντος, ἀμφὶ δ' ἄκρα Γυρέων ὀρθὸν ἵσταται νέφος,
σῆμα χειμῶνος, κιχάνει δ' ἐξ ἀελπτίης φόβος (105).

'Look, Glaucus! Already the sea is troubled by waves to its depths, and round the heights of Gyrae a cloud stands straight up, the sign of a storm, and fear comes from the unexpected.' If it were not for Heraclitus' testimony we might be tempted to take the lines simply as dramatic narrative, although it is not easy to see why Archilochus should write such description for its own sake. It seems best to believe Heraclitus, since he presumably knew the whole poem, and to associate the lines with 'the Thracian dangers'; but the precise geographical detail of the pillar of cloud rising over Gyrae, the cliffs at the south end of Tenos, is surprising. Tenos is far from Thasos: it lies in the central Aegean, north of Rhenea, Delos and Myconos, some thirty miles from Paros. According to Homer, Locrian Ajax was wrecked there on his way home from Troy (*Od.* 4.500ff.), and Archilochus must have mentioned it as a notorious dangerspot. The lines are vivid and structurally satisfying with the variation in the length of the units and the arresting enjambment.

Archilochus, as we have seen in the chapters on love and wine, wrote on themes other than political and social. The Spartan poet Tyrtaeus, perhaps his contemporary, seems to have used only Spartan history, politics and above all warfare as his material. About 735–715 B.C. Sparta had defeated her western neighbour Messenia and gained possession of the rich plain of Stenyclarus. Two generations later the Messenians tried to throw off Spartan domination, and the long Second Messenian War, in which Sparta eventually crushed her enemy, forms the background to Tyrtaeus' poetry.

In two fragments he speaks of the first war:

ἡμετέρῳ βασιλῆϊ, θεοῖσι φίλῳ Θεοπόμπῳ,
ὃν διὰ Μεσσήνην εἵλομεν εὐρύχορον,
Μεσσήνην ἀγαθὸν μὲν ἀροῦν, ἀγαθὸν δὲ φυτεύειν·
ἀμφ' αὐτὴν δ' ἐμάχοντ' ἐννέα καὶ δέκ' ἔτη
νωλεμέως αἰεὶ ταλασίφρονα θυμὸν ἔχοντες   5
αἰχμηταὶ πατέρων ἡμετέρων πατέρες·
εἰκοστῷ δ' οἱ μὲν κατὰ πίονα ἔργα λιπόντες
φεῦγον Ἰθωμαίων ἐκ μεγάλων ὀρέων (5).

'. . . to our king, Theopompus dear to the gods: thanks to him we captured spacious Messene, Messene good to plough and good to plant; over it they fought for nineteen years without ever ceasing, keeping a stout heart, those warrior fathers of our fathers; and in the twentieth year the enemy abandoned their rich fields and fled from the great mountains of Ithome.' This is good narrative poetry, if not particularly exciting; it is worth noting that the conventional adjectives which Tyrtaeus uses of Messenia and its fields are significant, since it was the fertility of the country that attracted the Spartans. Other epic touches are the epithet *talasiphrona*, used especially of Odysseus, and the chronological expression 'for nineteen years . . . in the twentieth year'. The balance of the third line, 'Messene good to plough and good to plant', makes it easily memorable, and it is not surprising that Plato calls it famous.

Tyrtaeus shows an unexpected sympathy for the condition of the defeated Messenians:

> ὥσπερ ὄνοι μεγάλοις ἄχθεσι τειρόμενοι,
> δεσποσύνοισι φέροντες ἀναγκαίης ὕπο λυγρῆς
> ἥμισυ παντὸς ὅσον καρπὸν ἄρουρα φέρει (6),

'like asses distressed by great loads, bringing their masters under grievous necessity a half of all the crops the land bears'. Homer compared Ajax, driven slowly back by the Trojans, to an ass beaten out of a cornfield by young boys (*Il.* 11.558ff.), and Semonides, writing about the same time as Tyrtaeus, compared one type of woman to a much-thumped ass working *sun . . . anankēi*, 'under necessity' (7.43ff.). Tyrtaeus' simile fits the situation nicely: the Messenians have heavy burdens to carry and are distressed by them.

We can only guess at the occasion on which poems of this kind might be performed. Some ancient authorities call Tyrtaeus *stratēgos*, 'general'; if he was and if he harangued his troops, he may have done so on the eve of battle to exhort them to valour and to show the greatness of Sparta by alluding to its history. Ancient scholars call one poem *Eunomia*, a term which refers both to the existence of good laws and to the happy condition of people who respect their laws and live at peace. One excerpt runs:

> αὐτὸς γὰρ Κρονίων καλλιστεφάνου πόσις Ἥρης
> Ζεὺς Ἡρακλείδαις ἄστυ δέδωκε τόδε,
> οἷσιν ἅμα προλιπόντες Ἐρινεὸν ἠνεμόεντα
> εὐρεῖαν Πέλοπος νῆσον ἀφικόμεθα (2.12ff.).

'for the son of Cronus, Zeus himself, husband of fair-garlanded Hera, gave this city to the descendants of Heracles, and with them we left windy Erineus and came to the broad island of Pelops.' This is the poet's version of the Dorian invasion and settlement in Sparta, sanctioned, he says, by Zeus himself; and since the next line has *glaukōpidos*, 'grey-eyed', he may have mentioned the help of Athena also. The lines probably gave the justification for obeying the kings, one aspect of 'eunomia', since the previous passage has the words 'let us obey' and 'closer to the race (of the gods?)', that is, the kings were of divine descent, being of the line of Heracles, son of Zeus. Zeus is described as 'husband of Hera' since Hera's cult was widespread in Laconia. 'Windy', Homer's epithet for Troy, is applied to Erineus, the place in the Doris of central Greece at the foot of the Pindus range which was regarded as the Dorians' homeland.

A fragment which deals with a later event in Spartan history may belong to the same poem:

> Φοίβου ἀκούσαντες Πυθωνόθεν οἴκαδ᾽ ἔνεικαν
>   μαντείας τε θεοῦ καὶ τελέεντ᾽ ἔπεα·
> ἄρχειν μὲν βουλῆς θεοτιμήτους βασιλῆας,
>   οἶσι μέλει Σπάρτης ἱμερόεσσα πόλις,
> πρεσβυγενέας τε γέροντας· ἔπειτα δὲ δημότας ἄνδρας   5
>   εὐθείαις ῥήτραις ἀνταπαμειβομένους
> μυθεῖσθαί τε τὰ καλὰ καὶ ἔρδειν πάντα δίκαια,
>   μηδέ τι βουλεύειν τῇδε πόλει <σκολιόν>.
> δήμου τε πλήθει νίκην καὶ κάρτος ἕπεσθαι.
>   Φοῖβος γὰρ περὶ τῶν ὧδ᾽ ἀνέφηνε πόλει (4).

'Having heard Phoebus they [i.e. the kings Polydorus and Theopompus] brought home from Pytho the oracles and sure words of the god: that the god-honoured kings, whose concern is the lovely city of Sparta, should begin counsel, along with the old men, senior in birth; then the people, countering with straight enactments, should say what is honourable and do all that is just, and give no crooked counsel to this city; so victory and strength would attend the assembly of the people. This was Phoebus' revelation to the city about these matters.' In these couplets, which deal with Delphic approval of the Spartan constitution, Tyrtaeus seems to have expanded four hexameter lines of the oracle (3, 5, 7, 9) by the addition of pentameters (4, 6, 8), which give little factual matter that is not in the hexameters but deck the prosaic material with touches of poetry, 'sure words', 'lovely Sparta' and the opposition of 'straight' and 'crooked' decisions.

Our four longest examples of Tyrtaeus' work are concerned with the battlefield. A papyrus fragment forecasts the course of the fighting:

> ὀρσέοντ]αι κοίλης ἀσπίσι φραξάμ[ενοι,
> χωρὶς Πάμφυλοί τε καὶ Ὑλλεῖς ἠδ[ὲ Δυμᾶνες,
>   ἀνδροφόνους μελίας χερσὶν ἀν[ασχόμενοι...
> ἀλλ᾽ εὐθὺς σύμπαντες ἀλοιήσεο[μεν ἐκείνους,
>   ἀ]νδράσιν αἰχμηταῖς ἐγγύθεν ἱσ[τάμενοι.
> δεινὸς δ᾽ ἀμφοτέρων ἔσται κτύπος [
>   ἀσπίδας εὐκύκλους ἀσπίσι τυπτ[ομένων (19.7-9, 12-15).

'. . . (they will rush) protecting themselves with hollow shields, Pamphyli and Hylleis and Dymanes separately, raising in their hands the man-killing spears . . . but straightway we shall all of us together thresh them, standing near the spearsmen. Grim will be the din of both sides as they strike the round shields against shields.' Tyrtaeus depicts the Spartan army fighting in its three Dorian tribal units and predicts victory. His language is partly traditional: 'man-killing' is Homeric and is usually applied to Hector, although it is used also of the hands of Achilles in *Iliad* 18; the 'round' shield is known from *Iliad* 5, but the 'hollow' shield is not Homeric: it is found first in Tyrtaeus, Mimnermus and Alcaeus as a description of the new hoplite shield with its offset rim. The use of *aloiō*, 'we shall thresh them', is also new and exciting.

In fr. 2 Tyrtaeus said that Sparta had been given to the descendants of Heracles by Zeus himself. Another passage begins by reminding the Spartans of their lineage:

> ἀλλ', Ἡρακλῆος γὰρ ἀνικήτου γένος ἐστέ,
> θαρσεῖτ'· οὔπω Ζεὺς αὐχένα λοξὸν ἔχει·
> μηδ' ἀνδρῶν πληθὺν δειμαίνετε, μηδὲ φοβεῖσθε,
> ἰθὺς δ' ἐς προμάχους ἀσπίδ' ἀνὴρ ἐχέτω,
> ἐχθρὴν μὲν ψυχὴν θέμενος, θανάτου δὲ μελαίνας   5
> κῆρας <ὁμῶς> αὐγαῖς ἠελίοιο φίλας.
> ἴστε γὰρ ὡς Ἄρεος πολυδακρύου ἔργ' ἀΐδηλα,
> εὖ δ' ὀργὴν ἐδάητ' ἀργαλέου πολέμου,
> καὶ μετὰ φευγόντων τε διωκόντων τ' ἐγένεσθε,
> ὦ νέοι, ἀμφοτέρων δ' ἐς κόρον ἠλάσατε (11.1-10).

'Come! You are the descendants of invincible Heracles, so be confident: Zeus is not turning his head aside. Do not fear the numbers of the enemy, and do not run away; let every man hold his shield straight towards the front line, counting life as hateful and the black spirits of death dear like the sun's rays. You realise how destructive are the works of Ares, bringer of many tears, and you know well the character of painful war: you have been with the pursuers and the pursued, young men, and have had enough of both.' The sequel is a long exhortation to face the enemy and fight with determination. The excerpt shows Tyrtaeus' composition at its finest. The phrase used of the continuing concern of Zeus for the Spartans, descended from his son Heracles, is more vivid than appears in translation: 'Zeus does not hold his neck aslant': Theognis used the words of a slave with his head lowered in subjection, but that is not likely to be the meaning here; in *Iliad* 13 Homer described Zeus' loss of sympathy for the Trojans by saying that he turned his eyes away from them. The couplet which prescribes the correct attitude to life and death is even more striking: it is an expansion of *mēde philopsukheite*, 'and do not love your lives', which Tyrtaeus uses elsewhere (10.18), and when he says that the warrior should love death like the sunlight, he makes the paradox complete, since the sunlight was the usual symbol for the world of the living. The couplet is carefully organised, so that it is enclosed by the opposites *ekhthrēn* and *philas*, 'hateful' and 'dear', in chiastic order. The adjectives used of Ares and his works are Homeric: in the *Iliad* we find *poludakrus*, 'bringer of many tears', applied to Ares and to battle, and *aidēlos* to Ares. Like Homer Tyrtaeus does not hide the grimness of war, and there is no trace of the attitude sometimes taken by the Homeric hero that war is desirable or enjoyable.

Elsewhere Tyrtaeus turns the thoughts of the Spartan warriors to the life of a beggar, which he depicts as the consequence of defeat:

τεθνάμεναι γὰρ καλὸν ἐνὶ προμάχοισι πεσόντα
   ἄνδρ' ἀγαθὸν περὶ ᾗ πατρίδι μαρνάμενον·
τὴν δ' αὐτοῦ προλιπόντα πόλιν καὶ πίονας ἀγροὺς
   πτωχεύειν πάντων ἔστ' ἀνιηρότατον,
πλαζόμενον σὺν μητρὶ φίλῃ καὶ πατρὶ γέροντι   5
   παισί τε σὺν μικροῖς κουριδίῃ τ' ἀλόχῳ.
ἐχθρὸς μὲν γὰρ τοῖσι μετέσσεται οὕς κεν ἵκηται,
   χρησμοσύνῃ τ' εἴκων καὶ στυγερῇ πενίῃ,
αἰσχύνει τε γένος, κατὰ δ' ἀγλαὸν εἶδος ἐλέγχει,
   πᾶσα δ' ἀτιμίη καὶ κακότης ἔπεται (10.1-10).

'For it is a fine thing to lie dead, having fallen in the front rank, a good man fighting for his country; but to leave one's city and rich fields and go begging is the most painful thing of all, roaming with dear mother and aged father, with little children and wedded wife. For he will be hated by those to whom he comes yielding to need and loathsome poverty: he disgraces his lineage and belies his splendid beauty, and all dishonour and evil accompany him.' There is strong Homeric influence, not only in the formulae, 'rich fields', 'dear mother', 'aged father', 'wedded wife', but in the picture of the beggar, details of which may be derived from Homer, whose Odysseus plays the part of beggar in his own home. Lines 7–8 are particularly close to *Od.* 14.156–7, which begin with *ekhthros gar*, 'for hated . . .', and contain the phrase *peniēi eikōn*, 'yielding to poverty'. Line 9, where the device of chiasmus is used again (*aiskhunei . . . genos, . . . eidos elenkhei*), recalls the words of Glaucus in *Iliad* 6, *mēde genos paterōn aiskhunemen*, 'and not to disgrace our fathers' lineage'. In line 10 *kakotēs*, 'evil', may refer to the beggar's loss of social status.

Tyrtaeus composed a more elaborate poem about courage (12), the opening lines of which are quoted above in the chapter on athletics, since his point is that athletic skill like wealth or eloquence is of no value in wartime, unless it is accompanied by fierce courage. Almost all of the poem is occupied by his reflections on this, the sole *aretē* or 'excellence' which counts in wartime, and it is only in the last couplet that he turns to exhortation, declaring that this is the *aretē* that every man should now aim at.

An older contemporary of Tyrtaeus, Callinus of Ephesus, composed poetry about the wars of his city. His longest fragment (quoted below, p. 209) spurs the Ephesians to battle, whether against their neighbours, the Magnesians, or against the invading Cimmerians we cannot tell. If we can trust the few surviving fragments and references, he paid less attention to the traditions and history of his city than Tyrtaeus, although one fragment of a prayer to Zeus remains:

Σμυρναίους δ' ἐλέησον (2),

'and pity the Smyrnaeans', Smyrna, Strabo tells us, being an old name for Ephesus.

* * *

The poetry of Tyrtaeus and Callinus was an effective and memorable means of exhortation and moral comment. Solon, the Athenian statesman, archon in 594/3 B.C., composed a poem of one hundred lines in elegiac couplets called 'Salamis' in later times, and Plutarch tells us that Solon ran into the agora and sang the poem, the opening lines of which were

αὐτὸς κῆρυξ ἦλθον ἀφ' ἱμερτῆς Σαλαμῖνος,
κόσμον ἐπέων ᾠδὴν ἀντ' ἀγορῆς θέμενος (1).

'I have come as a herald from lovely Salamis, having composed a song, an ornament of verses, instead of a speech.' Whether Plutarch is correct in saying that Solon 'sang the poem', literally 'went right through the elegy in song', is uncertain; what is of interest is Solon's phrase, 'a song, an ornamental thing made of verses, instead of a speech', poetry used to persuade an assembly. The gist of the poem was that the Athenians should continue the fight to capture Salamis from the Megarians. Diogenes Laertius in his life of Solon quotes two passages which were particularly effective:

εἴην δὴ τότ' ἐγὼ Φολεγάνδριος ἢ Σικινήτης
ἀντί γ' 'Αθηναίου πατρίδ' ἀμειψάμενος·
αἶψα γὰρ ἂν φάτις ἥδε μετ' ἀνθρώποισι γένοιτο·
·'Αττικὸς οὗτος ἀνήρ, τῶν Σαλαμιναφετέων' (2).

'Then I would rather change my country and belong to Pholegandros or Sicinos instead of Athens, for soon men would be speaking like this: "This fellow is from Attica, one of the Salamis-droppers"'; and

ἴομεν ἐς Σαλαμῖνα μαχησόμενοι περὶ νήσου
ἱμερτῆς χαλεπόν τ' αἶσχος ἀπωσόμενοι (3).

'Let us go to Salamis to fight for the lovely island and thrust harsh disgrace from us.' The ridicule of the two insignificant islands and the comic formation 'Salamis-droppers' are lively, more so than anything in Tyrtaeus, and reminiscent of iambic rather than elegiac verse. We shall meet the same device of quoting ridicule directly in the iambic fragment 33.

Our longest surviving example of Solon's poetry (13, quoted below in Chapter 7) contains his thoughts on ill-gotten gains, the punishment inflicted by Zeus, the false beliefs and hopes of mortals, and the uncertain outcome of their endeavours. Another poem has similar content but sets it firmly against the Athenian background and gives explicit warning and advice to the citizens:

> ἡμετέρη δὲ πόλις κατὰ μὲν Διὸς οὔποτ' ὀλεῖται
> αἶσαν καὶ μακάρων θεῶν φρένας ἀθανάτων·
> τοίη γὰρ μεγάθυμος ἐπίσκοπος ὀβριμοπάτρη
> Παλλὰς 'Αθηναίη χεῖρας ὕπερθεν ἔχει·
> αὐτοὶ δὲ φθείρειν μεγάλην πόλιν ἀφραδίῃσιν   5
> ἀστοὶ βούλονται χρήμασι πειθόμενοι,
> δήμου θ' ἡγεμόνων ἄδικος νόος, οἶσιν ἑτοῖμον
> ὕβριος ἐκ μεγάλης ἄλγεα πολλὰ παθεῖν·
> οὐ γὰρ ἐπίστανται κατέχειν κόρον οὐδὲ παρούσας
> εὐφροσύνας κοσμεῖν δαιτὸς ἐν ἡσυχίῃ (4.1-10).

'Our city shall never perish, according to the dispensation of Zeus and the purpose of the blessed immortal gods: so strong is Pallas Athena, our stout-hearted guardian, child of a mighty father, who holds her hands over us; but it is the citizens themselves who in their folly are ready to destroy the great city, putting their trust in possessions; and the mind of the people's leaders is unjust, and it is certain that they will suffer much distress for their great insolence, since they cannot keep check on their excessive wealth or conduct decently the present joys of their feasting in quietness.' The opening with its confident assertion of divine concern for the city is reminiscent of fragments 2 and 11 of Tyrtaeus, which refer to Zeus' care for Sparta. The unusual word-positioning of *kata men Dios oupot' oleitai/aisan* allows great emphasis to fall on the prediction *oupot' oleitai*, 'shall never perish'. Pallas Athena is dignified by an impressive list of epithets, *megathumos*, 'stout-hearted', appropriate for a warrior goddess, *episkopos*, 'guardian', used here for the first time of a deity keeping a watchful eye on a city, and *obrimopatrē*, 'daughter of a mighty father', Zeus himself. The first and last of these epithets were applied to Athena in the *Odyssey* also; the framework of the sentence, *toiē gar ... episkopos ... Pallas Athēnaiē* is also derived from Homer; and the last word of line 5, *aphra-diēisin*, is a common line-ending in Homer. But Homeric influence, so apparent in this introductory passage, is much less evident in what follows. The spirit is closer to Hesiod's warnings to his brother Perses and his account of the wrong-doing of the nobles; and the language anticipates that of Attic tragedy with its emphasis on *hubris*, 'insolence', and *koros*, 'excessive wealth, satiety'.

A few lines later when he describes the activity of the greedy Athenian nobles his tone is elevated:

οὐδὲ φυλάσσονται σεμνὰ Δίκης θέμεθλα,
ἣ σιγῶσα σύνοιδε τὰ γιγνόμενα πρό τ' ἐόντα,   15
   τῷ δὲ χρόνῳ πάντως ἦλθ' ἀποτεισομένη,
τοῦτ' ἤδη πάσῃ πόλει ἔρχεται ἕλκος ἄφυκτον,
   ἐς δὲ κακὴν ταχέως ἤλυθε δουλοσύνην,
ἣ στάσιν ἔμφυλον πόλεμόν θ' εὕδοντ' ἐπεγείρει,
   ὃς πολλῶν ἐρατὴν ὤλεσεν ἡλικίην·   20
ἐκ γὰρ δυσμενέων ταχέως πολυήρατον ἄστυ
   τρύχεται ἐν συνόδοις τοῖς ἀδικέουσι φίλαις.
ταῦτα μὲν ἐν δήμῳ στρέφεται κακά· τῶν δὲ πενιχρῶν
   ἱκνέονται πολλοὶ γαῖαν ἐς ἀλλοδαπὴν
πραθέντες δεσμοῖσί τ' ἀεικελίοισι δεθέντες. . .   25

οὕτω δημόσιον κακὸν ἔρχεται οἴκαδ' ἑκάστῳ,
   αὔλειοι δ' ἔτ' ἔχειν οὐκ ἐθέλουσι θύραι,
ὑψηλὸν δ' ὑπὲρ ἕρκος ὑπέρθορεν, εὗρε δὲ πάντως,
   εἰ καί τις φεύγων ἐν μυχῷ ᾖ θαλάμου (4.14-29).

'(But when men . . .) and do not defend the august foundations of Justice, who though silent knows both the present and the past, and in time always comes to exact punishment, this comes as an inescapable wound on the whole city, and it falls swiftly into foul slavery, which rouses civil strife and war from their sleep—war which destroys the lovely youth of many; for at the hands of the enemy the much-loved city is swiftly being wasted in associations dear to the unjust. These are the evils that are at large among the people, while many of the poor go to a foreign land, sold into slavery and bound in unseemly fetters. . . . Thus the public evil comes home to each individual: street doors can no longer keep it out: it jumps over a high fence and always finds its man, even if he runs and hides in the corner of his bedroom.' Solon relies heavily on personification: Justice, silent but aware and effective; sleeping War aroused; Evils at large like rampaging beasts; Public Evil making its way to individual homes and leaping fences. He is influenced by Hesiod, for whom Justice, Battles and the rest were real divinities whose parentage he knew; and the confident certainty that justice will prevail is also reminiscent of Hesiod; but the august foundations of her altar or temple are new to us. Some of the other startling expressions can be paralleled in earlier poets: the metaphorical 'wound' is in Archilochus (13.8), the 'much-loved' or 'lovely' city is Homeric (*Od.* 11.275), the man hiding in a corner of his house is in Callinus (1.15). The passage is impressive and yet clumsily thrown together: the relative clause within the relative clause (lines 19–20) and the repeated *takheōs*, 'swiftly', have an uncouth air.

The poem, or at least the passage, ends with impassioned praise of Eunomia, 'Lawfulness':

> ταῦτα διδάξαι θυμὸς Ἀθηναίους με κελεύει,　　　30
> 　　ὡς κακὰ πλεῖστα πόλει Δυσνομίη παρέχει·
> Εὐνομίη δ' εὔκοσμα καὶ ἄρτια πάντ' ἀποφαίνει,
> 　　καὶ θαμὰ τοῖς ἀδίκοις ἀμφιτίθησι πέδας·
> τραχέα λειαίνει, παύει κόρον, ὕβριν ἀμαυροῖ,
> 　　αὑαίνει δ' ἄτης ἄνθεα φυόμενα,　　　35
> εὐθύνει δὲ δίκας σκολιάς, ὑπερήφανά τ' ἔργα
> 　　πραΰνει· παύει δ' ἔργα διχοστασίης,
> παύει δ' ἀργαλέης ἔριδος χόλον, ἔστι δ' ὑπ' αὐτῆς
> 　　πάντα κατ' ἀνθρώπους ἄρτια καὶ πινυτά (4.30-9)

'This is what my heart bids me tell the Athenians, how Lawlessness brings much evil on a city, while Lawfulness makes everything orderly and sound and often puts fetters on the wrong-doers; she makes the rough smooth, checks excess, hides outrage in obscurity and withers the growing flowers of ruin; she straightens crooked judgements, softens proud deeds, checks the works of faction and checks the anger of grievous strife; thanks to her, all is sound and wise in the world of men.' Both the fervour with which Solon speaks and the imagery he uses are reminiscent of Old Testament prophecy, and Hesiod had written in the same spirit about the blessings that attend just men (*Op.* 225–37). Solon uses many literary devices: the antithesis of Lawlessness and Lawfulness, asyndeton and variation in the position of verb and object in line 34, anaphora ('checks . . . checks'), verbs placed at the beginnings of their clauses (lines 35–8), rhyme in *leiainei . . . hauainei, euthunei . . . praunei*, and *panta* and *artia* repeated in the last line to round off the passage. The concepts of *hubris*, 'insolence', and *koros*, 'excess', reappear along with *atē*, 'ruin'; and the whole is explicitly called 'instruction' or 'didactic poetry' in line 30: these are the political lessons which the Athenians must learn in order to survive.

The opening lines of another poem express his distress at the situation:

> γινώσκω, καί μοι φρενὸς ἔνδοθεν ἄλγεα κεῖται,
> 　　πρεσβυτάτην ἐσορῶν γαῖαν Ἰαονίης
> κλινομένην (4a).

'I know—and pain lies in my heart when I see it—that the oldest land of Ionia is being laid low.' There is doubt about the reading of the last word, which may be *kainomenēn*, 'is being slain'. Whichever is correct, there is an effect of shock, due partly to the placing of the word, partly to the personification. The proud description of Attica contributes to the effect, since maltreatment of the old is particularly deplorable.

Solon's reforms, known as the *seisachtheia*, the shaking-off of the load, were the cancellation of debts for which land or personal liberty was the security and the prohibition of borrowing on the security of the person. The peasants of Attica who had become serfs were set free and restored to their farms, and those who had been sold abroad as slaves were redeemed. Solon used verse to defend his actions as striking a balance between the claims of privileged and unprivileged:

> δήμῳ μὲν γὰρ ἔδωκα τόσον γέρας ὅσσον ἐπαρκεῖν,
> τιμῆς οὔτ᾽ ἀφελὼν οὔτ᾽ ἐπορεξάμενος·
> οἳ δ᾽ εἶχον δύναμιν καὶ χρήμασιν ἦσαν ἀγητοί,
> καὶ τοῖς ἐφρασάμην μηδὲν ἀεικὲς ἔχειν·
> ἔστην δ᾽ ἀμφιβαλὼν κρατερὸν σάκος ἀμφοτέροισι,
> νικᾶν δ᾽ οὐκ εἴασ᾽ οὐδετέρους ἀδίκως (5).

'For I gave the people as much privilege as would protect them, neither robbing them of honour nor giving too much; as for those who had power and were envied for their possessions, I took care that they too should suffer no insult. I took up my position holding my strong shield over both sides, and I did not allow either to triumph unjustly.' Solon's idea of fair play is reflected in the layout of his verses: one couplet for the common people, one for the nobility, and one in which he claims to have protected the interests of both sides. Some of the language is Homeric, and the metaphor from the battlefield has an epic ring, although *krateron sakos*, 'strong shield', is in fact a variation on the Homeric formula. Later in the poem Solon again uses language that Pindar and the tragic poets were to echo:

> δῆμος δ᾽ ὧδ᾽ ἂν ἄριστα σὺν ἡγεμόνεσσιν ἔποιτο,
> μήτε λίην ἀνεθεὶς μήτε βιαζόμενος·
> τίκτει γὰρ κόρος ὕβριν, ὅταν πολὺς ὄλβος ἔπηται
> ἀνθρώποις ὁπόσοις μὴ νόος ἄρτιος ἦ (6).

'Thus would the people best go along with their leaders—neither given too free a rein nor constrained forcibly; for satiety breeds insolence, when great prosperity goes along with men whose wits are not sound.' The couplets are clearly aimed at the nobility, who are told not to use force in their dealings with the people. The path to destruction is represented as a natural progression by the use of the metaphor *tiktei*: *koros*, 'satiety', is the parent of *hubris*, 'insolence'. These lines are a good instance of Solon's readiness to repeat a word (*hepesthai*, 'go along with') where no special purpose is served by the repetition and a modern poet would have looked for another verb. An isolated pentameter may come from the same poem:

ἔργμασιν ἐν μεγάλοις πᾶσιν ἁδεῖν χαλεπὸν (7),

'in great deeds it is hard to please everyone.'

By the end of Solon's life his kinsman Pisistratus had made himself tyrant of Athens. Solon foresaw the event and delivered his warning:

ἐκ νεφέλης πέλεται χιόνος μένος ἠδὲ χαλάζης,
βροντὴ δ' ἐκ λαμπρῆς γίγνεται ἀστεροπῆς.
ἀνδρῶν δ' ἐκ μεγάλων πόλις ὄλλυται, ἐς δὲ μονάρχου
δῆμος ἀϊδρίῃ δουλοσύνην ἔπεσεν.
λίην δ' ἐξάραντ' οὐ ῥᾴδιόν ἐστι κατασχεῖν
ὕστερον, ἀλλ' ἤδη χρὴ <τάδε> πάντα νοεῖν (9).

'From a cloud comes the might of snow and hail, and thunder follows the bright lightning; even so a city is destroyed by great men, and the people in its ignorance falls into slavery to a monarch. Raise a man too high and he cannot easily be checked afterwards: now is the time to think of all these things.' The laws of nature are adduced as a parallel for the laws of political life, and snow, hail and thunderstorm illustrate the destruction which will fall on the city; and of course the nature imagery serves to brighten Solon's unpoetic material. The word *monarkhos*, 'monarch, sole ruler', is first attested here and in Theognis; many words which were common in later Greek make their first appearance in Solon's poems.

When Pisistratus had seized power and had been given a bodyguard by the assembly, Solon had further comment:

εἰ δὲ πεπόνθατε λυγρὰ δι' ὑμετέρην κακότητα,
μὴ θεοῖσιν τούτων μοῖραν ἐπαμφέρετε·
αὐτοὶ γὰρ τούτους ηὐξήσατε ῥύματα δόντες,
καὶ διὰ ταῦτα κακὴν ἔσχετε δουλοσύνην.
ὑμέων δ' εἷς μὲν ἕκαστος ἀλώπεκος ἴχνεσι βαίνει,
σύμπασιν δ' ὑμῖν χαῦνος ἔνεστι νόος·
ἐς γὰρ γλῶσσαν ὁρᾶτε καὶ εἰς ἔπη αἱμύλου ἀνδρός,
εἰς ἔργον δ' οὐδὲν γιγνόμενον βλέπετε (11).

'And if you have suffered grievously through your baseness, do not try to blame the gods for your portion in this; for you yourselves exalted these men by giving them protection, and that was why you got your foul slavery. Each individual among you walks with the steps of a fox, but collectively you have a flabby mind: you concentrate on the tongue and words of a wheedler, and you never see the deed that is being done.' As in much of Solon's political poetry the couplets are self-contained: perhaps he thought of them as slogans to be remembered and quoted. The image of the fox, the type of cleverness, is arresting, as is the contrast between the intelligent individual and the stupid crowd.

4. Politics

Solon's trochaic and iambic poetry forms only a small part of his surviving work, but it is of the greatest importance in literary history since it shows an Athenian poet of the first half of the sixth century writing fluently in metres which were to be used by the tragic poets for speeches and dialogue some fifty years later. Indeed the content of his longest iambic fragment (36) has been compared to that of a speech from tragedy, and a trochaic passage (33) reveals a gift for lively characterization:

'οὐκ ἔφυ Σόλων βαθύφρων οὐδὲ βουλήεις ἀνήρ·
ἐσθλὰ γὰρ θεοῦ διδόντος αὐτὸς οὐκ ἐδέξατο·
περιβαλὼν δ' ἄγρην ἀγασθεὶς οὐκ ἐπέσπασεν μέγα
δίκτυον, θυμοῦ θ' ἁμαρτῇ καὶ φρενῶν ἀποσφαλείς·
ἤθελεν γάρ κεν κρατήσας, πλοῦτον ἄφθονον λαβὼν
καὶ τυραννεύσας Ἀθηνέων μοῦνον ἡμέρην μίαν,
ἀσκὸς ὕστερον δεδάρθαι κἀπιτετρίφθαι γένος.'

' "Solon has no depth of intelligence and no wisdom: God offered him blessings and he actually refused them. He rounded up his quarry, but in his astonishment did not pull the great net tight, failing both in courage and in good sense. Otherwise having once got power, he would have been ready to take over great wealth and be tyrant of Athens for just one day, even if it meant being flayed afterwards for a wineskin and having his family wiped out." ' In this version of the vulgar claptrap which greeted his refusal to become tyrant, he draws on colourful expressions from everyday speech; the last line has a strongly Aristophanic flavour.

Other trochaic lines have the loftier tone of the elegiac poetry:

εἰ δὲ γῆς ἐφεισάμην
πατρίδος, τυραννίδος δὲ καὶ βίης ἀμειλίχου
οὐ καθηψάμην μιάνας καὶ καταισχύνας κλέος,
οὐδὲν αἰδέομαι· πλέον γὰρ ὧδε νικήσειν δοκέω
πάντας ἀνθρώπους (32).

'If I spared my native land and did not turn my hand to tyranny and brute force, sullying and disgracing my good name, I am not ashamed, for I think that by so doing I shall the more easily surpass all my fellow men.'

The important iambic fragment 36 again presents Solon's defence of his legislation: he had been given power as *aisumnētēs* or arbitrator, and he claims that he did not abuse that power while carrying out his promises. His stout patriotism is evident in the lines on the expatriated Athenians.

ἐγὼ δὲ τῶν μὲν οὕνεκα ξυνήγαγον
δῆμον, τί τούτων πρὶν τυχεῖν ἐπαυσάμην;
συμμαρτυροίη ταῦτ' ἂν ἐν δίκῃ Χρόνου
μήτηρ μεγίστη δαιμόνων Ὀλυμπίων

ἄριστα, Γῆ μέλαινα, τῆς ἐγώ ποτε 5
ὅρους ἀνεῖλον πολλαχῇ πεπηγότας·
πρόσθεν δὲ δουλεύουσα, νῦν ἐλευθέρη.
πολλοὺς δ' ᾿Αθήνας πατρίδ' ἐς θεόκτιτον
ἀνήγαγον πραθέντας, ἄλλον ἐκδίκως,
ἄλλον δικαίως, τοὺς δ' ἀναγκαίης ὑπὸ 10
χρειοῦς φυγόντας γλῶσσαν οὐκέτ' ᾿Αττικὴν
ἱέντας, ὡς ἂν πολλαχῇ πλανωμένους,
τοὺς δ' ἐνθάδ' αὐτοῦ δουλίην ἀεικέα
ἔχοντας ἤθη δεσποτέων τρομεομένους
ἐλευθέρους ἔθηκα. ταῦτα μὲν κράτει 15
ὁμοῦ βίην τε καὶ δίκην συναρμόσας
ἔρεξα καὶ διῆλθον ὡς ὑπεσχόμην.
θεσμοὺς δ' ὁμοίως τῷ κακῷ τε κἀγαθῷ
εὐθεῖαν εἰς ἕκαστον ἁρμόσας δίκην
ἔγραψα. κέντρον δ' ἄλλος ὡς ἐγὼ λαβών, 20
κακοφραδής τε καὶ φιλοκτήμων ἀνήρ,
οὐκ ἂν κατέσχε δῆμον· εἰ γὰρ ἤθελον
ἃ τοῖς ἐναντίοισιν ἥνδανεν τότε,
αὖτις δ' ἃ τοῖσιν οὕτεροι φρασαίατο,
πολλῶν ἂν ἀνδρῶν ἥδ' ἐχηρώθη πόλις. 25
τῶν οὕνεκ' ἀλκὴν πάντοθεν ποιεόμενος
ὡς ἐν κυσὶν πολλῇσιν ἐστράφην λύκος.

'And which of my objectives, my reasons for assembling the people, had I not attained when I stopped? Best witness to this might be given for me in the court of Time by the mighty mother of the Olympian gods, black Earth, from whom I once removed the mortgage-markers fixed everywhere in her: she was a slave before, now she is free. Many I brought back to their native Athens, the divine foundation, men who had been sold as slaves, some unjustly, some justly, and those who had fled by dire necessity, no longer speaking the Attic language since they had been wandering far and wide; and those who in this very land suffered the disgrace of slavery, trembling at the moods of their masters, I set free. Now these things I did by force, uniting might and right, and I completed them as I had promised; but I proposed decrees for high and low alike, fitting straight justice to each. If some other man, unscrupulous and acquisitive, had taken the goad as I did, he would not have kept check on the people; if I had been willing to do what pleased their opponents at that time and later what the other side planned for them, this city would have been widowed of many men. So displaying courage on all sides I ranged like a wolf among a pack of dogs.'

These are the lines which point forward most clearly to Attic tragedy; they read not unlike a speech of self-justification made by a tragic character. Although the sentences are long, there is none of the discursiveness which marks Solon's elegiac couplets: each point is clearly made and then abandoned for the next. Some of the language, the first sentence for example, reads more like prose than poetry, but the imagery is impressive: no one had spoken of 'the court of Time': Anaximander, Solon's younger contemporary, may have owed his phrase

κατὰ τὴν τοῦ Χρόνου τάξιν (fr. 1DK),

'according to the assessment of Time', to him. That mother Earth should give testimony is remarkable since Solon seldom refers to the gods; even here she has a physical reality as the Attic soil in which the mortgage-posts were planted. The goad is the symbol for authority as in the hands of a charioteer keeping check on his horses; Sophocles used the image, and the 'reins' of power are found first in Aristophanes and Plato. Finally the simile of the wolf at bay among dogs, Homeric in inspiration, is notable for the conciseness of its expression.

Solon saw the iambic trimeter as the appropriate vehicle for *oneidos*, reproach: an iambic poem begins,

δήμῳ μὲν εἰ χρὴ διαφάδην ὀνειδίσαι,
ἃ νῦν ἔχουσιν οὔποτ' ὀφθαλμοῖσιν ἂν
εὕδοντες εἶδον (37.1-3).

'If I must reproach the people openly, what they now have they would never have seen even in their dreams.' He repeats his claim that he has behaved with moderation; another in the same position, he says, would not have checked the people or stopped

πρὶν ἀνταράξας πῖαρ ἐξεῖλεν γάλα (37.8),

'until he had churned the milk and removed the cream', presumably meaning that the other man would so have broken down the structure of society by supporting the claims of the common people that the nobility would have disappeared. He continues with another reference, metaphorical this time, to the boundary-markers:

ἐγὼ δὲ τούτων ὥσπερ ἐν μεταιχμίῳ
ὅρος κατέστην (37.9-10).

'But I as if in no-man's-land between them stood like a marker.'

*   *   *

Alcaeus, the lyric poet from Lesbos, differs markedly in temperament from his Athenian contemporary, Solon. Whereas Solon was a fair-minded reformer who could claim with justice that he had acted in the best interests of both nobles and common people, Alcaeus was a member of one noble family struggling against others in Mytilene. Solon was mocked for not seizing power himself when the opportunity came, whereas nothing would have pleased Alcaeus better than political power for himself or his family. Solon was an intelligent thinker who won a place among the Seven Sages of the Greek world, but Alcaeus inveighed against Pittacus, another of the Seven Sages, whose moderation and generosity are attested. Solon was a thinker, Alcaeus, to judge from his poetry, was ruled by his passions. But whereas Solon wrote elegiac and iambic poetry, some of it clumsy and tedious, Alcaeus composed vigorous lyrics to be sung for the entertainment of his aristocratic companions.

The critic Dionysius of Halicarnassus said of Alcaeus' style that if one removed the metre one would often find political rhetoric; and when Horace wanted a single epithet to characterize Alcaeus' songs, he chose the word *minaces*, 'threatening' (*Carm.* 4.9.7). Roughly half of his surviving poetry has a political content, and it is mainly from these fragments that this period of Lesbian history is reconstructed.

Alcaeus was born *c.* 630 or 620 B.C. A generation earlier the ruling family, the Penthilidae, who traced their ancestry through Penthilus and Orestes to Agamemnon, were overthrown, although they retained sufficient influence to make marriage into the family politically advantageous. Their overthrow was followed by rivalry among various noble families, each competing for power in Mytilene, and we hear of three successful contestants, Melanchrus, Myrsilus and Pittacus. Melanchrus was overthrown by Pittacus and Alcaeus' brothers in the period from 612 to 609, when Alcaeus himself seems to have been too young to take part. Shortly afterwards he fought against the Athenians in the war for possession of Sigeum, a vantage-point at the entrance to the Hellespont, and like Archilochus before him and Anacreon and Horace later he confessed to losing his shield. Herodotus says that he composed a poem about the incident and sent it to a friend Melanippus in Mytilene; Strabo quotes lines the text of which is corrupt but seems to run, 'Alcaeus is safe, but the Athenians hung up (the shield that was his protection?) in the holy temple of grey-eyed Athena' (428).

Various poems contained warnings that Myrsilus was hatching a tyrannical conspiracy. Heraclitus, writer of *Homeric Allegories* in perhaps the first century A.D., was emphatic that this was the correct interpretation of a storm scene in Alcaeus:

ἀσυννέτημμι τῶν ἀνέμων στάσιν·
τὸ μὲν γὰρ ἔνθεν κῦμα κυλίνδεται,
τὸ δ' ἔνθεν, ἄμμες δ' ὂν τὸ μέσσον
νᾶϊ φορήμμεθα σὺν μελαίνα,

χείμωνι μόχθεντες μεγάλῳ μάλα·   5

πὲρ μὲν γὰρ ἄντλος ἰστοπέδαν ἔχει,
λαῖφος δὲ πὰν ζάδηλον ἤδη,
καὶ λάκιδες μέγαλαι κὰτ αὖτο. . . (326.1-8).

'I fail to understand the direction of the winds: one wave rolls in from this side, another from that, and we in the middle are carried along in company with our black ship, much distressed in the great storm. The bilge-water covers the masthold; all the sail lets the light through now, and there are great rents in it . . .' Heraclitus says that one's first impression that this is a seascape is wrong: the poem, he says, is about Myrsilus and the tyranny he planned in Mytilene. It has sometimes been thought that Heraclitus was searching too diligently for allegory and finding it where none existed, but we possess scraps of a commentary on this poem which mention Myrsilus, and it is best to take Heraclitus at his word; the use of allegory may have offered protection against recrimination. The lines are a fine example of Alcaeus' craftsmanship. As he often does, he begins with a verb, an unusual one here and striking because of its length. The word *stasis* is well chosen, since it fits the storm description as 'the direction' of the winds and can also mean 'civil war'. Alcaeus makes clever use of the Alcaic stanza in lines 3–4, where the bumpy rhythm of line 3 is followed by the rapid dactylic movement of line 4 in illustration of the head-long rush of the ship. Assonance in line 1 and alliteration in 2 and 4–5 are effective, and the passage is a good example of paratactic construction, short units being linked by the simplest connectives.

Heraclitus continues with the first three lines of another poem of Alcaeus in which a storm at sea is described, and he offers the same interpretation, adding that Alcaeus as an island-dweller is too ready to use this allegory. A papyrus find added the beginning of several lines and, most important for the understanding of the poem, gave the word *monarkhian*, 'sole rule, tyranny', in line 27, so that Heraclitus' interpretation of the poem is again vindicated:

τόδ' αὖτε κῦμα τῶ προτέρω † νέμω †
στείχει, παρέξει δ' ἄμμι πόνον πόλυν
ἄντλην, ἐπεί κε νᾶος ἔμβα . . .

φαρξώμεθ' ὡς ὤκιστα [τοίχοις,
ἐς δ' ἔχυρον λίμενα δρό[μωμεν·

καὶ μή τιν' ὄκνος μόλθ[ακος ἀμμέων
λάβη· πρόδηλον γὰρ μέγ' [ἀέθλιον·
μνάσθητε τὼ πάροιθα μ[όχθω·
νῦν τις ἄνηρ δόκιμος γε[νέσθω.

καὶ μὴ καταισχύνωμεν [ἀνανδρίᾳ
ἔσλοις τόκηας γᾶς ὔπα κε[ιμένοις . . . (6).

'This wave in turn comes (like?) the previous one, and it will give us much trouble to bale out when it enters the ship's . . . Let us strengthen (the ship's sides) as quickly as possible, and let us race into a secure harbour; and let soft fear not seize any of us; for a great (ordeal) stands clear before us. Remember the previous (hardship): now let every man show himself steadfast. And let us not disgrace (by cowardice) our noble fathers lying beneath the earth . . .' The third and fourth stanzas make better sense if they are regarded as political in their reference, especially the call not to disgrace 'our noble fathers'.

Another papyrus scrap is valuable for the scholiast's paraphrase of a very fragmentary text: 'but, Mytileneans, so long as the log gives off smoke only, i.e. so long as he is not yet tyrant, extinguish it, check it quickly, lest the glow become brighter' (74). We cannot say whether Myrsilus or Pittacus was the smoking log of this unusual metaphor.

A long and sometimes difficult papyrus fragment attacks Pittacus for his treachery. It is likely that he had at one time been allied with Alcaeus and his brothers against Myrsilus and that he changed sides. Alcaeus writes in exile on Lesbos near a sacred precinct of Zeus, Hera and Dionysus:

>]. ρά . α τόδε Λέσβιοι
> . . .]. . . . εὔδειλον τέμενος μέγα
> ξῦνον κά[τε]σσαν, ἐν δὲ 6ώμοις
> ἀθανάτων μακάρων ἔθηκαν,
>
> κἀπωνύμασσαν ἀντίαον Δία,   5
> σὲ δ' Αἰολήαν [κ]υδαλίμαν θέον
> πάντων γενέθλαν, τὸν δὲ τέρτον
> τόνδε κεμήλιον ὠνύμασσ[α]ν
>
> Ζόννυσσον ὠμήσταν. ἄ[γι]τ' εὔνοον
> θῦμον σκέθοντες ἀμμετέρα[ς] ἄρας   10
> ἀκούσατ', ἐκ δὲ τῶν[δ]ε μόχθων
> ἀργαλέας τε φύγας ῤ[ύεσθε,
>
> τὸν Ὕρραον δὲ πα[ῖδ]α πεδελθέτω
> κήνων Ἐ[ρίννυ]ς ὥς ποτ' ἀπώμνυμεν
> τόμοντες ἄ . . [΄.]ν . .   15
> μηδάμα μηδένα τῶν ἐταίρων
>
> ἀλλ' ἢ θάνοντες γᾶν ἐπιέμμενοι
> κείσεσθ' ὑπ' ἄνδρων οἳ τότ' ἐπικ. ΄. ην
> ἤπειτα κακκτάνοντες αὔτοις
> δᾶμον ὑπὲξ ἀχέων ῤύεσθαι.   20
>
> κήνων ὁ φύσγων οὐ διελέξατο
> πρὸς θῦμον, ἀλλὰ 6ραϊδίως πόσιν

ἔ]μβαις ἐπ᾽ ὀρκίοισι δάπτει
τὰν πόλιν ἄμμι ... (129. 1-24).

'. . . the Lesbians established this great conspicuous precinct to be held in common, and put in it altars of the blessed immortals, and they entitled Zeus God of Suppliants and you, the Aeolian, Glorious Goddess, Mother of all, and this third they named Kemelios, Dionysus, eater of raw flesh. Come, with gracious spirit hear our prayer, and rescue us from these hardships and from grievous exile; and let their Avenger pursue the son of Hyrrhas, since once we swore, cutting (a lamb's throat?), never (to abandon?) any of our comrades, but either to die at the hands of men who at that time (came against us?) and to lie clothed in earth, or else to kill them and rescue the people from their woes. But Pot-belly did not talk to their hearts; he recklessly trampled the oaths underfoot and devours our city . . .' In the scraps which follow Myrsilus is named. Alcaeus prays for an end to exile and for vengeance on the traitor: *kēnōn Erinnus* must be the avenging spirit of those who died because of Pittacus' treachery. The alternatives of death and victory are tidily expressed, two lines to each, in 17–20, and the expressions 'clothed in earth', 'trampled the oaths underfoot' and 'devours the city' are vivid. 'Pot-belly' is only one of the insulting epithets applied to Pittacus: Diogenes Laertius quotes also *sarapous* and *sarapos*, 'splay-footed', *kheiropodēs*, 'with chapped feet', *gaurēx*, 'boaster', *gastrōn*, 'big-belly', *zophodorpidas*, 'diner in the dark', *agasurtos*, 'filthy'.

   Another difficult papyrus fragment is interesting for the picture of the exile's life addressed to a friend, Agesilaidas:

                    ... ὀ τάλαις ἔγω
ζώω μοῖραν ἔχων ἀγροϊωτίκαν
ἰμέρρων ἀγόρας ἄκουσαι
καρυ[ζο]μένας Ὠγεσιλαΐδα

καὶ β[ό]λλας· τὰ πάτηρ καὶ πάτερος πάτηρ   5
καγγ[ε]γήρασ᾽ ἔχοντες πεδὰ τωνδέων
τὼν [ἀ]λλαλοκάκων πολίταν,
ἔγ[ωγ᾽ ἀ]πὺ τούτων ἀπελήλαμαι

φεύγων ἐσχατίαισ᾽, ὠς δ᾽ Ὀνυμακλέης
ἔνθα[δ᾽] οἶος ἐοίκησα λυκαιμίαις...   10

οἴκημμι κ[ά]κων ἔκτος ἔχων πόδας,   16

ὄππα Λ[εσβί]αδες κρινόμεναι φύαν
πώλεντ᾽ ἐλκεσίπεπλοι, περὶ δὲ βρέμει
ἄχω θεσπεσία γυναίκων
ἴρα[ς ὀ]λολύγας ἐνιαυσίας ... (130.1-10, 16-20).

'. . . I, poor wretch, live with the lot of a rustic, longing to hear the assembly being summoned, Agesilaidas, and the council: the property in possession of which my father and my father's father have grown old among these mutually destructive citizens—from it I have been driven, an exile at the back of beyond, and like Onomacles I settled here alone in the wolf-thickets (?) . . .; . . . I dwell, keeping my feet out of trouble, where Lesbian women with trailing robes go to and fro being judged for beauty, and around rings the marvellous sound of the sacred yearly shout of women . . .' The richness of the detail is unexpected—the political life which he misses in exile, the family property he has had to leave, Onomacles, unknown but presumably a recluse or exile, the beauty-contests held, according to a commentator on Homer, in the precinct of Hera on Lesbos. The metrical structure of the stanza is unparalleled, although the elements are the familiar aeolic units. Alcaeus used a surprising number of metrical patterns, one aspect of his versatility.

Yet another four-line stanza is used for the following poem, from which it emerges that Pittacus at one time shared power with Myrsilus:

κῆνος δὲ παώθεις ᾿Ατρεῖδα[ν γένει
δαπτέτω πόλιν ὡς καὶ πεδὰ Μυρσίλω
θᾶς κ᾽ ἄμμε βόλλητ᾽ Ἄρευς ἐπὶ τ[ε]ύχε[α
τρόπην· ἐκ δὲ χόλω τῶδε λαθοίμεθ᾽ [αὖ·

χαλάσσομεν δὲ τὰς θυμοβόρω λύας   10
ἐμφύλω τε μάχας, τάν τις ᾿Ολυμπίων
ἔνωρσε, δᾶμον μὲν εἰς ἀυάταν ἄγων
Φιττάκῳ δὲ δίδοις κῦδος ἐπήρ[ατ]ον (70. 6-13).

'But let him, married into the family of the Atridae, devour the city as he did in company with Myrsilus, until Ares is pleased to turn us to arms; and may we forget this anger; and let us relax from the heart-eating strife and civil warring, which one of the Olympians has aroused among us, leading the people to ruin, but giving delightful glory to Pittacus.' The expression *paōtheis Atreidan genei* is an unusual, economical and perhaps ironic way of referring to Pittacus' marriage into the house of the Penthilidae who claimed descent from Agamemnon, son of Atreus. The metaphor of 'devouring' the city has been observed already in Alcaeus; Homer uses the verb of ravening animals. The last two lines have an effective antithesis between the people, ruined as Alcaeus sees it, and Pittacus in the position of authority.

News of the death of Myrsilus was greeted with high spirits:

νῦν χρῆ μεθύσθην|καί τινα πὲρ βίαν
πώνην, ἐπεὶ δὴ κάτθανε Μύρσιλος . . . (332).

'Now must men get drunk and drink with all their strength, since Myrsilus has died.' Horace echoed the sentiment and metre in his poem about the death of Cleopatra (*Carm.* 1.37 *nunc est bibendum*).

It seems that Alcaeus and his brother and possibly also Sappho were in exile at this time, and that Alcaeus' party hoped to return triumphantly thanks to foreign support:

Ζεῦ πάτηρ, Λῦδοι μὲν ἐπα[σχάλαντες
συμφόραισι δισχελίοις στά[τηρας
ἄμμ' ἔδωκαν, αἴ κε δυνάμεθ' ἴρ[αν
ἐς πόλιν ἔλθην,

οὐ πάθοντες οὐδάμα πῶσλον οὐ[δὲ]ν   5
οὐδὲ γινώσκοντες· ὁ δ' ὡς ἀλώπα[
ποικιλόφρων εὐμάρεα προλέξα[ις
ἤλπετο λάσην (69).

'Father Zeus, the Lydians, indignant at the turn of events, gave us two thousand staters in the hope that we could enter the holy city, although they had never received any benefit from us and did not know us; but he, with the cunning of a fox, predicted an easy outcome and thought we would not notice him.' The city may have been Mytilene or, if the text is read differently, Hiera, a city of old Lesbos. Lydian intervention is attested by scraps of a commentary on Alcaeus' poems. One would guess that Pittacus is the fox-like creature mentioned in line 6.

Whatever the details of the exiles and returns—three are mentioned in our sources—Aristotle says clearly in the *Politics* that Pittacus was elected tyrant 'to deal with the exiles, whose leaders were Antimenidas [Alcaeus' brother] and the poet Alcaeus'. As evidence that Pittacus' tyranny was extraordinary in that he was elected to office by the people, Aristotle quotes Alcaeus himself:

τὸν κακοπατρίδαν
Φίττακον πόλιος τὰς ἀχόλω καὶ βαρυδαίμονος
ἐστάσαντο τύραννον, μέγ' ἐπαίνεντες ἀόλλεες (348).

'They established base-born Pittacus as tyrant of that gutless, ill-starred city, all of them loud in his praise.' Here we have the crucial information from Pittacus' opponent himself that 'all' the Mytileneans made him tyrant; in other words he was a special brand of tyrant, who did not seize power by force but was given it in a crisis by popular consent as an *aisumnētēs* or elected tyrant. Most remarkably, he laid down his powers after ten years.

Alcaeus continued to protest. We have several stanzas of a long poem in which drastic measures are proposed: '. . . we must put (a noose?) on their necks and (kill them) by stoning. It would have been far better for the Achaeans if they had killed the man who did violence to the gods.' Alcaeus relates the story of Locrian Ajax, who raped Cassandra in Athena's shrine when the Greeks had taken Troy:

ἀλλ' ἀ μὲν] ἐν ναύω<ι> Πριάμω πάϊς
ἄγαλμ' 'Α]θανάας πολυλάϊδος
ἀμπῆχ'] ἐπαππένα γενήω,   10
δυσμέ]νεες δὲ πόλη' ἔπηπον

. . . Δαΐφοβόν τ' ἄμα
ἔπεφν]ον, οἰμώγα δ' [ἀπ]ὺ τείχεος
ὄρωρε, κα]ὶ παίδων ἀῦτα
Δαρδάνι]ον πέδιον κατῆχε·   15

Αἴας δὲ λ]ύσσαν ἦλθ' ὀλόαν ἔχων
ἐς ναῦο]ν ἄγνας Πάλλαδος, ἀ θέων
θνάτοι]σι θεοσύλαισι πάντων
αἰνο]τάτα μακάρων πέφυκε·

χέρρεσ]σι δ' ἄμφοιν παρθενίκαν ἔλων   20
σέμνωι] παρεστάκοισαν ἀγάλματι
ὔβρισσ'] ὀ Λόκρος, οὐδ' ἔδεισε
παῖδα Δ]ίος πολέμω δότε[ρ]ραν

γόργωπι]ν· ἀ δὲ δεῖνον ὐπ' [ὄ]φρυσι
σμ[|] [πε]λ[ι]δνώθεισα κὰτ οἴνοπα | 25
ἄϊξ[ε πόν]το[ν], ἐκ δ' ἀφάντοι[ς
ἐξαπ[ίν]ας ἐκύκα θυέλλαις . . . (298.8-27).

'But in the temple the daughter of Priam was embracing the statue of Athena, generous giver of booty, clasping its chin, while the enemy assailed the city; . . . they killed . . . and Deiphobus too, and lamentation (arose?) from the wall, and the shout of children filled the (Dardanian?) plain; and Ajax came in deadly madness to the temple of holy Pallas, who of all the blessed gods is most (terrible) to sacrilegious (mortals), and seizing the maiden with both hands as she stood by the (holy?) statue the Locrian (ravished her), without fear of the daughter of Zeus, giver of victory in war, grim-eyed; but she, . . . terribly beneath her brows, livid with anger (darted) over the wine-dark sea and suddenly stirred up hidden stormwinds . . .' The beginnings of the following twenty lines are preserved, one of which has a reference to the son of Hyrrhas, i.e. Pittacus; it would seem that after telling the story of Ajax Alcaeus returned to the theme of contemporary politics, and that it was Pittacus and his associates whose stoning he recommended in the earlier lines. He must have argued that if the Mytileneans did not themselves destroy Pittacus, the gods would take matters into their hands and many citizens would suffer in the end. The main interest of the poem is in Alcaeus' use of part of the Trojan story as a parallel for the contemporary situation; he devotes some nine stanzas to it, and enough is preserved to show how successfully he uses alcaic stanzas for concise and vivid narrative.

We have noted already the catalogue of abusive epithets applied by Alcaeus to Pittacus. In fr. 348 he calls him *kakopatridan*, 'base-born', and the adjective recurs elsewhere in the fragments. That he was in fact of low birth is quite unlikely, since he was at one time allied with Alcaeus' party and in sympathy with his aims; but Alcaeus seems to have sung at some length of Pittacus' parentage, calling his father a drunkard, perhaps adding that he was of Thracian birth, and abusing his mother also:

σὺ δὴ τεαύτας ἐκγεγόνων ἔχῃς
τὰν δόξαν οἴαν ἄνδρες ἐλεύθεροι
ἔσλων ἔοντες ἐκ τοκήων . . . ; (72.11-13).

'Do you, the son of such a mother, have the reputation that free men of noble parentage have . . .?' Pittacus' forbearance in view of these tirades is remarkable; in the words of the historian Diodorus, 'when he got hold of the poet Alcaeus, who had been his confirmed enemy and had reviled him most bitterly in his poems, he let him go, uttering the maxim that forgiveness is preferable to revenge.'

Alcaeus' political faction or *hetaireia* must have provided the audience for these songs, since their content presupposes that his listeners shared his aims. Loyalty, friendship, broken promises and deceit are recurring themes, presumably since alliances were short-lived and factions were formed and reformed from motives of ambition and greed as well as political principle. The evening drinking-party is the most likely occasion for the performance of the songs: the convivial and political themes are linked in the call for hard drinking to celebrate Myrsilus' death, and wine and sincerity are allied in fragments such as 'wine, dear boy, and truth' (366) and 'wine is a peep-hole into a man' (333).

*   *   *

The violent political life of Mytilene is hardly reflected at all in the fragments of Alcaeus' contemporary, Sappho; yet she too was exiled, presumably because her husband or her family was involved, and she spent some time in Sicily, probably at Syracuse, where her statue stood in later days in the town-hall. A fragmentary poem tells her daughter of the hardships:

σοὶ δ' ἔγω Κλέϊ ποικίλαν
οὐκ ἔχω πόθεν ἔσσεται
μιτράν<αν>· ἀλλὰ τῷ Μυτιληνάῳ . . . (98b. 1-3).

'For you, Cleis, I have no way of obtaining a decorated headband; but to the Mytilenean . . .' She goes on to mention the exile of the Cleanactidae, i.e. the family of Myrsilus. Other scraps speak with hostility of the Penthilidae, who formerly held power in Mytilene, and of other noble families.

Anacreon, described by Pausanias as the first poet after Sappho to make love his main theme, similarly paid scant attention to political themes. We know that he used the word *muthiētai*, 'talkers', with reference to the Samian fishermen who rebelled against the tyrant Polycrates (353), and we have the first stanza of a poem in which he praises the citizens of Magnesia who were under Persian rule:

γουνοῦμαί σ' ἐλαφηβόλε
ξανθὴ παῖ Διὸς ἀγρίων
    δέσποιν' "Αρτεμι θηρῶν·
ἥ κου νῦν ἐπὶ Ληθαίου
δίνῃσι θρασυκαρδίων   5
ἀνδρῶν ἐσκατορᾷς πόλιν
χαίρουσ', οὐ γὰρ ἀνημέρους
    ποιμαίνεις πολιήτας (348).

'I beseech you, deer-shooter, fair-haired child of Zeus, Artemis, queen of wild beasts, who now somewhere by the eddies of the Lethaeus look down on a city of bold-hearted men and rejoice, since the citizens whom you shepherd are not untamed.' The poem speaks of Magnesia as a courageous and civilised Greek city and perhaps continued with a request that Artemis preserve its citizens. The sentiment accords with the anti-Persian policy of Anacreon's patron, Polycrates.

*   *   *

Whereas Alcaeus attacked and insulted fellow aristocrats in his songs, Theognis of Megara inveighed against the other classes of society, the newly rich merchants and the once unprivileged poor. The question of the authorship of the poems transmitted under his name is hardly relevant here, since they are uniformly aristocratic in their outlook. They are more likely to belong to the sixth century than the late seventh, and to reflect the political upheavals which followed the rule of the tyrant Theagenes and persisted through most of the sixth century till the restoration of the aristocracy.

Theognis does not often speak of his own situation, but one poem shows that he lost his lands and may suggest that he was in exile abroad:

ὄρνιθος φωνήν, Πολυπαΐδη, ὀξὺ βοώσης
    ἤκουσ', ἥτε βροτοῖς ἄγγελος ἦλθ' ἀρότου
ὡραίου· καί μοι κραδίην ἐπάταξε μέλαιναν,
    ὅττι μοι εὐανθεῖς ἄλλοι ἔχουσιν ἀγρούς,   1200
οὐδέ μοι ἡμίονοι κυφὸν ἕλκουσιν ἄροτρον
    τῆς †ἄλλης μνηστῆς† εἵνεκα ναυτιλίης (1197-1202).

'I heard the voice of the clear-calling bird, son of Polypaus, which comes to mortals with news that it is time for ploughing; and it smote my black heart that others have my flowery fields and my mules do not drag the curving plough because of that . . . voyage.' Theognis refers poignantly to the south-ward flight of the crane in November and to the 'blackness' of his heart, presumably his angry resentment that he cannot plough his own fields. He may well have the passage of Hesiod in mind in which the crane's migration is said to mark the ploughing season: 'Take note when you hear the voice of the crane crying each year from the clouds above: she brings the signal for ploughing and indicates the season of rainy winter; and this eats the heart of the man who has no oxen' (*Op.* 448–51). Each passage ends with the sad condition of the man who cannot plough.

Theognis prays in darker mood for revenge on the men who stole his property:

> ἀλλά, Ζεῦ, τέλεσόν μοι, Ὀλύμπιε, καίριον εὐχήν·
> δὸς δέ μοι ἀντὶ κακῶν καί τι παθεῖν ἀγαθόν.
> τεθναίην δ', εἰ μή τι κακῶν ἄμπαυμα μεριμνέων
> εὑροίμην. δοίην δ' ἀντ' ἀνιῶν ἀνίας.
> αἶσα γὰρ οὕτως ἐστί. τίσις δ' οὐ φαίνεται ἡμῖν   345
> ἀνδρῶν, οἳ τἀμὰ χρήματ' ἔχουσι βίῃ
> συλήσαντες· ἐγὼ δὲ κύων ἐπέρησα χαράδρην
> χειμάρρῳ ποταμῷ πάντ' ἀποσεισάμενος.
> τῶν εἴη μέλαν αἷμα πιεῖν· ἐπί τ' ἐσθλὸς ὄροιτο
> δαίμων, ὃς κατ' ἐμὸν νοῦν τελέσειε τάδε (341-50).

'Come, Olympian Zeus, fulfil my timely prayer, and grant that in place of evils I experience some good. May I die if I do not find some respite from my evil cares. May I give distress for distress. For such is my lot; and there is in sight no vengeance on the men who have my possessions after forcibly carrying them off. I am the dog who crossed the torrent, having shaken off everything in the wintry river. May it be mine to drink their dark blood; and may a good daemon arise to accomplish this as I should wish it.' Theognis is probably alluding to some form of the fable in which a dog drops a piece of meat into the river she is crossing. Aesop's well-known version in which the dog loses her meat in her greediness to get the larger piece she sees reflected in the water is clearly not relevant, since, first, the wintry torrent would not give a reflection; secondly, the verb in 'having shaken off everything' is inappropriate; and, thirdly, Theognis would be accusing himself of greed. The gruesome prayer to drink his enemy's blood is reminiscent of Homer's language in the *Iliad*, where Zeus tells Hera that her malice would be satisfied only if she ate Priam and the Trojans raw. In this piece too the words are well-placed, the positioning of *sulēsantes* being especially effective.

In Theognis' view society had been turned upside-down by democratic reforms, and in some of his most famous lines he attacks the new class of citizens, rustics who now live in the city and claim to be the equals of the aristocracy:

Κύρνε, πόλις μὲν ἔθ' ἥδε πόλις, λαοὶ δὲ δὴ ἄλλοι,
οἳ πρόσθ' οὔτε δίκας ᾔδεσαν οὔτε νόμους,
ἀλλ' ἀμφὶ πλευραῖσι δορὰς αἰγῶν κατέτριβον,   55
ἔξω δ' ὥστ' ἔλαφοι τῆσδ' ἐνέμοντο πόλεος.
καὶ νῦν εἰσ' ἀγαθοί, Πολυπαΐδη· οἱ δὲ πρὶν ἐσθλοί
νῦν δειλοί. τίς κεν ταῦτ' ἀνέχοιτ' ἐσορῶν;
ἀλλήλους δ' ἀπατῶσιν ἐπ' ἀλλήλοισι γελῶντες,
οὔτε κακῶν γνώμας εἰδότες οὔτ' ἀγαθῶν.   60
μηδένα τῶνδε φίλον ποιεῦ, Πολυπαΐδη, ἀστῶν
ἐκ θυμοῦ χρείης οὕνεκα μηδεμιῆς·
ἀλλὰ δόκει μὲν πᾶσιν ἀπὸ γλώσσης φίλος εἶναι,
χρῆμα δὲ συμμείξῃς μηδενὶ μηδ' ὁτιοῦν
σπουδαῖον· γνώσῃ γὰρ ὀϊζυρῶν φρένας ἀνδρῶν,   65
ὥς σφιν ἐπ' ἔργοισιν πίστις ἔπ' οὐδεμία,
ἀλλὰ δόλους ἀπάτας τε πολυπλοκίας τ' ἐφίλησαν
οὕτως ὡς ἄνδρες μηκέτι σῳζόμενοι (53-68).

'Cyrnus, this city is still a city, but the people are different: in their earlier days they were acquainted with neither judgments nor laws; they wore out their goatskins against their ribs and lived outside the city like deer. And now they are the good men, son of Polypaus, and those who used to be fine men are now worthless. Who could endure this sight? They deceive each other, laughing at one another, and know nothing of bad or good. Make none of these citizens your friend, son of Polypaus, not sincerely at least, no matter what your need. Seem to be a friend to them all in your speech, but do not communicate any matter to any of them, nothing serious at any rate; for if you do, you will get to know the minds of miserable wretches—how there is no trustworthiness in their deeds, but they have come to love tricks, deceptions and convolutions, just like lost men.' The language defies translation, since the terms *agathoi*, 'good', *esthloi*, 'fine', and *deiloi*, 'worthless', are used in a social sense, although Theognis, speaking from the aristocratic viewpoint, no doubt intended the moral overtones; for him the old noble families who used to control the city are the *agathoi* or *esthloi*, the rustics are *kakoi*, 'bad' or 'worthless'. The terms are used consistently throughout the poems. The present lines are vigorous with the picture of the poor countrymen wearing out their goatskin jackets and the comparison with timid deer, keeping away from the society of men; the verb *enemonto*, 'lived', is applicable either to men dwelling in a place or to animals pasturing. Theognis uses his favourite device of enjambment for a lively effect in 62 *ek thumou*, 'sincerely', and 65 *spoudaion*, 'serious'. The noun *poluplokias*, 'convolutions', is unparalleled; and it is interesting to see Theognis counsel duplicity as the answer to the deceits of the other class.

It would seem that not all the Megarian nobility felt so strongly as Theognis about the new classes in society and that some were ready to marry for money, provoking one of the poet's finest protests:

> κριοὺς μὲν καὶ ὄνους διζήμεθα, Κύρνε, καὶ ἵππους
> εὐγενέας, καί τις 6ούλεται ἐξ ἀγαθῶν
> 6ήσεσθαι· γῆμαι δὲ κακὴν κακοῦ οὐ μελεδαίνει   185
> ἐσθλὸς ἀνήρ, ἤν οἱ χρήματα πολλὰ διδῷ,
> οὐδὲ γυνὴ κακοῦ ἀνδρὸς ἀναίνεται εἶναι ἄκοιτις
> πλουσίου, ἀλλ' ἀφνεὸν 6ούλεται ἀντ' ἀγαθοῦ.
> χρήματα μὲν τιμῶσι· καὶ ἐκ κακοῦ ἐσθλὸς ἔγημε
> καὶ κακὸς ἐξ ἀγαθοῦ· πλοῦτος ἔμειξε γένος.   190
> οὕτω μὴ θαύμαζε γένος, Πολυπαΐδη, ἀστῶν
> μαυροῦσθαι· σὺν γὰρ μίσγεται ἐσθλὰ κακοῖς (183-92).

'We seek rams and asses and horses, Cyrnus, that are of fine pedigree, and men want them to be bred from good stock; but a noble man does not mind marrying the base daughter of a base father if he gives him many possessions, nor does a woman refuse to be the wife of a base man provided he is rich: she chooses the affluent rather than the good. It is possessions that they respect, and the noble man marries a woman of bad family, the bad a woman of good family. Riches have confused race. In these circumstances, son of Polypaus, do not be surprised that the citizen race is being blurred, for noble is being mixed with base.' Megara's economy depended on its sheep-rearing and woollen industry, and the emphasis in the first sentence falls on *krious*, 'rams', and *eugeneas*, 'of fine pedigree'. There was a joke to the effect that it was better to be a Megarian's *krios* ('ram') than his *huios* ('son'). The poem again takes as its standpoint the ambiguous distinction between *agathos* and *esthlos*, 'good, noble', and *kakos*, 'bad' or 'base'. The aphorisms are striking: *khrēmata men timōsi*, 'it is possessions that they respect', and *ploutos emeixe genos*, 'riches have confused race'. The poem is well constructed and relies largely for its effect on the enjambment which gives a fine emphasis, for example, to *plousiou*, 'rich', in the third couplet.

Poverty is a recurrent theme in the poems, since Theognis, having fallen on hard times, is sensitive to the taunts of the new rich. One poem begins

> χρήματ' ἔχων πενίην μ' ὠνείδισας (1115),

'You have possessions, and you have reproached me with my poverty.' Elsewhere he adapts Hesiod's advice (*Op.* 717–18) in creating one couplet, and by adding the Homeric image of the balance produces an admirable short lyric:

μήποτέ τοι πενίην θυμοφθόρον ἀνδρὶ χολωθεὶς
μηδ' ἀχρημοσύνην οὐλομένην πρόφερε·
Ζεὺς γάρ τοι τὸ τάλαντον ἐπιρρέπει ἄλλοτε ἄλλῳ,
ἄλλοτε μὲν πλουτεῖν, ἄλλοτε μηδὲν ἔχειν (155-8).

'Never lose your temper and taunt a man with heart-breaking poverty or ruinous need: for Zeus tips the balance now in this man's favour, now in that: one day riches, the next day nothing.' Slavery is a disaster which Theognis views with realism but with none of Solon's compassion:

οὔποτε δουλείη κεφαλὴ ἰθεῖα πέφυκεν,
ἀλλ' αἰεὶ σκολιή, καὐχένα λοξὸν ἔχει.
οὔτε γὰρ ἐκ σκίλλης ῥόδα φύεται οὐδ' ὑάκινθος,
οὔτε ποτ' ἐκ δούλης τέκνον ἐλευθέριον (535-8).

'A slave's head is never erect but always bent, his neck crooked. For just as the squill does not produce roses or hyacinths, so no slave-woman ever produces a free-spirited child.'

Theognis like Solon wrote about the possibility that his city might fall under the sway of a tyrant. He distinguishes between the citizens, charitably described here as being 'of sound mind', and their leaders, whose behaviour is corrupt. It is hard to tell whether these leaders are the fellow-aristocrats of Theognis: he talks of 'our' evil insolence, but he identifies them with the 'bad':

Κύρνε, κύει πόλις ἥδε, δέδοικα δὲ μὴ τέκη ἄνδρα
εὐθυντῆρα κακῆς ὕβριος ἡμετέρης.   40
ἀστοὶ μὲν γὰρ ἔθ' οἵδε σαόφρονες, ἡγεμόνες δὲ
τετράφαται πολλὴν εἰς κακότητα πεσεῖν.
οὐδεμίαν πω, Κύρν', ἀγαθοὶ πόλιν ὤλεσαν ἄνδρες·
ἀλλ' ὅταν ὑβρίζειν τοῖσι κακοῖσιν ἄδῃ
δῆμόν τε φθείρωσι δίκας τ' ἀδίκοισι διδῶσιν   45
οἰκείων κερδέων εἵνεκα καὶ κράτεος,
ἔλπεο μὴ δηρὸν κείνην πόλιν ἀτρεμίεσθαι,
μηδ' εἰ νῦν κεῖται πολλῇ ἐν ἡσυχίῃ,
εὖτ' ἂν τοῖσι κακοῖσι φίλ' ἀνδράσι ταῦτα γένηται,
κέρδεα δημοσίῳ σὺν κακῷ ἐρχόμενα.   50
ἐκ τῶν γὰρ στάσιές τε καὶ ἔμφυλοι φόνοι ἀνδρῶν
μούναρχοί θ'· ἃ πόλει μήποτε τῇδε ἄδοι (39-52).

'Cyrnus, this city is pregnant, and I am afraid that it will give birth to a man who will be a corrector of our evil insolence. For though these fellow-citizens of ours are still of sound mind, the leaders are always poised to fall into much evil. No city yet, Cyrnus, has been destroyed by good men; but when it pleases the evil citizens to be insolent and they destroy the people and decide cases in favour of the unjust for the sake of private gain and power, do not expect that city to remain quiet long, not even if it now lies in great tranquillity, as long as these things are dear to the evil men—profits that bring public evil along with them. For from these come factions and murders of kinsmen and tyrants. May these things never please this city.' Theognis uses many of Solon's ideas and much of his vocabulary: both speak of civic *hubris* and public evil; both use *hēgemones* of the people's leaders and *monarkhos* of the tyrant whose rule is anticipated. Theognis also uses the rare noun *euthuntēr*, 'corrector', bringing attention to it by its positioning. The words *kakos* and *kakotēs* occur in almost every couplet, and besides emphasising the themes of present and future evil they help to build up an alliterative pattern with the repeated *k* sound, noticeable especially in line 46.

It is not surprising to find emphasis on the theme of loyalty. Like Alcaeus, Theognis was composing poetry for a circle of fellow-aristocrats in time of political upheaval. The loyalty might be expressed in true love, as in 87–92, already quoted in the chapter on love (p. 24). The following couplet stresses a wider loyalty:

> πιστὸς ἀνὴρ χρυσοῦ τε καὶ ἀργύρου ἀντερύσασθαι
> ἄξιος ἐν χαλεπῇ, Κύρνε, διχοστασίῃ (77-8).

'A trustworthy man is worth his weight in gold and silver, Cyrnus, in time of grievous dissension.' Homer had used a similar expression in a famous passage in the *Iliad* (22.351–2), where Achilles told Hector that he would accept no ransom for his corpse, not even if Priam offered Hector's weight in gold, although the expression may have been commonplace as in English. Theognis is unlike Alcaeus, however, in his readiness to advocate duplicity: we have seen something of this in lines 63–4, where he told Cyrnus to give the riff-raff the impression of friendship, 'from the tongue' only. It is more explicit in the following soliloquy:

> θυμέ, φίλους κατὰ πάντας ἐπίστρεφε ποικίλον ἦθος,
> ὀργὴν συμμίσγων ἥντιν' ἕκαστος ἔχει.
> πουλύπου ὀργὴν ἴσχε πολυπλόκου, ὃς ποτὶ πέτρῃ,   215
> τῇ προσομιλήσῃ, τοῖος ἰδεῖν ἐφάνη.
> νῦν μὲν τῇδ' ἐφέπου, τοτὲ δ' ἀλλοῖος χρόα γίνου.
> κρέσσων τοι σοφίη γίνεται ἀτροπίης (213-18).

'My heart, on all your friends turn a changeful disposition, mingling with yours the character each man has. Adopt the character of the convoluted octopus, which when near a rock takes on the appearance of the rock it consorts with. At one moment follow along in this direction, at the next change the colour of your skin. Wisdom is better than inflexibility.' Three lines of epic poetry which may be older than Theognis use the image of the octopus in exactly the same way, and it is common in later poets. Here as elsewhere

Theognis chooses his words effectively: *poikilos*, 'changeful', was used by Hesiod of the 'wily' Prometheus, but it suggests also the idea of 'many-coloured' and so prepares for the introduction of the octopus; *poluplokos*, 'convolved', has both a literal and a metaphorical use, the latter seen also in the noun *poluplokiē* which we have already met in Theognis; the verb *prosomileō* is used of the octopus 'consorting' with the rock, but it is normally used of social intercourse and so is appropriate here; and *atropiē*, 'inflexibility', is again apt, since the octopus is flexible both physically and in its colour-change.

* * *

Pindar's poetry was commissioned by wealthy patrons and displays the aristocratic outlook he shared with them. We have noted already in connection with athletics (p. 65) that he regarded birth and breeding as of first importance. The aristocratic government of Corinth provides an example of the political system he admired:

> ἐν τᾷ γὰρ Εὐνομίᾳ ναίει κασι-
>   γνήτα τε, βάθρον πολίων ἀσφαλές,
> Δίκα καὶ ὁμότροφος Εἰ-
>   ρήνα, τάμι' ἀνδράσι πλούτου,
> χρύσεαι παῖδες εὐβούλου Θέμιτος·
> ἐθέλοντι δ' ἀλέξειν
> Ὕβριν, Κόρου ματέρα θρασύμυθον (*Ol.* 13.6-10).

'For in that city dwells Lawfulness and her sisters, secure foundation for cities, Justice and she who was reared with her, Peace, the guardian of men's wealth, golden daughters of Themis who gives good counsel; and they are ready to ward off Insolence, bold-mouthed mother of Satiety.' This formidable array of powers, derived from Hesiod (*Theog.* 901–3), is led by Eunomia, 'Lawfulness', whom we have met in Solon as the personification of good laws, together with obedience to those laws. Kingship and tyranny were also acceptable to Pindar especially when like the Sicilians Theron and Hieron the ruler could point to a distinguished family tree. Pindar lavishes praise on such princes, but often follows immediately with a caution:

> νῦν δὲ πρὸς ἐσχατιὰν
>   Θήρων ἀρεταῖσιν ἱκάνων ἅπτεται
> οἴκοθεν Ἡρακλέος
>   σταλᾶν. τὸ πόρσω δ' ἐστὶ σοφοῖς ἄβατον
> κἀσόφοις. (*Ol.* 3.43-5).

'Now Theron has come by his excellences to the furthest limit and through his own resources lays hands on the pillars of Heracles. What lies beyond may not be trodden by the wise or by the unwise.' Pindar uses geographic imagery to illustrate Theron's prosperity and success—the pillars of Heracles were the mountains north and south of the straits of Gibraltar at the western extremity of the Mediterranean—and warns that his patron should not attempt more.

In a famous passage he mentions the three forms of government known in the Greek world of his time:

> ἐν πάντα δὲ νόμον εὐθύγλωσσος ἀνὴρ προφέρει,
> παρὰ τυραννίδι, χὠπόταν ὁ λάβρος στρατός,
> χὤταν πόλιν οἱ σοφοὶ τηρέωντι (*Pyth.* 2.86-8).

'Under every kind of regime it is the man of straightforward speech who comes to the front, in tyranny, or when a city is guarded by the boisterous mob or by the wise.' The loaded references to democracy and aristocratic oligarchy seem to show Pindar's sympathies unmistakeably, but it must be remembered that the lines are addressed to a successful tyrant, and that Pindar was ready also to sing the praises of democratic Athens in a dithyramb which provoked the admiration and gratitude of the Athenians and, we are told, the displeasure of his native Thebes: the opening lines were

> ὦ ταὶ λιπαραὶ καὶ ἰοστέφανοι καὶ ἀοίδιμοι,
> Ἑλλάδος ἔρει-
> σμα, κλειναὶ Ἀθᾶναι, δαιμόνιον πτολίεθρον (fr. 76).

'Gleaming, violet-crowned, famed in song, bulwark of Greece, renowned Athens, divine citadel.' The poem belongs to the decade after the Persian wars, and Pindar went on to speak of the battle of Artemisium,

> ὅθι παῖδες Ἀθαναίων ἐβάλοντο φαεννάν
> κρηπῖδ' ἐλευθερίας (fr. 77),

'where the sons of the Athenians laid the shining foundations of freedom'.

A very different poem was written about 478 B.C. by Timocreon, a Rhodian who had hoped that when the Persians departed Themistocles would restore him to his native city of Ialysus:

> ἀλλ' εἰ τύ γε Παυσανίαν ἢ καὶ τύ γε Ξάνθιππον αἰνεῖς
> ἢ τύ γε Λευτυχίδαν, ἐγὼ δ' Ἀριστείδαν ἐπαινέω
> ἄνδρ' ἱερᾶν ἀπ' Ἀθανᾶν
> ἐλθεῖν ἕνα λῷστον, ἐπεὶ Θεμιστοκλῆν ἤχθαρε Λατώ,
>
> ψεύσταν ἄδικον προδόταν, ὃς Τιμοκρέοντα ξεῖνον ἐόντα   5
> ἀργυρίοισι κοβαλικοῖσι πεισθεὶς οὐ κατᾶγεν
> πατρίδ' Ἰαλυσὸν εἴσ<ω>
> λαβὼν δὲ τρί' ἀργυρίου τάλαντ' ἔβα πλέων εἰς ὄλεθρον,

τοὺς μὲν κατάγων ἀδίκως, τοὺς δ' ἐκδιώκων, τοὺς δὲ
   καίνων·
ἀργυρίων δ' ὑπόπλεως Ἰσθμοῖ γελοίως πανδόκευε   10
ψυχρὰ <τὰ> κρεῖα παρίσχων·
οἱ δ' ἤσθιον κηΰχοντο μὴ ὥραν Θεμιστοκλέος γενέσθαι (727).

'Well, if you praise Pausanias and you, sir, Xanthippus and you Leotychidas, I commend Aristides as the best man to have come from holy Athens; for Themistocles was hated by Leto, Themistocles the liar, the criminal, the traitor, who was bribed with mischievous silver and would not take Timocreon home to his native Ialysus, although he was his guest-friend. Instead he accepted three talents of silver and sailed off to the devil, restoring some to their homes unjustly, chasing others out, bribing others. Gorged with silver, he made a ridiculous innkeeper at the Isthmus, serving up cold meat: the guests ate up and prayed that no attention be paid to Themistocles.' This vigorous poem begins with mention of five successful commanders in the Persian wars, Pausanias and Aristides who distinguished themselves at Plataea, Xanthippus and Leotychidas who destroyed the remnants of the Persian fleet at Mycale, and Themistocles whose policies had brought about the victory at Salamis, and moves into the attack on Themistocles. Why Leto should have been hostile to him is not clear. The detail of the 'innkeeping' at the Isthmus is also obscure, but it was there that the Greek commanders met to award the prizes for distinguished service against the Persians: each commander, says Herodotus, gave his first vote to himself, but most of the second votes went to Themistocles. The reference might be to a vote-catching dinner which turned out to be 'cold', a frost, or the innkeeping may all be metaphorical. At any rate the commanders departed without awarding any prize. Timocreon's choice of metre for this poem is another puzzle, since dactylo-epitrites are normally used for choral song, and it is hard to believe that this was other than a solo.

   Some of the scolia performed at parties in fifth-century Athens had a political content. Several versions have been transmitted to us of songs in praise of Harmodius and Aristogeiton, heroes of the Athenian democracy since they had killed Hipparchus, brother of Hippias who succeeded Pisistratus as tyrant. A fine elegiac couplet on the significance of the event was attributed to Simonides:

ἦ μέγ' Ἀθηναίοισι φόως γένεθ', ἡνίκ' Ἀριστογείτων Ἵππαρχον κτεῖνε καὶ Ἁρμόδιος (76D.).

'Truly a great light shone for the Athenians when Aristogeiton and Harmodius killed Hipparchus.' The scolia which follow are examples of the aeolic stanza which was commonly used; the poems may have been sung to a standard melody.

ἐν μύρτου κλαδὶ τὸ ξίφος φορήσω
ὥσπερ Ἁρμόδιος κ᾿ Ἀριστογείτων
ὅτε τὸν τύραννον κτανέτην
ἰσονόμους τ᾿ Ἀθήνας ἐποιησάτην (893).

'I shall carry my sword in a spray of myrtle, like Harmodius and Aristogeiton when they killed the tyrant and made Athens a city of equal rights.' As *eunomia*, 'lawfulness', had been seen by Pindar as the mark of oligarchy, so *isonomia*, 'equality of rights', became a catchword of the Athenian democracy.

φίλταθ᾿ Ἁρμόδι᾿, οὔ τί που τέθνηκας,
νήσοις δ᾿ ἐν μακάρων σέ φασιν εἶναι,
ἵνα περ ποδώκης Ἀχιλεὺς
Τυδεΐδην τέ φασιν Διομήδεα (894).

'Dearest Harmodius, you cannot be dead. No, they say you are in the isles of the blessed, where swift Achilles is and, so they say, Tydeus' son, Diomedes.' Various accounts were given of Achilles' after-life; Pindar placed him in the islands of the blessed, and also said that Diomedes was made immortal by Athena.

We have one song which must have been sung in the first place in Alcmaeonid circles, since it commemorates those members of the clan who lost their lives in an unsuccessful attempt to expel the tyrant Hippias:

αἰαῖ Λειψύδριον προδωσέταιρον,
οἵους ἄνδρας ἀπώλεσας, μάχεσθαι
ἀγαθούς τε καὶ εὐπατρίδας,
οἳ τότ᾿ ἔδειξαν οἵων πατέρων ἔσαν (907).

'Alas, Leipsydrion, betrayer of comrades! What men you destroyed, good fighters and nobly born, who showed then of what stock they came!' Leipsydrion was a strongpoint on Mount Parnes which the Alcmaeonids had fortified as the base of their operations. The poem has the dignity and reticence which mark the epitaphs of Simonides.

A popular song of a very different kind was sung by women on Lesbos as they worked their handmills:

ἄλει μύλ᾿ ἄλει·
καὶ γὰρ Πιττακὸς ἄλει
μεγάλας Μυτιλήνας βασιλεύων (869).

'Grind, mill, grind; for Pittacus used to grind while ruling great Mytilene.' The verb in the second line may be present tense, in which case the poem must have originated during Pittacus' term of office. The significance of the verb is also uncertain: it was explained by ancient writers as a reference to the statesman's daily exercise, but a metaphorical sense is more likely, with reference either to 'grinding' oppression of the people or to sexual activity; in those cases the song was composed by someone who shared Alcaeus' uncharitable view of the great statesman.

*   *   *

In this chapter we have considered the work of poets who for one reason or another made contemporary politics the subject of their verses. Some of the early lyric poets also displayed an interest in the past and composed accounts of the foundation and history of their cities. We have noticed that Tyrtaeus introduced the exploits of 'the fathers of our fathers' into his exhortations. Similarly the elegiac poet Mimnermus seems to have encouraged the Smyrnaeans to resist Alyattes by pointing to heroic exploits performed when Smyrna faced Gyges and his Lydians two or three generations earlier. The title of his poem, *Smurneis*, suggests a poem of some length. Another seventh-century poet, Semonides of Amorgos, is credited with a history of his birthplace Samos, *Arkhaiologia tōn Samiōn*, but we know nothing of it.

Later poets followed suit. Xenophanes is said to have written hexameter poems called 'The Foundation of Colophon', his birthplace, and 'The Colonisation of Elea', the city of south Italy where he may have spent some years of his life. In the fifth century the epic poet Panyassis, uncle of Herodotus, wrote a long poem, almost certainly in elegiac couplets, with the title *Ionica*; the notice in the *Suda* indicates that it began with early Athenian history, since it gives the contents as Codrus, Neleus and the Ionian colonies. Later fifth-century writers, Ion of Chios and Hellanicus, wrote their *Foundation of Chios* and *Foundations of Peoples and Cities* in prose, but in Hellenistic times the use of poetry for foundation accounts was revived.

CHAPTER FIVE

Friends and Enemies

In the first part of this chapter I discuss the poets' generalisations on the subject of friendships and enmities, and in the second part I consider their satirical poems.

Homer made the friendship of Achilles and Patroclus one of the most important themes in the *Iliad*. It is the death of Patroclus, whom Achilles allowed to go into battle wearing his own armour, that spurs Achilles into leaving his tent for the fighting, so ending the anger that had made him retire from the battlefield and allowing him to vent his new rage on Hector, the champion of Troy. Something of the tutor-pupil relationship in their association can be seen in Menoetius' words to his son Patroclus when the young men left home for Troy: 'My son, Achilles is of nobler lineage than you; but you are older than he is, although he is far stronger: give him wise advice, prompt him and show him the way, and he will obey you for the better' (*Il.* 11.786ff.). The intensity of Achilles' grief at Patroclus' death and Patroclus' wish that their bones should lie together in burial (23.82ff.) have led critics ancient and modern to see the relationship as erotic; but Homer, unlike the dramatist Aeschylus, does not make the eroticism explicit, and indeed points away from it by noting that the two heroes slept with slave-women (9.663ff.).

No other friendship is important in Homer. It was a different tie that led the Greek commanders to join Agamemnon and Menelaus in the fighting at Troy, the *xenia* which bound men of different cities to offer hospitality and help to each other in time of need. The clearest example of this relationship is given in *Iliad* 6, where Diomedes of Argos and Glaucus of Lycia, on the point of fighting each other, discover that they are *xenoi*: Homer can use the word *philos*, 'dear', in this context, but the adjective simply denotes the reciprocity of the relationship between the heroes and does not imply affection. Diomedes says, 'So now I am your dear *xenos* in the heart of Argos, you are mine in Lycia if I ever come to that country' (224f.). The appropriate treatment of 'guest-friends' is one of the principal themes of the *Odyssey*, found both in the stories of the hero's wanderings and in the emphasis on the suitors' abuse of hospitality. King Alcinous of the Phaeacians, who gave a practical demonstration of *xenia* in his treatment of Odysseus, was in a position to generalise:

ἐπεὶ οὐ μέν τι κασιγνήτοιο χερείων
γίγνεται ὅς κεν ἑταῖρος ἐὼν πεπνυμένα εἰδῇ (8.585-6).

'For a wise comrade is as good as a brother.' Hesiod has a few words on what we should call friendship among his social precepts in *Works and Days*:

μηδὲ κασιγνήτῳ ἶσον ποιεῖσθαι ἑταῖρον·
εἰ δέ κε ποιήσῃ, μή μιν πρότερος κακὸν ἔρξεις,
μηδὲ ψεύδεσθαι γλώσσης χάριν· εἰ δὲ σέ γ' ἄρχῃ
ἤ τι ἔπος εἰπὼν ἀποθύμιον ἠὲ καὶ ἔρξας,
δὶς τόσα τείνυσθαι μεμνημένος· εἰ δέ κεν αὖτις
ἡγῆτ' ἐς φιλότητα, δίκην δ' ἐθέλῃσι παρασχεῖν,
δέξασθαι· δειλός τοι ἀνὴρ φίλον ἄλλοτε ἄλλον
ποιεῖται· σὲ δὲ μή τι νόος κατελεγχέτω εἶδος (707-14).

'Do not make your comrade the equal of your brother; but if you do, do him no harm unprovoked and tell him no lies to win his favour with your tongue; and if he take the lead in offensive words or deeds against you, remember it and repay him double the amount; but if he wants to restore you to his friendship again and is willing to make amends, accept him. He is a bad man who keeps changing his friends: let your thinking not disgrace your appearance.' The idea of returning evil for evil, in double measure at that, is repellent, but it was normal Greek thinking at this period and for centuries afterwards. Archilochus puts it with customary bluntness:

ἕν δ' ἐπίσταμαι μέγα,
τὸν κακῶς μ' ἔρδοντα δεινοῖς ἀνταμείβεσθαι κακοῖς (126).

'One thing of first importance I know, how to pay back with grim evils the man who does evil to me.' In another poem he makes a similar claim:

ἐπ]ίσταμαί τοι τὸν φιλ[έο]ν[τα] μὲν φ[ι]λεῖν,
τὸ]ν δ' ἐχθρὸν ἐχθαίρειν τε καὶ κακο[
μύ]ρμηξ (23.14-16).

'I know how to love the man who loves me and to hate and (revile?) my enemy, just like the ant.' If this is the correct interpretation of the last word, Archilochus must be alluding to a fable as he often does. The expression *ton phileonta philein*, 'to love him who loves (me)', is Hesiodic (*Op.* 353) and may be proverbial.

Solon, civilised man that he was, prays on the same lines:

εἶναι δὲ γλυκὺν ὧδε φίλοις, ἐχθροῖσι δὲ πικρόν,
τοῖσι μὲν αἰδοῖον, τοῖσι δὲ δεινὸν ἰδεῖν (13.5-6).

'May I thus be sweet to my friends, bitter to my enemies, reverenced by my friends, a grim sight for the others.' Sappho's prayer for her brother is

> καὶ φίλοισ]ι *F*οῖσι χάραν γένεσθαι
> κὠνίαν ἔ]χθροισι (5.6-7).

'May he be a pleasure to his friends, a distress to his enemies.' All these poets saw the world in black and white, making a clear-cut distinction since prestige, security and welfare depended on one's 'friends', whereas we tend to have an extensive grey area occupied by those who are not particularly our friends or enemies, if we allow ourselves to think in terms of enmity at all.

Solon is reported to have said, 'Do not be quick to acquire friends; but when you have acquired them, do not reject them.' But it was Theognis who had most to say on the subject. We have seen already that his thinking was coloured by his division of the citizen body into the 'good' and the 'bad', that is, the aristocrats and the others, and that he advised Cyrnus to avoid the friendship of the bad. He makes the point most succinctly in this couplet:

> μήποτε τὸν κακὸν ἄνδρα φίλον ποιεῖσθαι ἑταῖρον,
> ἀλλ᾽ αἰεὶ φεύγειν ὥστε κακὸν λιμένα (113-14).

'Never make the bad man your comrade: always avoid him like a bad harbour.' Theognis nowhere makes more effective use of the nautical imagery of which he was so fond. He expands his advice elsewhere:

> ταῦτα μὲν οὕτως ἴσθι· κακοῖσι δὲ μὴ προσομίλει
> ἀνδράσιν, ἀλλ᾽ αἰεὶ τῶν ἀγαθῶν ἔχεο·
> καὶ μετὰ τοῖσιν πῖνε καὶ ἔσθιε, καὶ μετὰ τοῖσιν
> ἵζε, καὶ ἄνδανε τοῖς, ὧν μεγάλη δύναμις.
> ἐσθλῶν μὲν γὰρ ἄπ᾽ ἐσθλὰ μαθήσεαι· ἢν δὲ κακοῖσι   35
> συμμίσγῃς, ἀπολεῖς καὶ τὸν ἐόντα νόον.
> ταῦτα μαθὼν ἀγαθοῖσιν ὁμίλει, καί ποτε φήσεις
> εὖ συμβουλεύειν τοῖσι φίλοισιν ἐμέ (31-8).

'These, then, are the precepts you must know; and do not keep company with bad men but cling to the good always. Drink and eat with them, sit with them, please them—they have great power. For from fine men you will learn fine things, but if you mix with the bad you will destroy even the wits that you have. Learn this lesson, then, and keep company with the good, and one day you will say that I give sound advice to my friends.' Any doubt that Theognis uses 'the good' and 'the bad' in a political sense is dispelled by the cynical comment that it is 'the good' who have political power and influence.

A tolerant attitude must be adopted towards the faults of friends:

μήποτ' ἐπὶ σμικρᾷ προφάσει φίλον ἄνδρ' ἀπολέσσαι
πειθόμενος χαλεπῇ, Κύρνε, διαβολίῃ.
εἴ τις ἁμαρτωλῇσι φίλων ἐπὶ παντὶ χολοῖτο,   325
οὔποτ' ἂν ἀλλήλοις ἄρθμιοι οὐδὲ φίλοι
εἶεν· ἁμαρτωλαὶ γὰρ ἐν ἀνθρώποισιν ἕπονται
θνητοῖς, Κύρνε· θεοὶ δ' οὐκ ἐθέλουσι φέρειν (323-8).

'Never through paying heed to harsh slander, Cyrnus, destroy a friend for a slight cause. If someone were angry in every case at the faults of his friends, they would never be close or friendly. For in this world, Cyrnus, faults keep company with mortal men: it is gods who cannot endure them.' Text and interpretation are disputed. In the first sentence 'never . . . lose a friend' is an equally valid translation. The last couplet is more difficult: I think Theognis may have meant, 'Men are naturally prone to faults: only gods are perfect'; but it is doubtful if our present text could allow that interpretation, whether we translate *pherein* as 'endure them (in themselves)' or 'carry them'.

We have noted that in both his amatory and his political poems Theognis like Alcaeus was obsessed by thoughts of treachery. There was no question of tolerance in this context. Theognis often returns to the point:

ἄν τις ἐπαινήσῃ σε τόσον χρόνον ὅσσον ὁρῷης,
νοσφισθεὶς δ' ἄλλῃ γλῶσσαν ἵῃσι κακήν,
τοιοῦτός τοι ἑταῖρος ἀνὴρ φίλος οὔ τι μάλ' ἐσθλός,   95
ὅς κ' εἴπῃ γλώσσῃ λεῖα, φρονῇ δ' ἕτερα.
ἀλλ' εἴη τοιοῦτος ἐμοὶ φίλος, ὃς τὸν ἑταῖρον
γινώσκων ὀργὴν καὶ βαρὺν ὄντα φέρει
ἀντὶ κασιγνήτου. σὺ δέ μοι, φίλε, ταῦτ' ἐνὶ θυμῷ
φράζεο, καί ποτέ μου μνήσεαι ἐξοπίσω (93-100).

'If someone praises you so long as you can see him but speaks evil of you behind your back, that kind of comrade is no very good friend, the kind whose tongue speaks smoothly but whose thoughts are different. Let my friend be the kind who recognises his comrade's mood and puts up with him even when he is disagreeable as if he were a brother. Consider that in your heart, my friend, and you will remember me in time to come.' This passage too has textual difficulties, and it has been thought that the first couplet fits the sequel poorly on the ground that a different account of the characteristic behaviour of the bad friend is given in the second couplet. The most striking feature of the piece is the expression *anti kasignētou*, 'like a brother'; it gains force from the enjambment, a favourite structural device of Theognis. In the *Odyssey* the hospitable king Alcinous said that guest-friend and suppliant were *anti kasignētou*, 'like a brother' (8.546). We have seen, however, that Hesiod's advice was that one should not treat a comrade like a brother.

In one poem he appeals to Zeus:

Ζεὺς ἄνδϱ' ἐξολέσειεν Ὀλύμπιος, ὃς τὸν ἑταῖϱον
μαλθακὰ κωτίλλων ἐξαπατᾶν ἐθέλει (851-2).

'May Zeus the Olympian destroy the man who wants to deceive his comrade by
soft cajoling.' As often, a single word or phrase or image sets Theognis' stamp
on the poem, in this case the colourful and alliterative *malthaka kōtillōn*, 'with
the babbling of soft words' in Edmonds' translation. Elsewhere he turns to
Castor and Pollux, the heavenly twins who were noted for their strong bond of
friendship:

Κάστοϱ καὶ Πολύδευκες, οἳ ἐν Λακεδαίμονι δίῃ
    ναίετ' ἐπ' Εὐϱώτᾳ καλλιϱόῳ ποταμῷ,
εἴ ποτε βουλεύσαιμι φίλῳ κακόν, αὐτὸς ἔχοιμι·
    εἰ δέ τι κεῖνος ἐμοί, δὶς τόσον αὐτὸς ἔχοι (1087-90).

'Castor and Polydeuces, who dwell in holy Lacedaemon by the Eurotas, that
fair-flowing river, if ever I plot evil against a friend, may I get it myself; and
if he plots evil against me, may he get twice as much himself.' The idea of
repaying harm in double measure was seen also in Hesiod's lines on friendship.
Theognis expresses the Spartan associations of the twins in Homeric terms,
Lakedaimoni diēi, 'holy Lacedaemon', and the adjective *kalliroōi*, 'fair-flowing'.
The lyric poets were fond of naming a river as the distinctive feature of a city;
in summer a river with a fair flow is a rare blessing in Greece.
    The opposition of words and deeds is the basis of the following couplets:

μή μοι ἀνὴϱ εἴη γλώσσῃ φίλος, ἀλλὰ καὶ ἔϱγῳ·
    χεϱσίν τε σπεύδοι χϱήμασί τ', ἀμφότεϱα·
μηδὲ παϱὰ κϱητῆϱι λόγοισιν ἐμὴν φϱένα θέλγοι,
    ἀλλ' ἔϱδων φαίνοιτ' εἴ τι δύναιτ' ἀγαθόν (979-82).

'May no man be my friend with tongue only but in deed also; may he give
ready help with his hands and his possessions, both of them. May he not cast a
spell on my heart with his words beside the mixing-bowl but show his quality
by doing what good he can.' The mixing-bowl is the distinguishing feature of
the symposium, the obvious occasion for the conversation of friends and indeed
for the performance of these verses.
    Theognis gives his own versions of the appropriate behaviour towards
friends and enemies.

ἔν μοι ἔπειτα πέσοι μέγας οὐϱανὸς εὐϱὺς ὕπεϱθεν
    χάλκεος, ἀνθϱώπων δεῖμα χαμαιγενέων,
εἰ μὴ ἐγὼ τοῖσιν μὲν ἐπαϱκέσω οἵ με φιλεῦσιν,
    τοῖς δ' ἐχθϱοῖς ἀνίη καὶ μέγα πῆμ' ἔσομαι (869-72).

'May the great wide bronze heavens fall down on me, that terror of earth-born men, if I do not help those who love me and am not the distress and great woe of my enemies.' The elaboration of the first couplet with its epic language and enjambment forms a fine contrast with the starkness of the second. Theognis uses similar language to describe harsh times:

> ὤ μοι ἐγὼ δειλός· καὶ δὴ κατάχαρμα μὲν ἐχθροῖς,
> τοῖς δὲ φίλοισι πόνος δειλὰ παθὼν γενόμην (1107-8).

'Oh wretched me! See, I have become the joy of my enemies and the distress of my friends because I have suffered wretchedly.' He varies the terminology, using the unique compound form *katakharma*, 'joy' or perhaps 'malicious joy', and *ponos*, 'distress, trial, hardship'. The Greeks had a constant fear of providing merriment for enemies, neighbours or others who might be spiteful.

Both friends and enemies deserve *tisis*, 'repayment, requital', the giving of like for like:

> Ζεύς μοι τῶν τε φίλων δοίη τίσιν, οἵ με φιλεῦσιν,
> τῶν τ' ἐχθρῶν μεῖζον, Κύρνε, δυνησόμενον.
> χοὕτως ἂν δοκέοιμι μετ' ἀνθρώπων θεὸς εἶναι,
> εἴ μ' ἀποτεισάμενον μοῖρα κίχῃ θανάτου (337-40).

'May Zeus grant that I repay both my friends who love me and my enemies, Cyrnus, with my power greater than theirs; then I should seem a god among men if I made repayment before the fate of death overtook me.' The echo of the noun *tisin*, 'repayment', in the participle *apoteisamenon*, 'having made repayment', provides a circular structure for the little poem. As often, there is one memorable expression, here, 'a god among men', that gives a distinctive touch. We note again Theognis' concern with the reaction of the outside world.

Repayment is bluntly recommended in another poem:

> εὖ κώτιλλε τὸν ἐχθρόν· ὅταν δ' ὑποχείριος ἔλθῃ,
> τεῖσαί μιν πρόφασιν μηδεμίαν θέμενος (363-4).

'Talk softly to your enemy; but when you have him in your grasp, repay him and make no excuse about it.' The verb *kōtillein*, 'talk softly, cajole' with the implication of pulling the wool over someone's eyes, is a favourite of Theognis; the practice is forbidden in the case of a comrade (851–2), but is appropriate in dealing with an enemy. All the emphasis falls on the verb *teisai*, 'repay, punish, take vengeance on' the enemy.

The last couplet of Book I of the poems expresses Theognis' cynically jaundiced outlook:

> ἐχθρὸν μὲν χαλεπὸν καὶ δυσμενεῖ ἐξαπατῆσαι,
> Κύρνε· φίλον δὲ φίλῳ ῥάδιον ἐξαπατᾶν (1219-20).

'It is difficult, Cyrnus, even for an enemy to deceive his foe, easy for a friend to deceive his friend.'

True friendship is the theme of a short poem attributed to Phocylides:

γνήσιός εἰμι φίλος καὶ τὸν φίλον ὡς φίλον οἶδα,
τοὺς δὲ κακοὺς διόλου πάντας ἀποστρέφομαι.
οὐδένα θωπεύω πρὸς ὑπόκρισιν· οὓς δ' ἄρα τιμῶ,
τούτους ἐξ ἀρχῆς μέχρι τέλους ἀγαπῶ (17D.).

'I am a genuine friend, and I know my friend to be a friend; but I turn my back on all base men without exception. I flatter no one with insincerity; but those whom I honour I love from beginning to end.' This is in the spirit of much of Theognis' poetry and it may be roughly contemporary. If it is, the word *kakous*, 'base', may have social as well as moral application.

Pindar often talks of the relationship between his patron or host and himself in terms of friendship even when he can scarcely have known the other or was of markedly inferior social standing as in the case of Hieron, ruler of Syracuse. He sees the composition of the victory-song as a token of friendship and can call it *philion humnon*, 'a friendly song' (*Pyth.* 1.60), addressing Hieron with the words *ō phile*, 'my friend' (92). His finest lines on friendship are spoken by Polydeuces when he finds his brother Castor on the point of death:

οἴχεται τιμὰ φίλων τατωμένῳ
φωτί· παῦροι δ' ἐν πόνῳ πιστοὶ βροτῶν
καμάτου μεταλαμβάνειν (*Nem.* 10.78-9).

'Honour departs from a man when he is deprived of his friends. Among mortals few can be trusted to share one's toil in time of hardship.' The word *timē*, 'honour', denotes a man's status in society; there was a proverb, 'Prosperity has many friends', to which Theognis 929–30 and Pindar (*Pyth.* 5.1–4, *Isthm.* 2.11) refer.

But Pindar's view of the appropriate behaviour towards friends and enemies is the traditional one:

φίλον εἴη φιλεῖν·
ποτὶ δ' ἐχθρὸν ἅτ' ἐχθρὸς ἐὼν λύκοιο
δίκαν ὑποθεύσομαι,
ἀλλ' ἄλλοτε πατέων ὁδοῖς σκολιαῖς (*Pyth.* 2.83-5).

'May it be mine to love my friend; against my enemy, since I am his enemy, I shall run down like a wolf, treading crooked paths, now this way, now that.' The same morality appears in *Isthmian* 3/4.66:

χρὴ δὲ πᾶν ἔρδοντ' ἀμαυρῶσαι τὸν ἐχθρόν.

'One must use any means to enfeeble one's enemy.'

True friendship is the theme of three of the Attic scolia:

> εἴθ' ἐξῆν ὁποῖός τις ἦν ἕκαστος
> τὸ στῆθος διελόντ', ἔπειτα τὸν νοῦν
> ἐσιδόντα, κλείσαντα πάλιν,
> ἄνδρα φίλον νομίζειν ἀδόλῳ φρενί (889).

'If only it were possible to see what everyone is like by opening his breast and having looked at his mind to close it up again and regard the man as one's friend by reason of his guileless heart.' This reveals the same suspicious outlook as the poetry of Theognis, for example,

> κιβδήλου δ' ἀνδρὸς γνῶναι χαλεπώτερον οὐδέν (117),

'Nothing is harder to recognise than a counterfeit friend.' Euenus echoes the thought:

> ἡγοῦμαι σοφίης εἶναι μέρος οὐκ ἐλάχιστον
> ὀρθῶς γινώσκειν οἷος ἕκαστος ἀνήρ (3).

'I consider it not the least part of wisdom to recognise correctly what each man is like.' Eustathius, who quotes our scolion, mentions a fable of Aesop in which Momus, 'Blame', finds fault with Prometheus for not making a door in the breast when he created man.

The second song is also connected with fable:

> ὁ δὲ καρκίνος ὧδ' ἔφα
> χαλᾷ τὸν ὄφιν λαβών·
> 'εὐθὺν χρὴ τὸν ἑταῖρον ἔμ-
> μεν καὶ μὴ σκολιὰ φρονεῖν' (892).

'The crab, seizing the snake in its claws, spoke thus: "One's comrade should be straight and not think crooked thoughts."' One of Aesop's fables tells how the crab, before killing the snake for its treachery, said to it, 'You see, you should have been straight and honest and then you would not have been punished like this.'

The third song treats the theme of treachery in asclepiad metre:

> ὅστις ἄνδρα φίλον μὴ προδίδωσιν μεγάλην ἔχει
> τιμὴν ἔν τε βροτοῖς ἔν τε θεοῖσιν κατ' ἐμὸν νόον (908).

'He who does not betray his friend has great honour, in my view, both among mortals and among gods.'

*   *   *

Satire is just as much at home in friendship as in enmity. One of its objects is to make people laugh, as Iambe, said to have given her name to iambic verse, the usual medium for invective, made the sorrowing Demeter laugh, and one may satirise friends as well as enemies. In the symposium, where much of Greek lyric poetry must have been performed, the foibles of friends provided raw material no less than the iniquities of enemies. The case of Archilochus is instructive: he had a friend called Glaucus, son of Leptines, a real person whose cenotaph has been found on Thasos: he addressed political, moralising and other poems to him (15, 48, 96, 105, 131), but he also teased him about his hair-style in fine mock-epic:

τὸν κεροπλάστην ἄειδε Γλαῦκον (117),

'Sing of Glaucus, the horn-moulder.' Another friend, Pericles, is the recipient of solemn lines on the loss of friends in shipwreck and on the dispensation of fortune and fate (13, 16), but we have seen in Chapter Two that he was also admonished for gate-crashing parties. Charilaus, 'by far the dearest of my comrades' (168), was mocked for his gluttony (167).

These examples show the light-hearted side of Archilochus' satire, solemnly condemned two centuries later by Critias on the grounds that his abuse was directed at friends and enemies alike; but he was especially remembered in antiquity for the vicious attacks on Lycambes and his daughters which were said to have driven the victims to suicide. It is possible that this poetry also was performed at the symposium, but Martin West has argued that iambic verse of this kind was designed for public entertainment and was perhaps even acted by costumed performers; in his view Lycambes and his daughters may have been not real people, contemporaries of Archilochus, but 'stock characters in a traditional entertainment'. According to another view the recitation of the poems was intended as a public shaming of the wrong-doers.

Greek satire might be said to begin with Homer, since it is unmistakeable in his description of Thersites, the only common soldier whose role is of any importance in the *Iliad*:

ἄλλοι μέν ῥ᾽ ἕζοντο, ἐρήτυθεν δὲ καθ᾽ ἕδρας,
Θερσίτης δ᾽ ἔτι μοῦνος ἀμετροεπὴς ἐκολῴα,
ὅς ῥ᾽ ἔπεα φρεσὶν ᾗσιν ἄκοσμά τε πολλά τε ᾔδη,
μάψ ἀτὰρ οὐ κατὰ κόσμον ἐριζέμεναι βασιλεῦσιν,
ἀλλ᾽ ὅτι οἱ εἴσαιτο γελοίιον Ἀργείοισιν
ἔμμεναι. αἴσχιστος δὲ ἀνὴρ ὑπὸ Ἴλιον ἦλθεν·
φολκὸς ἔην, χωλὸς δ᾽ ἕτερον πόδα· τὼ δέ οἱ ὤμω
κυρτώ, ἐπὶ στῆθος συνοχωκότε· αὐτὰρ ὕπερθεν
φοξὸς ἔην κεφαλήν, ψεδνὴ δ᾽ ἐπενήνοθε λάχνη (2.211-19).

'Now the others sat down and were kept in check on the benches; Thersites alone, immoderate in speech, kept on brawling. He had a fund of insubordinate words for his pointless, disorderly quarrels with the kings and said what seemed likely to make the Greeks laugh. He was the ugliest man to come to Troy: he was bandy-legged and lame in one foot, and his shoulders were rounded, meeting in front of his chest; above, his head was pointed with a thin fuzz on it.' His attack on Agamemnon is a fine piece of invective, and he does not spare his fellow-soldiers either:

ὦ πέπονες, κάκ' ἐλέγχε', Ἀχαιίδες, οὐκέτ' Ἀχαιοί (235),

'You weaklings, foul disgraces, you women of Greece—I could not call you men . . .' The picture of Thersites has the exaggeration that is typical of satire, and it is marked off from the rest of Homer by a specialised vocabulary, many of the words being used here only in his poems.

Greek writers pointed to the *Margites* as an example of Homer's satirical composition, although the poem in fact belongs probably to the seventh or sixth century. Written in the hexameters of epic poetry with occasional iambic lines, it tells of Margites, the foolish son of rich parents, who 'knew how to do many things but knew it all badly':

πόλλ' ἠπίστατο ἔργα, κακῶς δ' ἠπίστατο πάντα (3).
τὸν δ' οὔτ' ἄρ' σκαπτῆρα θεοὶ θέσαν οὔτ' ἀροτῆρα
οὔτ' ἄλλως τι σοφόν· πάσης δ' ἡμάρτανε τέχνης (2).

'The gods made him neither a digger nor a plougher nor skilled in anything else: he failed in every craft.' In particular he failed in his marital responsibilities, unable to tell whether it was his father or his mother who had given birth to him, and unwilling to have intercourse with his wife in case she reported his behaviour to her mother.

Homer's skill in composing invective is most obvious in the account of the quarrel between Achilles and Agamemnon, where Achilles rounds on the other with a fine mixture of insult and irony:

οἰνοβαρές, κυνὸς ὄμματ' ἔχων, κραδίην δ' ἐλάφοιο,
οὔτε ποτ' ἐς πόλεμον ἅμα λαῷ θωρηχθῆναι
οὔτε λόχονδ' ἰέναι σὺν ἀριστήεσσιν Ἀχαιῶν
τέτληκας θυμῷ· τὸ δέ τοι κῆρ εἴδεται εἶναι.
ἦ πολὺ λώιόν ἐστι κατὰ στρατὸν εὐρὺν Ἀχαιῶν
δῶρ' ἀποαιρεῖσθαι, ὅς τις σέθεν ἀντίον εἴπῃ·
δημοβόρος βασιλεύς, ἐπεὶ οὐτιδανοῖσιν ἀνάσσεις·
ἦ γὰρ ἄν, Ἀτρεΐδη, νῦν ὕστατα λωβήσαιο (*Il.* 1. 225-32).

' "You drunkard with the eyes of a dog and the heart of a deer, you have never had the courage to arm yourself for battle with your soldiers or to join in an ambush with the Achaean nobles: you avoid that like death. Far better to stay in the wide camp of the Achaeans, taking away the prizes of anyone who contradicts you, eater of your people since the subjects you rule are feeble—or else, son of Atreus, you would now be maltreating them for the last time."' Odysseus, the finest speaker of the Greeks, matches this eloquence in his attack on Thersites (2.246ff.).

In later times iambics were regarded as the appropriate rhythm for personal abuse. The word *iambos* is found first in Archilochus:

καί μ' οὔτ' ἰάμβων οὔτε τερπωλέων μέλει (215),

'and neither iambics nor other delights are of interest to me.' Tzetzes, who quotes the line, says that Archilochus was mourning the drowning of his brother-in-law and used these words to answer friends who told him to give his attention to composition. Abuse of Lycambes is in iambic metre:

πάτερ Λυκάμβα, ποῖον ἐφράσω τόδε;
τίς σὰς παρήειρε φρένας,
ἧς τὸ πρὶν ἠρήρησθα; νῦν δὲ δὴ πολὺς
ἀστοῖσι φαίνεαι γέλως (172).

'Father Lycambes, what is this that you have thought up? Who unhinged those wits with which you used to be equipped? Nowadays you seem a great laughing-stock to the citizens.' This admirably direct poem begins with the ambiguous word 'father', a term of respect in some contexts but probably bitter here, since Lycambes had broken off the arrangement which would have made him the poet's father-in-law. The alliteration of *p* and *ph* gives an explosive effect. Archilochus continued with the fable of the eagle and the fox which we know from Aesop's collection: an eagle and a fox vowed mutual friendship, but the eagle stole the fox's cubs to feed its young; retribution followed when the eagle took a piece of burning meat from an altar: the nest caught fire and the young birds fell to the ground and were eaten by the fox. Scraps of Archilochus' version are preserved:

αἶνός τις ἀνθρώπων ὅδε,
ὡς ἄρ' ἀλώπηξ καἰετὸς ξυνεωνίην
ἔμειξαν (174).

'There is a tale told by men as follows: a fox and an eagle made an agreement.' The agreement between Lycambes and Archilochus must have been the link with the fable, and Archilochus no doubt prophesied retribution for Lycambes' faithlessness. The fable is told in leisurely fashion with generous use of direct speech: some third animal seems to have spoken of the eagle to the fox (unless the fox is soliloquising):

'ὁρᾷς ἵν' ἐστὶ κεῖνος ὑψηλὸς πάγος
τρηχύς τε καὶ παλίγκοτος;

ἐν τῷ κάθηται σὴν ἐλαφρίζων μάχην' (176).

' "You see where that high crag stands, rough and spiteful? There he sits, scorning your fighting ability." ' When the fox loses her cubs, she prays for vengeance:

ὦ Ζεῦ, πάτερ Ζεῦ, σὸν μὲν οὐρανοῦ κράτος,
σὺ δ' ἔργ' ἐπ' ἀνθρώπων ὁρᾷς
λεωργὰ καὶ θεμιστά, σοὶ δὲ θηρίων
ὕβρις τε καὶ δίκη μέλει' (177).

' "O Zeus, father Zeus, yours is the power over heaven; you oversee the deeds of men, their crimes and their lawful acts; you are concerned with the outrageous behaviour and the justice of beasts." ' This is fine composition in the paratactic manner, with each of the short clauses introduced by a form of the second person singular, *son men . . . su de . . . soi de. . . .*

Poems in which the metrical unit is a pair of lines, the longer followed by the shorter, were known as epodes. Another has an equally forthright introduction of a fable:

ἐρέω τιν' ὕμιν αἶνον, ὦ Κηρυκίδη,
ἀχνυμένη σκυτάλη·
πίθηκος ἤει θηρίων ἀποκριθεὶς
μοῦνος ἀν' ἐσχατιήν,
τῷ δ' ἄρ' ἀλώπηξ κερδαλῆ συνήντετο,
πυκνὸν ἔχουσα νόον (185).

'I shall tell you all a tale, Cerycides, I a sorrowful message-stick. A monkey, separated from the other beasts, was going alone into the wilds, when a crafty vixen met him with cunning in her mind.' Cerycides, not known elsewhere, is most likely to have been a real person, although this is disputed; and Archilochus may have referred to himself as a message-stick since the man's name suggested *kērux*, 'herald'. In Aesop's version of the fable the monkey, who has become king of the beasts, is made to look stupid by the vixen.

Although his scorpion tongue and heavy-worded hatreds were what later generations remembered about Archilochus, we know little else of his satirical writing beyond references to mockery of a seer called Batusiades (182–3) and a lecherous piper called Myclus (270) and to attacks on homosexuals (294). There are solitary iambic lines in which he makes fun of an old woman who continues to use perfumes (205) and talks of a hateful woman, 'thick about the ankles' (206). One well-known trochaic fragment may have been directed at Glaucus, since it was his hair-style that provoked mirth:

οὐ φιλέω μέγαν στρατηγὸν οὐδὲ διαπεπλιγμένον
οὐδὲ βοστρύχοισι γαῦρον οὐδ' ὑπεξυρημένον·

ἀλλά μοι σμικρός τις εἴη καὶ περὶ κνήμας ἰδεῖν
ῥοικός, ἀσφαλέως βεβηκὼς ποσσί, καρδίης πλέως (114).

'I do not love a tall general nor one with straddling legs, nor one who prides himself on his curls or shaves under the chin. Give me a short one, knock-kneed, walking firmly on his two feet and full of courage.' The generals are described in unusual words, although Homer's pictures of Thersites, Tydeus or even Odysseus may have been in Archilochus' mind.

Another prominent figure appears in amusing lines quoted as an example of polyptoton, a figure in which a noun is repeated in different cases. We have seen Anacreon use the device in one of his love poems (359).

νῦν δὲ Λεώφιλος μὲν ἄρχει, Λεωφίλου δ' ἐπικρατεῖν,
Λεωφίλῳ δὲ πάντα κεῖται, Λεώφιλον δ' ἄκουε <πᾶς> (115).

'But now Leophilus rules, Leophilus' is the power, to Leophilus everything belongs, hear Leophilus, everyone!' The text is uncertain; I have adopted West's suggestions which present the name in four different cases, nominative, genitive, dative and accusative, in the order in which they were given in antiquity. Without knowledge of the context we cannot say whether Archilochus was composing in light-hearted vein or was using the repetition of the name to convey ridicule or bitterness.

A fine piece of invective found on a fragment of papyrus has been attributed to Archilochus but is more probably the work of Hipponax:

κύμ[ατι] πλα[ζόμ]ενος·
κἂν Σαλμυδ[ησσ]ῷ γυμνὸν εὐφρονέστ[ατα   5
    Θρήϊκες ἀκρό[κ]ομοι
λάβοιεν – ἔνθα πόλλ' ἀναπλήσει κακὰ
    δούλιον ἄρτον ἔδων –
ῥίγει πεπηγότ' αὐτόν· ἐκ δὲ τοῦ χνόου
    φυκία πόλλ' ἐπέχοι,   10
κροτέοι δ' ὀδόντας, ὡς [κ]ύων ἐπὶ στόμα
    κείμενος ἀκρασίῃ
ἄκρον παρὰ ῥηγμῖνα κυμα[
    ταῦτ' ἐθέλοιμ' ἂν ἰδεῖν,
ὅς μ' ἠδίκησε, λ[ὰ]ξ δ' ἐπ' ὁρκίοις ἔβη,   15
    τὸ πρὶν ἑταῖρος [ἐ]ών (Hipponax 115).

'... he ... sent floundering by a wave; and at Salmydessus may the Thracians with their top-knots give him most kindly welcome and catch him naked—then he'll have a wretched time of it, eating slaves' bread—naked and stiff with cold; after the scum may much seaweed cover him; may he rattle his teeth, like a dog sprawled on his face, helpless, by the edge of the shore ... the waves. That is what I should like to see: he wronged me and trampled on his oaths, he who was once my comrade.' This most impressive piece of abuse is written in alternating iambic trimeter and dactylic hemiepes, and there is a corresponding mixture of Homeric and non-Homeric material. We may be reminded of Odysseus washed ashore on Phaeacia, and indeed there are one or two verbal reminiscences of that episode, but the picturesque detail is original and remarkable: the faithless friend ought to be washed up at Salmydessus, a Thracian place on the Black Sea notorious for its dangerous shallows and its well-organised wrecking industry; the local inhabitants, distinguished by their hair-style, are to welcome him in friendly fashion: nice irony here, if the text is correctly supplemented. The sequence of wishes in the optative mood is broken by the prediction of *anaplēsei*, 'he will have a wretched time of it', literally 'he will fill the measure of wretchedness', a Homeric expression given new interest by its juxtaposition with *edōn*, 'by eating'. The 'bread of slavery' echoes Homer's *doulion ēmar*, 'day of slavery'. The scum and seaweed and the dog-like figure on the beach complete the elaborate picture, and the poem finishes in contrast with three lines of blunt statement; each of the short units delivers its punch: 'that is what I should like to see' in summary; 'he wronged me', where the lack of antecedent in the Greek is brisk and concise; 'and trampled (or jumped) on his oaths', a lively variation of a Homeric expression; and the last words, '(he who was) once my comrade', which pack the entire justification for the poet's hostility into one bitter phrase.

A clever couplet on a woman or girl called Pasiphile, 'Love-all', is ascribed to Archilochus in our text of Athenaeus, but belongs more probably to the Hellenistic period:

συκῆ πετραίη πολλὰς βόσκουσα κορώνας,
εὐήθης ξείνων δέκτρια Πασιφίλη (331).

'Figtree on a rock, feeding many crows, easy-going hostess to strangers, Pasiphile.'

Semonides of Amorgos is best known for his satire on women, which is considered at the end of this chapter. He also directed personal invective against someone whose name is transmitted as Orodoecides, an odd form, perhaps a foreign name with the common Greek patronymic suffix; none of this poetry survives.

We have seen that Sappho made hostile political comment on women or girls of her acquaintance. She is also said by the sophist Maximus of Tyre to have had literary 'rivals', Andromeda and Gorgo: sometimes, he reports, she censures them, at other times she cross-examines them, and she uses irony just like Socrates. Scraps of her mockery survive: to Andromeda she says

† τίς δ' ἀγροῖωτις θέλγει νόον ...
ἀγροῖωτιν ἐπεμμένα στόλαν † ...
οὐκ ἐπισταμένα τὰ βράκε' ἕλκην ἐπὶ τῶν σφύρων; (57)

'And what country girl beguiles your mind . . . dressed in country garb . . . not knowing how to pull her rags over her ankles?' The text is faulty, but if the repeated *agroiōtis*, 'country, rustic', is authentic, it is acid. A girl called Atthis left Sappho's circle for Andromeda:

> Ἄτθι, σοὶ δ' ἔμεθεν μὲν ἀπήχθετο
> φροντίσδην, ἐπὶ δ' Ἀνδρομέδαν πότη (131).

'Atthis, the thought of me has become hateful to you, and you fly off to Andromeda.' We can only guess at the context of

> ἔχει μὲν Ἀνδρομέδα κάλαν ἀμοίβαν (133),

'Andromeda has a fine recompense.' The love-life of Gorgo too provoked hostile comment: one Pleistodica, also known as Archeanassa, will be called *sundugos*, 'yoke-mate', of Gorgo along with Gongyla (213); and Sappho says of a group of people that they 'have had quite enough of Gorgo',

> μάλα δὴ κεκορημένοις
> Γόργως (144).

Our longest example of Sappho's invective is aimed at a woman described by our sources as rich and uneducated:

> κατθάνοισα δὲ κείσῃ οὐδέ ποτα μναμοσύνα σέθεν
> ἔσσετ' οὐδὲ πόθα εἰς ὕστερον· οὐ γὰρ πεδέχῃς βρόδων
> τῶν ἐκ Πιερίας, ἀλλ' ἀφάνης κἀν Ἀίδα δόμῳ
> φοιτάσῃς πεδ' ἀμαύρων νεκύων ἐκπεποταμένα (55).

'But when you die you will lie there, and afterwards there will never be any recollection of you or any longing for you, since you have no share in the roses of Pieria; unseen in the house of Hades also, flown from our midst, you will go to and fro among the shadowy corpses.' Sappho presumably implies that she herself will enjoy immortality because of her poetry; indeed she may have said so elsewhere in the poem. The imagery of 'the roses of Pieria' is striking: Pieria in Macedonia was the birthplace of the Muses, but there is no other reference to its roses; we know only that Sappho is said to have loved the rose and to have used it in many similes to express female beauty (Philostratus *Ep.* 51).

Sappho employs mockery of a different sort in some of her epithalamia. Banter has often played a role in wedding ceremonies and is usually explained as an attempt to detract from the happiness of the occasion so as to ward off the envy of the gods. Sappho makes fun of the 'doorkeeper', the friend of the bridegroom whose duty was to prevent the bride's attendants from rescuing her:

θυρώρῳ πόδες ἐπτορόγυιοι,
τὰ δὲ σάμβαλα πεμπεβόεια,
πίσσυγγοι δὲ δέκ' ἐξεπόναισαν (110a).

'The doorkeeper's feet are seven fathoms long, his sandals are made from five ox-hides; ten cobblers worked hard to make them.' These simple lines were condemned by the critic Demetrius as 'cheap stuff, in the language of prose, not poetry'. Another song ran,

ἴψοι δὴ τὸ μέλαθρον –
ὐμήναον¹ –
ἀέρρετε τέκτονες ἄνδρες·
ὐμήναον.
γάμβρος † εἰσέρχεται ἴσος † Ἄρευι,   5
ἄνδρος μεγάλω πόλυ μέζων (111).

'On high raise up—Hymenaeus!—the roof, you carpenters—Hymenaeus! The bridegroom is coming, the equal of Ares, much larger than a large man.' Here too the humour is childish, directed at the great size of the bridegroom. Elsewhere Sappho compares a groom to Achilles, and in the present lines she may be mocking the convention that he like his doorman was of epic stature.

The invective of Alcaeus, Sappho's contemporary in Mytilene, has been considered in Chapter Four, since it is entirely political. Horace, contrasting him with Archilochus, says, 'He does not look for a father-in-law to besmirch with black verses, nor does he tie a noose round the neck of his fiancée with libellous song' (*Epist.* 1.19.30–1). Quintilian thought highly of 'that part of his work in which he attacks the tyrants' and found moral value in it (10.1.63), but on our evidence this is an unbalanced verdict: Alcaeus attacked the tyrants simply because he wanted to see himself or one of his associates in their place, as Strabo says (13.2.3), and the surviving fragments for all their attractiveness do not make the contribution to moral thinking that Quintilian claimed to see.

Anacreon was remembered as the poet of love and wine, but we have already seen an example of his satirical writing in fr. 427, in which a woman is told not to keep chattering, 'swilling down the hearth-cup with that battered Gastrodora': the name is more likely to be a comic creation than a real one. We know several witty epithets that he applied to whores: *pandosia*, 'giver of all', *leōphoros*, 'highway', and *poluumnos*, 'much-sung', all three used, says Eustathius, with more caution than violence. The second has turned up in a papyrus fragment, in what is probably the first line of a poem:

λεωφ]όρε λεωφόρ' Ἡρο[τ]ίμη (346 fr. 1.13),

'Herotima, you highway, you highway'; the suggestion is that she is a public thoroughfare, 'people-carrying'. The *Suda* adds another adjective, *maniokēpos*, 'sex-mad', in which the second element, *kēpos*, literally 'garden', is used with reference to the woman's genital region.

We have two examples of Anacreon's mockery of effeminates. One is an isolated line,

καὶ θάλαμος ἐν † ᾧ † κεῖνος οὐκ ἔγημεν ἀλλ᾽ ἐγήματο (424),

'and the chamber in which he did not marry but got married', the point of which is grammatical, since the middle voice, 'got married', is properly used of the woman, the active voice, 'married', of the man. The other is our longest example of Anacreon's satire and is directed against a society upstart:

πρὶν μὲν ἔχων βερβέριον, καλύμματ᾽ ἐσφηκωμένα,
καὶ ξυλίνους ἀστραγάλους ἐν ὠσὶ καὶ ψιλὸν περὶ
πλευρῇσι <δέρμ᾽ ἥει> βοός,
νήπλυτον εἴλυμα κακῆς ἀσπίδος, ἀρτοπώλισιν
κἀθελοπόρνοισιν ὁμιλέων ὁ πονηρὸς Ἀρτέμων,   5
κίβδηλον εὑρίσκων βίον,
πολλὰ μὲν ἐν δουρὶ τιθεὶς αὐχένα, πολλὰ δ᾽ ἐν τροχῷ,
πολλὰ δὲ νῶτον σκυτίνῃ μάστιγι θωμιχθείς, κόμην
πώγωνά τ᾽ ἐκτετιλμένος·
νῦν δ᾽ ἐπιβαίνει σατινέων χρύσεα φορέων κατέρματα   10
† παῖς Κύκης † καὶ σκιαδίσκην ἐλεφαντίνην φορεῖ
γυναιξὶν αὔτως <ἐμφερής> (388).

'He used to go about in an old cap, a wasped hood, with wooden dice in his ears and around his ribs a hairless oxhide, the unwashed wrapping of a wretched shield, that scoundrel Artemon, consorting with bread-women and ready whores, devising a fraudulent living; often he had his neck in the stocks, often on the wheel; often his back was flogged with a leather whip and his hair and beard plucked out. But nowadays the son of Cyce rides in a carriage wearing gold earrings, and he carries an ivory parasol exactly like the ladies.' Three-quarters of the poem are devoted to Artemon's squalid past, the last stanza to his disreputable present. The rhythm is free iambic, appropriate to invective. The detail is colourful and generously supplied, often in unfamiliar words which may have a colloquial flavour as in the diminutive forms *berberion*, 'cap', and *skiadiskē*, 'parasol'. The earrings, the parasol and the type of coach in which he rides are all marks of his effeminacy, and Anacreon notes the wooden dice which served as earrings when he was down and out. The poem is usually regarded as an example of savage indignation in the manner adopted centuries later by the Roman satirist Juvenal, but we are in no position to say that Artemon was not one of Anacreon's friends.

Hipponax, like Archilochus, was remembered for the savagery of his verses. There was a tale that the target of his invective, Bupalus, a Chian sculptor, was driven to suicide along with his brother like the victims of Archilochus. The poets of the Palatine Anthology wrote of his wasp-like sting; his tomb, they said, is covered with bramble and prickly wild pear, his ashes still make iambics to satisfy his hatred of Bupalus, and he barked even at his parents (*AP* 7.405, 408, 536). We rely on unsatisfactory evidence for our assessment of his work, mainly isolated lines quoted to illustrate his use of a difficult or rare word, together with shreds of papyrus texts and commentaries.

The picturesque quality of his insults can be seen in his rhetorical question,

> τίς ὀμφαλητόμος σε τὸν διοπλῆγα
> ἔψησε κἀπέλουσεν ἀσκαρίζοντα; (19)

'What navel-string-cutter wiped and washed your twitching body, you whom Zeus blasted?' The term for a midwife, found first here, has a comic ring, but it was used by the medical writer Hippocrates a century later; *dioplēx*, 'smitten by Zeus', occurs here only; and the verb *askarizō*, 'twitch', was unusual enough to require comment from the grammarians. The lines gain much of their effect from the metre, the 'limping iambic' which Hipponax seems to have invented; the rhythm is the regular iambic trimeter given a jolt by the unexpected long penultimate syllable, and the metrical distortion, like the coarse vocabulary and squalid subject-matter, must be due to Hipponax' wish to compose a deliberately vulgarised poetry.

The 'limping' character of the following trochaic lines may be used for a comic effect:

> λάβετέ μεο ταἰμάτια, κόψω Βουπάλῳ τὸν ὀφθαλμόν.
> ἀμφιδέξιος γάρ εἰμι κοὐκ ἁμαρτάνω κόπτων (120, 121).

'Hold my clothes, fellows, and I'll punch Bupalus in the eye.' 'I'm ambidextrous, and I don't miss when I punch.' The three long syllables -*ō koptōn*, together with the repetition of the verb, suggest a right, left, right to the head.

Hipponax' abuse is associated with narration of his amatory adventures with Arete, mistress of Bupalus; we must not see irony in her name since the word has three long syllables and, like the lady herself, has no connection with *aretē*, 'virtue'.

> ἐγὼ δὲ δεξιῷ παρ' Ἀρήτην
> κνεφαῖος ἐλθὼν ᾽ρῳδιῷ κατηυλίσθην (16).

'And I, with a heron on my right, came at dusk to Arete's and lodged there.' There is a mock-epic touch in the mention of the favourable omen.

τί τῷ τάλαντι Βουπάλῳ συνοίκησας; (15)

'Why did you live with that wretch Bupalus?' The story is detailed, squalid and funny:

ἐκ πελλίδος πίνοντες· οὐ γὰρ ἦν αὐτῇ
κύλιξ, ὁ παῖς γὰρ ἐμπεσὼν κατήραξε (13).

'(we) . . . drinking from a pail: she had no cup: her slave had fallen on it and smashed it.'

ἐκ δὲ τῆς πέλλης
ἔπινον· ἄλλοτ' αὐτός, ἄλλοτ' Ἀρήτη
προύπινεν (14).

'And I drank from the pail; I drank to Arete and she to me, turn about.' While they have sex on the floor Bupalus is told that he can go to hell:

κλαίειν κελεύ[ων Βού]παλον[(84.18).

Comic detail is supplied with equal generosity in other fragments:

ὁ δ' ἐξολισθὼν ἱκέτευε τὴν κράμβην
τὴν ἑπτάφυλλον, ἣν θύεσκε Πανδώρῃ
Ταργηλίοισιν ἔγκυθρον . . . (104.47-9).

'He slipped and made supplication to the cabbage, the seven-leaved cabbage he used to sacrifice in a pot to [Earth], the Giver of All, at the Thargelia . . .' Here as elsewhere the element of parody is conspicuous.

Insults are varied: Bupalus sleeps with his mother (*ho mētrokoitēs Boupalos*, 12.2, cf. 70.8), the painter Mimnes is *nikurtas*, 'slave born of a slave' (28.5), Sannus is both gluttonous and emaciated (118), Cicon, a seer, is *ammoros kauēs* (4), 'a luckless cormorant', *ouden aision prothespizōn* (4a), 'giving no favourable prophecy', the thief of a cloak is exposed:

πᾶς δὲ πέφηνε δόλος (117.11),

'and all your trickery has come to light.' Athenis, brother of Bupalus, is addressed at the beginning of one poem (70.11); elsewhere the audience is wide:

ὦ Κλαζομένιοι, Βούπαλος κατέκτεινεν (1),

'People of Clazomenae, Bupalus has killed (me?)'; Hipponax was said to have moved to Clazomenae when driven out of his native Ephesus. Hermes is addressed with the minimum of respect:

Ἑρμῆ κυνάγχα, μηονιστὶ Κανδαῦλα,
φωρῶν ἑταῖρε, δεῦρό μοι σκαπαρδεῦσαι (3a).

'Hermes, dog-throttler, "Candaules" in Maeonian, comrade of thieves, come and pull on the rope for me.' As god of thieves, Hermes helps by taking care of watchdogs. The Maeonian term among his epithets is only one of the Asiatic words found in the fragments: Hermes himself is *Kullēnēs palmun* (3), 'tsar of Cyllene', *palmus* being a Lydian word for 'king' which Hipponax uses several times. These foreign expressions must reflect the speech of the streets of the coastal cities of Asia and are another aspect of Hipponax' vulgarisation of poetry.

Witty couplets are attributed to Demodocus of Leros:

καὶ τόδε Δημοδόκου· Λέριοι κακοί· οὐχ ὁ μέν, ὃς δ' οὔ·
πάντες, πλὴν Προκλέους – καὶ Προκλέης Λέριος (2).

'This too belongs to Demodocus: the Lerians are bad; not one bad and another not; all bad, except Procles—and Procles is a Lerian.'

<καὶ τόδε Δημοδόκου· > Μιλήσιοι ἀξύνετοι μὲν
οὔκ εἰσιν, δρῶσιν δ' οἶά περ ἀξύνετοι (1).

'This too belongs to Demodocus: the Milesians are not fools, but they act like fools.' Strabo, however, quotes the first couplet as belonging to Phocylides of Miletus, the gnomic poet (*kai tode Phōkulideō*), and it is attractive to see the second couplet as Demodocus' riposte.

Καππαδόκην ποτ' ἔχιδνα κακὴ δάκεν· ἀλλὰ καὶ αὐτὴ
κάτθανε γευσαμένη αἵματος ἰοβόλου (4).

'A Cappadocian was once bitten by a foul snake; but it was the snake itself that died when she tasted his poisonous blood.' Concision of expression, fine positioning of the words, especially of *katthane*, 'died', and alliteration all contribute to the success of this splendid epigram.

Much of the poetry of Theognis, as we have seen, was prompted by contemporary politics, and as a dispossessed aristocrat he inveighs against the other classes of society. None of his invective is directed by name against individuals, however. Two fine pieces begin with the scornful *anthrōpe*, 'fellow':

ὤνθρωπ', εἰ γνώμης ἔλαχες μέρος ὥσπερ ἀνοίης
καὶ σώφρων οὕτως ὥσπερ ἄφρων ἐγένου,
πολλοῖς ἂν ζηλωτὸς ἐφαίνεο τῶνδε πολιτῶν
οὕτως ὥσπερ νῦν οὐδενὸς ἄξιος εἶ (453-6).

'Fellow, if you had been allotted a portion of wisdom equal to that of your folly and had been as sensible as you are senseless, you would have seemed as enviable to many of these citizens as you are now worthless in their eyes.' When Theognis recited this to his circle of friends, he must have made the identification plain: 'X said so-and-so; this is my answer.'

Friendship is the theme of another poem addressed to a nameless individual:

> ἄνθρωπ', ἀλλήλοισιν ἀπόπροθεν ὦμεν ἑταῖροι·
> πλὴν πλούτου παντὸς χρήματός ἐστι κόρος.
> δὴν δὴ καὶ φίλοι ὦμεν· ἀτὰρ τ' ἄλλοισιν ὁμίλει
> ἀνδράσιν, οἳ τὸν σὸν μᾶλλον ἴσασι νόον (595-8).

'Fellow, let us be comrades at a distance. There is satiety in everything except wealth. Let us be friends for a long time; but keep company with other men who understand your mind better than I do.' 'Comrades at a distance' is a contradiction in terms according to the proverb,

> τηλοῦ φίλοι ναίοντες οὐκ εἰσὶν φίλοι,

'friends who live far apart are no friends'. There is cynicism in the second line, emphasised by the alliteration: money is the only thing of which we cannot have too much. The poem depends on paradox: friendship normally implied pleasure in association, but its basic element was mutual obligation. Theognis wants this basic relationship preserved, no doubt for reasons of convenience, but dispenses with the personal contact.

A still more bitter poem on a ruined friendship follows in the manuscripts and has sometimes been regarded as the second half of the last piece:

> οὔ μ' ἔλαθες φοιτῶν κατ' ἀμαξιτόν, ἢν ἄρα καὶ πρὶν
> ἠλάστρεις, κλέπτων ἡμετέρην φιλίην.
> ἔρρε, θεοῖσίν τ' ἐχθρὲ καὶ ἀνθρώποισιν ἄπιστε,
> ψυχρὸν ὃς ἐν κόλπῳ ποικίλον εἶχες ὄφιν (599-602).

'You did not escape my notice when you travelled on the highway along which, it seems, you used to drive and so betrayed our friendship. To hell with you, you enemy of the gods, distrusted by men: you had a cold cunning snake in the fold of your tunic.' This is Theognis at his finest; the third line with the Homeric *erre* as its opening and the balance between 'god-hated' and 'man-distrusted' is particularly successful. The road which the treacherous friend has been taking again is presumably figurative, 'you went back to your old ways', although it could be regarded as the road leading to some rival, abandoned for Theognis and now back in favour. We have seen the snake as the type of crookedness and faithlessness in one of the scolia (892); its coldness is both literal and figurative—it lacks the warmth of the true friend; similarly *poikilos* may refer both to the appearance of the snake, its various colours or its rapid, sinuous movement, and to its inconstancy. We have seen Theognis prescribe the *poikilon ēthos*, 'changeful disposition', of the octopus (213ff.).

Timocreon figured in the last chapter as the author of a bitter attack on Themistocles (727). He also composed a metrical joke in which approximately the same words in different arrangement give a dactylic hexameter and a trochaic tetrameter:

Κηῖα με προσῆλθε φλυαρία οὐκ ἐθέλοντα·
οὐ θέλοντά με προσῆλθε Κηῖα φλυαρία (10).

'Nonsense from Ceos came to me against my will. Against my will there came to me nonsense from Ceos.' Ceos suggests Simonides, who was born on the island; and a mock epitaph for Timocreon was ascribed to Simonides in the Palatine Anthology; such ascriptions must be regarded with suspicion, but at least the chronology fits:

πολλὰ πιὼν καὶ πολλὰ φαγὼν καὶ πολλὰ κάκ' εἰπὼν
ἀνθρώπους κεῖμαι Τιμοκρέων Ῥόδιος (99D., 37 Page).

'Here I lie, Timocreon of Rhodes, having drunk much, having eaten much, having spoken much evil of men.' A variation on the theme was attributed to Simonides by the 'corrector' of our manuscript of the Anthology:

βαιὰ φαγὼν καὶ βαιὰ πιὼν καὶ πολλὰ νοσήσας
ὀψὲ μὲν ἀλλ' ἔθανον· ἔρρετε πάντες ὁμοῦ (A.P. 9.349).

'Having eaten little, having drunk little, having had much illness, I died, although it took a long time. To hell with you all!'

* * *

The long satire on the entire female sex by Semonides of Amorgos (7) is in a class of its own in Greek literature; only Phocylides' eight lines on the same subject (2D.) are comparable, and they are simply a much abbreviated version of Semonides' poem, transposed from iambic rhythm into hexameters. Mockery of women was nothing new: there is strong misogyny in Hesiod's account of Prometheus and Pandora; and male gatherings like the symposium must have been prone to merry contemplation of the women left at home. Semonides' innovation is the composition of a long poem—apart from epic it is the longest piece to survive from before the fifth century—devoted to abuse of the whole sex, and his creation of a catalogue in iambics instead of the customary dactylic hexameters.

In the first 93 lines of his poem Semonides describes ten types of women as made from eight different animals and from earth and sea. Animal fables must have influenced him: one from the Aesopic collection runs as follows: at the command of Zeus Prometheus made men and beasts; but Zeus noticed that the beasts were by far the more numerous and ordered him to destroy some of them and change them into men; he did as he was told, with the result that those who had not been made men in the first place had the bodies of men but the souls of beasts (228 Hausrath). Although Aesop himself belonged to the century after Semonides, fables like this one are likely to be of much earlier date.

χωρὶς γυναικὸς θεὸς ἐποίησεν νόον
τὰ πρῶτα. τὴν μὲν ἐξ ὑὸς τανύτριχος,
τῇ πάντ' ἀν' οἶκον βορβόρῳ πεφυρμένα
ἄκοσμα κεῖται καὶ κυλίνδεται χαμαί·
αὐτὴ δ' ἄλουτος ἀπλύτοις ἐν εἵμασιν   5
ἐν κοπρίῃσιν ἡμένη πιαίνεται (1-6).

'In the beginning the god created woman's mind separately: one woman from a bristly sow; in her house everything lies about in disorder and rolls on the ground, fouled with mud, and she herself, unwashed, in unwashed clothes, sits in the dungheap and grows fat.' This vigorous opening derives its effect from its brisk movement towards the final verb *piainetai* and from the obtrusive alliteration of line 4. The interpretation of the first word *khōris*, 'separately', is debated: Semonides may mean 'separately from man's mind', assuming that the second word *gunaikos*, 'woman's', made this clear; or he may simply be saying 'variously' by way of introducing his ten types.

τὴν δ' ἐξ ἀλιτρῆς θεὸς ἔθηκ' ἀλώπεκος
γυναῖκα πάντων ἴδριν· οὐδέ μιν κακῶν
λέληθεν οὐδὲν οὐδὲ τῶν ἀμεινόνων·
τὸ μὲν γὰρ αὐτῶν εἶπε πολλάκις κακόν,   10
τὸ δ' ἐσθλόν· ὀργὴν δ' ἄλλοτ' ἀλλοίην ἔχει (7-11).

'Another the god made from a wicked vixen, a woman who knows everything: no evil escapes her notice, nothing of the better sort either; for the latter she often calls bad, the former good. Her mood changes all the time.' The picture is less clear than the first: the vixen-woman is wicked and knowing or skilful; that nothing escapes her notice explains the second quality, that she calls the good bad and the bad good shows her wickedness; her changeable mood or character represents a third characteristic of the animal.

τὴν δ' ἐκ κυνὸς λιτουργόν, αὐτομήτορα,
ἣ πάντ' ἀκοῦσαι, πάντα δ' εἰδέναι θέλει,
πάντῃ δὲ παπταίνουσα καὶ πλανωμένη
λέληκεν, ἢν καὶ μηδέν' ἀνθρώπων ὁρᾷ.   15
παύσειε δ' ἄν μιν οὔτ' ἀπειλήσας ἀνήρ,
οὐδ' εἰ χολωθεὶς ἐξαράξειεν λίθῳ
ὀδόντας οὐδ' ἂν μειλίχως μυθεόμενος,
οὐδ' εἰ παρὰ ξείνοισιν ἡμένη τύχῃ·
ἀλλ' ἐμπέδως ἄπρηκτον αὐονὴν ἔχει (12-20).

'Another from a bitch, rascally, the image of her mother, who wants to hear everything and know everything, and prying and roaming in every direction barks even if there is nobody in sight. A man could not check her, either by threats or by losing his temper and knocking out her teeth with a stone, or by speaking gently, not even if she should be sitting with friends: non-stop she keeps up her unmanageable yapping.' This is fine, assured composition as in the opening lines; Semonides uses anaphora and alliteration effectively in 13–14, and again he moves to a fine climax.

<blockquote>
τὴν δὲ πλάσαντες γηίνην Ὀλύμπιοι
ἔδωκαν ἀνδρὶ πηρόν· οὔτε γὰρ κακὸν
οὔτ' ἐσθλὸν οὐδὲν οἶδε τοιαύτη γυνή·
ἔργων δὲ μοῦνον ἐσθίειν ἐπίσταται.
κοὐδ' ἢν κακὸν χειμῶνα ποιήσῃ θεός,   25
ῥιγῶσα δίφρον ἄσσον ἕλκεται πυρός (21-6).
</blockquote>

'Another the Olympians made of earth and gave to man, a feeble-minded thing: such a woman knows nothing, neither good nor bad, and of employments the only one she understands is eating. Even if the god brings a hard winter she shivers but does not draw her chair nearer the fire.' After three animals Semonides turns to earth, probably remembering that in Hesiod's account Hephaestus had used earth mixed with water to create Pandora (*Op.* 60–1). The illustrations of the clod-woman's ignorance are vivid, and the positioning of *pēron*, 'feeble-minded', and *rhigōsa*, 'shivering', is skilful.

<blockquote>
τὴν δ' ἐκ θαλάσσης, ἣ δύ' ἐν φρεσὶν νοεῖ·
τὴν μὲν γελᾷ τε καὶ γέγηθεν ἡμέρην·
ἐπαινέσει μιν ξεῖνος ἐν δόμοις ἰδών·
'οὐκ ἔστιν ἄλλη τῆσδε λωίων γυνὴ   30
ἐν πᾶσιν ἀνθρώποισιν οὐδὲ καλλίων·'
τὴν δ' οὐκ ἀνεκτὸς οὐδ' ἐν ὀφθαλμοῖς ἰδεῖν
οὔτ' ἄσσον ἐλθεῖν, ἀλλὰ μαίνεται τότε
ἄπλητον ὥσπερ ἀμφὶ τέκνοισιν κύων,
ἀμείλιχος δὲ πᾶσι κἀποθυμίη   35
ἐχθροῖσιν ἴσα καὶ φίλοισι γίγνεται·
ὥσπερ θάλασσα πολλάκις μὲν ἀτρεμὴς
ἔστηκ' ἀπήμων χάρμα ναύτῃσιν μέγα
θέρεος ἐν ὥρῃ, πολλάκις δὲ μαίνεται
βαρυκτύποισι κύμασιν φορεομένη·   40
ταύτῃ μάλιστ' ἔοικε τοιαύτη γυνὴ
ὀργήν· φυὴν δὲ πόντος ἀλλοίην ἔχει (27-42).
</blockquote>

'Another from the sea. She has two minds: one day she is all smiles and happiness: a stranger seeing her in her home will commend her: "There is no woman finer than this one in the whole world, none more beautiful"; the next day she is unbearable to see or to come near: then she has a mad unapproachable rage like a bitch around her puppies, implacable to all, the despair of friend and foe alike, just as the sea often stands calm and harmless in summertime, a great joy to sailors, but often again goes mad, rushing with thunderous waves. This kind of woman is most like it in temperament, and the ocean's nature is something else altogether.' After earth, the sea, Semonides' longest picture and, for the first ten lines at least, one of his best. Alliteration is again important in 28, where *gelāi*, 'laughs', is well-chosen since it can be used of a sunlit sea, and the comparison with the dog and her pups, found in Homer, is lively. In line 37 Semonides reverts for the only time in the poem to the material of which the woman was created, linking this new section to the previous lines by the repetition of *mainetai*, 'is mad', and drawing fine pictures of calm and storm: the three thundering words of 40 are expressive; but the last two lines are feeble summary. If the text of 42 is correct, *alloios*, 'of another sort', must have a sinister meaning as in the conversational use of 'something else altogether'.

> τὴν δ' ἔκ τε τεφρῆς καὶ παλιντριβέος ὄνου
> ἣ σύν τ' ἀνάγκη σύν τ' ἐνιπῆσιν μόγις
> ἔστερξεν ὧν ἅπαντα κἀπονήσατο   45
> ἀρεστά. τόφρα δ' ἐσθίει μὲν ἐν μυχῷ
> προνύξ, προῆμαρ, ἐσθίει δ' ἐπ' ἐσχάρῃ.
> ὁμῶς δὲ καὶ πρὸς ἔργον ἀφροδίσιον
> ἐλθόντ' ἑταῖρον ὁντινῶν ἐδέξατο (43-9).

'Another from an ash-grey much-thumped ass, who under compulsion and abuse puts up with it all and works satisfactorily. Meanwhile, she eats in the inner room all night and all day, and she eats by the fire-place. Equally she welcomes any friend who has come to make love.' The adjective *palintribēs* is unusual and colourful, 'thumped again and again', like the ass in Homer's simile (*Il.* 11.558ff.). The repetition of *esthiei*, 'eats', and of the prefix *pro-*, 'all night, all day', adds to the humour of the passage.

> τὴν δ' ἐκ γαλῆς δύστηνον οἰζυρὸν γένος·   50
> κείνη γὰρ οὔ τι καλὸν οὐδ' ἐπίμερον
> πρόσεστιν οὐδὲ τερπνὸν οὐδ' ἐράσμιον.
> εὐνῆς δ' ἀληνής ἐστιν ἀφροδισίης,
> τὸν δ' ἄνδρα τὸν παρεόντα ναυσίη διδοῖ.
> κλέπτουσα δ' ἔρδει πολλὰ γείτονας κακά,   55
> ἄθυστα δ' ἱρὰ πολλάκις κατεσθίει (50-6).

'Another from a weasel, a wretched, miserable sort: in her there is nothing beautiful, nothing desirable, nothing delightful, nothing lovable. She is mad about love-making but makes the partner who is with her sick. With her thievish ways she does her neighbours much damage, and she often eats up sacrifices that have not been burned.' This repulsive creature, the wild rather than the domestic weasel, is described in terms which remind us of Archilochus: his description of Thasos was

> οὐ γάρ τι καλὸς χῶρος οὐδ' ἐφίμερος
> οὐδ' ἐρατός (22),

'for it is no beautiful or desirable or lovable place'. Aristophanes refers to the thievish habits of the animal and to its foul smell, which is presumably what makes the partners sick.

> τὴν δ' ἵππος ἁβρὴ χαιτέεσσ' ἐγείνατο,
> ἣ δούλι' ἔργα καὶ δύην περιτρέχει,
> κοὔτ' ἂν μύλης ψαύσειεν οὔτε κόσκινον
> ἄρειεν οὔτε κόπρον ἐξ οἴκου βάλοι,   60
> οὔτε πρὸς ἱπνὸν ἀσβόλην ἀλεομένη
> ἵζοιτ'· Ἀνάγκη δ' ἄνδρα ποιεῖται φίλον.
> λοῦται δὲ πάσης ἡμέρης ἄπο ῥύπον
> δίς, ἄλλοτε τρίς, καὶ μύροις ἀλείφεται·
> αἰεὶ δὲ χαίτην ἐκτενισμένην φορεῖ   65
> βαθεῖαν ἀνθέμοισιν ἐσκιασμένην.
> καλὸν μὲν ὦν θέημα τοιαύτη γυνὴ
> ἄλλοισι, τῷ δ' ἔχοντι γίγνεται κακόν,
> ἢν μή τις ἢ τύραννος ἢ σκηπτοῦχος ᾖ,
> ὅστις τοιούτοις θυμὸν ἀγλαΐζεται (57-70).

'Another was produced by a delicate mare with a fine mane: she shies away from a slave's work and misery and would not touch a handmill or lift a sieve or throw the dung out of the house or sit by the stove, since she keeps clear of the soot; and she makes her husband the friend of Distress. She washes off her dirt twice every day, sometimes thrice, and she rubs herself with perfumes. She always wears her thick hair combed and shadowed with flowers. A woman like her is a beautiful sight for others but for her husband a calamity, unless he is a tyrant or a sceptred king, the kind who takes pride in such things.' Not all the detail of this fine portrait is certain: the reading *peritrekhei*, 'trots around, shies away from', is Lattimore's emendation of *peritrepei*, which some accept in the sense 'passes on to others'; and the interpretation of *anankē*, 'necessity, distress', in 62 is hotly disputed; if the meaning is indeed 'she makes her husband the friend of Distress', this will be a comment inserted appropriately enough in the catalogue of her expensive ways and repeated in 68.

> τὴν δ' ἐκ πιθήκου· τοῦτο δὴ διακριδὸν
> Ζεὺς ἀνδράσιν μέγιστον ὤπασεν κακόν.
> αἴσχιστα μὲν πρόσωπα· τοιαύτη γυνὴ
> εἶσιν δι' ἄστεος πᾶσιν ἀνθρώποις γέλως·

ἐπ' αὐχένα βραχεῖα κινεῖται μόγις,   75
ἄπυγος, αὐτόκωλος. ἂ τάλας ἀνήρ,
ὅστις κακὸν τοιοῦτον ἀγκαλίζεται.
δήνεα δὲ πάντα καὶ τρόπους ἐπίσταται
ὥσπερ πίθηκος οὐδέ οἱ γέλως μέλει·
οὐδ' ἄν τιν' εὖ ἔρξειεν, ἀλλὰ τοῦτ' ὁρᾷ   80
καὶ τοῦτο πᾶσαν ἡμέρην βουλεύεται,
ὅκως τιν' ὡς μέγιστον ἔρξειεν κακόν (71-82).

'Another from a monkey: this one is easily the greatest calamity Zeus gave men. Her face is the ugliest: a woman like her will go through the town laughed at by everyone. Short in the neck, she has difficulty in moving, no buttocks and all legs. Ah, the poor wretch who embraces such a disaster! She knows all arts and wiles like a monkey, and she does not mind when people laugh at her. She would do no one a good turn: she keeps her eye and mind on one thing all day—how to do most damage to people.' In presenting this ninth type, the last of the undesirable ones, Semonides contrives a climax: the monkey-woman is in a class by herself (*diakridon*), the greatest evil. The interjection *a talas anēr*, 'ah, the poor wretch', and the repeated *kakon*, 'evil' (72, 77, 82), also indicate heightened emotion.

τὴν δ' ἐκ μελίσσης· τήν τις εὐτυχεῖ λαβών·
κείνη γὰρ οἴη μῶμος οὐ προσιζάνει,
θάλλει δ' ὑπ' αὐτῆς κἀπαέξεται βίος.   85
φίλη δὲ σὺμ φιλέοντι γηράσκει πόσι
τεκοῦσα καλὸν κοὐνομάκλυτον γένος.
κἀριπρεπὴς μὲν ἐν γυναιξὶ γίγνεται
πάσῃσι, θείη δ' ἀμφιδέδρομεν χάρις.
οὐδ' ἐν γυναιξὶν ἥδεται καθημένη,   90
ὅκου λέγουσιν ἀφροδισίους λόγους.
τοίας γυναῖκας ἀνδράσιν χαρίζεται
Ζεὺς τὰς ἀρίστας καὶ πολυφραδεστάτας (83-93).

'Another from a bee: the man who takes her prospers, for on her alone does no blame settle, and his substance flourishes and increases thanks to her. She grows old with a husband whom she loves as he loves her, mother of a handsome and distinguished family. She is conspicuous among all women, and a divine beauty plays around her. She does not enjoy sitting among the women where they tell stories about love-making. Women like her are the best and wisest that Zeus gives men.' The bee-woman may be the only commendable type in the catalogue, but her portrait is painted with affection. The tone is lofty, with impressive epic words (*onomakluton, poluphradestatas*), anaphora (*philē . . . phileonti* 85) and the Homeric echoes of 89. The choice of words in 84–5 is appropriate to the description of the bee: *prosizanei*, 'settles', suggests an insect alighting on flowers, and *thallei* and perhaps *epaexetai*, 'flourishes, increases', fit the image of flowers.

> τὰ δ' ἄλλα φῦλα ταῦτα μηχανῇ Διὸς
> ἔστιν τε πάντα καὶ παρ' ἀνδράσιν μένει.   95
> Ζεὺς γὰρ μέγιστον τοῦτ' ἐποίησεν κακόν,
> γυναῖκας. ἤν τι καὶ δοκέωσιν ὠφελεῖν,
> ἔχοντί τοι μάλιστα γίγνεται κακόν·
> οὐ γάρ κοτ' εὔφρων ἡμέρην διέρχεται
> ἅπασαν, ὅστις σὺν γυναικὶ †πέλεται†,   100
> οὐδ' αἶψα Λιμὸν οἰκίης ἀπώσεται,
> ἐχθρὸν συνοικητῆρα, δυσμενέα θεόν.
> ἀνὴρ δ' ὅταν μάλιστα θυμηδεῖν δοκῇ
> κατ' οἶκον ἢ θεοῦ μοῖραν ἢ ἀνθρώπου χάριν,
> εὑροῦσα μῶμον ἐς μάχην κορύσσεται.   105
> ὅκου γυνὴ γάρ ἐστιν, οὐδ' ἐς οἰκίην
> ξεῖνον μολόντα προφρόνως δεχοίατο.
> ἥτις δέ τοι μάλιστα σωφρονεῖν δοκεῖ,
> αὕτη μέγιστα τυγχάνει λωβωμένη·
> κεχηνότος γὰρ ἀνδρὸς – οἱ δὲ γείτονες   110
> χαίρουσ' ὁρῶντες καὶ τόν, ὡς ἁμαρτάνει.
> τὴν ἣν δ' ἕκαστος αἰνέσει μεμνημένος
> γυναῖκα, τὴν δὲ τοὐτέρου μωμήσεται·
> ἴσην δ' ἔχοντες μοῖραν οὐ γιγνώσκομεν.
> Ζεὺς γὰρ μέγιστον τοῦτ' ἐποίησεν κακόν,   115
> καὶ δεσμὸν ἀμφέθηκεν ἄρρηκτον πέδην,
> ἐξ οὗ τε τοὺς μὲν Ἀίδης ἐδέξατο
> γυναικὸς εἵνεκ' ἀμφιδηριωμένους (94-118).

'But those other tribes of women, thanks to the planning of Zeus, all exist and remain with men; for this is the greatest evil Zeus has created—women. Even if they seem to be giving some help, mischief is surely being done to the husband. For that man never goes through a whole day in cheerfulness who lives with a woman; he will not readily push Starvation out of his house, that enemy under his roof, that hostile deity. Just when a man most feels like having a good time at home, thanks to a god's dispensation or to a man's favour, she finds some fault and arms herself for the fray. For where there is a woman, they could not even give a kindly welcome to a guest who has come to the house. And the one who seems to be most respectable in fact commits the greatest outrages; for while the husband gapes . . .—and the neighbours enjoy seeing how wide of the mark he is too. Every man will be careful to commend his own wife but will find fault with the other man's wife: we fail to realise that we all have the same fate. For this is the greatest evil Zeus has created, and he has shackled us with this chain, an unbreakable fetter, ever since Hades welcomed those warriors who were fighting for the sake of a woman.' In case the message of the first 93 lines did not sink in, Semonides adds 25 lines of generalisation; indeed he may have composed more, since it is not certain that the poem ended at 118: in one view he had just begun a list of mythological examples of ruinous women, commencing with Helen of Troy; but it seems more likely that Stobaeus, who quotes the poem in his *Anthology*, transmitted it in its entirety, and one could argue that *gunaikos heineka*, 'for the sake of a woman', is a suitable opening for the last line of a poem on women, and that *amphidēriōmenous*, the longest word of the poem, makes an impressive ending, just as *poluphradestatas*, the second-longest word, marks the end of the first section (93). The style of the final passage is elevated, with Homeric words (*korussetai*, *-dēriōmenous*), impressively constructed lines (102, 116), enjambment (twice with the word for women, 97, 113!), the personification of 'Starvation' and the repeated statement that woman is the greatest evil (96f., 115), itself echoing the description of the hideous monkey-woman (72). In 110 Semonides apparently resorts to aposiopesis, the figure of speech in which a sentence is left uncompleted: the details of the wife's outrageous behaviour are left to the imagination.

CHAPTER SIX

Gods and Heroes

By the middle of the seventh century when our first extant lyric poetry was composed gods and heroes had been celebrated in three types of poetry: in the Homeric poems the gods played an important role, and characteristic features of their appearance, interests or attributes were reflected by formulaic expressions; Hesiod's *Theogony* gave a systematic account of the origin and genealogies of the gods; and the earliest of the Homeric Hymns, for example the hymns to Demeter, to Delian Apollo and to Aphrodite, had been addressed to individual gods and given an account of their nature and exploits. All three types of poetry were composed in dactylic hexameters.

Xenophanes wrote, 'Since from the beginning the learning of all men has been in accordance with Homer . . .' (9D.), and Herodotus gave it as his opinion that it was Hesiod and Homer who taught the Greeks the lineage, titles, honours, exploits and appearance of their gods (2.53). Homer's picture of the gulf between gods and men was copied by the lyric poets: the gods are immortal and live an easy life on Mount Olympus, whereas men are *ephēmeroi*, 'living one day at a time' (Semonides 1.3), no more permanent than the leaves of the trees (Semonides 29D., Mimnermus 2). The gods, Zeus above all, are in control of the world, and man stumbles along blindly (Semonides 1, Solon 13). Yet the gods bridge the gulf and intervene personally in this world to support their favourites and destroy those who have offended them: Homer's Athena talks to Achilles or Odysseus, and similarly Sappho can record the comforting words spoken by Aphrodite when she appeared in answer to her prayer (1). The poets' prayers themselves owe many of their features to the prayers of Homeric heroes. Where metre allows, as in elegiac couplets, a poet will repeat a Homeric formula: Mimnermus has *khrusēs Aphroditēs*, 'golden Aphrodite' (1.1), and *rhododaktulos Eōs*, 'rose-fingered Dawn' (12.3); or he will use a variation of Homer's epithet: Solon's *Hēphaistou polutekhneō*, 'Hephaestus of many skills' (13.49), recalls Homer's *Hēphaistos klutotekhnēs*, 'Hephaestus famed for his skills'.

Hesiod's achievement in the *Theogony* was to impose order on a large body of mythological material, principally by his use, perhaps in some cases his construction, of the family-trees of the gods. Many of his versions of their interrelationships and attributes became standard; when Solon, for example, begins a long poem with an invocation to the Muses,

> Μνημοσύνης καὶ Ζηνὸς Ὀλυμπίου ἀγλαὰ τέκνα,
> Μοῦσαι Πιερίδες (13.1-2),

'Glorious children of Memory and Olympian Zeus, Muses of Pieria', he follows Hesiod's account of their parentage and birthplace. Among Hesiod's gods are Justice, Lawfulness, Famine and so on, and Solon, Semonides and later poets likewise regarded these as divine powers to whom mankind is subject. Furthermore, the *Theogony* and *Works and Days* alike represent Zeus as closely concerned with justice, a connection which does not emerge clearly in Homer, and this view of the greatest of the gods as being also the god of justice was to have a pervasive influence on later Greek thought. At the end of the *Theogony* our text states a new theme, *gunaikōn phulon*, 'the company of women'; this formed a transition to *The Catalogue of Women*, a poem, fragments of which are extant, usually attributed to Hesiod in antiquity but possibly no earlier than 600 B.C. Its subject was the heroines who had intercourse with gods and gave birth to distinguished children, for example, Coronis, mother of Asclepius by Apollo, and like the authentic works of Hesiod it had great influence on later writers.

The Homeric Hymns are a collection of 34 hymns to various gods, composed in epic language but later than Homer if we date the *Iliad* and *Odyssey* to the second half of the eighth century: some may belong to the seventh century, e.g. the hymn to Demeter, some are demonstrably much later, e.g. the hymn to Ares. Four of them, to Demeter, Apollo (in fact two hymns, to Delian and Pythian Apollo), Hermes and Aphrodite, are several hundred lines long, others have only a few lines and contain little more than an invocation. Their importance for lyric poetry lies in the facts that they were literary works, performed like Homer by travelling rhapsodes, rather than hymns intended for cult purposes, and that they described the characteristics and exploits of the gods, often, as in the hymn to the Dioscuri, in short compass. It is instructive to compare Alcaeus' poem to the Dioscuri with it, but one must remember that the Homeric Hymn is in dactylic, not lyric, metre, and that there is no certainty that it was composed before Alcaeus' time.

In addition to these works of literature a few examples of cult hymns have survived, some of which may be of great antiquity: a good example is the hymn to Dionysus sung by the women of Elis:

> ἐλθεῖν ἥρω Διόνυσε
> Ἀλείων ἐς ναὸν
> ἁγνὸν σὺν Χαρίτεσσιν
> ἐς ναὸν
> τῷ βοέῳ ποδὶ δύων,
> ἄξιε ταῦρε,
> ἄξιε ταῦρε (871).

'Come, hero Dionysus, to the holy temple of the Eleans along with the Graces, entering the temple with your ox foot, worthy bull, worthy bull.' The details of the text are uncertain, but we note the use of repeated phrases, a feature of later hymn-writing, and the metre which, although it has dactylic elements, is not the dactylic hexameter of Homer, Hesiod and the Hymns but a freer lyric rhythm. It is remarkable that Dionysus should be invoked as 'hero' rather than as god; his animal form is familiar to us from Euripides' *Bacchae*, where he is requested to appear to his worshippers in the shape of a bull (1017).

*   *   *

Various shadowy figures, mythical rather than historical, were said to have composed hymns. Herodotus says that the ancient hymns still sung in his day on Delos were the work of Olen of Lycia (4.35), and Pausanias calls him the composer of the oldest Greek hymns (9.27.2), quoting from the hymns to Hera (2.13.3), Achaeia (5.7.8) and Eileithyia (8.21.3). Pamphos and Orpheus were said to have composed hymns to Eros and Demeter, Musaeus a hymn to Demeter, and so on.

One of the earliest Greek poets for whom a firm date is given is Eumelus of Corinth, who belongs to the second half of the eighth century. Most of his poems were epics, composed in dactylic hexameters, but two lines survive from a *prosodion* or processional hymn which he wrote for the Messenians to perform at Delos:

τῷ γὰρ Ἰθωμάτᾳ καταθύμιος ἔπλετο Μοῖσα
ἁ καθαρὰ καὶ ἐλεύθερα σάμβαλ' ἔχοισα (696).

'For the god of Ithome took pleasure in the Muse, the pure Muse wearing her free sandals.' Ithome is the mountain fortress of Messenia, Zeus its god. The first line is dactylic hexameter, the second a dactylic pentameter of lyric type.

In the middle of the seventh century Terpander of Lesbos, founder of the first 'school' of music in Sparta, composed hexameter 'preludes', which are thought to have resembled the Homeric Hymns; nothing survives. Shortly afterwards various musicians of the second 'school', Thaletas of Gortyn, Xenodamus of Cythera and Xenocritus of Italian Locri are said to have composed paeans, hymns in honour of Apollo.

We are on firmer ground with Archilochus, notorious for his invective poetry but associated also with the worship of Dionysus, Apollo and perhaps Demeter. In two poems he describes himself as 'leading off' a religious song:

αὐτὸς ἐξάρχων πρὸς αὐλὸν Λέσβιον παιήονα (121),

'myself leading off the Lesbian paean to the accompaniment of the pipe'. The paean must have been developed on Lesbos, perhaps by Terpander. The verb *exarkhein* is a technical word used of the singer or instrumentalist who starts off a choral performance, presumably by indicating the pitch and giving a down-beat or by singing or playing the first phrase. Archilochus uses it again in a well-known fragment:

ὡς Διωνύσου ἄνακτος καλὸν ἐξάρξαι μέλος
οἶδα διθύραμβον οἴνῳ συγκεραυνωθεὶς φρένας (120),

'since I know how to lead off the beautiful song of Dionysus, the dithyramb, when my mind is blitzed by the wine'. This is our earliest reference to the dithyramb, the hymn in honour of Dionysus. The drunkenness of the 'leader' does not suggest a formal hymn so much as some artless formula of praise. We know, however, from the inscription on the Parian Monument, set up to honour the local poet, Archilochus, that he composed a hymn for Dionysus; the beginnings of four or five lines have survived on the monument, together with scraps of a narrative which can be interpreted as follows: at a festival on Paros Archilochus improvised verses about Dionysus and taught them to a chorus of citizens; but they were considered too ribald—a reference to unripe grapes and sweet figs probably had sexual overtones, and Dionysus seems to have been called *Oipholios*, 'the Fucker'—and Archilochus was brought to court; but the men of Paros became impotent, and when they consulted the Delphic oracle they were told to respect Archilochus. It looks as though he succeeded in introducing a fertility rite of Dionysus, presumably with phallic worship, to the island.

The worship of Demeter also was important on Paros; Archilochus' grandfather was said to have been associated with the introduction of her rites to the Parian colony on Thasos, and Archilochus was said, perhaps incorrectly, to have composed a hymn called *Iobakkhoi*, 'Hail, Bacchants', part of which referred to Demeter and Persephone:

Δήμητρος ἁγνῆς καὶ Κόρης
τὴν πανήγυριν σέβων (322),

'revering the festal assembly of holy Demeter and the Maiden'. He addressed Hephaestus in one poem, asking for his assistance (108).

Mythological themes seem to have been of little concern to him, but we know of his poem on Deianira, in which he narrated her wooing by Achelous, the assault on her by the centaur Nessus and Heracles' killing of the centaur (286–8).

Arion is the earliest poet known to have worked for a patron: he is associated especially with the court of Periander, tyrant of Corinth at the end of the seventh century, and he composed dithyrambs which he taught to Corinthian choirs. Herodotus (1.23) and Aristotle in fact say that he 'invented' the dithyramb, but that is to take no account of Archilochus' poetry. Herodotus says he gave names to his dithyrambs, perhaps titles descriptive of their contents, but neither titles nor fragments remain. He is said to have composed a hymn of thanks to Poseidon when he was rescued after shipwreck by a dolphin, but the lines quoted as the hymn by Aelian (939 *PMG*) are not authentic.

The elegiac and iambic poets wrote little that could be classed as hymns, but they were fond of referring or appealing to the gods at the beginnings of their poems or of new sections of poems. We have seen that Tyrtaeus introduces a long exhortation to bravery with a reminder that the Spartans are descended from Zeus (via Heracles and his son Hyllus) :

> ἀλλ', Ἡρακλῆος γὰρ ἀνικήτου γένος ἐστέ,
> θαρσεῖτ'· οὔπω Ζεὺς αὐχένα λοξὸν ἔχει (11.1-2).

'Come! You are the descendants of invincible Heracles, so be confident : Zeus does not hold his neck aslant.' The sense must be that Zeus is sympathetic and has not averted his eyes from the fortunes of his people. Solon writes similarly that Athens has a strong protectress in Pallas Athene, who 'holds her hands over us' (4.1–4), and Theognis begins poems by referring to the guardianship of Zeus and of Apollo (757ff., 773ff.). Solon's long poem about money-making opens, as we have noted, with a formal invocation of the Muses; elsewhere he speaks of the inscrutability of the gods' intentions (17). Semonides began a gloomy poem on the powerlessness of mankind by contrasting the power of Zeus:

> ὦ παῖ, τέλος μὲν Ζεὺς ἔχει βαρύκτυπος
> πάντων ὅσ' ἐστὶ καὶ τίθησ' ὅκῃ θέλει,
> νοῦς δ' οὐκ ἐπ' ἀνθρώποισιν . . . (1.1-3).

'Boy, loud-thundering Zeus holds the end (i.e. controls the outcome) of everything that is and arranges it as he wishes. Men have no intelligence . . .'

Mimnermus wrote a poem in elegiacs about the never-ending hardship endured by the Sun, perhaps in order to make the point that not only man but even the Sun-god has a life full of toil:

> Ἠέλιος μὲν γὰρ ἔλαχεν πόνον ἤματα πάντα,
> οὐδέ κοτ' ἄμπαυσις γίγνεται οὐδεμία
> ἵπποισίν τε καὶ αὐτῷ, ἐπεὶ ῥοδοδάκτυλος Ἠὼς
> Ὠκεανὸν προλιποῦσ' οὐρανὸν εἰσαναβῇ·
> τὸν μὲν γὰρ διὰ κῦμα φέρει πολυήρατος εὐνή,   5
> κοίλη Ἡφαίστου χερσὶν ἐληλαμένη
> χρυσοῦ τιμήεντος, ὑπόπτερος, ἄκρον ἐφ' ὕδωρ
> εὕδονθ' ἁρπαλέως χώρου ἀφ' Ἑσπερίδων
> γαῖαν ἐς Αἰθιόπων, ἵνα δὴ θοὸν ἅρμα καὶ ἵπποι
> ἑστᾶσ', ὄφρ' Ἠὼς ἠριγένεια μόλῃ.   10
> ἔνθ' ἐπεβήσεθ' ἑῶν ὀχέων Ὑπερίονος υἱός (12).

'For the Sun got as his portion toil for all his days, and there is never any respite for him and his horses when once rose-fingered Dawn leaves Ocean and climbs the heavens. He is carried over the waves by the lovely bed, a hollow, winged bed made of precious gold by the hands of Hephaestus which rapidly carries him asleep over the surface of the water from the country of the Hesperides to the land of the Ethiopians, where his swift chariot and horses stand till early-born Dawn comes. Then the son of Hyperion mounts his chariot.' Mimnermus lingers over his description of the Sun's bed, adding epithets without connectives. His language is melodious, his manner fluent; only two of the couplets end with a strong stop.

Alcman is the first writer of choral poetry about whom we can speak with some confidence. The ancients deliberated whether he was born in Lydia or Sparta, but it is certain and more important that his poetry was composed in the Laconian dialect for Spartan audiences. His *melē*, songs, were arranged in six books by some Alexandrian scholar: there may have been two books of partheneia, 'maiden-songs', and we hear also of hymns and wedding-songs, but it is often difficult to assign our fragments to one of these genres.

Apollo is addressed more than once; for example,

Fάδοι Διὸς δόμῳ χορὸς ἁμὸς καὶ τοί, Fάναξ (45),

'May our choir please the house of Zeus and you, lord'; and he is associated with the Muses in fr. 46 under the title (W)ekatos, 'Far-shooter'. Elsewhere he is *Lētoidēs* (48), 'Leto's son', *Lukaios* (49, 50), 'Lycian', and a player of the pipes (51). The words *khrusokoma philomolpe* (S1), 'golden-haired, song-lover', are also likely to have been directed at him. He was worshipped in Sparta at the festival of Carnea, which Alcman mentions (52), and some of our scraps must have come from hymns performed then. Paeans could be sung in the men's messes:

θοίναις δὲ καὶ ἐν θιάσοισιν
ἀνδρείων παρὰ δαιτυμόνεσσι πρέπει παιᾶνα κατάρχην (98).

'At feasts and the gatherings of the men's mess it is fitting to begin the paean among the banqueters.'

Apollo's sister, Artemis, was also worshipped in and near Sparta, and she too appears in the fragments of Alcman's poetry. It is not certain that he was the author of the invocation

Ἄρταμι ῥύτειρα τόξων (170),

'Artemis, drawer of the bow'; but he is said to have summoned her from countless mountains, cities and rivers. The words

Ἀρτέμιτος θεράποντα (54),

'the servant of Artemis', are his and may possibly refer to himself, and the description

Ϝεσσαμένα πέρι δέρματα θηρῶν (53),

'clad in the skins of beasts', would fit her. Another scrap refers to

θριδακίσκας τε καὶ κριβανωτώς (94),

'cakes and loaves', used in the festival of Artemis the Maiden.
    Athena is addressed as

Ϝάνασσα Διὸς θύγατερ (43),

'lady, daughter of Zeus'; and Aphrodite is asked to appear,

Κύπρον ἱμερτὰν λιποῖσα καὶ Πάφον περιρρύταν (55),

'leaving lovely Cyprus and sea-girt Paphos'. The Dioscuri were worshipped with divine honours in Therapnae, and Alcman refers to them more than once:

σιοῖσί τ' ἀνθρώποισί τ' αἰδοιεστάτοι
ναίοισι νέ[ρθεν γᾶς ἀειζώοι] σιόδματον τέγος
Κάστωρ τε πώλων ὠκέων δματῆρες, ἱππόται σοφοί,
καὶ Πωλυδεύκης κυδρός (2: Page's restoration).

'Most revered by gods and men they dwell, for ever alive, beneath the earth in a god-built house, Castor and glorious Polydeuces, tamers of swift steeds, skilled horsemen.' Their horses were called Xanthus and Cyllarus (25).
    Dionysus was worshipped on the slopes of Mount Taygetus which towers above the vale of Sparta, and six well-known lines are probably addressed to a Bacchante:

πολλάκι δ' ἐν κορυφαῖς ὀρέων, ὄκα
σιοῖσι Ϝάδη πολύφανος ἑορτά,
χρύσιον ἄγγος ἔχοισα, μέγαν σκύφον,
οἷά τε ποιμένες ἄνδρες ἔχοισιν,
χερσὶ λεόντεον ἐν γάλα θεῖσα
τυρὸν ἐτύρησας μέγαν ἄτρυφον Ἀργειφόντα (56).

'Often on the peaks of the mountains, when the feast with its many torches pleases the gods, holding a golden vessel, a great bowl such as shepherds hold, you put in it with your hands the milk of a lioness and made a great firm cheese for the Slayer of Argus [Hermes].' The rhetorician Menander says that according to 'a Laconian poet' Dionysus could milk lionesses; the miracle has its parallels in the feats described in Euripides' *Bacchae*.

Tyche, Fortune, is personified as

> Εὐνομίας <τε> καὶ Πειθῶς ἀδελφὰ
> καὶ Προμαθήας θυγάτηρ (64),

'sister of Lawfulness and Persuasion and daughter of Forethought'.

The Muse is addressed more often by Alcman than any other deity. This may be due in part at least to the importance of her cult in Sparta: she had a temple of her own, and the army made sacrifice to her before battle. Alcman is said to have called the Muses the daughters of Uranus and Ge, Heaven and Earth (67: cf. 5 fr. 2 i 28), so linking them with the most ancient gods; yet more than once he invokes the Muse as 'daughter of Zeus' (27, 28), and he links them with Mnemosyne, Memory (8.9), although we cannot be certain that he made them the children of Zeus and Memory as Hesiod did. Among their epithets are *Olumpiades* (3 fr. 1.1), 'Olympian', and *ōraniaphi* (28), 'heavenly'.

A fragmentary commentary on one of Alcman's poems (5) gives his eccentric account of creation: the basic material, *hulē*, was first organised by Thetis, whose name may have been linked with the verb *tithenai*, 'to place'; then Poros, the Contriver, appeared 'like a beginning', followed by Tekmor, 'Termination'. This cosmogony must have been related in one of Alcman's hymns.

Our two longest examples of Alcman's work are papyrus fragments of *partheneia*, hymns for girls' choirs. One of them (3) refers to the *puleōn*, which an ancient authority describes as a garland offered by Spartans to Hera, so that the poem may have been performed at a gathering in her honour. Two parts of the poem are reasonably well preserved. The first stanza, supplemented by Page, runs as follows:

> Μώσαι 'Ολ]υμπιάδες, περί με φρένας
> ἱμέρῳ νέα]ς ἀοιδᾶς
> πίμπλατ'· ἰθύ]ω δ' ἀκούσαι
> παρθενηΐ]ας ὀπὸς
> πρὸς αἰθέ]ρα καλὸν ὑμνιοισᾶν μέλος   5
>   ].οι
> ὕπνον ἀ]πὸ γλεφάρων σκεδ[α]σεῖ γλυκὺν
>   ]ς δέ μ' ἄγει πεδ' ἀγῶν' ἴμεν
> ἆχι μά]λιστα κόμ[αν ξ]ανθὰν τινάξω (3.1-9).

'Olympian Muses, fill my heart with longing for a new song: I am eager to hear the maiden voice of girls singing to the heavens a fair melody . . . (it) will scatter sweet sleep from my eyes . . . and leads me to go to the gathering where more than anywhere else I shall toss my yellow hair.' The lines are probably sung by a solo singer who introduces the song of the whole choir. If

v. 8 is correctly supplemented with the word *Antheia*]*s*, the gathering will be in honour of Hera Antheia, the goddess of flowers worshipped at Argos.

Fifty lines later the girls are singing of Astymeloisa, who seems to lead their worship, and the tone of their song is strongly erotic:

> λυσιμελεῖ τε πόσῳ, τακερώτερα
> δ' ὕπνω καὶ σανάτω ποτιδέρκεται,
> οὐδέ τι μαψιδίως γλυκ[ῆα κ]ήνα ·
>
> ᾽Αστυμέλοισα δέ μ' οὐδὲν ἀμείβεται,
> ἀλλὰ τὸ]ν πυλεῶν' ἔχοισα   65
> ὥ]τις αἰγλά[ε]ντος ἀστὴρ
> ὠρανῶ διαιπετὴς
> ἢ χρύσιον ἔρνος ἢ ἁπαλὸ[ν ψίλ]ον
>   ]ν
>   ]. διέβα ταναοῖς πο[σί ·   70
> καλλίκ]ομος νοτία Κινύρα χ[άρ]ις,
> ἤν, ἐπὶ π]αρσενικᾶς χαίταισιν ἴσδει ·
>
> ἦ μὰν ᾽Α]στυμέλοισα κατὰ στρατὸν
> ἔρχεται] μέλημα δάμῳ . . .
>
> ἆσ]σον [ἰο]ῖσ' ἁπαλᾶς χηρὸς λάβοι,   80
> αἶψα κ' [ἐγὼν ἱ]κέτις κήνας γενοίμαν (61-74, 80-1).

'. . . with desire that loosens the limbs, and she looks (at me?) more meltingly than sleep or death, and not (without reason is she sweet?) But Astymeloisa makes no answer to me: holding the garland, like a star flying through the shining heavens, or a golden branch or soft down . . . she went over with her long feet; see, (giving beauty to her tresses?) the moist charm of Cinyras sits on the maiden's hair. Truly Astymeloisa goes through the host the darling of the people . . . May she come nearer and take my soft hand; quickly I would become her suppliant.' The song is beautiful and at the same time enigmatic. It has striking imagery, particularly in the mention of the girl's glances that are more melting than sleep or death, allusiveness in the elaborate periphrasis of 'the moist charm of Cinyras', by which Cyprian perfume is meant, and a lightness of touch, for example, in the description of Astymeloisa ('darling of the town') as *meléma damôi*, 'darling of the people'. The metre is a lively combination of dactyls and trochees.

Our longest fragment of Alcman (1), a papyrus with seventy nearly complete lines preceded by thirty-four half-lines, displays the same features. The text has been known since 1863, but there is little agreement over its interpretation. It bristles with difficulties, both in points of detail and in major questions such as the identity of the deity in whose honour it was sung. The stanzas are of fourteen lines, the metre strongly trochaic with dactyls in the last two lines, and there may have been ten stanzas in all. The scholar Proclus says of partheneia that they praise both gods and men; it would appear that Alcman devoted the first five stanzas to his invocation and mythical matter, the second five to the more light-hearted personal section in which two girls, Agido and Hagesichora, are prominent.

Our text begins with a list of the sons of the mythical Spartan king Hippocoon, who were killed by their cousins, Castor and Polydeuces, with the aid of Heracles. Such catalogues—ten warriors are listed by name—seem to have been a valued element of early hexameter poetry. The passage ends with a generalisation:

> μή τις ἀνθ]ρώπων ἐς ὡρανὸν ποτήσθω
> μηδὲ πη]ρήτω γαμῆν τὰν Ἀφροδίταν
> Κυπρίαν F]άν[α]σσαν ἢ τιν'
>] ἢ παίδα Πόρκω
> εἰναλίω· Χά]ριτες δὲ Διὸς δ[ό]μον
> ἀμφιέπου]σιν ἐρογλεφάροι (16-21).

'Let not any man fly to heaven, nor try to marry Aphrodite, the Cyprian queen, or any . . . or a daughter of Porcus of the sea: the house of Zeus is managed by the Graces of the seductive eyes.' Some such attempt must have been made by the sons of Hippocoon, who are described elsewhere as 'rival suitors' of Castor and Polydeuces; but what was possible for the heavenly twins, sons of Zeus, was ruled out for the human sons of Hippocoon. The next section of the hymn is so damaged that we cannot tell whether Alcman is concluding the story of the Hippocoontidae or giving a second example of the punishment of hybris: 'and they suffered unforgettably, having devised evil.'

The following section, the first that is complete on the papyrus, begins with further moralising and then moves from this gloomy material to the cheerfulness of the secular theme:

> ἔστι τις σιῶν τίσις·
> ὁ δ' ὄλβιος, ὅστις εὔφρων
> ἀμέραν [δι]απλέκει
> ἄκλαυτος· ἐγὼν δ' ἀείδω
> Ἀγιδῶς τὸ φῶς· ὁρῶ   40
> F' ὥτ' ἄλιον, ὄνπερ ἄμιν
> Ἀγιδὼ μαρτύρεται
> φαίνην· ἐμὲ δ' οὔτ' ἐπαινῆν
> οὔτε μωμήσθαι νιν ἁ κλεννὰ χοραγὸς
> οὐδ' ἁμῶς ἐῆ· δοκεῖ γὰρ ἤμεν αὔτα   45
> ἐκπρεπὴς τὼς ὥπερ αἴτις
> ἐν βοτοῖς στάσειεν ἵππον

παγὸν ἀεθλοφόρον καναχάποδα
τῶν ὑποπετριδίων ὀνείρων (36-49).

'There is such a thing as the vengeance of the gods. That man is blessed who in wisdom weaves to the end the web of his day, unweeping. My song is the radiance of Agido: I see her as the sun, which Agido summons to appear for us; but our distinguished chorus-leader in no way allows *me* to praise or blame her; for she herself appears supreme, just as if one were to put a horse among cattle, a sturdy prize-winning horse of echoing hooves, such as one dreams of in the shade of a rock.' Difficulties arise at once, and space allows only a statement of one position with no consideration of alternative views. Agido is stated as the theme of the singers, only to be displaced at once by 'our chorus-leader', clearly Hagesichora, whose name, which means Leader of the Chorus, will soon be given. The imagery of light is important, the comparison with the prize horse striking.

η οὐχ ὁρῇς; ὁ μὲν κέλης 50
Ἐνητικός· ἁ δὲ χαίτα
τᾶς ἐμᾶς ἀνεψιᾶς
Ἁγησιχόρας ἐπανθεῖ
χρυσὸς [ὡ]ς ἀκήρατος·
τό τ᾽ ἀργύριον πρόσωπον, 55
διαφάδαν τί τοι λέγω;
Ἁγησιχόρα μὲν αὕτα·
ἁ δὲ δευτέρα πεδ᾽ Ἀγιδὼ τὸ Ϝεῖδος
ἵππος Ἰβηνῷ Κολαξαῖος δραμήται·
ταὶ Πεληάδες γὰρ ἁμιν 60
Ὀρθρίᾳ φᾶρος φεροίσαις
νύκτα δι᾽ ἀμβροσίαν ἅτε σήριον
ἄστρον ἀυηρομέναι μάχονται (50-63).

'Why, don't you see? The race-horse is Venetic, but the hair of my cousin Hagesichora blossoms like pure gold, and her silver face—why do I tell you plain? This is Hagesichora here; but the second after Agido in beauty shall race like a Colaxaean horse against an Ibenian. For, you see, as we bring a plough to Orthria the Pleiads fight against us, rising like the star Sirius through the ambrosial night.' Some of the obscurity in this stanza might have been dispelled by gestures on the part of the girls. For example, the contrast between the Venetic race-horse and Hagesichora (*men . . . de*) makes it likely that Agido is the race-horse, even although it was Hagesichora who was compared a moment earlier to the prize horse. If so, the chorus once more turn immediately from praise of Agido to praise of Hagesichora, but this time proclaim, still with equine imagery, that any third girl who might be mentioned is far less beautiful than Agido. The emphasis on the good looks of these girls is now explained: at the festival the choir, a family group if the word 'cousin' is taken literally, is competing against another choir called the Peleiades, either 'Pleiads' or 'Doves', and success will depend partly on the physical appearance of the girls and their leaders. The star-imagery harks back to the emphasis on light in the previous stanza. At line 61 we seem to be given the name of the deity who is being honoured: Orthria means 'she of the Dawn', and a marginal comment in the papyrus identifies her with Orthia or Ortheia, a goddess of fertility and vegetation equated in later times with Artemis; Artemis Orthia had a rich shrine in Sparta. Why she should be a dawn-goddess is not clear. In line 87 'Aotis', 'she who dwells in the East', may have the same reference: there was a cult of *Artemis proseōia*, 'Artemis towards the East', in Euboea.

> οὔτε γάρ τι πορφύρας
> τόσσος κόρος ὥστ' ἀμύναι,   65
> οὔτε ποικίλος δράκων
> παγχρύσιος, οὐδὲ μίτρα
> Λυδία, νεανίδων
> ἰανογ[λ]εφάρων ἄγαλμα,
> οὐδὲ ταὶ Ναννῶς κόμαι,   70
> ἀλλ' οὐ[δ'] Ἀρέτα σιειδής,
> οὐδὲ Σύλακίς τε καὶ Κλεησισήρα,
> οὐδ' ἐς Αἰνησιμβρ[ό]τας ἐνθοῖσα φασεῖς·
> Ἀσταφίς [τ]έ μοι γένοιτο
> καὶ ποτιγλέποι Φίλυλλα   75
> Δαμαρ[έ]τα τ' ἐρατά τε Fιανθεμίς·
> ἀλλ' Ἀγησιχόρα με τηρεῖ (64-77).

'For we have not such abundance of purple as to ward them off, no intricate snake-bracelet of solid gold, no, nor a headdress from Lydia, that adornment of dark-eyed girls, nor the hair of Nanno, nor again godlike Areta nor Thylacis and Cleësithera; nor will you go to Aenesimbrota's and say, "May I have Astaphis; may Philylla look my way and Damarata and lovely Vianthemis": no, Hagesichora is my protection.' The choir lists the assets which they do not themselves possess, moving from dress and jewellery to the beauty of various girls (listed in the second catalogue of the poem), and taking comfort from the protection afforded by Hagesichora. If *tērei*, 'protects', is the correct reading, the military metaphor of *makhontai* (63), *amunai* (65) and later *irēnas* (91) is maintained; but the papyrus may have had the word *teirei*, which some explain as 'Hagesichora distresses me' (since I cannot help loving her). The identity of Aenesimbrota is obscure: she may have been the mother or the teacher of the four girls whose names follow.

> οὐ γὰρ ἁ κ[α]λλίσφυρος
> Ἀγησιχ[ό]ρ[α] πάρ' αὐτεῖ,

'Αγιδοῖ [δ' ἴκτ]αρ μένει   80
θωστήρ[ιά τ'] ἄμ' ἐπαινεῖ;
ἀλλὰ τᾶν [εὐχάς], σιοί,
δέξασθε· [σι]ῶν γὰρ ἄνα
καὶ τέλος· [χο]ροστάτις,
Fείποιμί κ', [ἐ]γὼν μὲν αὐτὰ   85
παρσένος μάταν ἀπὸ θράνω λέλακα
γλαύξ· ἐγὼ[ν] δὲ τᾶ μὲν 'Αώτι μάλιστα
Fανδάνην ἐρῶ· πόνων γὰρ
ἄμιν ἰάτωρ ἔγεντο·
ἐξ 'Αγησιχόρ[ας] δὲ νεάνιδες   90
ἰρ]ήνας ἐρατ[ᾶ]ς ἐπέβαν (78-91).

'For is not Hagesichora of the lovely ankles with us here? Does she not wait
near Agido and commend our festival? Accept their prayers, gods: for to the
gods belong fulfilment and completion. Chorus-leader, I shall say these words:
I am myself a girl screeching pointlessly like an owl from a rafter; but I do
wish most of all to please Aotis, since she has proved the healer of our toils; but
thanks to Hagesichora girls trod the paths of lovely peace.'

We return to the religious ceremony—and to the obscurity which veils it
from us. Hagesichora and Agido are both offering prayer to the gods, now
plural; and the chorus wish to please Aotis, the Dawn-goddess, who has healed
their toils: are they referring to the labour of preparing for the ceremony and
the public performance, toils which 'Aotis' has healed in the past by granting
victory? And is the final reference to the paths of peace another metaphor for
victory, which at the human level has been due to Hagesichora's leadership?

τῷ] τε γὰρ σηραφόρῳ
αὐ]τῶς εδ[
τ[ῷ] κυβερνάτᾳ δὲ χρὴ
κ[ἠ]ν νᾶϊ μάλιστ' ἀκούην·
ἁ δὲ τᾶν Σηρην[ί]δων
ἀοιδοτέρα μ[ὲν οὐχί,
σιαὶ γάρ, ἀντ[ὶ δ' ἕνδεκα
παίδων δεκ[ὰς ἅδ' ἀείδ]ει·
φθέγγεται δ' [ἄρ'] ὥ[τ' ἐπὶ] Ξάνθω ῥοαῖσι
κύκνος· ἁ δ' ἐπιμέρῳ ξανθᾷ κομίσκᾳ (92-101).

'For like the trace-horse . . .; and in a ship too one ought to obey the helmsman
above all; and she is of course not more melodious than the Sirens, for they are
goddesses; but this our choir of ten sings as well as eleven girls; why, its voice is
like that of the swan on the waters of Xanthus; and she with her lovely yellow
hair (is a fine leader and will bring us victory?).' The papyrus text breaks off
only four lines before the end of the poem which is marked by a coronis in the

margin. Hagesichora is almost certainly the main subject of the final stanza: she steers the choir in the dance as the trace-horse the chariot and the helmsman the ship. We gather that the choir had ten members and guess that the rival choir had eleven. The tone is confident as befits the end of a competitive song.

It is easy to be dismayed by the countless problems of interpretation and by the parochialism of the allusions; but one cannot miss the gaiety of the metre, the variety and vividness of the imagery, and the sprightliness with which the girls allude to themselves, their leaders and their rivals. Ancient critics noted that partheneia were less solemn than other genres of choral poetry, and there is a decided lack of solemnity in at least the last five stanzas of Alcman's poem.

*   *   *

The second great figure in the history of choral lyric is Stesichorus of Himera in north Sicily. His work, which belongs to the first half of the sixth century, differs markedly from that of Alcman: whereas Alcman composed for Spartan audiences and recounted Spartan myth, Stesichorus drew on the sagas which were the heritage of all Greece, the tales of the Trojan War, the Argonauts, Heracles, the Theban story, Meleager. His use of epic material and dactylic rhythms led critics to call him 'most Homeric'; like Homer he used formulaic epithets generously, sometimes giving them an unexpected twist in their application, he was fond of direct speech, and he avoided moralising. The titles of a dozen of the poems in his twenty-six books are known, and at least one, the *Geryoneis*, ran to 780 lines, perhaps even to 1300. This great length has led scholars to wonder whether the performance was really choral rather than solo, but we cannot say with confidence that poems of this length were beyond the capacities of a choir: Pindar's fourth *Pythian* has 299 long lines, the equivalent of 500–600 of Stesichorus' short lines, and dramatic choirs, for example in the *Agamemnon*, had a large amount to learn. Moreover, Stesichorus composed his poem in triads, i.e. in a system of three stanzas called strophe, antistrophe and epode, in which strophe and antistrophe have the same metrical pattern: the *Geryoneis*, for example, has triads of 9+9+8 lines, and there are at least 30 triads, perhaps 50; and it has always been assumed that such triadic structure was related to the movements of a dancing chorus.

Stesichorus' poetry is concerned with heroes rather than gods, although like most Greek narrative poets he allows divine intervention in the exploits of his heroes. We hear of his 'paeans', and Clement of Alexandria says he invented the 'hymn', but our knowledge of the contents of his poetry does not square with this information.

The stories of Heracles provided the material for several poems, the *Geryoneis*, *Cycnus*, *Cerberus* and perhaps *Scylla*, and the papyrus fragments of the *Geryoneis* give some idea of his manner. The story of the tenth labour of

Heracles is known from Hesiod, Apollodorus and vase-paintings: he had to fetch the cattle of Geryon from Erytheia, an island near the stream of Ocean, without demand or payment. Geryon, son of Chrysaor and Callirrhoe (who was daughter of the Titan Oceanus), was king of Tartessus in Spain and reputedly the strongest man alive. He had three heads, six hands and three bodies joined at the waist. His cattle were guarded by the herdsman, Eurytion, son of Ares, and his two-headed watchdog, Orthus. Heracles reached Erytheia after adventures with the Sun-god and Oceanus, killed Orthus with his club, despatched Eurytion in the same way, began to march off with the herd, fought against Geryon, whom he killed with a poisoned arrow, and so drove off the cattle.

Much of this material is found in our fragments of the poem, together with further detail which indicates how discursive Stesichorus was: for example, Heracles at one point drinks from a large cup 'which Pholus had given him after mixing it': this alludes to Heracles' entertainment by the centaur on the occasion of his fourth labour, the quest for the Erymanthian boar. His journey to Erytheia in the Sun-god's cup must have been described in leisurely fashion: the end of the episode runs,

> ἆμος δ' Ὑπεριονίδα <ἲ>ς
> δέπας ἐσκατέβαινεν χρύσεον ὄ-
> φρα δι' Ὠκεανοῖο περάσαις
> ἀφίκοιθ' ἱαρᾶς ποτὶ βένθεα νυ-
> κτὸς ἐρεμνᾶς   5
> ποτὶ ματέρα κουριδίαν τ' ἄλοχον
> παίδας τε φίλους,
> ὁ δ' ἐς ἄλσος ἔβα δάφναισι κατα-
> σκιόεν ποσὶ παῖς Διὸς . . . (S 17).

'And when the mighty son of Hyperion was entering the golden cup so that he might cross over Ocean and reach the depths of holy, black night and his mother and wedded wife and dear children, he [Heracles], son of Zeus, entered on foot the grove that was shadowed with laurels.' One begins to see the point of Quintilian's criticism, 'redundat atque effunditur', 'he is redundant and effusive'. The birthplace of Eurytion is described and possibly events of his early childhood. It seems that Menoites, who tended the cattle of Hades nearby, takes the news of Heracles' arrival to Geryon and urges him not to forget his parents by fighting Heracles and dying at his hands; Geryon makes lengthy reply. His mother Callirrhoe adds her prayers. There is a council of the gods, in which Athena, protectress of Heracles, addresses Poseidon, Geryon's paternal grandfather. Heracles debates how to kill Geryon and decides on a poisoned arrow:

> στυγε[ρ]οῦ
> θανάτοι]ο [τέλος

κ]εφ[αλ]ᾷ πέρι [   ] ἔχων, πεφορυ-
γ]μένος αἵματ[ι   ]ι τε χολᾷ,

ὀλεσάνορος αἰολοδε[ίρ]ου   5
ὀδύναισιν Ὕδρας· σιγᾷ δ' ὅγ' ἐπι-
κλοπάδαν [ἐ]νέρεισε μετώπῳ·
διὰ δ' ἔσχισε σάρκα [καὶ] ὀ[στ]έα δαίμονος αἴσᾳ·
διὰ δ' ἀντικρὺ σχέθεν οἰ[σ]τὸς ἐπ' ἀ-
κροτάταν κορυφάν,   10
ἐμίαινε δ' ἄρ' αἵματι πορφ[υρέῳ
θώρακά τε καὶ βροτόεντ[α μέλεα·

ἀπέκλινε δ' ἄρ' αὐχένα Γαρ[υόνας
ἐπικάρσιον, ὡς ὅκα μ[ά]κω[ν   15
ἅτε καταισχύνοισ' ἁπαλὸν [δέμας
αἶψ' ἀπὸ φύλλα βαλοῖσα ν[(S 15 ii).

'. . . (an arrow) having about its head the end of hateful death, defiled with blood . . . and gall, the pains of the man-killing, dapple-necked Hydra; and in silence he cunningly thrust it in his forehead; and it cut through the flesh and bones by the god's dispensation; and the arrow held straight on to the crown of his head, and he stained with his dark gore his breastplate and bloody limbs; and Geryon twisted his neck at an angle, as a poppy which, spoiling its tender form, swiftly shedding its petals . . .' Some of the features of the narrative are obviously Homeric, and in particular the memorable image of the poppy is in *Iliad* 8.306–8; but a considerable amount is not Homeric, for example, the apposition of the words 'blood and gall' and the word 'pains'— Heracles after killing the Hydra had removed its poisonous blood and gall— and the epithets applied to the Hydra. Again the discursiveness of the narrative is remarkable.

This one example must suffice, but the fragments of the *Sack of Troy*, *Wooden Horse*, *Eriphyle* and a poem about the sons of Oedipus all exhibit the features of the *Geryoneis*.

References to the gods are for the most part subordinate to the needs of the narrative. We are told that Stesichorus, an innovator in his use of mythology (193.17–18), was the first to have Athena leap fully-armed at birth from Zeus' forehead (233); this was probably no more than a passing allusion to her, perhaps in one of the Heracles poems since she is his protectress. He invoked the Muse at the beginning of some, perhaps all, of his poems. One fragment contrasts Apollo and Hades:

<χορεύ>ματά τοι μάλιστα
παιγμοσύνας <τε> φιλεῖ μολπάς τ' Ἀπόλλων,

κήδεα δὲ στοναχάς τ' Ἀίδας ἔλαχε (232).

'Apollo loves dances and merriment and songs most of all, Hades got as his portion mourning and lamentations.' Poseidon was described as

κοιλωνύχων ἵππων πρύτανιν (235),

'lord of the hollow-hoofed horses'.

The poems which deal with Helen are perhaps to be regarded as a unique example of a divine theme in Stesichorus, since she had a cult in Sparta and elsewhere, and certainly wields divine power in her blinding of the poet. In telling her story he first of all seems to have given the usual version: she went with Paris to Troy and was there during the war. Blinded for his pains he recanted and said in his palinode,

οὐκ ἔστ' ἔτυμος λόγος οὗτος,
οὐδ' ἔβας ἐν νηυσὶν ἐυσσέλμοις
οὐδ' ἵκεο πέργαμα Τροίας (192).

'That story is not true, you did not go in well-benched ships, and you did not come to the citadel of Troy'; whereupon he regained his sight. In this second version he made the Greeks and Trojans fight over the phantom (*eidōlon*) of Helen, while the real Helen was in Egypt.

Ibycus, a native of Rhegium and the second great poet of the Greek west, wrote narrative poetry so similar to that of Stesichorus that scholars argued over the authorship of the *Funeral Games of Pelias*. His themes were the same, the stories of Heracles, Meleager, the Argonauts, and the Trojan War and its sequel, and the features of his style the same. But he had a double career and finished as a court poet of Polycrates, tyrant of Samos. It was probably to cater for the sexual preference of this court that he sang of the rape of the boy Ganymede by Zeus and of the boy Tithonus by Dawn (289), of the handsome Endymion (284) and of the love of Talos for Rhadamanthys (309).

*   *   *

Sappho invoked Aphrodite in two poems which were considered in Chapter One; the first (1) is private rather than public poetry, but there is room for doubt in the case of the second (2), in which she requested Aphrodite to appear and 'gracefully pour nectar that mingles with our festivity'. A single line remains of another invocation of the goddess:

ἢ σε Κύπρος ἢ Πάφος ἢ Πάνορμος (35),

'either Cyprus or Paphos or Panormus (detains) you'. The poets commonly listed places in which the god might be found so that the invocation should be appropriate and therefore successful. In the present case there is a difficulty over the words 'Cyprus or Paphos', since Paphos is in Cyprus: we may either take Sappho to mean 'Paphos in particular' or follow editors who emend the text to 'Cyprus and Paphos'.

A prayer addressed by Sappho to Aphrodite and the Nereids (5) may be classed as a *propemptikon*, a poem in which a wish is expressed for a safe journey. Sappho's brother Charaxus had caused her chagrin by his entanglement with a notorious courtesan of Naucratis called Rhodopis: Sappho prays for his safe voyage from Egypt, a happy homecoming and a mending of his ways.

Κύπρι καὶ] Νηρήϊδες, ἀβλάβη[ν μοι
τὸν κασί]γνητον δ[ό]τε τυίδ' ἴκεσθα[ι
κὤσσα F]οι θύμῳ κε θέλη γένεσθαι
πάντα τε]λέσθην,

ὄσσα δὲ πρ]όσθ' ἄμβροτε πάντα λῦσα[ι   5
καὶ φίλοισ]ι Fοῖσι χάραν γένεσθαι
κὠνίαν ἔ]χθροισι, γένοιτο δ' ἄμμι
πῆμ' ἔτι μ]ηδ' εἷς·

τὰν κασιγ]νήταν δὲ θέλοι πόησθαι
ἔμμορον] τίμας . . . (5.1-10)

'Cyprian and Nereids, grant that my brother come here unharmed and that all he wishes in his heart to happen be accomplished, and that he redeem all his previous errors and be a joy to his friends and the distress of his enemies; from now on may no one (trouble?) us; may he be ready to give his sister her due honour . . .' Cyprian Aphrodite was doubly qualified to be the recipient of the prayer: as well as being goddess of love she was a sea-goddess like the Nereids, having emerged at birth from the sea near Cyprus. Another poem ends with a prayer to Aphrodite:

Κύ]πρι, κα[ί σ]ε πι[κροτάτ]αν ἐπεύρ[οι,
μη]δὲ καυχάσ[α]ιτο τόδ' ἐννέ[ποισα
Δ]ωρίχα, τὸ δεύ[τ]ερον ὡς πόθε[ννον
εἰς] ἔρον ἦλθε (15b. 9-12).

'. . . Cyprian, and may she (he?) find you very harsh; and may she, Doricha, not boast, telling how he came the second time to a longed-for love.' Doricha is said to be another name for Rhodopis, but our fragment does not make it clear whether Sappho requests Aphrodite to deal harshly with the girl or with her brother.

Elsewhere Sappho seems to be promised world-wide glory by Cyprian Aphrodite (65), and she is said to have called Peitho, 'Persuasion', her daughter (90). No deity appears more frequently in the fragments, yet there is scarcely any hint of public poetry: almost everything points to private song, composed for the pleasure of her friends. Among the other gods Hera seems to have been of some importance to her. We have scraps of a prayer in which Sappho may have asked her for a safe voyage for herself or another (17); this too seems to be private poetry, but an anonymous poem in the Palatine Anthology (9.189) calls on the women of Lesbos to come to Hera's precinct and dance for her, 'and Sappho will lead you, lyre in hand'; we have no way of saying whether the writer based this on the content of Sappho's poetry or was simply using his imagination. She mentioned Artemis once in an unknown context (84) and also Castor and Polydeuces (68a); somewhere she described Apollo's appearance (208), and she sang of the Moon's love for Endymion (199). She gave conflicting versions of Eros' parentage: he was child of Uranus and Ge, Heaven and Earth, but elsewhere child of Uranus and Aphrodite (198).

There are two types of verse, however, which cannot be divorced from the public life of Lesbos: her poetry about Adonis and her wedding-songs. The worship of Adonis had reached Asia Minor from Syria by way of Cyprus. In the following lines we seem to have a dialogue between worshippers lamenting the annual death of Adonis, Aphrodite's favourite, and a priestess representing Aphrodite:

> κατθνάσκει, Κυθέρη', ἄβρος Ἄδωνις· τί κε θεῖμεν;
> καττύπτεσθε, κόραι, καὶ κατερείκεσθε χίτωνας (140a).

'Delicate Adonis is dying, Cytherea. What are we to do? Beat your breasts, girls, and tear your clothes.' The ionic rhythm may be appropriate to the passionate lamentation, and the second line is strongly alliterative. We are told that Sappho linked Adonis and Oetolinus, a cult name of Linus, another youth whose death was bewailed; that the cry,

> ὦ τὸν Ἄδωνιν (168),

'Alas for Adonis!', was used in her poetry; and that she told how Aphrodite placed the corpse of Adonis among lettuces (211b. iii).

Sappho's wedding-songs have already been mentioned in Chapter Five because of the satirical element apparent in some of them. Lyricism is commoner than satirical tone, however:

> ὄλβιε γάμβρε, σοὶ μὲν δὴ γάμος ὡς ἄραο
> ἐκτετέλεστ', ἔχης δὲ πάρθενον ἂν ἄραο . . .
> σοὶ χάριεν μὲν εἶδος, ὄππατα δ' . . .
> μέλλιχ', ἔρος δ' ἐπ' ἰμέρτῳ κέχυται προσώπῳ
> . . . τετίμακ' ἔξοχά σ' Ἀφροδίτα (112).

'Happy bridegroom, your marriage has been fulfilled as you prayed, you have the girl for whom you prayed . . .; (to the bride) your form is graceful, your eyes . . . gentle, and love streams over your beautiful face . . . Aphrodite has honoured you outstandingly.' The repetition of *arao*, 'you prayed', is unexpected but effective, and it adds to the melodious quality of the lines. Other excerpts from the epithalamia are better known:

> Ἔσπερε πάντα φέρων ὅσα φαίνολις ἐσκέδασ' Αὔως,
> †φέρεις ὄιν, φέρεις† αἶγα, φέρεις ἄπυ μάτερι παῖδα (104a).

'Hesperus, you who bring everything that shining Dawn scattered, you bring the sheep, you bring the goat, you bring the child back to its mother.' Sappho may have continued by saying that the Evening Star fails to bring the bride back to her parents.

> οἶον τὸ γλυκύμαλον ἐρεύθεται ἄκρῳ ἐπ' ὔσδῳ,
> ἄκρον ἐπ' ἀκροτάτῳ, λελάθοντο δὲ μαλοδρόπηες·
> οὐ μὰν ἐκλελάθοντ', ἀλλ' οὐκ ἐδύναντ' ἐπίκεσθαι (105a).

'As the sweet-apple reddens on the bough-top, on the top of the topmost bough; the apple-gatherers have forgotten it—no, not forgotten it: they could not reach it.' Sappho is comparing the bride to the apple, and she lingers over the simile to elaborate it. So with

> οἴαν τὰν ὐάκινθον ἐν ὤρεσι ποίμενες ἄνδρες
> πόσσι καταστείβοισι, χάμαι δέ τε πόρφυρον ἄνθος . . . (105c).

'Like the hyacinth which shepherds tread underfoot in the mountains, and on the ground the purple flower . . .' Poem 62 of Catullus, which probably contains reminiscences of Sappho's poem, suggests that it is the bride's virginity that is crushed like a mountain flower.

Two narrative passages were in all likelihood parts of epithalamia in which Sappho described a divine or heroic wedding:

> κῆ δ' ἀμβροσίας μὲν
> κράτηρ ἐκέκρατ',
> Ἔρμαις δ' ἔλων ὄλπιν θέοισ' ἐοινοχόησε.
> κῆνοι δ' ἄρα πάντες
> καρχάσι' ἦχον
> κἄλειβον, ἀράσαντο δὲ πάμπαν ἔσλα γάμβρῳ (141).

'There a bowl of ambrosia had been mixed, and Hermes took the jug and poured wine for the gods. They all held drinking-cups, and they offered libations and prayed for all manner of blessings on the bridegroom.' Sappho may be singing of the wedding of Peleus and Thetis which the gods attended.

A longer fragment (44) describes the wedding of Hector and Andromache with picturesque detail: this excerpt begins two lines after the opening of a proclamation by Idaeus, the Trojan herald:

Ἔκτωρ καὶ συνέταιρ[ο]ι ἄγοισ' ἐλικώπιδα   5
Θήβας ἐξ ἱέρας Πλακίας τ' ἀ[π' ἀι]ν<ν>άω
ἄβραν Ἀνδρομάχαν ἐνὶ ναῦσιν ἐπ' ἄλμυρον
πόντον· πόλλα δ' [ἐλί]γματα χρύσια κάμματα
πορφύρ[α] καταΰτ[με]να, ποίκιλ' ἀθύρματα,
ἀργύρα τ' ἀνάριθμα ποτήρια κἀλέφαις.'   10
ὣς εἶπ'. ὀτραλέως δ' ἀνόρουσε πάτ[η]ρ φίλος·
φάμα δ' ἦλθε κατὰ πτόλιν εὐρύχορον φίλοις·
αὔτικ' Ἰλίαδαι σατίναι[ς] ὐπ' ἐυτρόχοις
ἆγον αἰμιόνοις, ἐπ[έ]βαινε δὲ παῖς ὄχλος
γυναίκων τ' ἄμα παρθενίκα[ν] τ . . [. .]οσφύρων,   15
χῶρις δ' αὖ Περάμοιο θύγ[α]τρες[(44.5-16).

' "Hector and his comrades are bringing the lively-eyed, graceful Andromache from holy Thebe and ever-flowing Placia in their ships over the salt sea; and there are many golden bracelets and (perfumed?) purple robes, ornate trinkets and countless silver drinking-cups and ivory." So he spoke, and nimbly his dear father leapt up, and the news went to his friends throughout the spacious city. At once the sons of Ilus [Trojans] yoked the mules to the smooth-running carriages, and the whole crowd of women and (tender?-) ankled maidens climbed on board. Apart (drove) the daughters of Priam.' The strongly dactylic rhythm and the use of epic forms rather than Sappho's own Lesbian dialect may be due to the epic theme. The poem ends as follows:

αὖλος δ' ἀδυ[μ]έλης [κίθαρίς] τ' ὀνεμίγνυ[το
καὶ ψ[ό]φο[ς κ]ροτάλ[ων, λιγέ]ως δ' ἄρα πάρ[θενοι   25
ἄειδον μέλος ἄγν[ον, ἴκα]νε δ' ἐς αἴθ[ερα
ἄχω θεσπεσία γελ[
πάντα δ' ἦς κὰτ ὄδο[ις
κράτηρες φίαλαί τ' ὀ[. . .]υεδε[. .]. . εακ[.] . [
μύρρα καὶ κασία λίβανός τ' ὀνεμείχνυτο·   30
γύναικες δ' ἐλέλυσδον ὄσαι προγενέστερα[ι,
πάντες δ' ἄνδρες ἐπήρατον ἴαχον ὄρθιον
Πάον' ὀνκαλέοντες ἐκάβολον εὐλύραν,
ὔμνην δ' Ἔκτορα κ'Ἀνδρομάχαν θεοεικέλο[ις (24-34).

'The sweet-sounding pipe and cithara were mingled and the noise of castanets, and maidens sang clearly a holy song, and a marvellous echo reached the sky . . . and everywhere in the streets . . . bowls and cups . . . myrrh and cassia and frankincense were mingled. The elder women cried out joyfully, and all the men sent forth a lovely high-pitched strain calling on Paean, the Archer skilled in the lyre [Apollo], and they sang in praise of the godlike Hector and Andromache.' The detail is derived not from epic poetry but from contemporary life in Mytilene: myrrh, cassia, frankincense, the castanets and the woman's carriages are all unknown to Homer. Lesky wondered if the theme of Hector and Andromache was too ill-omened for a song designed for a real wedding, but there is no trace of foreboding in the poem, only happiness and merriment.

Alcaeus is important as the earliest writer of short literary hymns. Little of the texts remains, but if we supplement the few quotations by the information given in later writers we can form a clear idea of their scope. Alcaeus addressed the god directly, gave his parentage and other attributes, and recorded his exploits in brief compass, some hymns probably extending to no more than five short stanzas. He used the same metres and dialect as in his other poetry.

A poem such as Horace's hymn to Mercury (*Carm.* 1.10) gives a good impression of the form and scale, since the commentator Porphyrio tells us that it was based on Alcaeus' hymn to Hermes (308). The opening survives:

χαῖρε, Κυλλάνας ὁ μέδεις, σὲ γάρ μοι
θῦμος ὕμνην, τὸν κορύφαισ' ἐν αὔταις
Μαῖα γέννατο Κρονίδᾳ μίγεισα
παμβασίληι.

'Greetings, ruler of Cyllene—for it is of you that I wish to sing, you whom Maia bore on the very mountain-peaks, having lain with Cronus' son, king of all.' There are resemblances with the opening of the Homeric hymn to Hermes:

Ἑρμῆν ὕμνει, Μοῦσα, Διὸς καὶ Μαιάδος υἱόν,
Κυλλήνης μεδέοντα καὶ Ἀρκαδίης πολυμήλου,
ἄγγελον ἀθανάτων ἐριούνιον, ὃν τέκε Μαῖα,
νύμφη ἐϋπλόκαμος, Διὸς ἐν φιλότητι μιγεῖσα . . .

'Sing, Muse, of Hermes, son of Zeus and Maia, ruler of Cyllene and Arcadia with its many flocks, messenger of the immortals, luck-bringer, whom Maia, the lovely-haired nymph, bore after lying in love with Zeus . . .' But the differences between the hymns are important: the Homeric hymn is in hexameters and extends to almost 600 lines, whereas Alcaeus compresses his material and can derive special effects from the Sapphic stanza, for example, when he emphasises the majesty of Zeus by placing the impressive *pambasilēi*, 'king of all', in the short fourth line. Alcaeus begins with the formula *khaire*, 'greetings', which regularly comes at the end of the Homeric hymns; and he seems to have continued with references to the midwifery of the Graces and the nursing of the Seasons, material which is not in the Homeric hymn for all its length. In any case it must be remembered that we cannot say that the Homeric hymn was the earlier of the two, tempting though it may be to see

Alcaeus' poem as a condensed lyric version of it. Pausanias tells us that Alcaeus described Hermes' theft of the cattle of Apollo, and Porphyrio adds that the mischievous young god went further and made Apollo laugh by stealing his quiver, an episode which the Homeric hymn mentions only in passing and in a different context (514–15).

When the Alexandrian editor arranged Alcaeus' poems, he gave pride of place to the hymn to Apollo, making it the first poem of Book 1. Alcaeus used his favourite Alcaic stanza on this occasion: the first line is

ὦναξ Ἄπολλον, παῖ μεγάλω Δίος (307a),

'Lord Apollo, son of great Zeus'. Not much more of the text survives, but fortunately the sophist Himerius gives a paraphrase of the contents: Zeus equipped his son with golden headband, lyre and swan-drawn chariot and sent him to Delphi to declare justice to the Greeks; but Apollo went instead to the land of the Hyperboreans and spent a year there before going to Delphi. Himerius in florid language, his own rather than Alcaeus', describes the account of the god's arrival as follows: 'what with the blaze of summer and the presence of Apollo, the poet's lyre also adopts a summer wantonness . . .: nightingales sing for him the sort of song that one might expect birds to sing in Alcaeus, swallows too and cicadas, not proclaiming their own fortunes in the world but telling of the god in all their songs. Castalia flows in poetic fashion with waters of silver, and Cephisus rises in flood . . .' In this hymn too we can observe a fundamental difference from the Homeric hymn to Apollo in the account it gives of Apollo's coming to Delphi.

Something is known of his hymns to the other gods. The line

Νύμφαις ταῖς Δίος ἐξ αἰγιόχω φαῖσι τετυχμέναις (343),

'They say that the Nymphs, created by aegis-bearing Zeus, . . .' was the opening of a poem; it may be correct to accept the emendation to the vocative case *Numphai* and to regard the poem as a hymn like those to Hermes and Apollo. There is good evidence for a hymn to Hephaestus: we are told that Alcaeus sang of his birth, and it is likely that he told how Hera banished her lame son from Olympus and how he was eventually restored by Dionysus (349). We have a garbled version of the first stanza of a hymn to Athena Itonia, whose worship belongs to Coronea in Boeotia: Alcaeus may have visited the place. There are some striking lines which may come from a hymn to Eros:

. . . δεινότατον θέων,
<τὸν> γέννατ' εὐπέδιλλος Ἴρις
χρυσοκόμα Ζεφύρῳ μίγεισα (327),

'the most grim of gods, whom Iris of the fair sandals bore, having lain with golden-haired Zephyr'. Plutarch, who quotes the lines, refers to scholars who saw symbolic significance in the west wind and the rainbow as parents of Love.

A poem in which Castor and Pollux are invoked may have been a hymn or a prayer for a safe voyage or even another example of the ship of state metaphor with allegorical reference to Mytilene:

δεῦτέ μοι νᾶ]σον Πέλοπος λίποντε]ς,
παῖδες ἴφθ]ιμοι Δ[ίος] ἠδὲ Λήδας,
εὐνόῳ] θύ[μ]ῳ προ[φά]νητε, Κάστορ
καὶ Πολύδε[υ]κες·

οἳ κὰτ εὔρηαν χ[θόνα] καὶ θάλασσαν   5
παῖσαν ἔρχεσθ' ὠ[κυπό]δων ἐπ' ἴππων,
ῥῆα δ' ἀνθρώποι[ς] θα[ν]άτω ῥύεσθε
ζακρυόεντος,

εὐσδ[ύγ]ων θρῴσκοντ[ες ἐπ'] ἄκρα νάων
π]ήλοθεν λάμπροι πρό[τον' ὀν]τρ[έχο]ντες   10
ἀργαλέᾳ δ' ἐν νύκτι φ[άος φέ]ροντες
νᾶϊ μ[ε]λαίνᾳ (34a).

'Come hither, leaving the island of Pelops, strong sons of Zeus and Leda; appear with kindly heart, Castor and Polydeuces, who go on swift horses over the broad earth and all the sea, and easily rescue men from chilling death, leaping on the peaks of their well-benched ships, brilliant from afar as you run up the fore-stays, bringing light to the black ship in the night of trouble . . .' The Dioscuri are summoned from the Peloponnese, since they are especially associated with Sparta. The reference in lines 10–11 is to St. Elmo's fire, the electrical discharge which causes a glow about the mast-head and rigging of ships: Alcaeus represents it as a token of the presence of the Dioscuri, although the light that they bring to the ship (11–12) may, by a metaphor found in Homer, be 'deliverance' also. Alcaeus composed his poem in the Sapphic stanza, and there were probably three more stanzas after line 12. He is generous in his use of traditional epithets—broad earth, swift horses, well-benched ships, black ship—but he knows how to gain effect from his choice and placing of adjectives: *zakruoentos*, 'chilling', shocks by its position and its length; and the 'black' ship is in contrast with the brilliance and light of the Dioscuri. The lines show Alcaeus' composition at its most elegant, smooth and melodious. He makes discreet use of alliteration in lines 1, 10 and 11; it may be fortuitous that the consonant *b* is absent as in Sappho's hymn to Aphrodite (1).

We have the beginning of a hymn to the river Hebrus:

Ἔβρε, κ[άλ]λιστος ποτάμων πὰρ Α[ἶνον
ἐξί[ησθ' ἐς] πορφυρίαν θάλασσαν

Θραϰ[ίας ἐϱ]ευγόμενος ζὰ γαίας
.] ιππ[.] . [. .] ι·

ϰαί σε πόλλαι παϱθένιϰαι 'πέπ[οισιν
. . . .]λων μήϱων ἀπάλαισι χέϱ[σι
. . . .]α· θέλγονται τὸ [σ]ὸν ὡς ἄλει[ππα
θή[ϊο]ν ὕδωϱ (45).

'Hebrus, you flow, the most beautiful of rivers, past Aenus into the turbid sea, surging through the land of Thrace . . . and many maidens visit you (to bathe?) their (lovely) thighs with tender hands; they are enchanted (as they handle?) your divine water like unguent . . .' The river, now called the Maritza, may seem a curious subject for a hymn; it formed the southern end of a trade-route to the Black Sea; more important for a poet from Lesbos, the town of Aenus at its mouth was a joint foundation of Mytilene and Cyme, and, more important still, the head of Orpheus had been carried down the river and over the sea to Lesbos, where it was buried at Antissa, and the presence of his head and lyre were said to have made Lesbos such a musical island.

The heroes and heroines of mythology were also important to Alcaeus. We have seen already that he could tell a myth briefly in order to establish a point: the criminal behaviour of Locrian Ajax was offered as a parallel to that of Pittacus (298), and the tale of Sisyphus' ultimate failure to escape death was told to support the hedonistic advice of a drinking-song (38A); similarly Sappho spoke of Helen to illustrate the power of love. Some of the mythological material, however, does not seem to be used for any such purpose: so far as we can tell, the story is told for its own sake. This is true of a short poem (44), possibly complete in eight lines, in which Alcaeus tells of the wrath of Achilles and of Thetis' plea to Zeus, the theme of *Iliad* 1.495ff., and of a longer fragment in which he sings of the adultery of Paris and Helen and the consequent deaths of many Trojan warriors (283).

Disapproval of Helen is more explicit in four stanzas, perhaps a complete poem, in which she is unfavourably compared with Thetis, wife of Peleus and mother of Achilles:

ὠς λόγος, ϰάϰων ἄ[χος ἔννεϰ' ἔϱγων
Πεϱϱάμῳ ϰαὶ παῖσ[ί ποτ', 'Ὤλεν', ἦλθεν
ἐϰ σέθεν πίϰϱον, π[ύϱι δ' ὤλεσε Ζεῦς
Ἴλιον ἴϱαν.

οὐ τεαύταν Αἰαϰίδαι[ς ἄγαυος
πάντας ἐς γάμον μάϰ[αϱας ϰαλέσσαις
ἄγετ' ἐϰ Νή[ϱ]ηος ἔλων [μελάθϱων
πάϱθενον ἄβϱαν

ἐς δόμον Χέϱϱωνος· ἔλ[υσε δ' ἄγνας

ζῶμα παρθένω· φιλό[τας δ' ἔθαλε
Πήλεος καὶ Νηρεῖδων ἀρίστ[ας,
ἐς δ' ἐνίαυτον

παῖδα γέννατ' αἰμιθέων [φέριστον
ὄλβιον ξάνθαν ἐλάτη[ρα πώλων·
οἱ δ' ἀπώλοντ' ἀμφ' Ἐ[λένα Φρύγες τε
καὶ πόλις αὔτων (42).

'As the story goes, because of evil deeds bitter grief came once to Priam and his sons from you, Helen, and Zeus destroyed holy Ilium with fire. Not such was the delicate maiden [Thetis] whom the noble son of Aeacus [Peleus] married, inviting all the blessed gods to the wedding, taking her from the halls of Nereus to the home of Chiron; he loosened the pure maiden's girdle, and the love of Peleus and the best of Nereus' daughters flourished; and within the year she bore a son, the finest of demigods, blessed driver of chestnut horses. But they perished for Helen's sake—the Phrygians and their city [Troy].' The emphasis in the narrative is unexpected: Thetis was not a model wife nor a happy mother; Greeks as well as Trojans died for Helen; and Achilles, child of Thetis and 'finest of demigods', was conspicuously the destroyer of Trojans.

Homeric heroes appear elsewhere in Alcaeus: Achilles is called 'ruler of Scythia' (354) in allusion to the story that after his death he lived in a kind of Elysium near the Danube delta. We meet Salaminian Ajax as well as the despicable Locrian:

Κρονίδα βασίληος γένος Αἴαν τὸν ἄριστον πεδ' Ἀχίλλεα (387),

'Ajax, descendant of king Zeus, Cronus' son, best after Achilles'. And the Phaeacians, familiar from the *Odyssey*, are said to have had their origin in the drops of blood shed by Uranus when he was castrated by his son Cronus (441). Non-homeric heroes appear too: Heracles, killer of the Hydra (443), Endymion, assured by Zeus that he may choose the time of his own death (317), Perseus, identified by the *kibisis*, the wallet in which he carried Medusa's head (255).

Anacreon's fame depends on the short poems on love and wine which he sang at the tyrant's courts of Samos and Athens. We have seen that some of them begin with appeals to gods: in 357 he prays to Dionysus for help in winning the love of Cleobulus, and in 348 to Artemis for the well-being of the city of Magnesia. Two other addresses to deities are inscrutable:

κλῦθί μεο γέροντος, εὐέθειρα χρυσόπεπλε κούρα (418),

'Hear an old man's prayer, maiden of the lovely hair and golden robe'; and ἥλιε καλλιλαμπέτη (451),

'Fair-shining sun'.

There are a few hints that he composed choral poetry: the fifth-century politician and poet Critias writes of Anacreon's 'songs for women's melodies' and of 'female choirs' performing 'night-long rites' (500), and a papyrus commentary on the *Iliad* seems to quote from Anacreon's partheneia (501). We hear also of 'cletic' hymns, in which a god is summoned, but perhaps the prayers to Artemis and Dionysus were in the mind of the scholar who mentions them (502b). The truth of the matter is probably expressed in the saying attributed to him, that he wrote hymns to boys rather than to gods because 'they are our gods'.

*   *   *

Xenophanes, poet and critic of morals and religion, has harsh words for the traditional literary treatment of the gods:

πάντα θεοῖς ἀνέθηκαν Ὅμηρός θ' Ἡσίοδός τε
ὅσσα παρ' ἀνθρώποισιν ὀνείδεα καὶ ψόγος ἐστίν,
κλέπτειν μοιχεύειν τε καὶ ἀλλήλους ἀπατεύειν (10).

'Homer and Hesiod have attributed to the gods everything that is matter for reproach and blame among men, thieving, adultery, deception of each other.' He mocked the anthropomorphic view of the gods in other hexameter lines:

ἀλλ' εἰ χεῖρας ἔχον βόες <ἵπποι τ'> ἠὲ λέοντες
ἢ γράψαι χείρεσσι καὶ ἔργα τελεῖν ἅπερ ἄνδρες,
ἵπποι μέν θ' ἵπποισι, βόες δέ τε βουσὶν ὁμοίας
καί <κε> θεῶν ἰδέας ἔγραφον καὶ σώματ' ἐποίουν
τοιαῦθ' οἷόν περ καὐτοὶ δέμας εἶχον ἕκαστοι (13).

'But if oxen and horses and lions had hands or could draw with hands and make works of art like men, horses would draw the forms of gods like horses, oxen like oxen, and they would make their bodies like the shapes they each have.' So in what seems to be an iambic line followed by a hexameter:

ἀλλ' οἱ βροτοὶ δοκέουσι γεννᾶσθαι θεούς,
τὴν σφετέρην δ' ἐσθῆτα ἔχειν φωνήν τε δέμας τε (12).

'But mortals think they are the begetters of gods and that gods have *their* clothes and voices and shapes'; and still more tellingly,

Αἰθίοπές τε <θεοὺς σφετέρους> σιμοὺς μέλανάς τε,
Θρῆκες τε γλαυκοὺς καὶ πυρρούς <φασι πέλεσθαι> (14).

'Ethiopians say their gods are snub-nosed and black, Thracians that theirs are blue-eyed and red-haired.' But this was almost a lone voice of protest.

In the manuscripts of Theognis four addresses to various gods have been placed at the beginning of the collection of poems as forming an appropriate prelude. The first two are directed to Apollo, god of music:

> ὦ ἄνα Λητοῦς υἱέ, Διὸς τέκος, οὔποτε σεῖο
> λήσομαι ἀρχόμενος οὐδ' ἀποπαυόμενος,
> ἀλλ' αἰεὶ πρῶτόν τε καὶ ὕστατον ἔν τε μέσοισιν
> ἀείσω· σὺ δέ μοι κλῦθι καὶ ἐσθλὰ δίδου (1-4).

'O lord, son of Leto, child of Zeus, I shall never forget you either at my beginning or at my ending: always I shall sing of you first and last and in the middle. Do you hear me and grant me good fortune.' Theognis uses 'polar' expressions to indicate that he will sing of Apollo at all times.

> Φοῖβε ἄναξ, ὅτε μέν σε θεὰ τέκε πότνια Λητώ,
> φοίνικος ῥαδινῇς χερσὶν ἐφαψαμένη,
> ἀθανάτων κάλλιστον, ἐπὶ τροχοειδέϊ λίμνῃ
> πᾶσα μὲν ἐπλήσθη Δῆλος ἀπειρεσίη
> ὀδμῆς ἀμβροσίης, ἐγέλασσε δὲ γαῖα πελώρη,
> γήθησεν δὲ βαθὺς πόντος ἁλὸς πολιῆς (5-10).

'Lord Phoebus, when the goddess, the lady Leto, clutching the palm-tree with her slender arms, brought you forth beside the wheel-shaped lake to be the fairest of the gods, all of wide Delos was filled with an ambrosial scent, the huge earth laughed, and the deep waters of the grey sea rejoiced.' Theognis handles the theme with the joyful lyricism found also in Alcaeus' hymn to Apollo; in both poems, as in the Homeric hymn to Delian Apollo (118, 135–39), nature rejoices at his coming. No prayer is expressed in the present poem; instead we have a brief narrative such as we might find in a hymn.

> Ἄρτεμι θηροφόνη, θύγατερ Διός, ἣν Ἀγαμέμνων
> εἵσαθ', ὅτ' ἐς Τροίην ἔπλεε νηυσὶ θοῇς,
> εὐχομένῳ μοι κλῦθι, κακὰς δ' ἀπὸ κῆρας ἄλαλκε·
> σοὶ μὲν τοῦτο θεὰ σμικρόν, ἐμοὶ δὲ μέγα (11-14).

'Artemis, killer of wild beasts, daughter of Zeus, whose image Agamemnon set up when he was about to sail to Troy in his swift ships, hear my prayer and ward off evil fates, a small thing for you, goddess, but great for me.' Theognis alludes to the sanctuary of Artemis established in his own city of Megara by Agamemnon before the Trojan expedition sailed. It has been thought that the poem is a prayer for a safe voyage, but this is far from certain, since the plural *kēras*, 'fates', is wide in its application.

> Μοῦσαι καὶ Χάριτες, κοῦραι Διός, αἵ ποτε Κάδμου

ἐς γάμον ἐλθοῦσαι καλὸν ἀείσατ' ἔπος,
'ὅττι καλὸν φίλον ἐστί, τὸ δ' οὐ καλὸν οὐ φίλον ἐστί'·
τοῦτ' ἔπος ἀθανάτων ἦλθε διὰ στομάτων (15-18).

'Muses and Graces, daughters of Zeus, who once sang beautiful words when you came to the marriage of Cadmus, "What is beautiful is dear, what is not beautiful is not dear": these were the words that passed your immortal lips.' Here the invocation seems to be complete in the simple address to the goddesses of song. Like the other gods, they attended the wedding of the human Cadmus with the divine Harmonia.

Among the other poems of the collection are prayers to Zeus and the other gods (757ff.) and to Apollo (773ff.) to protect 'this city', and the prayer to Castor and Polydeuces to supervise the behaviour of friend to friend (1087ff.). Most of the other references are to the god or gods as controllers of the world and givers of good or evil. Theognis makes a typically humorous and cynical comment when he complains that despite his poetic ability he has not been able to please all his fellow-citizens:

οὐδὲν θαυμαστόν, Πολυπαΐδη· οὐδὲ γὰρ ὁ Ζεὺς
οὔθ' ὕων πάντεσσ' ἁνδάνει οὔτ' ἀνέχων (25-6).

'No wonder, son of Polypaus, since not even Zeus pleases everyone either by raining or by stopping.' A similar idea is expressed at 803f. Elsewhere he bluntly finds fault with the dispensation of Zeus:

Ζεῦ φίλε, θαυμάζω σε· σὺ γὰρ πάντεσσιν ἀνάσσεις
τιμὴν αὐτὸς ἔχων καὶ μεγάλην δύναμιν,
ἀνθρώπων δ' εὖ οἶσθα νόον καὶ θυμὸν ἑκάστου,
σὸν δὲ κράτος πάντων ἔσθ' ὕπατον, βασιλεῦ·
πῶς δή σευ, Κρονίδη, τολμᾷ νόος ἄνδρας ἀλιτροὺς
ἐν ταὐτῇ μοίρῃ τόν τε δίκαιον ἔχειν . . . (373-8).

'Dear Zeus, I am surprised at you. You are ruler of all and alone have honour and great power; you know well the heart and mind of each man, and your power, o king, is highest of all. How then, son of Cronus, can your heart abide to hold the wicked and the just in the same esteem . . .?' The indignation is tempered by the pleasant familiarity with which he berates the ruler of all.

Hipponax was equally at home with his superiors:

ὦ Ζεῦ, πάτερ <Ζεῦ>, θεῶν Ὀλυμπίων πάλμυ,
⁻ʹ μοὐκ ἔδωκας ἀργύρου <κασίγνητον>; (38).

'O Zeus, father Zeus, tsar of the Olympian gods, why have you not given me silver's brother?' If West's emendation is correct, Hipponax refers to gold, as he elsewhere calls the fig-tree 'the vine's sister' (48). Whatever the text, there is a comic combination of the formal prayer (with the surprise of the Lydian word for 'ruler') and the cheeky complaint, and the metre is the limping iambic with its disconcerting jolt. A request to Hermes is in the same spirit and metre:

> Ἑρμῆ, φίλ' Ἑρμῆ, Μαιαδεῦ, Κυλλήνιε,
> ἐπεύχομαί τοι· κάρτα γὰρ κακῶς ῥιγῶ
> καὶ βαμβαλύζω ...
> δὸς χλαῖναν Ἱππώνακτι καὶ κυπασσίσκον
> καὶ σαμβαλίσκα κἀσκερίσκα καὶ χρυσοῦ
> στατῆρας ἑξήκοντα τοὐτέρου τοίχου (32).

'Hermes, dear Hermes, son of Maia, Cyllenian, I pray to you, for I am shivering damnably and my teeth are chattering. . . . Give Hipponax a cloak and a nice wee tunic and nice wee sandals and nice wee boots and sixty staters of gold from the other wall.' The words for cloak, tunic and sandals are probably all oriental, and the use of the diminutive forms with -iskos in coaxing speech is likely to be colloquial. The expression 'from the other wall' is not convincingly explained: it might refer to stealing from the next house, since Hermes is god of thieves, or to the more comfortable side of a ship. The following lines are in the same vein:

> ἐμοὶ δὲ Πλοῦτος –ἔστι γὰρ λίην τυφλός–
> ἐς τὠκί' ἐλθὼν οὐδάμ' εἶπεν· ''Ἱππῶναξ,
> δίδωμί τοι μνᾶς ἀργύρου τριήκοντα
> καὶ πόλλ' ἔτ' ἄλλα·'' δείλαιος γὰρ τὰς φρένας (36).

'And Wealth—he's too blind—never came to my house and said, ''Hipponax, I give you thirty minas of silver and much else besides.'' He's weak in the head.'

Two foreign goddesses whose cult was introduced into Greece some hundred years after the time of Hipponax, are mentioned in an unknown context:

> καὶ Διὸς κούρη Κυβήβη καὶ Θρεϊκίη Βενδῖς (127),

'Cybebe, daughter of Zeus, and Thracian Bendis'. Cybebe is the Lydian form of Cybele's name, and Hipponax may be alluding to cults practised in Ephesus with its mixed population.

Heroic figures naturally play a small role in this scurrilous poetry, and it is surprising to find three lines in typical limping iambics about the Thracian Rhesus who came to the aid of Priam but was killed by Odysseus and Diomedes on the night after his arrival (*Il.* 10.434ff.):

> ἐπ' ἁρμάτων τε καὶ Θρεϊκίων πώλων
> λευκῶν, ἰαύων ἐγγὺς Ἰλίου πύργων,
> ἀπηναρίσθη Ῥῆσος, Αἰνειῶν πάλμυς (72).

'(Having come?) in his chariot with its white Thracian horses Rhesus, tsar of the Aeneians, was slain as he slept near the walls of Troy.' The metre and the Lydian term *palmus*, 'tsar', suggest that Hipponax' purpose was less than serious, perhaps parody. There are scraps of evidence that he composed a comic version of the *Odyssey* (74, 77), and elsewhere he seems to have listed some of the labours of Heracles (102).

*   *   *

We have reached the great age of choral lyric poetry which extends for a century from *c.* 535 B.C., the probable date of Simonides' earliest work, to the death of Pindar in 438. Simonides, Pindar and Bacchylides, to name the most distinguished, wrote religious poetry of several genres, hymns, paeans, dithyrambs, processionals, maiden-songs, hyporchemata (dance-songs) and others.

Time has been unkind to Simonides. He won fifty-six victories in dithyrambic contests, but not a scrap of the texts has survived. We know only that in a dithyramb called *Memnon* he set Memnon's burial-place in Syria (539), which suggests that he did not deal exclusively with legends of Dionysus in his dithyrambs but used other heroic material. Similarly we have only a few papyrus shreds of his paeans (519, especially frr. 35, 55), and these contain few consecutive words. We have seen that in at least one of his victory-songs he concentrated on a mythological theme, the exploits of Castor and Polydeuces, to such an extent that his patron, Scopas, is said to have cut his fee by half.

Simonides also composed hymns of a different sort. Leonidas and the Spartans who died and were buried with him at Thermopylae are commemorated in this short song:

τῶν ἐν Θερμοπύλαις θανόντων
εὐκλεὴς μὲν ἁ τύχα, καλὸς δ' ὁ πότμος,
βωμὸς δ' ὁ τάφος, πρὸ γόων δὲ μνᾶστις, ὁ δ' οἶκτος ἔπαινος·
ἐντάφιον δὲ τοιοῦτον εὐρὼς
οὔθ' ὁ πανδαμάτωρ ἀμαυρώσει χρόνος.   5
ἀνδρῶν ἀγαθῶν ὅδε σηκὸς οἰκέταν εὐδοξίαν
Ἑλλάδος εἵλετο· μαρτυρεῖ δὲ καὶ Λεωνίδας,
Σπάρτας βασιλεύς, ἀρετᾶς μέγαν λελοιπὼς
κόσμον ἀέναόν τε κλέος (531).

'Of those who died at Thermopylae glorious is the fortune, fair the fate; their tomb is an altar, for lamentation they have remembrance, for pity praise. Such a funeral-gift neither mould nor all-conquering time shall destroy. This precinct of noble men chose the glory of Greece as its inhabitant; witness to this is Leonidas himself, king of Sparta, who left behind a great adornment of valour and imperishable glory.' The hymn derives its solemn dignity from its imaginative treatment of the subject and from the paratactic simplicity of its structure. Interest is added by the variation in the order of subject and predicate in lines 2–3 and by the application of Homer's adjective *pandamatōr*, 'all-conquering', which Homer uses of sleep, to time. The occasion and place of performance are disputed, but the words 'at Thermopylae' and 'this precinct' suggest a shrine, nowhere else attested, in Sparta; the altar of line 3 presumably stood there, and Simonides' hymn must have been composed for a ceremonial occasion of remembrance. It is possible that his *Sea-fight at Artemisium* (532–5) was also a hymn, written to commemorate the battle of the Greek fleet against the Persians. Some scholars regard a prayer to the Fates (1018), quoted by Stobaeus in his anthology, as the work of Simonides.

One of the most remarkable fragments of his poetry narrates the story of Danae and her baby son Perseus, who had been put to sea in a chest by her father Acrisius because of a prophecy that his grandson would kill him. It is impossible now to say whether it formed part of a dithyramb, a dirge or even a victory-ode.

```
                    ὅτε λάρνακι
ἐν δαιδαλέᾳ
ἄνεμός τέ μιν πνέων
κινηθεῖσά τε λίμνα δείματι
ἔρειπεν, οὐκ ἀδιάντοισι παρειαῖς                        5
ἀμφί τε Περσέι βάλλε φίλαν χέρα
εἶπέν τ᾽· 'ὦ τέκος, οἷον ἔχω πόνον·

σὺ δ᾽ ἀωτεῖς, γαλαθηνῷ
δ᾽ ἤθεϊ κνοώσσεις
ἐν ἀτερπέι δούρατι χαλκεογόμφῳ                          10
<τῷ>δε νυκτιλαμπεῖ
κυανέῳ δνόφῳ ταθείς·
ἅλμαν δ᾽ ὕπερθε τεᾶν κομᾶν
βαθεῖαν παριόντος
κύματος οὐκ ἀλέγεις, οὐδ᾽ ἀνέμου                        15
φθόγγον, πορφυρέᾳ
κείμενος ἐν χλανίδι, πρόσωπον καλόν.
εἰ δέ τοι δεινὸν τό γε δεινὸν ἦν,
καί κεν ἐμῶν ῥημάτων
λεπτὸν ὑπεῖχες οὖας.                                    20

κέλομαι δ᾽, εὗδε βρέφος,
εὑδέτω δὲ|πόντος, εὑδέτω δ᾽ ἄμετρον κακόν·
μεταβουλία δέ τις φανείη,
Ζεῦ πάτερ, ἐκ σέο·
ὅττι δὲ θαρσαλέον ἔπος εὔχομαι                          25
ἢ νόσφι δίκας,
σύγγνωθί μοι᾽ (543).
```

'. . . When in the intricately-carved chest the blasts of wind and the troubled water prostrated her in fear, with streaming cheeks she put her loving arm about Perseus and said, "My child, what suffering is mine! But you sleep, and in your babyish way you slumber in the dismal boat with its brazen bolts, stretched out in this darkness that is so blue and luminous in the night. You pay no attention to the deep salt water above your hair as the wave passes by nor to the sound of the wind, lying in your purple blanket, a lovely face. If the danger were danger to you, why, you would turn your tiny ear to my words. Sleep, my baby, I tell you; and let the sea sleep, and let our vast trouble sleep. Let some change of heart appear from you, father Zeus. If anything in my prayer is audacious or unjust, pardon me." ' Simonides was regarded in antiquity as the master of pathos, and the sad tenderness of Danae's words is rightly admired. Her speech begins with short clauses, but the style becomes more elaborate than is usual in Simonides, with accumulated adjectives in lines 10–11, uncommon epithets (*adiantoisi*, 'unwet', *galathēnōi*, 'babyish', *nuktilampei*, 'night-shining' if the text is correct, *ametron*, 'vast') and other rare words (*aōteis* and *knoōsseis*, 'slumber', *metaboulia*, 'change of heart'), and anaphora in lines 21–2 (*heude . . . heudetō . . . heudetō*). If line 17 is correctly interpreted, the child is 'a lovely face' since only the face appears from the mantle.

The collected works of Pindar included one book of Hymns, one of Paeans, two each of Dithyrambs and Prosodia (Processional-songs), three of Partheneia and two of Hyporchemata (Dance-songs). Papyrus discoveries have furnished extensive parts of the texts but no complete example of any type. The four books of Victory-songs survive intact, and they too, as we have seen, are full of references to gods and heroes for all their secular purpose; one of them indeed begins with the words

ἀναξιφόρμιγγες ὕμνοι,
τίνα θεόν, τίν' ἥρωα, τίνα δ' ἄνδρα κελαδήσομεν; (*Ol.* 2.1–2).

'Hymns that rule the lyre, what god, what hero, what man shall we celebrate?' The answer in this case is Zeus, god of Olympia, Heracles, founder of the Games, and of course the victor, Theron of Acragas. Whether his commission is for a sacred or a secular poem, Pindar finds it appropriate to introduce the gods. His view of them is traditional, not essentially different from Homer's, and he has no truck with the rationalisation of the Ionian thinkers whom he considered

ἀτελῆ σοφίας καρπὸν δρέπειν (fr. 209),

'to gather an ineffectual harvest of wisdom'. I shall first discuss some examples of his religious poetry and then note passages of the victory-odes which have relevance to gods and heroes.

We know of hymns addressed to Persephone, to Apollo Ptoios, worshipped in the sanctuary on Mount Ptoion in Pindar's own land of Boeotia, and to Zeus Ammon, whose shrine was in Libya. A famous hymn, which must have been composed for his city of Thebes, begins with a list of possible mythological themes, all Theban:

'Ισμηνὸν ἢ χρυσαλάκατον Μελίαν
ἢ Κάδμον ἢ Σπαρτῶν ἱερὸν γένος ἀνδρῶν
ἢ τὰν κυανάμπυκα Θήβαν
    ἢ τὸ πάντολμον σθένος Ἡρακλέος
ἢ τὰν Διωνύσου πολυγαθέα τιμὰν
    ἢ γάμον λευκωλένου Ἁρμονίας
ὑμνήσομεν; (fr. 29).

'Shall we sing of Ismenus or of Melia with her golden distaff or of Cadmus or of the holy race of the Sown Men or of Thebe with her dark-blue headband or the all-daring strength of Heracles or the joyful honouring of Dionysus or the marriage of white-armed Harmonia?' The lines are quoted in connection with Corinna's advice to the young Pindar that he should make use of myth in his poetry: he reacted by composing this preamble, whereupon she said that he 'should sow with the hand and not the whole sack'. The story may be apocryphal, and the long sequence of alternative Theban themes is paralleled at the beginning of one of his mature odes, *Isthmian 7*. His purpose on both occasions may have been to display the unique richness of Theban mythology. Later in the poem Pindar's theme is the marriage of Zeus and Themis, and here at least there is no lack of imaginative power:

πρῶτον μὲν εὔβουλον Θέμιν οὐρανίαν
χρυσέαισιν ἵπποις Ὠκεανοῦ παρὰ παγᾶν
Μοῖραι ποτὶ κλίμακα σεμνὰν
    ἆγον Οὐλύμπου λιπαρὰν καθ' ὁδὸν
σωτῆρος ἀρχαίαν ἄλοχον Διὸς ἔμμεν·
    ἁ δὲ τὰς χρυσάμπυκας ἀγλαοκάρ-
πους τίκτεν ἀλαθέας Ὥρας (fr. 30).

'First the Fates brought celestial Themis of the wise counsel in their golden chariot from the springs of Ocean to the holy stairway of Olympus along a shining path, to be the wife of saviour Zeus in olden times; and she bore the unerring Seasons with their gold headbands and lovely wrists.' In the same poem Pindar told how Zeus created Apollo and the Muses to celebrate in words and music his great achievements.

Fragments of more than twenty-five paeans survive, and since some are of considerable length we can speak with greater confidence of Pindar's treatment of this genre. Most were written for performance in Apollo's sanctuaries at Delos, Delphi, the Ismenion in Thebes or Mount Ptoion in Boeotia, but a few bear titles indicating that they were for the worship of another god, Zeus of Dodona, or of a hero, Aeacus on Aegina, Electryon at Argos. A version of the cry *Iē, Paian*, 'Hail, Paean', in which Apollo is invoked as Healer, forms a refrain in many of the hymns: in *Paean 2*, written for the Ionian colony of Abdera on the Thracian coast, Pindar is concerned with the survival of the city in its hostile environment, and he ends each of the three triads with the prayer

ἰὴ ἰὲ Παιάν, ἰὴ ἰέ · Παιὰν
δὲ μήποτε λείποι (35f., 71f., 107f.),

'Hail, hail, Paean, hail, hail! May Paean never abandon (us)!'

It is surprising to find a paean for the island of Ceos, since it had famous poets of its own in Simonides and Bacchylides. Indeed Pindar allows the choir of Ceans to pay tribute to them:

ἤτοι καὶ ἐγὼ σ[κόπ]ελον ναίων δια-
γινώσκομαι μὲν ἀρεταῖς ἀέθλων
Ἑλλανίσιν, γινώσκ[ο]μα[ι] δὲ καὶ
μοῖσαν παρέχων ἅλις (*Paean* 4. 21-4).

'Truly even I, although I dwell on a rock, am known for my deeds of prowess in the Greek games, known too for supplying poets in abundance.' Pindar's phrase is *moisan parekhōn*, 'supplying the Muse', that is, the arts of music and poetry over which she presides.

One of his paeans for his own people, the Thebans, begins with reference to the eclipse of the sun in 463 B.C.:

ἀκτὶς ἀελίου, τί πολύσκοπε μήσεαι,
ὦ μᾶτερ ὀμμάτων, ἄστρον ὑπέρτατον
ἐν ἀμέρᾳ κλεπτόμενον; <τί δ'> ἔθηκας ἀμάχανον
ἰσχύν <τ'> ἀνδράσι καὶ σοφίας ὁδόν,
ἐπίσκοτον ἀτραπὸν ἐσσυμένα;
ἐλαύνεις τι νεώτερον ἢ πάρος; (*Paean* 9.1-6).

'Beam of the sun, far-seeing one, what can you be planning, mother of eyes, supreme star stolen in the daytime? Why did you make resourceless the strength of man and the way to wisdom by speeding along a darkened path? Are you bringing something hitherto unknown?' This is in Pindar's boldest manner; the cry *ō mater ommatōn*, 'mother of eyes', must mean that the sun is the source of the light which is indispensable for man's eyes. He follows these lines with a catalogue of disasters that may be portended by the eclipse, war, crop failure, snowstorm and so on. But fifteen lines later he is relating Theban myth, on this occasion the story of Melia, bride of Apollo and mother of the prophet Tenerus. Myth seems to have been as prominent in the paeans as in the victory-songs.

In a long paean composed for the Delphians he told how Neoptolemus, son of Achilles, was killed by Apollo at Delphi:

ὤ[μο]σε [γὰϱ θ]εός,
γέ[ϱον]θ᾽ ὅ[τι] Πϱίαμον
π[ϱ]ὸς ἑϱκεῖον ἤναϱε βωμὸν ἐ[π-
   εν]θοϱόντα, μή νιν εὔφϱον᾽ ἐς οἶ[x]ον   115
μήτ᾽ ἐπὶ γῆϱας ἱξέ-
   μεν βίου· ἀμφιπόλοις δὲ
x]υϱιᾶν πεϱὶ τιμᾶν
δηϱι]αζόμενον xτάνεν
<ἐν> τεμέ]νεῖ φίλῳ γᾶς παϱ᾽ ὀμφαλὸν εὐϱύν.   120
   <ἰὴ> ἰῆτε νῦν, μέτϱα παιηό-
   ν]ων ἰῆτε, νέοι (*Paean* 6. 112-22).

'For the god had sworn that since he had killed old Priam who had leapt upon the household altar he should not reach his home to find a welcome nor reach life's old age; and while he was quarrelling with the attendants over the appointed dues he slew him in his own precinct at the spacious navel of the earth. Hail, cry hail, cry aloud due measure of paeans, young men!' This fine example of rapid and vivid narrative is followed abruptly by praise of the island of Aegina with its naval strength and its hospitable ways. Pindar tells how Zeus loved the nymph Aegina, and the following damaged lines speak of the boundless excellences of the line of Aeacus, offspring of this union. The line of course led through Peleus and Achilles to Neoptolemus. In his seventh *Nemean*, written to celebrate the victory of an Aeginetan boy, he gives a different version of the killing, ascribing it to a human agent, noting the distress of the Delphians, and referring to the honours fate had decreed for a descendant of Aeacus in Delphi.

Less survives from Pindar's dithyrambs, but the remnants are of the greatest interest. In the second, which carried the alternative titles *The Descent of Heracles* and *Cerberus*, he begins by speaking of the old dithyramb:

πϱὶν μὲν ἕϱπε σχοινοτένειά τ᾽ ἀοιδὰ
   διθυϱάμβων
xαὶ τὸ σὰν xίβδηλον ἀνθϱώποισιν ἀπὸ στομάτων (70b. 1-2).

'Previously the song of the dithyrambs came like a rope drawn out long, and the *san* came impure from men's mouths.' Pindar scoffs first at the length of the earlier compositions and perhaps also at their continuity, since he preferred an episodic narrative style, and secondly, although interpretation here is uncertain, at their sibilant harshness: *san* is the Doric equivalent of *sigma*, and Pindar seems to be following in the steps of his teacher Lasus, who so disapproved of the sound that he wrote an 'asigmatic' ode from which he banished it completely. The lines which follow this introduction are fragmentary, but Pindar may have claimed to open new doors for the dithyramb. He goes on immediately to speak of the rites of Dionysus as they are observed by the Olympian gods close by the very sceptre of Zeus:

σεμνᾷ μὲν κατάρχει
Ματέρι πὰρ μεγάλᾳ ῥόμβοι τυπάνων,
ἐν δὲ κέχλαδ[εν] κρόταλ᾽ αἰθομένα τε   10
   δαῖς ὑπὸ ξανθαῖσι πεύκαις·
ἐν δὲ Ναΐδων ἐρίγδουποι στοναχαὶ
μανίαι τ᾽ ἀλαλαί τ᾽ ὀρίνεται ῥιψαύχενι
   σὺν κλόνῳ.
ἐν δ᾽ ὁ παγκρατὴς κεραυνὸς ἀμπνέων   15
πῦρ κεκίνη[ται τό|τ᾽] Ἐνυαλίου
ἔγχος, ἀλκάεσσά [τ]ε Παλλάδο[ς] αἰγὶς
μυρίων φθογγάζεται κλαγγαῖς δρακόντων.
ῥίμφα δ᾽ εἶσιν Ἄρτεμις οἰοπολὰς ζεύ-
   ξαισ᾽ ἐν ὀργαῖς   20
Βακχίαις φῦλον λεόντων ἀ[γρότερον Βρομίῳ,
ὁ δὲ κηλεῖται χορευοίσαισι κα[ὶ θηρῶν ἀγέλαις (70b. 8-23).

'In the presence of the august Great Mother begins the whirling of tambourines; there are castanets ringing out, and the torch blazing under the gold-green pines; there are the Naiads' noisy groanings, and madness and yelling are roused amid the neck-tossing uproar. There whirls the all-powerful thunderbolt breathing its fire, and the spear of Enyalius [Ares], and the brave aegis of Pallas [Athena] resounds with the hiss of a thousand serpents. Swiftly comes Artemis, the solitary goddess, who in the Bacchic frenzy has yoked the savage breed of lions for Bromius [Dionysus]; and he is spellbound by the dancing herds of very beasts.' The power of the wild Dionysiac influence is depicted in language similar to that sung by Euripides' chorus in the *Bacchae*. What is astonishing is that it is the very gods of Olympus who are gripped by the 'Bacchic frenzy', not only the Mother Goddess, who has her own ecstatic rites, or the wild water-nymphs but the warrior gods themselves, Zeus of the thunderbolt, Ares and Athena; Artemis, the huntress, has yoked lions— Alcman had mentioned the milking of a lioness—and Dionysus is enchanted by the beasts' dance. Pindar's choice of words, as in *rhomboi tupanōn* for the circling movement of tambourines or the pictorial *rhipsaukheni sun klonōi* of the uncontrolled dancers, heads thrown back, creates an atmosphere without parallel in the rest of his poetry.

At least three dithyrambs were written for the Athenians, and the opening of one of them was much loved in Athens:

ὦ ταὶ λιπαραὶ καὶ ἰοστέφανοι καὶ ἀοίδιμοι,
Ἑλλάδος ἔρει-
σμα, κλειναὶ Ἀθᾶναι, δαιμόνιον πτολίεθρον (fr. 76).

'O gleaming, violet-crowned, glorious, bulwark of Hellas, famous Athens, divine citadel.' The adjective *liparos*, 'gleaming', is a conventional term of praise, applied by Pindar to a variety of cities; we must not think of the buildings of the Acropolis, destroyed by the Persians and not yet rebuilt. 'Violet-crowned' might refer to the actual decoration of buildings in time of festival, or, as our next dithyramb suggests, to Athenian fondness for garlands of violets; but earlier poets had applied it to Aphrodite and to the Muses, and it may be chosen here because of its associations with divinity. Pindar gives Athens, 'bulwark of Hellas', credit for saving all Greece in the Wars; another scrap of the poem mentions the battle of Artemisium,

> ὅθι παῖδες Ἀθαναίων ἐβάλοντο φαεννὰν
> κρηπῖδ' ἐλευθερίας (77),

'where the sons of the Athenians laid the shining foundation of freedom'.

In another dithyramb written for performance in Athens (75) Pindar begins by inviting the Olympian gods to attend and receive garlands of bound violets and 'these songs plucked in spring-time',

> τᾶν τ' ἐαριδρόπων ἀοιδᾶν,

and a few lines later he speaks of the glories of spring. Greek poets did not write about nature for its own sake, but they were ready to describe its beauties as part of some wider theme. Pindar was clearly alive to its delights:

> φοινικοεάνων ὁπότ' οἰχθέντος Ὡρᾶν θαλάμου
> εὔοδμον ἐπάγοισιν ἔαρ φυτὰ νεκτάρεα.   15
> τότε βάλλεται, τότ' ἐπ' ἀμβρόταν χθόν' ἐραταὶ
> ἴων φόβαι, ῥόδα τε κόμαισι μείγνυται,
> ἀχεῖ τ' ὀμφαὶ μελέων σὺν αὐλοῖς,
> οἰχνεῖ τε Σεμέλαν ἑλικάμπυκα χοροί (75.14-19).

'. . . when the chamber of the crimson-robed Seasons is opened, and the nectar-sweet plants bring fragrant spring. Then, then the lovely locks of violets are cast over the immortal earth, roses are twined in the hair, the voices of songs ring out to the sound of pipes, and choirs attend Semele of the circling headband.' With mention of Semele, mother of Dionysus, Pindar reverts to the dithyrambic theme, although he may have seen Dionysiac forces at work in the rich growth of spring. His epithets have a strongly pictorial quality, and it is they, together with bold phrasing like *omphai meleōn*, 'the voices of songs', that a modern reader notices. It is instructive to see what the critic Dionysius, who quotes the lines, found in them. Pindar provides him with the sole example among the lyric poets of the 'austere' style: he finds the lines strong, weighty and dignified, harsh and rough, though not painfully so, and possessing an old-fashioned austere beauty. Surprisingly he concentrates his criticism on what he calls the harshness of the juxtaposition of final *n* with the mute consonants *t, ph, kh* and also *l*, of which there are a dozen cases in the 19 lines he quotes; examples given above are *tan t'*, *ambrotan khthon'* and *iōn phobai*. The combination is jarring to his ear, since *nt* and the others cannot occur within single syllables (a word like *anti* would be divided *an-ti*), and there must be a gap between the consonants if each is properly pronounced. Most modern readers would find no difficulty and might be ready to call the lines smooth and euphonious.

Little remains of the processional-songs. One, perhaps in honour of Artemis, began

> τί κάλλιον ἀρχομένοισιν ἢ καταπαυομένοισιν
> ἢ βαθύζωνόν τε Λατὼ
> καὶ θοᾶν ἵππων ἐλάτειραν ἀεῖσαι; (fr. 89a).

'What finer theme for beginning or ending than to sing of low-girdled Leto and of the goddess who drives swift horses?' Pindar used myth in this genre also; he seems to have told how the gods were pursued to Egypt by the monster Typhos and changed themselves into animal form there to escape him (fr. 91). This sounds like one of the myths that he might have found hard to accept, given his strong sense of what was appropriate to divinity; but he may have told in the same poem how Zeus imprisoned the monster under Mount Etna and killed it.

Thanks to papyrus finds we have considerably more of the partheneia, and our knowledge of them is supplemented by the judgment of the critic Dionysius that they differed in style from other Pindaric poetry: whereas the rest was composed in the 'archaic and austere style', they were not, although they too had a nobility and dignity (*Dem.* ch. 39). The Plutarchian treatise *On Music* similarly implies that partheneia lacked solemnity, those of Simonides, Pindar and Bacchylides no less than Alcman's (1136f). In the second Partheneion the girls' chorus sings,

> ἐμὲ δὲ πρέπει
> παρθενήϊα μὲν φρονεῖν
> γλώσσᾳ τε λέγεσθαι (94b. 33-5).

'For me it is fitting to think a maiden's thoughts and utter a maiden's speech.' Pan is a suitably light-hearted theme (95–100).

Proclus said that partheneia praised both gods and man. The second Partheneion, the best preserved, is of the type called the *Daphnēphorikon*, a hymn sung to pipe accompaniment (14) at the Theban festival of Apollo Ismenios, when bay (*daphnē*: 8, 69) was carried in the procession. The girls begin by singing that Apollo has come to give undying honour to Thebes, but they move at once from the god to his human worshippers:

> ἀλλὰ ζωσαμένα τε πέπλον ὠκέως
> χεϱσίν τ' ἐν μαλακαῖσιν ὄϱπαϰ' ἀγλαὸν
> δάφνας ὀχέοισα πάν-
> δοξον Αἰολάδα σταθμὸν
> υἱοῦ τε Παγώνδα   10
> ὑμνήσω στεφάνοισι θάλ-
> λοισα παϱθένιον κάϱα (94b. 6-12).

'But quickly girding up my robe and holding in my soft hands a splendid branch of bay I shall sing of the all-glorious dwelling of Aeoladas and his son Pagondas, my maiden head blossoming with garlands.' Later they sing,

> πιστὰ δ' Ἀγασικλέει
> μάϱτυς ἤλυθον ἐς χοϱὸν
> ἐσλοῖς τε γονεῦσιν
> ἀμφὶ πϱοξενίαισι (38-41).

'I have come to the dance as a trusty witness for Agasicles and his noble parents, out of friendship.' Agasicles, son of Pagondas, must have been the *daphnēphoros*, the boy who carried the bay in procession. The chorus lists the honours the family has won in horse-racing in Boeotia and Olympia, and continues with directions for the procession:

> Δαμαίνας πα[ῖ, ἐ]να[ισίμ]ῳ νῦν μοι ποδὶ
> στείχων ἀγέο· [τ]ὶν γὰϱ ε[ὔ]φϱων ἕψεται
> πϱώτα θυγάτηϱ [ὁ]δοῦ
> δάφνας εὐπετάλου σχεδ[ὸ]ν
> βαίνοισα πεδίλοις,   70
> Ἀνδαισιστϱότα ἂν ἐπά-
> σκησε μήδεσ[ι] . . . (66-72).

'Son of Damaena [Pagondas], now lead the way for me, marching with propitious foot; for you will be joyfully followed along the way by your daughter first, walking in her sandals near the leafy bay, your daughter whom Andaesistrota has trained in (varied?) arts.' As in Alcman's partheneia the main participants are mentioned by name; Andaesistrota may be the girl's mother, wife of Pagondas, or her trainer. Again as in Alcman, the girls sing of their dress and adornments, though with less gaiety and with no trace of eroticism when they mention their leader. On one occasion Pindar seems to echo language used by Alcman's choir, although the result is typically bold and more complex than the original: Alcman's girls say of their leader, 'and she is of course not more melodious than the Sirens, for they are goddesses, but . . .' (1.96–8); Pindar's sing,

> σειρῆνα δὲ κόμπον
> αὐλίσκων ὑπὸ λωτίνων
> μιμήσομ' ἀοιδαῖς
> κεῖνον, ὃς Ζεφύρου τε σιγάζει πνοὰς
> αἰψηράς . . . (13-17).

'In my songs to the accompaniment of lotus-wood pipes I shall copy that Siren-vaunt, which silences the swift blasts of Zephyr . . . ' Pindar has equated the girls' vaunt, that is, their praise of the achievements of the Theban family, with the Siren whose song worked magic.

The nature of the hyporchemata or dance-songs remains enigmatic, but Proclus says that they were composed in honour of the gods, and two fragments make statements about divine power:

> θεοῦ δὲ δείξαντος ἀρχὰν
> ἕκαστον ἐν πρᾶγος, εὐθεῖα δὴ
> κέλευθος ἀρετὰν ἑλεῖν,
> τελευταί τε καλλίονες (108a).

'When the god has revealed the beginning for any exploit, the path to grasp excellence is a straight one and the ends are finer.'

> θεῷ δὲ δυνατὸν μελαίνας
> ἐκ νυκτὸς ἀμίαντον ὄρσαι φάος,
> κελαινεφέϊ δὲ σκότει
> καλύψαι σέλας καθαρὸν
> ἁμέρας (108b).

'For the god it is possible to rouse unsullied light out of black night, and to hide the pure light of day in the black cloud of darkness.' In such passages he uses the singular *theos* to refer to the gods in general, although he may have Zeus in mind as the supreme god; so in the fragment

> τί θεός; τὸ πᾶν (140d),

'What is god? Everything.'

In the victory-odes he can sing of the god's power in language of startling beauty:

> θεὸς ἅπαν ἐπὶ ἐλπίδεσσι τέκμαρ ἀνύεται,
> θεός, ὃ καὶ πτερόεντ' αἰετὸν κίχε, καὶ θαλασ-
> σαῖον παραμείβεται

δελφῖνα, καὶ ὑψιφϱόνων τιν' ἔκαμψε βϱοτῶν,
ἑτέϱοισι δὲ κῦδος ἀγήϱαον παϱέδωκ' (*Pyth*. 2.49-52).

'The god accomplishes his every purpose in accordance with his expectations, the god who can overtake even the winged eagle and pass the dolphin in the sea, and can bend any proud mortal and give undying glory to others.' Zeus is omnipotent:

Ζεὺς τά τε καὶ τὰ νέμει,
Ζεὺς ὁ πάντων κύϱιος (*Isthm*. 5.52-3).

'Zeus grants this and that, Zeus the master of all.' In the first *Pythian* Pindar prays to Apollo for the success of Hieron's new city of Etna, and continues,

ἐκ θεῶν γὰϱ μαχαναὶ πᾶσαι βϱοτέαις ἀϱεταῖς,
καὶ σοφοὶ καὶ χεϱσὶ βιαταὶ πεϱίγλωσ-
σοί τ' ἔφυν (41-2).

'For from the gods come all the resources for men's excellences, and thanks to them they are wise or strong of hand or eloquent.' This passage, like that from the second *Pythian*, is given prominence by its position at the opening of a triad. The gods' power is beyond belief:

ἐμοὶ δὲ θαυμάσαι
θεῶν τελεσάντων οὐδέν ποτε φαίνεται
ἔμμεν ἄπιστον (*Pyth*. 10.48-50).

'For me nothing of the gods' doing seems too incredible for wonder'. Their designs cannot be known:

τί ἔλπεαι σοφίαν ἔμμεν, ἂν ὀλίγον τοι
ἀνὴϱ ὑπὲϱ ἀνδϱὸς ἴσχει;
οὐ γὰϱ ἔσθ' ὅπως τὰ θεῶν
βουλεύματ' ἐϱευνάσει βϱοτέᾳ φϱενί·
θνατᾶς δ' ἀπὸ ματϱὸς ἔφυ (fr. 61).

'Why do you count as wisdom that in which man slightly surpasses man? He shall never discover the gods' plans with his human mind, since he is born of a mortal mother.'

Pindar's strongly religious cast of mind will not allow him to tell stories which bring discredit on the gods. In the first *Olympian* he rejects the tale that Demeter ate Pelops' flesh:

ἐμοὶ δ' ἄποϱα γαστϱίμαϱ-
γον μακάϱων τιν' εἰπεῖν· ἀφίσταμαι·
ἀκέϱδεια λέλογχεν θαμινὰ κακαγόϱους (52-3).

'For me it is impossible to call any of the gods a glutton. I stand clear. Lack of profit has often come the way of evil-speakers.' The tale of the eaten flesh, says Pindar, was put about by neighbours envious of Pelops' fortune in being loved by Poseidon. So in connection with the story that Heracles fought against the gods at Pylos he cries,

> ἀπό μοι λόγον
> τοῦτον, στόμα, ῥῖψον·
> ἐπεὶ τό γε λοιδορῆσαι θεοὺς
> ἐχθρὰ σοφία . . .
>   ἔα πόλεμον μάχαν τε πᾶσαν
> χωρὶς ἀθανάτων (*Ol.* 9.35-8, 40-1).

'Throw away that tale, my mouth! For to revile the gods is a hateful skill . . . Keep war and all fighting apart from the gods.' By *sophia*, 'wisdom, skill', he must mean the poet's skill.

Myth forms the centre-piece of most of the longer victory-songs, and the great heroes, half-men and half-gods in the sense that they had one divine parent, make many appearances. Heracles is of greatest importance to Pindar, especially in the odes for Olympic victories since he was regarded as the founder of the Olympic games.

> κωφὸς ἀνήρ τις, ὃς Ἡρακλεῖ στόμα μὴ περιβάλλει,
> μηδὲ Διρκαίων ὑδάτων ἀὲ μέ-
>   μναται, τά νιν θρέψαντο καὶ Ἰφικλέα (*Pyth.* 9.87-8).

'Dumb is the man who does not set his mouth to sing of Heracles and does not remember for ever the waters of Dirce which nourished him and Iphicles.' He was born in Thebes, 'mother' of Pindar also (*Isthm.* 1.1). The first *Nemean* tells the miraculous tale of the baby who strangled two serpents sent to kill him by an angry Hera, thanks to 'his extraordinary spirit and strength' (56–7); and Teiresias prophesied his great achievements and their reward:

> αὐτὸν μὰν ἐν εἰρή-
> να τὸν ἅπαντα χρόνον <ἐν> σχερῷ
> ἡσυχίαν καμάτων μεγάλων
> ποινὰν λαχόντ' ἐξαίρετον
> ὀλβίοις ἐν δώμασι, δεξάμενον
> θαλερὰν Ἥβαν ἄκοιτιν καὶ γάμον
> δαίσαντα πὰρ Δὶ Κρονίδᾳ,
>   σεμνὸν αἰνήσειν νόμον (69-72).

'Heracles himself will as choice recompense win rest from his great labours in the dwelling of the blessed, will take blooming Hebe as his wife, celebrating his marriage in the presence of Zeus, son of Cronus, and will praise his august rule, at peace for all time continuously.' Thus given a final home on Olympus he can be called *hērōs theos* (*Nem.* 3.22), a hero become god. References to his labours and his *aretai*, deeds of prowess, fill the victory-odes: Pindar saw him as the supreme contestant, a model for lesser athletes.

Other heroes were likewise singled out for special honours after death. Pelops won his bride by his victory in the chariot-race in Elis:

> νῦν δ᾽ ἐν αἱμακουρίαις
> ἀγλααῖσι μέμικται,
> Ἀλφεοῦ πόρῳ κλιθείς,
> τύμβον ἀμφίπολον ἔχων πολυξενω-
>   τάτῳ παρὰ βωμῷ· τὸ δὲ κλέος
> τηλόθεν δέδορκε τᾶν Ὀλυμπιάδων ἐν δρόμοις
> Πέλοπος (*Ol.* 1.90-5).

'Now he has been awarded splendid blood-sacrifices where he lies at the crossing of the Alpheus with a much-visited tomb near the altar where strangers throng; and the glory of the Olympic festival shines afar among the race-courses of Pelops.' Others were honoured by a renewal of life after death: Peleus, Cadmus and Achilles dwell in the island of the blest (*Ol.* 2.68–80), Castor and Polydeuces spend half of their days on Olympus (*Nem.* 10.55ff.). Certainly all these were related to the gods by blood or by marriage; such beliefs go back to Homer, who in the *Odyssey* gives the prediction of Proetus that Menelaus will live on in the Elysian plain since he is husband of Helen and so son-in-law of Zeus (*Od.* 4.561ff.); but Pindar uses them to illustrate the happiness that man can achieve by his effort.

*   *   *

Bacchylides, the contemporary of Pindar, wrote precisely the same types of religious choral song, but except for the dithyrambs we can say little about their content. He wrote a hymn to Hecate, addressing her as *Hekata daidophore*, 'torch-bearer', and *Nuktos megalokolpou thugater*, 'daughter of great-bosomed Night' (fr. 1B). Hesiod, who sang her praises in *Theogony* 411ff., made her the child of Perses and Asteria; Bacchylides' description suggests rather the moon-goddess with whom she is sometimes identified. If the phrases are typical, he used compound adjectives as freely in his hymns as in his victory-odes. One hymn may be addressed to Demeter or her daughter Persephone, and one to Apollo is classed as 'apopemptic', a hymn for the departure of a god on his travels as opposed to a 'cletic' hymn which invited him to appear. Bacchylides is the only poet who is said to have composed this type, and we are told that he described the places and peoples which the god was leaving and those he planned to visit.

The only paean of which we have much knowledge was written for the cult of

Apollo Pythaeus at Asine in the Argolid. It told how Heracles moved the Dryopes from Delphi to Asine, and how Melampus in later times established there an altar and precinct of Apollo Pythaeus. The poem contained an impassioned account of the blessings brought by peace; the passage may have been part of a prayer to Apollo for quiet prosperity:

τίκτει δέ τε θνατοῖσιν εἰ-
  ρήνα μεγαλάνορα πλοῦτον
καὶ μελιγλώσσων ἀοιδᾶν ἄνθεα
δαιδαλέων τ' ἐπὶ βωμῶν
θεοῖσιν αἴθεσθαι βοῶν ξανθᾷ φλογὶ   65
μηρί' εὐμάλλων τε μήλων
γυμνασίων τε νέοις
αὐλῶν τε καὶ κώμων μέλειν.
ἐν δὲ σιδαροδέτοις πόρπαξιν αἰθᾶν
ἀραχνᾶν ἱστοὶ πέλονται   70
ἔγχεα τε λογχωτὰ ξίφεα
  τ' ἀμφάκεα δάμναται εὐρώς . . .
χαλκεᾶν δ' οὐκ ἔστι σαλπίγγων κτύπος,   75
οὐδὲ συλᾶται μελίφρων
ὕπνος ἀπὸ βλεφάρων
ἀῷος ὃς θάλπει κέαρ.
συμποσίων δ' ἐρατῶν βρίθοντ' ἀγυιαί,
παιδικοί θ' ὕμνοι φλέγονται (fr. 4. 61-80).

'Peace gives birth to noble wealth for mortals, to the flowers of honey-tongued songs, to the burning for gods of thighs of oxen and fleecy sheep in yellow flame on elaborate altars, to young men's concern with the gymnasium, with pipes and revelry. On iron-pinned shieldgrips are found the spinnings of red-brown spiders, and sharp-pointed spears and double-edged swords are subdued by rust . . . There is no din of bronze trumpets, and sleep, honey for the mind, still soothing the heart at daybreak, is not pillaged from men's eyelids. The streets are laden with lovely feasts, and the songs of boys rise like flame.' The themes of war and peace occupied Pindar also: his eighth *Pythian* begins with a hymn to *Hēsukhia*, Peace or Quiet; he called war *gluku* . . . *apeiroisi* (fr. 110), 'a sweet thing for those who have not experienced it', and described *stasis*, 'civil strife', as *penias doteiran, ekhthran kourotrophon* (fr. 109), 'giver of poverty, hateful nurse for young men'. Bacchylides elaborates these ideas: Peace brings forth 'noble' wealth, as Pindar calls Peace herself 'noble'; and young men live to exercise in the gymnasium and to enjoy the riotous processions (*kōmoi*) that followed the symposium. This is choral poetry at its most elaborate, with a profusion of epithets, bold phrases—'flowers of songs', 'streets laden with feasts', 'flaming songs'—and a succession of sharp images loosely connected in the paratactic manner. It seems unlikely that Bacchylides

often inserted such displays of virtuosity in his religious poems, since antho-
logists like Stobaeus, who quotes the present passage, would have seized on
them.

Only a few phrases of the processional-songs and hyporchemata or dance-
songs survive, nothing at all of the partheneia; but parts of a dozen dithyrambs,
including two complete poems, turned up on papyrus with the victory-odes.
Bacchylides' concept of the dithyramb differs from Pindar's. It is not a poem
in which the praise of Dionysus is sung or his powers or exploits described;
none of our examples mentions or alludes to the god except for the *Io*, the
closing lines of which speak of Io's descendants, Cadmus, Semele and Dionysus,
'the rouser of Bacchic rites . . . and lord of garlanded choirs' (19.49–51). One
poem, called the *Eitheoi* (*The Youths*) or *Theseus*, can hardly be distinguished
from a paean: the Athenians, when their protector Theseus is miraculously
preserved, *paianixan* (17.129), 'shouted paeans', and Bacchylides continues
with the closing prayer,

> Δάλιε, χοροῖσι Κηΐων
> φρένα ἰανθεὶς
> ὄπαζε θεόπομπον ἐσθλῶν τύχαν (130-2).

'Delian [Apollo], rejoice in your heart at the choirs of the Ceans and grant a
heaven-sent fortune of blessings.' In another he speaks of paeans and addresses
Pythian Apollo, perhaps making reference to the god's holiday in Thrace,
before going on to sing of Heracles (16.8–12). The hymn must have been a
dithyramb sung at Delphi during the three months of the year when Apollo
was absent.

The dithyramb has become simply a narrative choral song, still in triadic
form; our examples are from 35 to 132 lines in length. Sometimes Homeric
material is used, notably in the *Sons of Antenor*, where the story of the pre-war
mission of Odysseus and Menelaus to Troy to request the return of Helen
(*Iliad* 3.205ff.) is told with a strong reminiscence of the epic manner:

> Μοῦσα, τίς πρῶτος λόγων ἄρχεν δικαίων; (15.47)

'Muse, who was the first to make the claim for justice?' In Homer Antenor
recalled Menelaus' speech as being that of a man of few words, brief but clear.
Bacchylides finds the laconic manner congenial: he presents the speech in
fourteen short lines, and ends the poem with the end of the speech. Odysseus'
words, which Homer describes as falling like snowflakes in winter, are omitted
completely, and the failure of the Greek plea is taken for granted. The abrupt
ending is typical of Bacchylides' dithyrambs: an episode in a well-known story
is highlighted, and that is all. There is no attempt to round it off: the moment
is what matters. Sometimes a myth of local interest is chosen, that of Messenian

Idas for the Spartans (20), that of Theseus in a dithyramb which was almost certainly for the Athenians (18).

The interaction of gods and heroes is the theme of *The Youths* (or *Theseus*: dith. 17). Theseus, the Athenian, is sailing to Crete with his fourteen young compatriots, fodder for the Minotaur; Minos, king of Crete, is also on board, and when he assaults one of the girls, 'chafed' by Aphrodite, Theseus rounds on him for this outrage: Minos may be son of Zeus, he cries, but he is himself the son of Poseidon. Minos appeals to Zeus to give sign of his fatherhood, and Zeus answers with a lightning-flash. Theseus, challenged to recover a ring which Minos throws into the sea, Poseidon's element, emerges triumphantly; and with the poet's prayer to Apollo the song has ended. Theseus has defied the tyrant on this occasion; no mention is made of the sequel in which he kills the Minotaur and so saves the young Athenians. The narrative is concentrated, and the heroes' spoken words occupy some two-fifths of the whole. The passage in which Theseus accepts Minos' challenge exemplifies the rapid narrative style and the poet's powers of vivid description; vase-painters were fond of the underwater scene:

ἵετο δ᾽ ὠκύπομπον δόρυ· σόει   90
    νιν βορεὰς ἐξόπιν πνέουσ᾽ ἄητα·
    τρέσσαν δ᾽ Ἀθαναίων
ἠϊθέων <πᾶν> γένος, ἐπεὶ
ἥρως θόρεν πόντονδε, κα-
    τὰ λειρίων τ᾽ ὀμμάτων δά-   95
    κρυ χέον, βαρεῖαν ἐπιδέγμενοι ἀνάγκαν.
φέρον δὲ δελφῖνες ἁλι-
    ναιέται μέγαν θοῶς
Θησέα πατρὸς ἱππί-
    ου δόμον· ἔμολέν τε θεῶν   100
    μέγαρον. τόθι κλυτὰς ἰδὼν
ἔδεισε<ν> Νηρῆος ὀλ-
    βίου κόρας· ἀπὸ γὰρ ἀγλα-
    ῶν λάμπε γυίων σέλας
ὧτε πυρός, ἀμφὶ χαίταις   105
    δὲ χρυσεόπλοκοι
δίνηντο ταινίαι· χορῷ δ᾽ ἔτερ-
    πον κέαρ ὑγροῖσι ποσσίν.
εἰδέν τε πατρὸς ἄλοχον φίλαν
σεμνὰν βοῶπιν ἐρατοῖ-   110
    σιν Ἀμφιτρίταν δόμοις·
ἅ νιν ἀμφέβαλεν ἀϊόνα πορφυρέαν,

    κόμαισί τ᾽ ἐπέθηκεν οὔλαις
    ἀμεμφέα πλόκον,

τόν ποτέ οἱ ἐν γάμῳ
δῶκε δόλιος Ἀφροδίτα ῥόδοις ἐρεμνόν.
ἄπιστον ὅ τι δαίμονες
θέωσιν οὐδὲν φρενοάραις βροτοῖς·
νᾶα πάρα λεπτόπρυμναν φάνη· φεῦ,
οἵαισιν ἐν φροντίσι Κνώσιον   120
ἔσχασεν στραταγέταν, ἐπεὶ
μόλ' ἀδίαντος ἐξ ἁλὸς
θαῦμα πάντεσσι, λάμ-
    πε δ' ἀμφὶ γυίοις θεῶν δῶρ', ἀγλαό-
    θρονοί τε κοῦραι σὺν εὐ-
    θυμίᾳ νεοκτίτῳ   125
ὠλόλυξαν, ἔ-
    κλαγεν δὲ πόντος· ἠΐθεοι δ' ἐγγύθεν
νέοι παιάνιξαν ἐρατᾷ ὀπί (17.90-129).

'And the ship was rushing swiftly along: Boreas, a breeze blowing astern, was speeding it; and all the group of young Athenians trembled when the hero leapt into the sea, and they shed tears from their lily eyes in expectation of a woeful doom. And dolphins, sea-dwellers, were swiftly carrying great Theseus to the home of his father, god of horses, and he reached the hall of the gods. There he saw the glorious daughters of blessed Nereus and was awestruck; for from their splendid limbs there shone a gleam as of fire, and round their hair were twined ribbons with gold inwoven; and they were delighting their hearts by dancing with liquid feet. And he saw his father's dear wife, august ox-eyed Amphitrite, in the lovely house; she put purple linen about him and set on his thick hair a faultless garland which once at her marriage guileful Aphrodite had given her, dark with roses. Nothing that the gods perform is beyond the belief of sane mortals: he appeared beside the ship with its slender prow. Whew, in what thoughts did he check the commander of Cnossus [Minos], when he came unwet from the sea, a miracle for all, and the gods' gifts shone on his limbs, and the splendid-throned maidens [the Nereids] cried out with newly-founded joy, and the sea rang out; and close by him the youths raised a paean with lovely voice.' This literal translation may perhaps bring out the shortness of the units, almost all linked by the simplest connectives, whether the verb is in the imperfect tense and draws a picture or in the aorist and denotes an action. The epithets are important: sometimes they are traditional, as when he calls Amphitrite 'ox-eyed', reminding us of the Homeric Hera, or Aphrodite 'guileful', as in Sappho, Theognis and Simonides; but sometimes they are new and astonishing: the 'lily' eyes of the young Athenians might well have come from Pindar, and the 'liquid' feet of the dancing sea-nymphs quaintly suggest supple movement. The exclamation *pheu*, 'whew', is a lively representation of a whistle of surprise.

One remarkable dithyramb, the *Theseus* (18), is in a class of its own: it is a dramatic lyric, consisting of four speeches, two in which a chorus of Athenians asks questions, two in which their king Aegeus answers them. The symmetry is made complete by the rejection of triadic structure in favour of four identically-patterned stanzas, one for each speech. As in the other dithyrambs Bacchylides chooses a moment of excitement and suspense, Theseus' approach to Athens, omitting preliminaries and outcome; but here his fondness for direct speech, inherited from Homer and Stesichorus, has reached its limit in the dialogue form. Tragedy was of course being composed in his lifetime: he was a younger contemporary of Aeschylus; but no tragedy shows the extreme metrical parallelism of this lyric dialogue.

Like Pindar and perhaps Simonides before him Bacchylides makes myth the centrepiece of his victory-songs. Sometimes he will choose a story of local interest: for a victor from Ceos, his own island, he tells at some length the supernatural events leading to the birth of Euxantius, founding ruler of the island's main city, Iulis (1); for Automedes of Phlius he tells myths associated with the local river, the Asopus (9); for an Aeginetan he sings, as Pindar also did, of the descendants of the hero Aeacus, concentrating on the exploits of Achilles and Ajax at Troy (13). The interaction of gods and men is a prominent theme: Croesus was miraculously rescued from the pyre by a grateful Apollo (3); the daughters of Proetus, who boasted that their father's palace at Tiryns was finer than Hera's temple in Argos, were afflicted with madness by Hera and finally cured by Artemis (11); Meleager was harried to death by Artemis' implacable anger, left unexplained in the poem (5). In this ode, Bacchylides' most beautiful and poignant composition, the spirit of Meleager tells his sad tale to Heracles, who has gone down to the underworld to fetch Cerberus: Artemis, angry with Meleager's father Oeneus, sent a boar to ravage the plain of Calydon; Meleager and his family succeeded at last in killing it, but Artemis, not satisfied, made the victors fight among themselves over the boar's hide; Meleager killed two brothers of his mother, Althaea, who retaliated by throwing on the fire the log on which his life depended:

τύχον μὲν

Δαἲπύλου Κλύμενον   145
παῖδ' ἄλκιμον ἐξεναρί-
ζων ἀμώμητον δέμας,
πύργων προπάροιθε κιχήσας·
τοὶ δὲ πρὸς εὐκτιμέναν
φεῦγον ἀρχαίαν πόλιν   150

Πλευρῶνα· μίνυθεν δέ μοι ψυχὰ γλυκεῖα·
γνῶν δ' ὀλιγοσθενέων,
αἰαῖ· πύματον δὲ πνέων δάκρυσα τλά[μων,
ἀγλαὰν ἥβαν προλείπων' (5.144-54).

'I happened to be slaying Clymenus, valiant son of Daipylus, faultless in body, having caught him in front of the wall; and the others were fleeing towards well-built Pleuron, that ancient city; and my sweet life was diminished within me; and I realised that I had little strength left, alas! And as I breathed my last I wept, poor wretch, at leaving behind my glorious youth.' The staccato manner effectively portrays the despair of the young man, dying in his moment of triumph as he slays a fine warrior. Truly this world is a vale of tears, and Heracles weeps for the only time in his life. When he turns from thoughts of the futility of man's life to contemplate what can be achieved, he asks if Meleager left a sister in his father's house. Meleager speaks of Deianira; and the listener feels a renewed chill of despair since he knows that this young woman will be the cause of Heracles' death and will take her own life in remorse.

The influence of the gods is pervasive in the poetry of Bacchylides. Certainly he never interrupts the flow of narrative to comment as Pindar does on the nature of godhead: there is nothing more remarkable than the formulaic

> ἄπιστον ὅ τι δαίμονες
> θέωσιν οὐδὲν φρενοάραις βροτοῖς (17.117-18).

'Nothing that the gods perform is beyond the belief of sane mortals.' Bacchylides does not claim any special relationship with the gods as Pindar did: he is not their *mantis*, 'prophet', and he does not claim that gods or heroes appeared to him directly. But they make their presence felt, not only in his tales of the heroic past but in the lives of the victors whose achievements he praises. The great games were part of a religious ceremony, and victory is granted by the appropriate god, Zeus at Olympia (6.1, 8.26), Apollo at Delphi (4.1, 11.15), Poseidon at the Isthmus (1.155, where 'the high-throned son of Cronus' is less likely to be Zeus), Zeus or 'the daemon' at Nemea (13.58ff., 9.27). Conversely victory may be refused by a god (11.34). Other patron deities may promote the interests of their charges: Artemis of Metapontion grants victory at Delphi to a boy from her city (11.37), and Athena honours the Athenian trainer Menander (13.190ff.). Zeus gives political power (3.11, 70, 5.199), Ares success in war (5.34), Apollo medical skill (1.148). Gods who have a special connection with a victor's city are addressed at the beginnings of odes, Demeter and Persephone, whose priest Hieron was (3.1ff.), Hestia in the celebration of a Thessalian victory (14B. 1ff.). Metapontion is *theotimon astu*, 'a god-honoured city' (11.12), since Artemis makes her home there:

> σὺν δὲ τύχα
> ναίεις Μεταπόντιον, ὦ
> χρυσέα δέσποινα λαῶν·
> ἄλσος τέ τοι ἱμερόεν
> Κάσαν παρ' εὔυδρον (11.115-19).

'With happy fortune you dwell in Metapontion, golden queen of your people; and you have a lovely grove by the Casas with its fine water.' Bacchylides' own island of Ceos has as founder of its city Euxantius, son of Minos and so grandson of Zeus (1.112ff.).

A host of minor deities moves among the Olympian gods. *Phēma*, Fame, is invoked at the beginning of two poems (2, 10) and is asked to carry the news of triumph to the victor's home. *Nika*, Victory, keeps company with Zeus on Olympus and judges the outcome of prowess for gods and men (11.1ff., 5.33). A passage in the thirteenth ode, written for a victor from Aegina, declares that the island is honoured and governed by *Areta* (Excellence), *Eukleia* (Glory) and *Eunomia* (Lawfulness). Menelaus in the *Antenoridae* makes no mention of Helen, whose return he is demanding, but preaches a brief sermon: his opening text is the protest made by Zeus near the beginning of the *Odyssey*, the remainder is strongly Hesiodic:

ὦ Τρῶες ἀρηΐφιλοι,   50
Ζεὺς ὑψιμέδων ὃς ἅπαντα δέρκεται
οὐκ αἴτιος θνατοῖς μεγάλων ἀχέων,
ἀλλ' ἐν μέσῳ κεῖται κιχεῖν
πᾶσιν ἀνθρώποις Δίκαν ἰθεῖαν, ἁγνᾶς
Εὐνομίας ἀκόλουθον καὶ πινυτᾶς Θέμιτος·   55
ὀλβίων παῖδές νιν αἱρεῦνται σύνοικον.
ἁ δ' αἰόλοις κέρδεσσι καὶ ἀφροσύναις
ἐξαισίοις θάλλουσ' ἀθαμβὴς
Ὕβρις, ἃ πλοῦτον δύναμίν τε θοῶς
ἀλλότριον ὤπασεν, αὖτις   60
    δ' ἐς βαθὺν πέμπει φθόρον,
    κε]ίνα καὶ ὑπερφιάλους
Γᾶς] παῖδας ὤλεσσεν Γίγαντας· (15.50-63).

' "Warloving men of Troy, high-ruling Zeus, who sees all things, is not responsible for the great troubles of mortals; no, it is open to all men to reach straightforward Justice, the attendant of holy Lawfulness and prudent Themis [Law]: happy the man whose sons choose her to dwell with them. But shameless Outrage, luxuriating in shifty cunning and lawless folly, she who swiftly gives a man another's wealth and power and then hurls him into deep ruination,—it was she who destroyed the insolent sons of Earth, the Giants." '

The correct attitude towards the gods is the theme of myths told in both victory-odes and dithyrambs. Croesus showed piety by the richness of his offerings to Apollo, and Hiero has followed suit:

θεὸν θ[εό]ν τις
ἀγλαϊζέθω· γὰρ ἄριστος [ὄ]λβων (3.21-2).

'Let all men honour the god, the god! That is the best prosperity.' The Cean myth of the first ode deals with hospitality given to the gods and rewarded when Dexithea ('Welcomer of gods') became mother to a line of kings. The dithyramb *The Youths* contrasts the arrogance of Minos with the protective valour of Theseus. The eleventh ode tells of the boasting of Proetus' daughters, the madness inflicted on them by Hera and its ultimate healing by Artemis.

Bacchylides' invocations of the Muses show another aspect of his religious outlook. Few poems have no invocation, and he often singles out one of the Muses, Clio and Urania four times each, Calliope once, to appeal to her. He calls himself 'famed servant of Urania of the gold headband' (5.13–4), and 'divine, i.e. divinely-inspired, spokesman of the violet-eyed Muses' (9.3).

*   *   *

It remains to say something of the minor contemporaries of Simonides, Pindar and Bacchylides. Some are little more than names; for example, Tynnichus of Chalcis, composer of a famous paean: Aeschylus, asked to write one for the Delphians, refused on the grounds that he could not match Tynnichus' poem, and Socrates in Plato's *Ion* 534d calls it 'almost the most beautiful of all lyric poems; truly, as he himself calls it, a discovery of the Muses'.

Lasus of Hermione was a famous musician who was said to have taught Pindar. He was associated especially with the musical elaboration of the dithyramb and with the introduction of dithyrambic contests at Athens in the time of the tyrants. We have little of his poems: the *Centaurs*, in which he avoided using the letter sigma, may have been a dithyramb (704); another asigmatic song was his hymn to Demeter of Hermione, the opening of which was:

> Δάματρα μέλπω Κόραν τε Κλυμένοι' ἄλοχον
> μελιβόαν ὕμνον ἀναγνέων
> Αἰολίδ' ἄμ βαρύβρομον ἁρμονίαν (702).

'I sing to Demeter and the Maiden [Persephone], wife of Clymenus [Hades], leading my honeyed hymn through the deep-sounding Aeolian tuning.' He draws attention to the musical idiom of his song, perhaps because it was new to choral poetry.

Another Peloponnesian, Pratinas of Phlius, was famous as the first to write satyr-plays; but a piece of vigorous poetry, in which a chorus turns on the piper-accompanist, complaining of the mad din at Dionysus' altar and stating the preeminence of song over pipe-music (708), may come from a dithyramb rather than a satyr-play. The last two lines are

θρίαμβε διθύραμβε κισσόχαιτ' ἄναξ,
<ἄκου'> ἄκουε τὰν ἐμὰν Δώριον χορείαν (708.15-16).

'Thriambus, dithyrambus, lord with ivy in your hair, hear, hear my Dorian dance-song.' Pratinas applies to Dionysus the epithet 'dithyrambus' from which the hymn took its name.

Myrtis was a Boeotian like Pindar and is said to have been his teacher. She used local legend in her poetry, but all we have of her work is Plutarch's summary of her lyric narrative about the Boeotian hero Eunostus (716). Another Boeotian poetess, Corinna, wrote lyrics of the same type, and we have long papyrus fragments on the subjects of a singing-match between the Boeotian mountains Helicon and Cithaeron and the fortunes of the nine daughters of Asopus (654). The titles of other works, *Boeotus, Seven against Thebes, Euonymie, Iolaus, Return (of Orion)*, confirm the local interest of her work, and the mysterious title (*w*)*eroia* may mean 'heroic tales'. But it is not certain that she was a contemporary of Myrtis and Pindar, although legend connected her with them, and she may belong rather to the third century B.C.

Tiny quotations from the work of Telesilla of Argos survive. One poem begins

ἁ δ' Ἄρτεμις, ὦ κόραι,
φεύγοισα τὸν Ἀλφεόν (717),

'Artemis, maidens, fleeing from Alpheus . . .', and must have told how the goddess, pursued by the river-god, went to Ortygia in Sicily. The address to 'maidens' is puzzling: the poetry might be private, like most of Sappho's; but although Sappho sings for her companions (160), she does not address them like this. When writing the cult-song for Adonis, however, she does use the vocative form *korai* (140a), and Alcman in what seems to be a prelude for a partheneion (26) addresses the girls of the choir (*parsenikai meligarues*, 'honey-voiced maidens'). Perhaps this is a similar prelude. Telesilla mentioned the gods, especially their local cults, in other poems: we hear of the temple of Artemis at Epidaurus (720) and that of Apollo Pythaeus at Hermione (719). She may have composed a 'song to Apollo' (718), and she spoke of Niobe's children, who were destroyed by Apollo and Artemis (721). She may have written a poem about the marriage of Zeus and Hera, the goddess of her native city (726).

Another poetess from the Peloponnese, Praxilla of Sicyon, wrote about Adonis, as Sappho had done: when asked by the inhabitants of the underworld what was the most beautiful thing he had left behind, he says,

κάλλιστον μὲν ἐγὼ λείπω φάος ἠελίοιο,
δεύτερον ἄστρα φαεινὰ σεληναίης τε πρόσωπον
ἠδὲ καὶ ὡραίους σικύους καὶ μῆλα καὶ ὄγχνας (747).

'The most beautiful thing I leave behind is the sun's light; second, the shining stars and the moon's face; also ripe cucumbers and apples and pears.' The lines caused amusement to later critics and gave rise to a saying, 'sillier than Praxilla's Adonis'; but they have their own beauty, and mention of ripe vegetables and fruits is not out of place on the lips of a fertility god. Praxilla also wrote dithyrambs, one of which was called *Achilles*; a hexameter line survives in which Achilles is addressed (748).

In Athens one Lamprocles may have written a hymn for Pallas Athena: according to the scholiast the words *Pallada persepolin*, 'Pallas, sacker of cities', quoted by Aristophanes (*Clouds* 967ff.) as an example of the good old-fashioned style, are the beginning of the poem. He was known also for his dithyrambs. The tragic poet Ion of Chios wrote dithyrambs too: in one he told how Antigone and Ismene were burned to death in the temple of Hera by their nephew, Laodamas, son of Eteocles (740), in another how Aegaeon, child of the Sea, was summoned by Thetis to protect Zeus (741). He also wrote a hymn to *Kairos*, Opportunity, perhaps for the cult of the deity at Olympia, and in it he called him in the Hesiodic manner the youngest son of Zeus. Ion's more famous contemporary, Sophocles, wrote a paean for the worship of Asclepius which was introduced to Athens in 420 B.C.: a broken inscription found near the god's temple gives the opening words, an address to Coronis, mother by Apollo of Asclepius, 'the god who wards off suffering' (737b).

The metrical pattern of the Attic scolia could be used for a brief prayer or hymn:

Παλλὰς Τριτογένει' ἄνασσ' Ἀθηνᾶ,
ὄρθου τήνδε πόλιν τε καὶ πολίτας
ἄτερ ἀλγέων καὶ στάσεων
καὶ θανάτων ἀώρων, σύ τε καὶ πατήρ (884).

'Pallas, Trito-born, queen Athena, uphold this city and its citizens, free from pains and strifes and untimely deaths, you and your father.' Even in this short stanza the poet finds it appropriate to begin by listing epithets of the goddess; 'Trito-born' is not well understood, but the first unit may denote water as in the names of the marine deities Triton and Amphitrite.

ὦ Πὰν Ἀρκαδίας μεδέων κλεεννᾶς,
ὀρχηστὰ βρομίαις ὀπαδὲ Νύμφαις,
γελάσειας ὦ Πὰν ἐπ' ἐμαῖς
εὐφροσύναις, ἀοιδαῖς κεχαρημένος (887).

'Pan, ruler of famous Arcadia, dancer, comrade of the bacchant Nymphs, laugh, Pan, at my merriment, rejoicing in my songs.' The first four words form the opening of one of Pindar's partheneia (fr. 95). Pan's worship was introduced to Athens after the battle of Marathon, when the god had cheered the runner Philippides as he crossed the Peloponnesian mountains on his way to request help from Sparta.

CHAPTER SEVEN

Life and Death

Homer describes the death of Patroclus with the words,

ὣς ἄρα μιν εἰπόντα τέλος θανάτοιο κάλυψεν·
ψυχὴ δ' ἐκ ῥεθέων πταμένη Ἀιδόσδε βεβήκειν,
ὃν πότμον γοόωσα, λιποῦσ' ἀνδροτῆτα καὶ ἥβην (*Il.* 16.855-7).

'When he had spoken these words, the end that is death covered him; and his soul, flying from his limbs, went off to the house of Hades, lamenting its doom now that it had left behind its manhood and youth.' No Homeric hero regards death as a happy release: it is a lamentable exchange of the sunlight for the darkness of the underworld, of the varied pleasures of this world for the nothingness of the next.

One account of these pleasures is given by Odysseus to his hosts, the Phaeacians: 'I declare that there is nothing more joyful than when festivity reigns among a whole people, and the banqueters in a house listen to a singer, sitting in their places, and the tables are full of bread and meats, and the wine-pourer draws the wine from the mixing-bowl and takes it and pours it in the cups. To my mind this is perhaps the finest thing of all.' Food, drink and song are the pleasures Odysseus has just enjoyed, and as a well-mannered guest it is these that he commends. The gifts of golden Aphrodite or of sleep might have been mentioned in other circumstances. Menelaus lists sleep, love, sweet song and the perfect dance as desirable activities (*Il.* 13.636-37). Pride of possession and the giving of gifts were both sources of pleasure. Even fighting and lamentation could bring delight.

Death is the negation of all this. The *psyche* or 'soul' of Patroclus flies out of his body: 'soul' is a misleading translation if it suggests that Homer could talk of Patroclus' 'soul' while he was alive. Perhaps the *psyche* should be regarded as breath since the verb *psukhein* can mean 'to blow'. It is insubstantial; when the 'ghost' of Patroclus appeared to request burial for his body, it had his exact appearance, but when Achilles tried to embrace it, it went beneath the earth like smoke, *tetriguia*, 'with a squeak'. Book 11 of the *Odyssey* recounts the hero's journey to Hades. The seer Teiresias, whom he must consult, talks of 'this joyless place' (*aterpea khōron*, 94); when Odysseus tries to embrace his mother, she 'flies' through his arms 'like a shadow or a dream' (207); Agamemnon's once supple limbs have lost all their strength (393); and Achilles, most glorious warrior of all, cries,

> βουλοίμην κ' ἐπάρουρος ἐὼν θητευέμεν ἄλλῳ,
> ἀνδρὶ παρ' ἀκλήρῳ, ᾧ μὴ βίοτος πολὺς εἴη,
> ἢ πᾶσιν νεκύεσσι καταφθιμένοισιν ἀνάσσειν (489-91).

'I would rather be on earth again as serf to another, some poor man with little to live on, than rule over all these dead spirits.' This was the existence, or rather the negation of existence, that awaited all mortals. Andromache, speaking of her dead husband Hector, says that dogs and then worms will eat his body, and that she will burn his clothes, since he will have no need of them (*Il.* 22.508–14). An exception to this view of the dead is implicit in Homer's description of the offerings made by Achilles at the pyre of Patroclus: he sacrifices not only sheep and cattle but honey and oil, four horses, two dogs and twelve young Trojans, possessions that Patroclus might use after his death. Moreover Hector can declare that his fame as a warrior will never die (*Il.* 7.91).

The prospect of the descent to Hades lies always before the Homeric warrior:

> ἐν δὲ ἰῇ τιμῇ ἠμὲν κακὸς ἠδὲ καὶ ἐσθλός·
> κάτθαν' ὁμῶς ὅ τ' ἀεργὸς ἀνὴρ ὅ τε πολλὰ ἐοργώς (*Il.* 9.319-20).

'We are all held in the same esteem, both the bad and the good [i.e. both the coward and the brave warrior]. He who achieves nothing and he who achieves much die alike.' Achilles, who spoke these words, knows that death is inevitable even for him:

> οὐχ ὁράᾳς οἷος καὶ ἐγὼ καλός τε μέγας τε;
> πατρὸς δ' εἴμ' ἀγαθοῖο, θεὰ δέ με γείνατο μήτηρ·
> ἀλλ' ἔπι τοι καὶ ἐμοὶ θάνατος καὶ μοῖρα κραταιή·
> ἔσσεται ἢ ἠὼς ἢ δείλη ἢ μέσον ἦμαρ
> ὁππότε τις καὶ ἐμεῖο Ἄρη ἐκ θυμὸν ἕληται (*Il.* 21.108-12).

'Do you not see how handsome and tall I am? My father was a noble man, my mother a goddess; but death and strong fate await me too. There will be a daybreak or an evening or a noon when someone will take my life in the fighting.' The same great warrior uses death as the image of what is most repellent: 'he is as hateful to me as the gates of Hades' (*Il.* 9.312).

A man's lot in life is the gift of the gods, and it is a miserable one. Achilles makes the most memorable statement of the pessimism which prevails in Homer:

> ὣς γὰρ ἐπεκλώσαντο θεοὶ δειλοῖσι βροτοῖσι,

ζώειν ἀχνυμένοις· αὐτοὶ δέ τ' ἀκηδέες εἰσί.
δοιοὶ γάρ τε πίθοι κατακείαται ἐν Διὸς οὔδει
δώρων οἷα δίδωσι κακῶν, ἕτερος δὲ ἑάων·
ᾧ μέν κ' ἀμμίξας δώῃ Ζεὺς τερπικέραυνος,
ἄλλοτε μέν τε κακῷ ὅ γε κύρεται, ἄλλοτε δ' ἐσθλῷ·
ᾧ δέ κε τῶν λυγρῶν δώῃ, λωβητὸν ἔθηκε,
καί ἑ κακὴ βούβρωστις ἐπὶ χθόνα δῖαν ἐλαύνει,
φοιτᾷ δ' οὔτε θεοῖσι τετιμένος οὔτε βροτοῖσιν (*Il.* 24.525-33).

'The gods have spun for wretched mortals a life of sorrow, while they themselves are carefree. Two jars stand at the threshold of Zeus holding the gifts he
gives, one of evils, the other of blessings. If Zeus, hurler of the thunderbolt,
gives a man a mixture of them, he sometimes meets with evil, sometimes with
good; if he gives him gifts from the urn of misery, he treats him outrageously:
evil famine drives him over the divine earth, and he goes about honoured by
neither gods nor mortals.' Peleus and Priam are Achilles' examples of men who
have had mixed fortunes. We note that no man is given gifts from the urn of
blessings only, and that a man's merits make no difference to his fortune.

Homer makes the Lycian Glaucus comment sadly on man's life. Diomedes
has asked him his lineage, and his reply begins:

'Τυδεΐδη μεγάθυμε, τί ἦ γενεὴν ἐρεείνεις;
οἵη περ φύλλων γενεή, τοίη δὲ καὶ ἀνδρῶν.
φύλλα τὰ μέν τ' ἄνεμος χαμάδις χέει, ἄλλα δέ θ' ὕλη
τηλεθόωσα φύει, ἔαρος δ' ἐπιγίγνεται ὥρη.
ὣς ἀνδρῶν γενεὴ ἡ μὲν φύει, ἡ δ' ἀπολήγει' (*Il.* 6.145-9).

'Great-hearted son of Tydeus, why do you ask about my lineage? As the
generation of leaves, so is that of men. Some leaves are cast on the ground by the
wind; but the trees flourish and grow others when springtime follows. Even so
one generation of men grows up and another ceases.' The unimportance of it
all is Glaucus' theme, and the image of the leaves illustrates both the short span
of man's life and his impermanence.

Pessimism outweighs optimism in the poems of Hesiod. Certainly the
Theogony presents the rule of Zeus in glowing colours as being associated with
Lawfulness, Justice, Peace, the Graces and the Muses, all of whom are his
daughters, and the *Works and Days* begins with the praises of Zeus and
describes the infallible operations of Justice. But Hesiod tells two 'tales' which
indicate how far man's life has declined from its pristine happiness. The first is
the story of Pandora, sent to earth by Zeus after Prometheus had stolen fire for
the benefit of men:

'τοῖς δ' ἐγὼ ἀντὶ πυρὸς δώσω κακόν, ᾧ κεν ἅπαντες
τέρπωνται κατὰ θυμόν, ἑὸν κακὸν ἀμφαγαπῶντες' (57-8).

' "To balance the gift of fire I shall give them a disastrous thing in which they may all take pleasure while embracing their own disaster." ' Pandora arrives, beautiful and finely-dressed, false, wheedling and deceitful, and is accepted by men. When she opens her jar, toil, trouble and disease fly out among men, and only Hope remains. Misogyny is one form of Hesiod's pessimism.

His second tale is an account of the five successive races of men. The golden race knew no sorrow, toil or old age; they lived happily and died easily; the silver generation were foolish, criminal, impious, and were destroyed by Zeus; the bronze race were violent and warlike and destroyed each other. The fourth race, the race of heroes or demigods, is formed by the warriors who died fighting at Thebes and Troy, the figures of Greek epic; they were an improvement over their immediate predecessors, and some live on in the islands of the blessed. Hesiod introduces the fifth race with the words,

μηκέτ' ἔπειτ' ὤφελλον ἐγὼ πέμπτοισι μετεῖναι
ἀνδράσιν, ἀλλ' ἢ πρόσθε θανεῖν ἢ ἔπειτα γενέσθαι (174-5).

'Would that I were not part of the fifth race of men, but had either died earlier or been born later.' The iron men know only toil and sorrow. Ties of family and hospitality will be broken, evil will be commended, not good, might will be right.

Gloom was the literary inheritance of the lyric poets. Most of them express a similar pessimism, and only occasionally is a more confident note heard. No one before the writers of fifth-century Athens expresses the view that the present might actually be an improvement on the past.

* * *

One of Archilochus' fragments recasts a Homeric expression of pessimism: Odysseus, talking of human feebleness, says that while man prospers he never sees hardship ahead, but when the gods send it he must endure it in turn, however reluctantly:

τοῖος γὰρ νόος ἐστὶν ἐπιχθονίων ἀνθρώπων
οἷον ἐπ' ἦμαρ ἄγηισι πατὴρ ἀνδρῶν τε θεῶν τε (*Od.* 18.136-7).

'For the mind of mortal man is as the day brought by the father of men and gods.' To put it prosaically, our view of life is coloured by the circumstances of any given day. Archilochus, whose outlook often led him to echo Odysseus, turns the lines into trochaics:

τοῖος ἀνθρώποισι θυμός, Γλαῦκε Λεπτίνεω πάϊ,
γίνεται θνητοῖς, ὁποίην Ζεὺς ἐφ' ἡμέρην ἄγη,
καὶ φρονέουσι τοῖ' ὁποίοις ἐγκυρέωσιν ἔργμασιν (131, 132).

'The spirit of mortal men, Glaucus, son of Leptines, is as the day brought by Zeus, and their thoughts are as the events they encounter.' Hermann Fraenkel has argued that this is the meaning of man's 'ephemeral' nature: he is 'subject to day and liable to its vicissitudes'.

Archilochus speaks more than once of these vicissitudes:

> τοῖς θεοῖς †τ᾽ εἰθεῖάπαντα†· πολλάκις μὲν ἐκ κακῶν
> ἄνδρας ὀρθοῦσιν μελαίνῃ κειμένους ἐπὶ χθονί,
> πολλάκις δ᾽ ἀνατρέπουσι καὶ μάλ᾽ εὖ βεβηκότας
> ὑπτίους κλίνουσ᾽· ἔπειτα πολλὰ γίνεται κακά,
> καὶ βίου χρήμῃ πλανᾶται καὶ νόου παρήορος (130).

'All things (are easy?) for the gods. Often they set upright after misfortune men who are lying on the black earth, often again they overthrow and put flat on their backs men with a very firm stance; thereafter much misfortune befalls this man, and he roams in need of a livelihood, unhinged in mind.' The gods are both powerful and unpredictable. Communing with his own 'heart' as the Homeric hero often does, he speaks of the *rhusmos*, the 'rhythm', that is, the recurrent pattern or pendulum swing of man's fortunes:

> θυμέ, θύμ᾽ ἀμηχάνοισι κήδεσιν κυκώμενε,
> †αναδευ†, δυσμενέων δ᾽ ἀλέξεο προσβαλὼν ἐναντίον
> στέρνον, †ἐν δοκοῖσιν † ἐχθρῶν πλησίον κατασταθεὶς
> ἀσφαλέως· καὶ μήτε νικέων ἀμφάδην ἀγάλλεο
> μηδὲ νικηθεὶς ἐν οἴκῳ καταπεσὼν ὀδύρεο,   5
> ἀλλὰ χαρτοῖσίν τε χαῖρε καὶ κακοῖσιν ἀσχάλα
> μὴ λίην· γίνωσκε δ᾽ οἷος ῥυσμὸς ἀνθρώπους ἔχει (128).

'My heart, my heart, thrown into turmoil by bewildering troubles, (rise up?), defend yourself and thrust your chest forward to meet the foe . . . standing steadfastly close to the enemy. Neither exult openly in victory nor fall down and weep at home in defeat: rather rejoice in your joys and be vexed by your misfortunes—but not too greatly. Recognise the pattern that rules mankind.' The text of lines 2 and 3 is corrupt but seems to introduce the military metaphors of 4 and 5. The words *mē liēn*, in enjambment like *asphaleōs* of line 4, are to be taken with both of the verbs in line 6: rejoice (but not too much), be vexed (but not too much). One must not take things lying down; but there is no room for an exaggerated response to success or failure, since circumstances may change again tomorrow: *mēden agan*, 'nothing in excess'. The emotional repetition of *thume*, 'my heart', the alliteration of *k* and *kh* in lines 1 and 6 and the rhyme of *agalleo* (4) and *odureo* (5) all contribute to the effect of this fine poem, which may well be complete as it stands.

The sun's eclipse in the year 648 B.C. gave Archilochus another image for the power of Zeus and the unpredictability of man's life:

'χρημάτων ἄελπτον οὐδέν ἐστιν οὐδ' ἀπώμοτον
οὐδὲ θαυμάσιον, ἐπειδὴ Ζεὺς πατὴρ Ὀλυμπίων
ἐκ μεσημβρίης ἔθηκε νύκτ' ἀποκρύψας φάος
ἡλίου λάμποντος, ὑγρὸν δ' ἦλθ' ἐπ' ἀνθρώπους δέος·
ἐκ δὲ τοῦ καὶ πιστὰ πάντα κἀπίελπτα γίγνεται   5
ἀνδράσιν. μηδεὶς ἔθ' ὑμέων εἰσορέων θαυμαζέτω,
μηδ' ἐὰν δελφῖσι θῆρες ἀνταμείψωνται νομὸν
ἐνάλιον καί σφιν θαλάσσης ἠχέεντα κύματα
φίλτερ' ἠπείρου γένηται, τοῖσι δ' ὑλήειν ὄρος' (122.1-9).

'There is nothing one should not expect, nothing one should swear to be impossible, nothing for one to marvel at, since Zeus, father of Olympians, made night from noon, concealing the light of the shining sun, and limp fear came over men. From now on anything is credible and anything is to be expected by men. Let none of you marvel henceforth at what he sees, not even if beasts exchange their pasture for the watery home of the dolphins, and the roaring waves of the sea become dearer than dry land to beasts, the wooded mountain dearer to dolphins.' Aristotle, who quotes the first line of the poem, adds a piece of information which is of the greatest interest and value and is at the same time unnerving, since it means that when dealing with fragments we can never be certain that Archilochus is speaking in his own person: the fault-finding of Archilochus, he says, is put in the mouth of the father who is speaking of his daughter. A papyrus scrap which gives the ends of the following lines mentions one Archenactides and, two lines later, marriage. Presumably the father and daughter are Lycambes and Neobule, to whom Archilochus was betrothed, but we cannot be certain about the identification or about the girl's misdemeanour; all that we can infer is that the father says, 'The eclipse shows that anything is possible, and my daughter's behaviour confirms it.'

One isolated hexameter, addressed to a friend like many of Archilochus' poems, states simply,

πάντα Τύχη καὶ Μοῖρα, Περίκλεες, ἀνδρὶ δίδωσιν (16).

'All things, Pericles, are given to man by Fortune and Fate', a bleak comment on human powerlessness.

But although Archilochus expresses so frequently and so vividly the grimness of man's condition, it does not follow that he adopts or advises a spirit of passive resignation. On the contrary, he displays a sturdy attitude of confident independence and a buoyancy in life's stormy seas. We have already seen his forthright remarks on the type of commander who appeals to him, not the tall long-legged general with his curls and elegant shave, but the short knock-kneed one who is full of courage (114). It is likely that he is talking of real people known to him; but the officer whom he rejects is in the Homeric mould, and it is probably correct to see in the lines a protest against traditional aristocratic values. Certainly the suggestion that a commander's outward appearance could bely his inner character runs counter to Homer's view of the noble warrior. Archilochus' use of the first person singular is important too: *ou phileō . . . alla moi*, 'I do not love . . .; give me instead . . .' The poet's insistence that his likes and dislikes are important to others marks the transition from the epic to the lyric age.

Another piece, this time in iambics, has a similar opening:

'οὔ μοι τὰ Γύγεω τοῦ πολυχρύσου μέλει
οὐδ' εἶλέ πώ με ζῆλος οὐδ' ἀγαίομαι
θεῶν ἔργα, μεγάλης δ' οὐκ ἐρέω τυραννίδος·
ἀπόπροθεν γάρ ἐστιν ὀφθαλμῶν ἐμῶν' (19).

' "I don't care about wealthy Gyges and his riches, nor have I ever been jealous of him. I am not envious of what the gods bring about, and I have no desire to be a great tyrant: that is quite out of my range of vision." ' Gyges was the king of Lydia during the first thirty years of Archilochus' life; but Archilochus is not speaking here in his own person: Aristotle tells us that here, as in the case of the eclipse poem, the poet is setting his own views in the mouth of another, this time an unknown figure called Charon the carpenter; and since these lines form the beginning of the poem, it must have continued or ended with 'So said Charon the carpenter'. The view he expresses is exactly the opposite of that attributed by Solon to the vulgar Athenians who were astonished that he passed by the opportunity to become tyrant: he should have been tyrant of Athens for just one day, even if it meant being flayed for a wineskin the next (33).

The values of a sturdy realist are displayed in the famous poem on the loss of his shield:

ἀσπίδι μὲν Σαΐων τις ἀγάλλεται, ἣν παρὰ θάμνῳ
ἔντος ἀμώμητον κάλλιπον οὐκ ἐθέλων,
αὐτὸν δ' ἐξεσάωσα. τί μοι μέλει ἀσπὶς ἐκείνη;
ἐρρέτω· ἐξαῦτις κτήσομαι οὐ κακίω (5).

'One of the Saians is rejoicing in the shield which I left reluctantly by a bush. It was a blameless piece of equipment too! But I saved myself. What does that shield matter to me? It can go to hell! I'll get another one some day just as good.' There is nothing here of the idealism of the Spartan mother's farewell to her son: 'Return with your shield or on it'; and the anti-heroic thought is expressed in Homer's own language, notably *agalletai*, 'rejoices', *amōmēton*, 'blameless', *erretō*, 'it can go', and in elegiac couplets which come closer to Homer's hexameters than any other lyric form. There may be a pun in *Saiōn* (1) and *exesaōsa* (3): the words occur at the same point in the hexameter line.

Cynicism is displayed also when he speaks of the disrespect shown to the dead. His contemporaries, Callinus and Tyrtaeus, exhorting soldiers who were about to risk their lives, did not depict death in this sombre colouring: when the Ephesians were at war with the neighbouring city of Magnesia, or perhaps when they faced the Cimmerian invasion, Callinus bolstered their spirits with these lines:

καί τις ἀποθνήσκων ὕστατ' ἀκοντισάτω.   5
τιμῆέν τε γάρ ἐστι καὶ ἀγλαὸν ἀνδρὶ μάχεσθαι
    γῆς πέρι καὶ παίδων κουριδίης τ' ἀλόχου
δυσμενέσιν· θάνατος δὲ τότ' ἔσσεται, ὁππότε κεν δὴ
    Μοῖραι ἐπικλώσωσ'· ἀλλά τις ἰθὺς ἴτω
ἔγχος ἀνασχόμενος καὶ ὑπ' ἀσπίδος ἄλκιμον ἦτορ   10
    ἔλσας, τὸ πρῶτον μειγνυμένου πολέμου.
οὐ γάρ κως θάνατόν γε φυγεῖν εἱμαρμένον ἐστὶν
    ἄνδρ', οὐδ' εἰ προγόνων ἦ γένος ἀθανάτων.
πολλάκι δηϊοτῆτα φυγὼν καὶ δοῦπον ἀκόντων
    ἔρχεται, ἐν δ' οἴκω μοῖρα κίχεν θανάτου.   15
ἀλλ' ὁ μὲν οὐκ ἔμπης δήμω φίλος οὐδὲ ποθεινός,
    τὸν δ' ὀλίγος στενάχει καὶ μέγας, ἤν τι πάθη·
λαῷ γὰρ σύμπαντι πόθος κρατερόφρονος ἀνδρὸς
    θνήσκοντος, ζώων δ' ἄξιος ἡμιθέων·
ὥσπερ γάρ μιν πύργον ἐν ὀφθαλμοῖσιν ὁρῶσιν·   20
    ἔρδει γὰρ πολλῶν ἄξια μοῦνος ἐὼν (1.5-21).

'Let every man among you hurl his spear for the last time at the moment of death. For it is honourable and glorious for a man to fight for his country, his children and his wedded wife against the enemy. Death will come whenever the spinning Fates decree it. Come then, let every man go straight ahead, holding high his spear and keeping a stout heart cooped up under his shield in the first shock of the battle. For it is fated that no man escape death, even if he is descended from the immortal gods. Often a man escapes from the fighting and the clash of spears and goes his way, only for the fate of death to overtake him in his house. But such a man is not loved and missed by the people, whereas the other is mourned by both great and small if anything happen to him; for the whole populace misses a stout-hearted warrior when he dies; and while alive he is the equal of the demigods: they look on him as a bastion, for single-handed he does the work of many men.' Callinus' language is Homeric from beginning to end, and the simile of the bastion is also Homeric (*Od.* 11.556), though not the vivid picture of the soldier who escapes death on the battlefield only to die at home, or of the stout heart 'tucked' or 'concentrated' behind the shield. Tyrtaeus used similar language and arguments when haranguing the Spartans:

ὃς δ' αὖτ' ἐν προμάχοισι πεσὼν φίλον ὤλεσε θυμόν,

ἄστυ τε καὶ λαοὺς καὶ πατέρ' εὐκλεΐσας,
πολλὰ διὰ στέρνοιο καὶ ἀσπίδος ὀμφαλοέσσης   25
καὶ διὰ θώρηκος πρόσθεν ἐληλαμένος,
τόνδ' ὀλοφύρονται μὲν ὁμῶς νέοι ἠδὲ γέροντες
ἀργαλέῳ τε πόθῳ πᾶσα κέκηδε πόλις,
καὶ τύμβος καὶ παῖδες ἐν ἀνθρώποις ἀρίσημοι
καὶ παίδων παῖδες καὶ γένος ἐξοπίσω·   30
οὐδέ ποτε κλέος ἐσθλὸν ἀπόλλυται οὐδ' ὄνομ' αὐτοῦ,
ἀλλ' ὑπὸ γῆς περ ἐὼν γίνεται ἀθάνατος,
ὅντιν' ἀριστεύοντα μένοντά τε μαρνάμενόν τε
γῆς πέρι καὶ παίδων θοῦρος Ἄρης ὀλέσῃ (12.23-34).

'Again, he who falls in the front rank and loses his life after bringing honour to
his town and the populace and his father, struck by many blows from in front
through his chest, through his bossed shield and his breastplate—*he* is mourned
by young and old alike, and the whole city grieves for him in sore longing, and
his tomb and his children are conspicuous among men, and his children's
children and his descendants after them: his fair glory never dies nor his name,
but though he is under the earth he is immortal—the man who while displaying
his excellence, holding his ground and fighting for his land and his children,
is destroyed by fierce Ares.'

Archilochus' words are

οὔτις αἰδοῖος μετ' ἀστῶν οὐδὲ περίφημος θανὼν
γίνεται· χάριν δὲ μᾶλλον τοῦ ζοοῦ διώκομεν
<οἱ> ζοοί· κάκιστα δ' αἰεὶ τῷ θανόντι γίνεται (133).

'After death no one is respected or much renowned among the citizens. We
who are alive pursue rather the favour of the living. The worst always befalls
the dead.' Callinus and Tyrtaeus share the Homeric view that a hero's death
can give immortality, but Archilochus again rejects the traditional value.
Another contemporary, the iambic poet Semonides, puts the cynical view even
more concisely:

τοῦ μὲν θανόντος οὐκ ἂν ἐνθυμοίμεθα,
εἴ τι φρονοῖμεν, πλεῖον ἡμέρης μιῆς (2).

'If we have any sense, we shall not keep the dead in mind for more than one
day.' This reads like a black version of Odysseus' words in the *Iliad* (19.228–
29), 'We must bury the dead, steeling our hearts and weeping for them only one
day.'

Yet the dead man must not be mocked either:

οὐ γὰρ ἐσθλὰ κατθανοῦσι κερτομεῖν ἐπ' ἀνδράσιν (134).

'For it is not a fine thing to mock dead men': *de mortuis nil nisi bonum*. Here Archilochus comes closer to conventional thinking: Solon is said to have proposed a law forbidding the Athenians to speak ill of the dead. An epitaph on a physician from Phocis runs

χαῖρε Χάρων, οὐδείς τυ κακῶς λέγει οὐδὲ θανόντα,
πολλοὺς ἀνθρώπων λυσάμενος καμάτου (Friedländer *Epigr*. 86).

'Greetings, Charon: no one speaks ill of you, not even now that you are dead, for you ransomed many men from sickness.'

Archilochus wrote a poem for his friend Pericles when citizens had been lost at sea:

κήδεα μὲν στονόεντα, Περίκλεες, οὔτε τις ἀστῶν
   μεμφόμενος θαλίης τέρψεται οὐδὲ πόλις·
τοίους γὰρ κατὰ κῦμα πολυφλοίσβοιο θαλάσσης
   ἔκλυσεν· οἰδαλέους δ᾽ ἀμφ᾽ ὀδύνης ἔχομεν
πνεύμονας. ἀλλὰ θεοὶ γὰρ ἀνηκέστοισι κακοῖσιν,   5
   ὦ φίλ᾽, ἐπὶ κρατερὴν τλημοσύνην ἔθεσαν
φάρμακον. ἄλλοτέ τ᾽ ἄλλος ἔχει τάδε· νῦν μὲν ἐς ἡμέας
   ἐτράπεθ᾽, αἱματόεν δ᾽ ἕλκος ἀναστένομεν,
ἐξαῦτις δ᾽ ἑτέρους ἐπαμείψεται. ἀλλὰ τάχιστα
   τλῆτε γυναικεῖον πένθος ἀπωσάμενοι (13).

'No citizen nor city, Pericles, will delight in feasting, censuring tearful lamentation: such were the men whom the waves of the roaring sea have washed away, so that our lungs are swollen with grief. But the gods, my friend, provided steadfast endurance as the remedy for incurable evils. One man suffers today, another tomorrow; now the trouble has assailed us, and we bewail a bloody wound, but it will move on to others in time. Come then, all of you, thrust away womanish grief at once and endure.' The poem is probably complete and is well-constructed, with the emphatic final *tlēte*, 'endure', echoing *tlēmosunēn*, 'endurance', of the central couplet. After the first couplet there is enjambment each time, violent in lines 5 and 7, so there is no trace of monotony in the composition. The 'swollen lungs' of the mourners suggest the physical condition of the drowned men, and there are medical metaphors throughout, 'incurable evils', 'remedy', 'bloody wound'. Archilochus presents a logical argument: we have lost fine friends; but there is a remedy in endurance, and we must therefore endure. His response to disaster is not meek resignation: he calls for the quality which brought *polutlas*, 'much-enduring', Odysseus through adversity. The *rhusmos* or pattern of men's lives is offered here as their consolation. In another poem, written when his brother-in-law had been drowned, his response to disaster is even more confident:

οὔτε τι γὰρ κλαίων ἰήσομαι, οὔτε κάκιον

θήσω τερπωλὰς καὶ θαλίας ἐφέπων (11).

'For I shall not cure it by weeping nor make it worse by indulging in pleasures and parties.'

We saw that Semonides' long tirade on women (7) relied for its comic effect on a pervasive pessimism: the monkey-woman is 'the greatest calamity Zeus gave man' (72), woman is the greatest evil Zeus created (96, 115). He composed another poem in iambics in which he set out the blindness of men's aspirations:

> ὦ παῖ, τέλος μὲν Ζεὺς ἔχει βαρύκτυπος
> πάντων ὅσ' ἐστὶ καὶ τίθησ' ὅκη θέλει.
> νόος δ' οὐκ ἐπ' ἀνθρώποισιν· ἀλλ' ἐπήμεροι
> ἃ δὴ βοτὰ ζόουσιν, οὐδὲν εἰδότες
> ὅκως ἕκαστον ἐκτελευτήσει θεός.   5
> ἐλπὶς δὲ πάντας κἀπιπειθείη τρέφει
> ἄπρηκτον ὁρμαίνοντας· οἱ μὲν ἡμέρην
> μένουσιν ἐλθεῖν, οἱ δ' ἐτέων περιτροπάς.
> νέωτα δ' οὐδεὶς ὅστις οὐ δοκεῖ βροτῶν
> Πλούτῳ τε κἀγαθοῖσιν ἵξεσθαι φίλος.   10
> φθάνει δὲ τὸν μὲν γῆρας ἄζηλον λαβόν,
> πρὶν τέρμ' ἵκηται· τοὺς δὲ δύστηνοι βροτῶν
> φθείρουσι νοῦσοι· τοὺς δ' Ἄρει δεδημημένους
> πέμπει μελαίνης Ἀίδης ὑπὸ χθονός.
> οἱ δ' ἐν θαλάσσῃ λαίλαπι κλονεόμενοι   15
> καὶ κύμασιν πολλοῖσι πορφυρῆς ἁλός
> θνήσκουσιν, εὖτ' ἂν μὴ δυνήσωνται ζόειν.
> οἱ δ' ἀγχόνην ἄψαντο δυστήνῳ μόρῳ
> καὐτάγρετοι λείπουσιν ἡλίου φάος.
> οὕτω κακῶν ἄπ' οὐδέν· ἀλλὰ μυρίαι   20
> βροτοῖσι κῆρες κἀνεπίφραστοι δύαι
> καὶ πήματ' ἐστίν. εἰ δ' ἐμοὶ πιθοίατο,
> οὐκ ἂν κακῶν ἐρῷμεν οὐδ' ἐπ' ἄλγεσι
> κακοῖς ἔχοντες θυμὸν αἰκιζοίμεθα (1).

'Boy, loud-thundering Zeus holds the outcome of everything that is and arranges it as he wishes. There is no intelligence in men: they live one day at a time like beasts without any knowledge of how the god will end each thing, and hope and confidence feed us all as we ponder the impossible: some wait for a day to come, some for the turning of years. Every man believes that next year he will turn out to be the friend of Wealth and Blessings. But unenviable age gets in ahead of one man before he reaches his goal; other mortals are destroyed by wretched diseases; others, laid low by the god of war, Hades escorts under the black earth; others at sea, battered by a gale and many waves of the dark brine, die when they have no longer the power to live; others fasten on a noose for wretched death and of their own choice leave the sun's light. Thus no evil is absent: mortals have a thousand deaths and undreamt-of miseries and troubles. Let them take my advice: we should not love our misery nor torture ourselves by letting our minds dwell on evil pains.' The opening words show that the poem is didactic: Semonides is passing on his wisdom to a member of the next generation, as Theognis did later. The message is the contrast between the omnipotence of Zeus and the limited vision of mortals. Hesiod's Pandora had left men with hope; but hope could be illusory—Solon uses the adjective *kouphos*, 'lightweight' (13.36)—and men are frustrated by age, sickness or death. The last lines of the poem are unclear, but tend towards an expression of hedonism.

There is the same movement in another poem, this time in elegiac couplets. The view that the author is Semonides of Amorgos is not accepted by scholars who find it too modern in language and manner and ascribe it rather to the great Simonides of Ceos; but in the simplicity of its thought it is close to Semonides, and he and other early writers, Solon and Mimnermus, expressed similar ideas.

> ἓν δὲ τὸ κάλλιστον Χῖος ἔειπεν ἀνήρ·
> 'οἵη περ φύλλων γενεή, τοίη δὲ καὶ ἀνδρῶν.'
>   παῦροι μὴν θνητῶν οὔασι δεξάμενοι
> στέρνοις ἐγκατέθεντο· πάρεστι γὰρ ἐλπὶς ἑκάστῳ
>   ἀνδρῶν, ἥ τε νέων στήθεσιν ἐμφύεται.   5
> θνητῶν δ' ὄφρα τις ἄνθος ἔχῃ πολυήρατον ἥβης,
>   κοῦφον ἔχων θυμὸν πόλλ' ἀτέλεστα νοεῖ·
> οὔτε γὰρ ἐλπίδ' ἔχει γηρασέμεν οὔτε θανεῖσθαι
>   οὐδ', ὑγιὴς ὅταν ᾖ, φροντίδ' ἔχει καμάτου.
> νήπιοι, οἷς ταύτῃ κεῖται νόος, οὐδὲ ἴσασιν   10
>   ὡς χρόνος ἔσθ' ἥβης καὶ βιότου ὀλίγος
> θνητοῖς. ἀλλὰ σὺ ταῦτα μαθὼν βιότου ποτὶ τέρμα
>   ψυχῇ τῶν ἀγαθῶν τλῆθι χαριζόμενος (29 Diehl, Sim. 8 West).

'And this was the best thing the man of Chios ever said: "As the generation of leaves, so is that of men." Few mortals having heard it with their ears have deposited it within their breasts. For hope is present with each man, hope which grows in the hearts of the young. As long as a mortal has the lovely flower of youth, he ponders with light heart many impossibles; for he neither expects to grow old or die, nor when he is healthy does he worry about illness. Fools, to think like that and not realise that mortals' time for youth and life is brief: you must take note of this, and since you are near the end of your life endure, indulging yourself with good things.' The excerpt begins with the famous quotation from the *Iliad* (6.146) which Mimnermus also used as the starting-point for reflections on the brevity of youth. Again we find emphasis on the delusions of *elpis*, 'hope' or 'expectation' of the impossible; again, a reminder that age and death must come and will come soon; again the advice *tlēthi*, 'endure', made more explicit here by the reference to 'good things'. Another two lines may well have been followed by the same advice:

πολλὸς γὰρ ἥμιν ἐστὶ τεθνάναι χρόνος,
ζῶμεν δ' ἀριθμῷ παῦρα <παγ> κακῶς ἔτεα (3).

'There is a long time for us to be dead in, and the years of our lives are few in in number and wholly bad.'

It is curious that we have few texts of Alcman which make generalisations about life and death. The anthologist Stobaeus does not once quote him, perhaps daunted by the difficulty of his dialect. In the one long partheneion which is well preserved Alcman shows the tendency to insert *sententiae*, the brief pieces of moralising that are so familiar in later choral poetry. He ends the mythical section of his poem with the words

ἄλαστα δὲ
Ϝέργα πάσον κακὰ μησαμένοι.
ἔστι τις σιῶν τίσις·
ὁ δ' ὄλβιος ὅστις εὔφρων
ἀμέραν [δι]απλέκει
ἄκλαυτος (1.34-9).

'And they suffered unforgettably, having devised evil. There is such a thing as the vengeance of the gods. That man is blessed who with right intention weaves to the end the web of his day, unweeping.' It is not certain whether *euphrōn* means 'with right intention' or 'in merriment' (in which case the adjective 'unweeping' repeats the idea); nor is it certain whether Alcman was thinking of the single day or was using *hamera* in the sense of a man's life. In any case the pessimism of so much archaic Greek poetry is evident here also. Early in the poem Alcman had mentioned Aisa and Poros as the oldest or most venerable (*geraitatoi*) of the gods (13–14): Aisa is the goddess who allots man's 'portion' in life, Poros is the Contriver or the 'Way and Means', who provides him with invention. Elsewhere Poros appears along with *Tekmōr* (Termination) as 'beginning and end' in Alcman's account of creation.

To judge from our fragments, eating and drinking were the foremost activities in Alcman's life, and he calls himself *ho pamphagos Alkman* (17.4), 'Alcman who eats anything'; in his description of the seasons spring is the time of empty cupboards:

ὥρας δ' ἔσηκε τρεῖς, θέρος
καὶ χεῖμα κὠπώραν τρίταν
καὶ τέτρατον τὸ Ϝῆρ, ὅκα
σάλλει μέν, ἐσθίην δ' ἄδαν
οὐκ ἔστι (20).

'And he [Zeus?] made three seasons, summer and winter and autumn, the third, and spring, the fourth, when things flourish but there is not enough to eat.' But our picture is unbalanced, since a disproportionate number of our fragments are quotations from Athenaeus' *Scholars at Dinner*, where one of the principal topics for discussion was food and wine.

Alcman often speaks of himself, and in hexameter lines which must have formed the prelude for a partheneion he speaks whimsically of his old age:

> οὔ μ' ἔτι, παρσενικαὶ μελιγάρυες ἱαρόφωνοι,
> γυῖα φέρην δύναται· βάλε δὴ βάλε κηρύλος εἴην,
> ὅς τ' ἐπὶ κύματος ἄνθος ἅμ' ἀλκυόνεσσι ποτήται
> νηδεὲς ἦτορ ἔχων, ἁλιπόρφυρος ἱαρὸς ὄρνις (26).

'Honey-toned, strong-voiced maidens, my limbs can no longer carry me. How I wish I were a cerylus that flies over the froth of the wave along with the halcyons with fearless heart, the strong sea-blue bird.' The cerylus was a fabulous bird, often associated with the halcyon, which D'Arcy Thompson calls 'a symbolic or mystical bird, early identified with the kingfisher'. The names of the fabled birds, the rich epithets and the escapist wish contribute to the powerful effect of the lines.

*   *   *

No Greek poet expresses more frequently or more cogently the grimness of old age than Mimnermus in his elegiac verses. He was remembered as a gentle love-poet, and a collection of his poems was later given the name of the girl Nanno whom he is said to have loved. But in the fragments that have been transmitted to us the praise of love is eclipsed by the damnation of age.

> τίς δὲ βίος, τί δὲ τερπνὸν ἄτερ χρυσῆς Ἀφροδίτης;
>   τεθναίην, ὅτε μοι μηκέτι ταῦτα μέλοι,
> κρυπταδίη φιλότης καὶ μείλιχα δῶρα καὶ εὐνή,
>   οἵ' ἥβης ἄνθεα γίνεται ἁρπαλέα
> ἀνδράσιν ἠδὲ γυναιξίν· ἐπεὶ δ' ὀδυνηρὸν ἐπέλθῃ   5
>   γῆρας, ὅ τ' αἰσχρὸν ὁμῶς καὶ κακὸν ἄνδρα τιθεῖ,
> αἰεί μιν φρένας ἀμφὶ κακαὶ τείρουσι μέριμναι,
>   οὐδ' αὐγὰς προσορῶν τέρπεται ἠελίου,
> ἀλλ' ἐχθρὸς μὲν παισίν, ἀτίμαστος δὲ γυναιξίν·
>   οὕτως ἀργαλέον γῆρας ἔθηκε θεός (1).

'What is life, what pleasure is there without golden Aphrodite? May I die when these things no longer concern me—secret friendship, gentle gifts, love-making, such things as are the flowers of youth to be plucked by men and women. But when painful old age comes on, making a man both ugly and base, foul cares always distress his heart, and he finds no pleasure in looking at the sun's rays: he is hateful to boys, dishonoured by women; so grievous did the god make old age.' This fine poem, famous enough to be quoted by Horace and branded as licentious by Plutarch, may well be complete, one of the short poems admired for their sweetness by Callimachus. Its language is Homeric, but it has the stamp of the lyric poet. Its structure is interesting and varied: the arresting rhetorical questions of line 1 are followed by the wish, underlined by the alliteration of line 2, that death may come as soon as the season for loving is over; the brisk catalogue of love's delights is summed up in metaphor, 'the flowers of youth, for plucking by men and women'; mention of youth is followed at once by the introduction of old age, and the second half of the piece is given over to a succession of short clauses which pile up the horrors of age; the closing pentameter is self-contained, an unusual device which makes its summary more effective.

For one poem Mimnermus uses Homer's image of the leaves (*Il.* 6.146ff.), as Semonides did also; but while Homer's point was that the succession of one generation of mankind to another is like the seasonal changes of a tree, Mimnermus says that the season of youth comes into being and decays as swiftly as the leaves:

> ἡμεῖς δ᾽ οἷά τε φύλλα φύει πολυάνθεμος ὥρη
> ἔαρος, ὅτ᾽ αἶψ᾽ αὐγῆς αὔξεται ἠελίου,
> τοῖς ἴκελοι πήχυιον ἐπὶ χρόνον ἄνθεσιν ἥβης
> τερπόμεθα, πρὸς θεῶν εἰδότες οὔτε κακὸν
> οὔτ᾽ ἀγαθόν· Κῆρες δὲ παρεστήκασι μέλαιναι,   5
> ἡ μὲν ἔχουσα τέλος γήραος ἀργαλέου,
> ἡ δ᾽ ἑτέρη θανάτοιο· μίνυνθα δὲ γίνεται ἥβης
> καρπός, ὅσον τ᾽ ἐπὶ γῆν κίδναται ἠέλιος.
> αὐτὰρ ἐπὴν δὴ τοῦτο τέλος παραμείψεται ὥρης,
> αὐτίκα δὴ τεθνάναι βέλτιον ἢ βίοτος·   10
> πολλὰ γὰρ ἐν θυμῷ κακὰ γίνεται· ἄλλοτε οἶκος
> τρυχοῦται, πενίης δ᾽ ἔργ᾽ ὀδυνηρὰ πέλει·
> ἄλλος δ᾽ αὖ παίδων ἐπιδεύεται, ὧν τε μάλιστα
> ἱμείρων κατὰ γῆς ἔρχεται εἰς Ἀίδην·
> ἄλλος νοῦσον ἔχει θυμοφθόρον· οὐδέ τίς ἐστιν   15
> ἀνθρώπων ᾧ Ζεὺς μὴ κακὰ πολλὰ διδοῖ (2).

'But we, as the leaves that the flowery springtime produces, when suddenly they swell under the sun's rays, like them for a brief span we enjoy the flowers of youth, knowing neither good nor evil from the gods; but black Death-spirits stand near us, one holding the end that is painful old age, the other the end that is death; and the harvest of youth is brief, as long only as the sun takes to spread its light over the earth. But when this season of youth passes, at once it is better to be dead than to live, for many evils arise to vex the heart: at one time a man's substance is consumed and the painful life of poverty is his; another man lacks children and longing for them above all else goes below the earth to Hades; another has a life-destroying disease; and there is no man to whom Zeus does not give much evil.' The image of the leaves and sun in lines 1 and 2 is varied by the mention of youth's harvest and the sun's rising in line 8. The expression *pēkhuion epi khronon*, 'for a cubit's length of time', has no precursor that we know. The idea of two alternative *Kēres*, Death-spirits or Fates, is of course Homeric: Achilles had the alternative *kēres* of dying young and glorious at Troy and of returning home to live a long but inglorious life (*Il*. 9.410–16); their personification here is striking: the two black Fates stand by the side of a man, holding age and death. As in the last fragment the poem—or it may be a section of a longer poem—ends with brief summary.

Another poem, perhaps complete, is found partly in the manuscripts of Theognis, partly in Stobaeus under Mimnermus' name:

> αὐτίκα μοι κατὰ μὲν χροιὴν ῥέει ἄσπετος ἱδρώς,
> πτοιῶμαι δ' ἐσορῶν ἄνθος ὁμηλικίης
> τερπνὸν ὁμῶς καὶ καλόν · ἐπὶ πλέον ὤφελεν εἶναι ·
> ἀλλ' ὀλιγοχρόνιον γίνεται ὥσπερ ὄναρ
> ἥβη τιμήεσσα · τὸ δ' ἀργαλέον καὶ ἄμορφον   5
> γῆρας ὑπὲρ κεφαλῆς αὐτίχ' ὑπερκρέμαται,
> ἐχθρὸν ὁμῶς καὶ ἄτιμον, ὅ τ' ἄγνωστον τιθεῖ ἄνδρα,
> βλάπτει δ' ὀφθαλμοὺς καὶ νόον ἀμφιχυθέν (5).

'At once copious sweat flows over my skin and I am terrified when I look at the flower of my contemporaries, both delightful and fair—it should last longer. But short-lived as a dream is precious youth: painful and unsightly old age immediately hangs over a man's head; both hateful and dishonoured, it makes a man unrecognisable and harms his sight and his wits, overwhelming him.' The imagery shifts: youth is a flower; it is as brief as a dream; age is poured over a man, overwhelming him like sleep or grief in Homer.

Stobaeus quotes two more couplets:

> τὸ πρὶν ἐὼν κάλλιστος, ἐπὴν παραμείψεται ὥρη,
> οὐδὲ πατὴρ παισὶν τίμιος οὔτε φίλος (3).

'He may be most handsome before; but when youth's season passes, he is not honoured or loved, not even by his own children.'

> Τιθωνῷ μὲν ἔδωκεν ἔχειν κακὸν ἄφθιτον <ὁ Ζεὺς>
> γῆρας, ὃ καὶ θανάτου ῥίγιον ἀργαλέου (4).

'To Tithonus Zeus gave an everlasting evil as his portion—old age, which is more wretched than painful death.' Tithonus was a good choice to illustrate the gloomy thought: the Homeric hymn to Aphrodite tells how the goddess Dawn fell in love with the Trojan youth and persuaded Zeus to grant him immortality; but she forgot to ask that he should remain young for ever, and he grew ever older and more feeble.

Hermann Fraenkel has observed that the melancholy which hangs over all these lines might have been partly dispelled if the poems had been transmitted complete, since one fragment runs

σὴν αὐτοῦ φϱένα τέϱπε (7.1),

'Give pleasure to your heart'. Praise of conviviality, wine and love may at least sometimes have been his response to thoughts about the brevity of youth.

Mimnermus is linked to Solon by an anecdote in Diogenes Laertius' *Lives of the Philosophers*: his couplet,

αἲ γὰϱ ἄτεϱ νούσων τε καὶ ἀϱγαλέων μελεδωνέων
ἑξηκονταέτη μοῖϱα κίχοι θανάτου (6),

'Oh that without diseases and painful cares the fate of death might overtake me in my sixtieth year', provoked the sturdier Athenian to emend the lines:

ἀλλ' εἴ μοι καὶ νῦν ἔτι πείσεαι, ἔξελε τοῦτο,
μηδὲ μέγαιϱ' ὅτι σέο λῷον ἐπεφϱασάμην,
καὶ μεταποίησον, Λιγυαστάδη, ὧδε δ' ἄειδε·
'ὀγδωκονταέτη μοῖϱα κίχοι θανάτου' (20).

'But if even now you take my advice, remove that line, and bear me no ill-will that I thought of something better than you; change it, Ligyastades, and sing it like this: "Oh that the fate of death might overtake me in my eightieth year."' If 'Ligyastades' is correct, Solon is playing on the name of Mimnermus' father, Ligyrtyades, to form a patronymic meaning 'son of the clear-voiced singer'. The unusually harsh alliteration of *d* at the end of line 3 may perhaps be used in mockery.

Solon made other comments on age and death: his line

γηϱάσκω δ' αἰεὶ πολλὰ διδασκόμενος (18),

'And as I grow old I learn much all the time', confirms that he had a more robust outlook than the Ionian Mimnermus.

μηδέ μοι ἄκλαυτος θάνατος μόλοι, ἀλλὰ φίλοισι
καλλείποιμι θανὼν ἄλγεα καὶ στοναχάς (21).

'And may my death not come unwept, but when I am dead may I leave my friends sorrow and grief.' Cicero translated the lines, but found Solon's prayer inferior to that of the early Latin poet Ennius:

> nemo me lacrimis decoret, neque funera fletu
> faxit,

'Let no one honour me with tears nor conduct my funeral with weeping.'

Solon composed a curious poem in which he set out the ten ages of man, giving one couplet to each except for the seventh and eighth, which he combines:

> παῖς μὲν ἄνηβος ἐὼν ἔτι νήπιος ἕρκος ὀδόντων
>   φύσας ἐκβάλλει πρῶτον ἐν ἔπτ' ἔτεσιν.
> τοὺς δ' ἑτέρους ὅτε δὴ τελέσῃ θεὸς ἔπτ' ἐνιαυτούς,
>   ἥβης ἐκφαίνει σήματα γιγνομένης.
> τῇ τριτάτῃ δὲ γένειον ἀεξομένων ἔτι γυίων   5
>   λαχνοῦται, χροιῆς ἄνθος ἀμειβομένης.
> τῇ δὲ τετάρτῃ πᾶς τις ἐν ἑβδομάδι μέγ' ἄριστος
>   ἰσχύν, ἥν τ' ἄνδρες σήματ' ἔχουσ' ἀρετῆς.
> πέμπτῃ δ' ὥριον ἄνδρα γάμου μεμνημένον εἶναι
>   καὶ παίδων ζητεῖν εἰσοπίσω γενεήν.   10
> τῇ δ' ἕκτῃ περὶ πάντα καταρτύεται νόος ἀνδρός,
>   οὐδ' ἔρδειν ἔθ' ὁμῶς ἔργ' ἀπάλαμνα θέλει.
> ἑπτὰ δὲ νοῦν καὶ γλῶσσαν ἐν ἑβδομάσιν μέγ' ἄριστος
>   ὀκτώ τ'· ἀμφοτέρων τέσσερα καὶ δέκ' ἔτη.
> τῇ δ' ἐνάτῃ ἔτι μὲν δύναται, μαλακώτερα δ' αὐτοῦ   15
>   πρὸς μεγάλην ἀρετὴν γλῶσσά τε καὶ σοφίη.
> τὴν δεκάτην δ' εἴ τις τελέσας κατὰ μέτρον ἵκοιτο,
>   οὐκ ἂν ἄωρος ἐὼν μοῖραν ἔχοι θανάτου (27).

'The immature boy, having grown "the barrier of his teeth" when still a baby, casts them for the first time within seven years. When god completes the second seven years he shows the signs of developing puberty. In the third, while his limbs are still growing, his chin turns woolly as his skin changes its bloom. In the fourth group of seven everyone is easily at his finest in strength, which men have as sign of excellence. In the fifth it is time for a man to think of marriage and seek a family of children to follow him. In the sixth a man's mind is disciplined in all respects, and he no longer wishes as before to perform the impossible. In seven sevens he is easily at his best in intelligence and speech and in eight sevens too: together they make fourteen years. In the ninth he is still strong, but his speech and wisdom are feebler by the standard of great excellence. If a man completed the tenth, reaching its full measure, he would not be too young to have death's portion.'

In Herodotus' account of Solon's conversation with Croesus (1.32.2) Solon again gives seventy years as the normal span. That did not of course prevent him from wishing that death might come in his eightieth year (20.4): Solon there opts for ten years more than the norm in reaction to Mimnermus' wish for ten years less, and in any case the Greek number 'seventieth' cannot be fitted straightforwardly into elegiac couplets. Solon's division of man's life into ten ages did not become canonical: seven was the commonest number and is used by the medical writer Hippocrates in the fifth century as by Shakespeare in *As You Like It* (2.7). Solon clearly finds it difficult to characterise the ten ages and gives up when he reaches the seventh and eighth; and although the content of the lines is interesting enough, there are no striking turns of phrase as in Shakespeare. The ordinal numbers, which Shakespeare wisely omits, are intractable material, and the phrase, 'together they make fourteen years' (line 14) is prosaic stuff. We may also find the repetition of the line-ending *meg' aristos* in 7 and 13 feeble, although it is not certain that such repetition was unattractive to Solon's audience.

Two isolated couplets deal with the human condition:

> οὐδὲ μάκαρ οὐδεὶς πέλεται βροτός, ἀλλὰ πονηροὶ
> πάντες ὅσους θνητοὺς ἠέλιος καθορᾷ (14).

'Nor is any mortal happy: all the humans on whom the sun looks down are wretched.' The emphasis on 'mortal' men (*brotos, thnētous*) suggests that Solon would use the word 'happy' only for the gods. But a man can be 'fortunate':

> ὄλβιος, ᾧ παῖδές τε φίλοι καὶ μώνυχες ἵπποι
> καὶ κύνες ἀγρευταὶ καὶ ξένος ἀλλοδαπός (23).

'Fortunate he who has dear children and single-hoofed horses and hunting dogs and a guest-friend abroad.' Solon's family belonged to the hunting and shooting aristocracy; but the life of the man whose basic needs for food and clothes and shoes and love are met is just as desirable:

> ἴσόν τοι πλουτέουσιν, ὅτῳ πολὺς ἄργυρός ἐστι
> καὶ χρυσὸς καὶ γῆς πυροφόρου πεδία
> ἵπποι θ' ἡμίονοί τε, καὶ ᾧ μόνα ταῦτα πάρεστι,
> γαστρί τε καὶ πλευραῖς καὶ ποσὶν ἁβρὰ παθεῖν,
> παιδός τ' ἠδὲ γυναικός, ἐπὴν καὶ ταῦτ' ἀφίκηται,   5
> ὥρη, σὺν δ' ἥβη γίνεται ἁρμοδίη.
> ταῦτ' ἄφενος θνητοῖσι· τὰ γὰρ περιώσια πάντα
> χρήματ' ἔχων οὐδεὶς ἔρχεται εἰς Ἀΐδεω,
> οὐδ' ἂν ἄποινα διδοὺς θάνατον φύγοι, οὐδὲ βαρείας
> νούσους, οὐδὲ κακὸν γῆρας ἐπερχόμενον (24).

'Equal is the wealth of the man who has much silver and gold and plains of wheat-bearing earth and horses and mules and the man who has only this—comfort for belly and sides and feet and, when the time for these things comes, the beauty of a boy or a woman and youth to fit theirs. That is wealth for mortals; for no one when he goes to Hades takes all those superfluous possessions with him, nor by offering a price might he escape death or grievous diseases or the onset of evil age.' Solon is the earliest writer to express the thought that man cannot take his property with him when he dies.

We have already considered in Chapter Four the poem in which Solon warns the rich Athenians that their lawless behaviour will be the undoing of the city (p. 92 above). In another poem (13), the longest piece in elegiacs to survive from the archaic period, his starting-point is the unjust acquisition of wealth; but he moves from one topic to another and by the end of the poem has discussed the justice of Zeus and the false hopes, the aspirations and the greed of men and their dependence on Fate and the gods. The course of the poem is most clearly seen if it is examined section by section:

> Μνημοσύνης καὶ Ζηνὸς Ὀλυμπίου ἀγλαὰ τέκνα,
>   Μοῦσαι Πιερίδες, κλῦτέ μοι εὐχομένῳ·
> ὄλβον μοι πρὸς θεῶν μακάρων δότε καὶ πρὸς ἁπάντων
>   ἀνθρώπων αἰεὶ δόξαν ἔχειν ἀγαθήν·
> εἶναι δὲ γλυκὺν ὧδε φίλοις, ἐχθροῖσι δὲ πικρόν,   5
>   τοῖσι μὲν αἰδοῖον, τοῖσι δὲ δεινὸν ἰδεῖν (1-6).

'Glorious children of Memory and Olympian Zeus, Pierian Muses, hear my prayer: grant me prosperity from the blessed gods, and from all men always to have a good reputation; and so to be sweet to my friends, bitter to my enemies, respected by the former, a grim sight for the latter.' Solon begins by appealing to the Muses, since as a poet he has a special relationship with them; but his prayer is not that they will help him in his lengthy poem but that they act as intermediaries, granting prosperity from the gods, a good name from men. If he is prosperous and glorious, his friends will be happy to have him as a friend, his enemies will be alarmed. We have seen that this way of thinking was prevalent in archaic Greek writers and goes back to Homer.

> χρήματα δ᾽ ἱμείρω μὲν ἔχειν, ἀδίκως δὲ πεπᾶσθαι
>   οὐκ ἐθέλω· πάντως ὕστερον ἦλθε δίκη.
> πλοῦτον δ᾽ ὃν μὲν δῶσι θεοί, παραγίγνεται ἀνδρὶ
>   ἔμπεδος ἐκ νεάτου πυθμένος ἐς κορυφήν·   10
> ὃν δ᾽ ἄνδρες μετίωσιν ὑφ᾽ ὕβριος, οὐ κατὰ κόσμον
>   ἔρχεται, ἀλλ᾽ ἀδίκοις ἔργμασι πειθόμενος
> οὐκ ἐθέλων ἕπεται, ταχέως δ᾽ ἀναμίσγεται ἄτη·
>   ἀρχὴ δ᾽ ἐξ ὀλίγου γίγνεται ὥστε πυρός,
> φλαύρη μὲν τὸ πρῶτον, ἀνιηρὴ δὲ τελευτᾷ·   15
>   οὐ γὰρ δὴν θνητοῖς ὕβριος ἔργα πέλει.
> ἀλλὰ Ζεὺς πάντων ἐφορᾷ τέλος, ἐξαπίνης δὲ
>   ὥστ᾽ ἄνεμος νεφέλας αἶψα διεσκέδασεν

ἠρινός, ὃς πόντου πολυκύμονος ἀτρυγέτοιο
  πυθμένα κινήσας, γῆν κάτα πυροφόρον   20
δῃώσας καλὰ ἔργα θεῶν ἕδος αἰπὺν ἱκάνει
  οὐρανόν, αἰθρίην δ' αὖτις ἔθηκεν ἰδεῖν·
λάμπει δ' ἠελίοιο μένος κατὰ πίονα γαῖαν
  καλόν, ἀτὰρ νεφέων οὐδὲν ἔτ' ἔστιν ἰδεῖν—
τοιαύτη Ζηνὸς πέλεται τίσις, οὐδ' ἐφ' ἑκάστῳ   25
  ὥσπερ θνητὸς ἀνὴρ γίγνεται ὀξύχολος,
αἰεὶ δ' οὔ ἑ λέληθε διαμπερές, ὅστις ἀλιτρὸν
  θυμὸν ἔχει, πάντως δ' ἐς τέλος ἐξεφάνη·
ἀλλ' ὁ μὲν αὐτίκ' ἔτεισεν, ὁ δ' ὕστερον· οἳ δὲ φύγωσιν
  αὐτοί, μηδὲ θεῶν μοῖρ' ἐπιοῦσα κίχῃ,   30
ἤλυθε πάντως αὖτις· ἀναίτιοι ἔργα τίνουσιν
  ἢ παῖδες τούτων ἢ γένος ἐξοπίσω (7-32).

'Money I long to have, but I do not wish to acquire it unjustly: justice assuredly comes later. Wealth that the gods give stands firm by a man's side from its very foundation to its topmost point; wealth that men seek with violence comes in no orderly manner, but trusting in unjust deeds it attends unwillingly, and soon infatuation is involved: its beginning, like that of fire, is slight: at first it is trivial, in the end grievous: the deeds of violence do not last long for mortals. No, Zeus oversees the outcome of all things, and suddenly, as a wind swiftly scatters the clouds in spring, a wind which after stirring up the bottom of the billowy unharvestable sea and laying waste the fair fields on the wheat-bearing land reaches the gods' abode, the heavens sheer above, and makes the sky clear again to see; and the sun's might shines in beauty over the rich earth, and there is nothing of the clouds to be seen now—such is the vengeance of Zeus; nor is he quick to anger on each occasion like a mortal, but there is no escaping his notice always and for ever for the man who has a sinful heart: assuredly he is shown up in the end. But one man pays the price at once, another later; those who themselves escape, whom divine fate does not come to attack—assuredly it reaches them later: innocents pay for the crimes, either their children or their descendants after them.' The first of Solon's prayers is now modified: he wants wealth, but he will not have it unjustly. Wealth acquired through *hubris*, 'violence', brings *atē*, 'infatuation, blindness', which is followed by punishment; in one of his political poems he added an earlier link in the chain: it is excessive wealth in irresponsible hands that breeds 'violence' (5.9–10). Herodotus and the tragic poets followed Solon's thinking. The images of the passage are interesting: wealth seems first of all to be a building, firm from foundation to rooftop (10), or perhaps a tree or standing grain, but it is personified too and stands by a man's side; the personification is stronger a moment later, when ill-gotten wealth is a disorderly attendant. The beginning of *atē* is 'as of fire', a brief simile, typical of elegiac poetry; but at line 18 Solon begins a long simile, Homeric in scale and language, taking his illustration from nature as he often did: the wind represents the speed and thoroughness of Zeus' power.

θνητοὶ δ' ὧδε νοέομεν ὁμῶς ἀγαθός τε κακός τε·
εὐθηνεῖν αὐτὸς δόξαν ἕκαστος ἔχει,
πρίν τι παθεῖν· τότε δ' αὖτις ὀδύρεται· ἄχρι δὲ τούτου   35
χάσκοντες κούφαις ἐλπίσι τερπόμεθα.
χὤστις μὲν νούσοισιν ὑπ' ἀργαλέῃσι πιεσθῇ,
ὡς ὑγιὴς ἔσται, τοῦτο κατεφράσατο·
ἄλλος δειλὸς ἐὼν ἀγαθὸς δοκεῖ ἔμμεναι ἀνήρ,
καὶ καλὸς μορφὴν οὐ χαρίεσσαν ἔχων·   40
εἰ δέ τις ἀχρήμων, πενίης δέ μιν ἔργα βιᾶται,
κτήσασθαι πάντως χρήματα πολλὰ δοκεῖ (33-42).

'Thus do we mortals reckon, both good and bad alike: each individual thinks he is prospering until something happens to him, and then in his turn he weeps; but until then, wide-mouthed, we take pleasure in lightweight hopes; and the man who is hard pressed by grievous diseases reckons that he will be healthy, another, a coward, thinks he is a fine man, another that he is handsome, although he has an unpleasing appearance; and if a man is penniless and a life of poverty oppresses him, he expects that he will assuredly acquire great wealth.' Solon had spoken in the last section of the eventual punishment inflicted on the criminal by Zeus who 'oversees the outcome of all things': men, both good and wicked, are deluded by false beliefs and false hopes. There is a short catalogue of examples: the invalid, the coward, the ugly man, the poor man who hopes to be wealthy one day. Solon has reverted to the theme of money-making and now gives another catalogue, this time listing the ways in which men seek wealth:

σπεύδει δ' ἄλλοθεν ἄλλος· ὁ μὲν κατὰ πόντον ἀλᾶται
ἐν νηυσὶν χρήζων οἴκαδε κέρδος ἄγειν
ἰχθυόεντ' ἀνέμοισι φορεόμενος ἀργαλέοισιν,   45
φειδωλὴν ψυχῆς οὐδεμίαν θέμενος·
ἄλλος γῆν τέμνων πολυδένδρεον εἰς ἐνιαυτὸν
λατρεύει, τοῖσιν καμπύλ' ἄροτρα μέλει·
ἄλλος Ἀθηναίης τε καὶ Ἡφαίστου πολυτέχνεω
ἔργα δαεὶς χειροῖν ξυλλέγεται βίοτον,   50
ἄλλος Ὀλυμπιάδων Μουσέων πάρα δῶρα διδαχθείς,
ἱμερτῆς σοφίης μέτρον ἐπιστάμενος·
ἄλλον μάντιν ἔθηκεν ἄναξ ἑκάεργος Ἀπόλλων,
ἔγνω δ' ἀνδρὶ κακὸν τηλόθεν ἐρχόμενον,
ᾧ συνομαρτήσωσι θεοί· τὰ δὲ μόρσιμα πάντως   55
οὔτε τις οἰωνὸς ῥύσεται οὔθ' ἱερά·
ἄλλοι Παιῶνος πολυφαρμάκου ἔργον ἔχοντες
ἰητροί, καὶ τοῖς οὐδὲν ἔπεστι τέλος·

πολλάκι δ᾽ ἐξ ὀλίγης ὀδύνης μέγα γίγνεται ἄλγος,
κοὐκ ἄν τις λύσαιτ᾽ ἤπια φάρμακα δούς·
τὸν δὲ κακαῖς νούσοισι κυκώμενον ἀργαλέαις τε
ἁψάμενος χειροῖν αἶψα τίθησ᾽ ὑγιῆ (43-62).

'And men set about acquiring it in different ways: one roams the sea desiring to bring home a profit in his ships, the fishy sea, swept along by distressing winds and not hoarding his life at all; another, cleaving the earth with its many trees, works for hire all the year—*their* concern is the curving plough; another, skilled in the works of Athene and the craftsman Hephaestus, gathers together his living with his hands, another, to whom the Olympian Muses have taught their gifts, by his skill in the measure of lovely poetry; another Lord Apollo, the far-worker, has made a seer, and he recognises from afar the evil that is approaching a man—if the gods attend him; but assuredly what is fated will be warded off neither by bird or omen nor by sacrifices; others, who have the craft of the healer Paeon, are doctors, and they have no certain conclusion: often from a small ache a great pain develops, and no one could ransom the man by giving soothing drugs, while the invalid racked by grievous diseases he swiftly restores to health by a touch of his hands.' This begins as a list of methods of money-making, but the emphasis changes and we find ourselves contemplating the uncertainty and lack of finality in human endeavours. The seer can only predict the evil that is coming; and even the startling emphasis on the 'fishy' sea may be sinister, since Homer calls fish 'eaters of raw flesh' (*Il.* 24.82).

Μοῖρα δέ τοι θνητοῖσι κακὸν φέρει ἠδὲ καὶ ἐσθλόν,
δῶρα δ᾽ ἄφυκτα θεῶν γίγνεται ἀθανάτων·
πᾶσι δέ τοι κίνδυνος ἔπ᾽ ἔργμασιν, οὐδέ τις οἶδεν　　　　65
ἢ μέλλει σχήσειν χρήματος ἀρχομένου·
ἀλλ᾽ ὁ μὲν εὖ ἔρδειν πειρώμενος οὐ προνοήσας
ἐς μεγάλην ἄτην καὶ χαλεπὴν ἔπεσεν,
τῷ δὲ κακῶς ἔρδοντι θεὸς περὶ πάντα δίδωσιν
συντυχίην ἀγαθήν, ἔκλυσιν ἀφροσύνης (63-70).

'Fate it is that brings good and ill to mortals, and the gifts of the immortal gods are inescapable. In all deeds there is danger, and no one knows where he will come ashore when some affair is beginning; no, the man who is trying to act correctly often falls into great, harsh ruin without foreseeing it, while to the man who acts wrongly god gives success in all respects, deliverance from his folly.' These lines sum up what has preceded: Fate, not man, is in control; man has no idea how his undertakings will end. There is grim humour in the description of the gods' gifts as 'inescapable'.

πλούτου δ᾽ οὐδὲν τέρμα πεφασμένον ἀνδράσι κεῖται·

οἳ γὰρ νῦν ἡμέων πλεῖστον ἔχουσι βίον,
διπλάσιον σπεύδουσι· τίς ἂν κορέσειεν ἅπαντας;
κέρδεά τοι θνητοῖς ὤπασαν ἀθάνατοι,
ἄτη δ' ἐξ αὐτῶν ἀναφαίνεται, ἣν ὁπότε Ζεὺς   75
πέμψῃ τεισομένην, ἄλλοτε ἄλλος ἔχει (71-6).

'But of wealth no limit stands revealed to men; for those of us who now have most resources are eager to double them. Who could satisfy us all? Profit is given to mortals by the immortals, and infatuation appears after profit: one gets it today, another tomorrow, whenever Zeus sends it to take vengeance.' The connection with the previous lines is tenuous: perhaps the 'success' of line 70 leads to 'wealth' in 71, perhaps Solon has decided to go back to the beginning again. He finishes with emphasis on the certainty of Zeus' vengeance and man's uncertainty about when it will fall.

* * *

Given that Stesichorus was 'most Homeric', one might have expected his heroes to utter generalisations about life and death; but Stobaeus the anthologist quotes no more than a couple of lines (244, 245), and the papyrus fragments confirm that he kept to the specific situation, even when opportunity arose for a piece of moralising: Geryon, for example, warned by Menoites that Heracles may kill him, begins a speech of some length by saying, 'Do not try to frighten me with talk of chilling death: if I am immortal and ageless (he cannot kill me); but if I must reach old age among mortals on earth, better to die now' (S 11). The two *sententiae* quoted by Stobaeus are both on the subject of death and have the ring of Archilochus and Semonides:

ἀτελέστατα γὰρ καὶ ἀμάχανα τοὺς θανόντας
κλαίειν (244).

'For it is quite futile and unhelpful to weep for the dead.'

θανόντος ἀνδρὸς πᾶσ' ἀπώλ<ετ>' ἁ ποτ' ἀνθρώπων χάρις (245).

'When a man dies, all the glory he has from men perishes.' Ibycus, whose choral poetry resembled that of Stesichorus, provided Stobaeus with no quotations at all.

The writers of solo song, Sappho, Alcaeus and Anacreon, also concentrate on the immediate situation, the girl or the boy, the wine, politics. Love is the theme of much of Sappho's poetry, and if she makes a general pronouncement about beauty, it serves to lead into the praise of Anactoria:

ο]ἰ μὲν ἰππήων στρότον, οἰ δὲ πέσδων,
οἰ δὲ νάων φαῖσ' ἐπ[ὶ] γᾶν μέλαι[ν]αν

ἔ]μμεναι κάλλιστον, ἔγω δὲ κῆν' ὄτ-
τω τις ἔραται (16.1-4).

'Some say that a host of cavalrymen is the fairest thing on the black earth,
some a host of infantry, others of ships. I say it is what one loves.' Thoughts of
death sometimes intrude: a girl's departure brings the reaction,

τεθνάκην δ' ἀδόλως θέλω (94.1),

'Honestly I wish to die'. In another poem she seems to be addressing Hermes,
guide of souls to the underworld:

εἶπον · 'ὦ δέσποτ' ἐπ.[
ο]ὐ μὰ γὰρ μάκαιραν [ἔγωγ'
ο]ὐδὲν ἄδομ' ἔπερθα γᾶ[ς ἔοισα,

κατθάνην δ' ἴμερός τις [ἔχει με καὶ
λωτίνοις δροσόεντας [ὄ-
χ[θ]οις ἴδην Ἀχέρ[οντος' (95.8-13).

'I said, "Lord, . . . for by the blessed (goddess) . . . I get no pleasure from
being above the earth, and a longing grips me to die and see the dewy, lotus-
covered banks of Acheron . . ."' She forthrightly predicts that some woman,
whom the Muses have not inspired, will be forgotten after death:

κατθάνοισα δὲ κείσῃ οὐδέ ποτα μναμοσύνα σέθεν
ἔσσετ' οὐδὲ πόθα εἰς ὕστερον · οὐ γὰρ πεδέχῃς βρόδων
τῶν ἐκ Πιερίας, ἀλλ' ἀφάνης κἀν Ἀΐδα δόμῳ
φοιτάσῃς πεδ' ἀμαύρων νεκύων ἐκπεποταμένα (55).

'But when you die you will lie there, and afterwards there will never be any
recollection of you or any longing for you, since you have no share in the roses
of Pieria; unseen in the house of Hades also, flown from our midst, you will go
to and fro among the shadowy corpses.' The woman will enjoy no immortality,
but will inhabit an underworld of nothingness as Homer pictured it. Sappho
foretold that she herself would never be forgotten (147, 193, perhaps 65). It
seems that she proscribed mourning when her own death should come:

οὐ γὰρ θέμις ἐν μοισοπόλων †οἰκίᾳ†
θρῆνον ἔμμεν' · οὔ κ' ἄμμι πρέποι τάδε (150).

'For it is not right that there should be lamentation in the house of those who
serve the Muses. That would not be fitting for us.'
　　Alcaeus had his share of troubles, and he sings,

κὰτ τὰς πόλλα παθοίσας κεφάλας <κάκ>χεέ μοι μύρον (50).

'Pour perfume over my head which has suffered much.' We have seen that he often recommends the pleasures of the symposium as the antidote for sorrow (73, 335, 346), and that he gives the inevitability of death as a reason for hard drinking (38A). It is rare for him to generalise: he refers to poverty twice:

> ὡς γὰρ δή ποτ' 'Αριστόδα-
> μον φαῖσ' οὐκ ἀπάλαμνον ἐν Σπάρτᾳ λόγον
> εἴπην· χρήματ' ἄνηρ, πένι-
> χρος δ' οὐδ' εἷς πέλετ' ἔσλος οὐδὲ τίμιος (360).

'For they say that Aristodemus once expressed it shrewdly at Sparta: "Money is the man, and no poor man is good or honourable." ' Aristodemus was one of the Seven Sages of the Greek world. The only lines of Alcaeus used by Stobaeus in his anthology are

> ἀργάλεον Πενία κάκον ἄσχετον, ἃ μέγαν
> δάμνα λᾶον 'Αμαχανίᾳ σὺν ἀδελφέᾳ (364).

'Poverty is a grievous thing, an ungovernable evil, who with her sister Helplessness lays low a great people.' One or two very fragmentary lines have the words *hubris*, 'outrage', and *atasthaloi*, 'wicked', and speak of 'throwing down' and 'raising up' (76), probably with reference to divine power as in Archilochus (130); others have 'god', 'justice' and something like the lines in Archilochus and Semonides, 'Zeus controls the outcome' (200). In 39.10 he has

> παρὰ μοῖραν Διός οὐδὲ τρίχ[,

'Against the will of Zeus not even hairs (fall?).'

Anacreon's short graceful lines in lyric metres are not the medium for solemn pronouncements. One fragment, however, seems to preach moderation, *mēden agan*, 'nothing in excess':

> ἐγὼ δ' οὔτ' ἂν 'Αμαλθίης
> βουλοίμην κέρας οὔτ' ἔτεα
> πεντήκοντά τε κἀκατὸν
> Ταρτησσοῦ βασιλεῦσαι (361).

'I would not wish for Amalthea's horn nor to be king of Tartessus for a hundred and fifty years.' Amalthea was the she-goat who nursed the infant Zeus: her horns flowed with ambrosia and nectar and were the prototype of the horn of plenty (*cornu copiae*). Tartessus was a district and city at the mouth of the Guadalquivir in Spain; according to Herodotus king Arganthonius ruled over it for eighty of his one hundred and twenty years (1.163, 165). Anacreon, whose dates overlap with those of the king, exaggerates the figure.

The theme of one of his best-known poems is the finality of death:

πολιοὶ μὲν ἡμὶν ἤδη
κρόταφοι κάρη τε λευκόν,
χαρίεσσα δ' οὐκέτ' ἤβη
πάρα, γηραλέοι δ' ὀδόντες,
γλυκεροῦ δ' οὐκέτι πολλὸς   5
βιότου χρόνος λέλειπται·

διὰ ταῦτ' ἀνασταλύζω
θαμὰ Τάρταρον δεδοικώς·
Ἀίδεω γὰρ | ἐστι δεινὸς
μυχός, ἀργαλῆ δ' ἐς αὐτὸν   10
κάτοδος· καὶ γὰρ ἑτοῖμον
καταβάντι μὴ ἀναβῆναι (395).

'My temples are already grey and my hair is white; graceful youth is no more with me, my teeth are old, and no long span of sweet life remains now. So I often weep in fear of Tartarus: the recess of Hades is grim and the road down to it grievous; and it is certain that he who goes down does not come up again.' This catalogue of woes is effectively expressed in the short clauses and paratactic structure, and the frequent enjambment prevents any sense of monotony. Word-position is particularly striking in lines 3 and 5, where the adjectives *khariessa*, 'graceful', and *glukerou*, 'sweet', are immediately cancelled by the negative *ouketi*, 'no more'. The rare verb *anastaluzō*, 'I weep', makes an impressive opening for the second half of the poem, and the repeated *kata-*, 'down', in lines 11 and 12 underlines the message. But Anacreon sets these gloomy thoughts in slight, frivolous anacreontic lines, so that the poem has 'a somewhat macabre air', as Kirkwood puts it. In another poem he expresses a wish for death as the only release from his 'troubles', by which he may mean the anxious life of the lover:

ἀπό μοι θανεῖν γένοιτ'· οὐ γὰρ ἂν ἄλλη
λύσις ἐκ πόνων γένοιτ' οὐδάμα τῶνδε (411a).

'May death be mine, for there could be no other release from these present troubles.' Here too the gay ionic metre lightens the melancholy theme. The rhyming *genoit' ou* is remarkable.

Anacreon wrote two lines about a young friend who died in battle:

ἀλκίμων σ' ὦ 'ριστοκλείδη πρῶτον οἰκτίρω φίλων·
ὤλεσας δ' ἤβην ἀμύνων πατρίδος δουληΐην (419).

'Foremost among my brave friends, Aristocleides, I pity you: you lost your youth, keeping slavery from your country.' This is probably not an epitaph to be carved in stone on a tomb but a brief lament to be performed among friends. The same is true of a piece attributed to Anacreon in the Palatine Anthology:

καὶ σέ, Κλεηνορίδη, πόθος ὤλεσε πατρίδος αἴης
θαρσήσαντα νότου λαίλαπι χειμερίῃ·
ὥρη γάρ σε πέδησεν ἀνέγγυος· ὑγρὰ δὲ τὴν σὴν
κύματ᾽ ἀφ᾽ ἱμερτὴν ἔκλυσεν ἡλικίην (102D.).

'You too, Cleënorides, were destroyed by your desire for your fatherland, when you put your trust in the wintry blast of the south wind; for the weather, with which no covenant can be made, shackled you, and the wet waves washed away your lovely youth.' This is a short commemorative elegy, but true epitaph is also attributed to him:

καρτερὸς ἐν πολέμοις Τιμόκριτος, οὗ τόδε σᾶμα·
Ἄρης δ᾽ οὐκ ἀγαθῶν φείδεται, ἀλλὰ κακῶν (101D.).

'Timocritus, whose tomb this is, was strong in the wars: Ares spares not the brave but the cowards.' Attributions in the Palatine Anthology are unreliable, especially in the case of early poets, and we cannot be certain about Anacreon's authorship; but epitaphs in elegiac metre appear first about 560 B.C., and this couplet might well be his work.

*   *   *

Thanks to Mimnermus and Solon the elegiac couplet had become the established medium for poetry of a reflective character. Its form helped the poet to marshal his ideas into brief, striking phrases, often made more memorable by the balance and sometimes even the internal rhyme of the pentameter. Most of the poems attributed to Theognis are *gnōmai*, pithy expressions in two or four lines of some general thought. Often they are offered as advice from older man to younger, and the name of Cyrnus, son of Polypaus, appears frequently:

σοὶ δ᾽ ἐγὼ εὖ φρονέων ὑποθήσομαι, οἷάπερ αὐτός,
Κύρν᾽, ἀπὸ τῶν ἀγαθῶν παῖς ἔτ᾽ ἐὼν ἔμαθον (27-8).

'But with kindly intent, Cyrnus, I shall give you such advice as I learned from the good men when I was still a boy.' 'The good men', as we have seen, are the aristocrats, and the collection of poems represents aristocratic thinking on a variety of topics.

Theognis lost his property in the political upheavals of Megara, and poverty is one of his favourite themes:

μήποτέ τοι πενίην θυμοφθόρον ἀνδρὶ χαλεφθεὶς
μηδ᾽ ἀχρημοσύνην οὐλομένην πρόφερε·
Ζεὺς γάρ τοι τὸ τάλαντον ἐπιρρέπει ἄλλοτε ἄλλως,
ἄλλοτε μὲν πλουτεῖν, ἄλλοτε μηδὲν ἔχειν (155-8).

'Never in a fit of anger taunt a man with heart-breaking poverty or ruinous need; for Zeus tips the balance now this way, now that: one day riches, the next day nothing.' The poem echoes two lines of Hesiod's *Works and Days*:

μηδέ ποτ' οὐλομένην πενίην θυμοφθόρον ἀνδρὶ
τέτλαθ' ὀνειδίζειν, μακάρων δόσιν αἰὲν ἐόντων (717-18).

'And do not ever bring yourself to reproach a man with ruinous heart-breaking poverty, the gift of the blessed immortals.' Theognis' lines are enlivened by Homer's image of the scales, but in the *Iliad* Zeus tips them only to decide the outcome of fighting.

In the case of the following lines it is uncertain whether we are dealing with one, two or three poems (173-8, 179-80, 181-2):

ἀνδρ' ἀγαθὸν πενίη πάντων δάμνησι μάλιστα,
  καὶ γήρως πολιοῦ, Κύρνε, καὶ ἠπιάλου.
ἣν δὴ χρὴ φεύγοντα καὶ ἐς βαθυκήτεα πόντον   175
  ῥιπτεῖν καὶ πετρέων, Κύρνε, κατ' ἠλιβάτων.
καὶ γὰρ ἀνὴρ πενίη δεδμημένος οὔτε τι εἰπεῖν
  οὔτ' ἔρξαι δύναται, γλῶσσα δέ οἱ δέδεται.
χρὴ γὰρ ὁμῶς ἐπὶ γῆν τε καὶ εὐρέα νῶτα θαλάσσης
  δίζησθαι χαλεπῆς, Κύρνε, λύσιν πενίης.   180
τεθνάμεναι, φίλε Κύρνε, πενιχρῷ βέλτερον ἀνδρὶ
  ἢ ζώειν χαλεπῇ τειρόμενον πενίη (173-82).

'Poverty more than anything else lays low the good man, more than grey age, Cyrnus, or fever. To escape it he should dive into the depths of the sea, Cyrnus, or from a sheer cliff. A man laid low by poverty can say nothing, can do nothing. His tongue is tied. He should go over land or over the broad back of the sea to seek escape from cruel poverty. Death, my dear Cyrnus, is better for a poor man than a life oppressed by cruel poverty.' The opening sentence reminds us that this theme is of concern to the aristocrat, Theognis' 'good man': it is he who is in danger of losing his possessions and who ought to take what action he may to avoid it; for someone who thinks in these terms, the 'bad' man will already be poor. The couplets are notable for the rhyme within each pentameter, a device of which Theognis is especially fond. Perhaps Poverty is seen as a cruel goddess; she is certainly alive in the following lines:

γνωτή τοι Πενίη γε καὶ ἀλλοτρίη περ ἐοῦσα·
  οὔτε γὰρ εἰς ἀγορὴν ἔρχεται οὔτε δίκας·
πάντη γὰρ τοὔλασσον ἔχει, πάντη δ' ἐπίμυκτος,
  πάντη δ' ἐχθρὴ ὁμῶς γίνεται, ἔνθα περ ᾖ (267-70).

'Poverty is recognisable even when she is someone else's; for she comes into neither the agora nor the lawcourt. Everywhere she gets the worst of it, everywhere she is scoffed at, everywhere she is hated equally, no matter where she is.'

If possible one should leave something for one's heirs:

> φείδεσθαι μὲν ἄμεινον, ἐπεὶ οὐδὲ θανόντ' ἀποκλαίει
> οὐδείς, ἢν μὴ ὁρᾷ χρήματα λειπόμενα (931-2).

'Better to go sparingly; for no one weeps for the dead, unless he sees possessions left behind.' Theognis displays the cynicism of Archilochus and Semonides but gives it a twist by putting it in a financial context. He can offer more uplifting advice when he pleases:

> οὐδένα θησαυρὸν παισὶν καταθήσῃ ἀμείνω
> αἰδοῦς, ἥ τ' ἀγαθοῖς ἀνδράσι, Κύρν', ἕπεται (409-10).

'You will store away no better treasure for your children, Cyrnus, than the respect which attends good men.'

Occasionally couplets set out opposing views:

> εἴη μοι πλουτοῦντι κακῶν ἀπάτερθε μεριμνέων
> ζώειν ἀβλαβέως μηδὲν ἔχοντι κακόν (1153-4).

'May I live wealthy, far from evil cares, unharmed, with no evil fortune.'

> οὐκ ἔραμαι πλουτεῖν οὐδ' εὔχομαι, ἀλλά μοι εἴη
> ζῆν ἀπὸ τῶν ὀλίγων μηδὲν ἔχοντι κακόν (1155-6).

'I do not desire wealth, nor do I pray for it: may I live off little, with no evil fortune.' We saw that Archilochus put similar words in the mouth of Charon the carpenter (19), and that Solon too praised the simple life (24). The views of Hesiod and Solon on ill-gotten gains appear in a new setting:

> βούλεο δ' εὐσεβέων ὀλίγοις σὺν χρήμασιν οἰκεῖν
> ἢ πλουτεῖν ἀδίκως χρήματα πασάμενος.
> ἐν δὲ δικαιοσύνῃ συλλήβδην πᾶσ' ἀρετή 'στιν,
> πᾶς δέ τ' ἀνὴρ ἀγαθός, Κύρνε, δίκαιος ἐών (145-8).

'Choose to be a pious man dwelling with few possessions rather than to be wealthy by acquiring possessions unjustly. To put it briefly, all excellence is contained in justice, and every just man, Cyrnus, is a good man.'

> χρήματα μὲν δαίμων καὶ παγκάκῳ ἀνδρὶ δίδωσιν,
> Κύρν'· ἀρετῆς δ' ὀλίγοις ἀνδράσι μοῖρ' ἕπεται (149-50).

'God gives money even to a villain, Cyrnus; few men are attended by the gift of virtue.'

The Greeks were fond of merit lists of the type 'the best thing is . . ., next best . . ., third . . .' and so on. The following couplet gives 'the best' in three different categories:

κάλλιστον τὸ δικαιότατον, λῷστον δ' ὑγιαίνειν·
πρᾶγμα δὲ τερπνότατον, τοῦ τις ἐρᾷ, τὸ τυχεῖν (255-6).

'The finest thing is the most just; the most advantageous is health; the most delightful is to get what one desires.' Various versions of the couplet are found in late writers, and Aristotle says that it was inscribed on the temple of Leto at Delos.

παύροις ἀνθρώπων ἀρετὴ καὶ κάλλος ὀπηδεῖ·
ὄλβιος, ὃς τούτων ἀμφοτέρων ἔλαχεν (933-4).

'Few are attended by virtue and beauty: lucky the man who has both.'

μηδὲν ἄγαν σπεύδειν· πάντων μέσ' ἄριστα· καὶ οὕτως,
Κύρν', ἕξεις ἀρετήν, ἥν τε λαβεῖν χαλεπόν (335-6).

'Do not be too eager in anything. The middle course is best in all things. Thus, Cyrnus, you will attain excellence, which is a hard thing to get.' Theognis begins with the famous Delphic maxim *mēden agan*, 'nothing in excess', expanding it by mention of the middle way, moderation, avoidance of extremes, a text on which many sermons were to be preached.

The theme of the brevity of youth is common in Theognis:

ἡμεῖς δ' ἐν θαλίῃσι φίλον καταθώμεθα θυμόν,
ὄφρ' ἔτι τερπωλῆς ἔργ' ἐρατεινὰ φέρῃ.
αἶψα γὰρ ὥστε νόημα παρέρχεται ἀγλαὸς ἥβη·   985
οὐδ' ἵππων ὁρμὴ γίνεται ὠκυτέρη,
αἵ τε ἄνακτα φέρουσι δορυσσόον ἐς πόνον ἀνδρῶν
λάβρως, πυροφόρῳ τερπόμενοι πεδίῳ (983-8).

'Let us devote our hearts to merriment while enjoyment of delights still brings pleasure; for glorious youth passes quickly like a thought; the pace of horses is not swifter, carrying their master furiously to where men toil with the lance and rejoicing in the wheat-bearing plain.' Theognis uses the Homeric 'swift as a thought' (*Od.* 7.36) for his first image, and unexpectedly expands the second with a couplet rich in epic language. The Homeric epithet *purophoros* suggests a plain flat and fertile enough for crops.

ἥβῃ τερπόμενος παίζω· δηρὸν γὰρ ἔνερθεν
γῆς ὀλέσας ψυχὴν κείσομαι ὥστε λίθος
ἄφθογγος, λείψω δ' ἐρατὸν φάος ἠελίοιο·
ἔμπης δ' ἐσθλὸς ἐὼν ὄψομαι οὐδὲν ἔτι (567-70).

'I enjoy myself, taking pleasure in my youth; for when I have lost my life I shall lie for a long time beneath the earth like a stone, dumb; and I shall leave behind the lovely light of the sun. Even though I am a good man I shall no longer see anything.' The melancholy thought had been well expressed by Mimnermus, but Theognis creates a fine poem on the theme. The simile, 'I shall lie like a stone', is his own, and the enjambment is important: not only does it link the two couplets, making a tighter unit from them, but it places great emphasis on the isolated adjective *aphthongos*, 'dumb': the years of song and conversation will be at an end.

> ἄφρονες ἄνθρωποι καὶ νήπιοι, οἵτε θανόντας
> κλαίουσ᾽, οὐδ᾽ ἥβης ἄνθος ἀπολλύμενον.
> τέρπεό μοι, φίλε θυμέ· τάχ᾽ αὖ τινες ἄλλοι ἔσονται
> ἄνδρες, ἐγὼ δὲ θανὼν γαῖα μέλαιν᾽ ἔσομαι (1069-70b).

'Foolish and childish those who weep for the dead and not for the loss of youth's flower. Enjoy yourself, my heart: soon others in turn will be men, and I shall die and be black earth.' It is not certain that the couplets form one poem, but they fit together easily. 'The flower of youth', found in Homer, is a favourite expression of Theognis; the participle with it, *apollumenon*, suggests 'death' or 'destruction' no less than 'loss'. In the second couplet enjambment places emphasis on the word *andres*, 'men', which is thrown into contrast with *egō* ('I on the other hand') and *gaia*, 'earth'.

The gloomiest thought of all is expressed in language which was echoed by Sophocles and Bacchylides among others:

> 'πάντων μὲν μὴ φῦναι ἐπιχθονίοισιν ἄριστον'
> μηδ᾽ ἐσιδεῖν αὐγὰς ὀξέος ἠελίου,
> 'φύντα δ᾽ ὅπως ὤκιστα πύλας Ἀΐδαο περῆσαι'
> καὶ κεῖσθαι πολλὴν γῆν ἐπαμησάμενον (425-8).

' "Best of all things for mortals is not to have been born" and not to have seen the rays of the keen sun; "best, once born, to pass through the gates of Hades as soon as possible" and to lie prostrate with a great heap of earth scraped on top.' Theognis may have taken the hexameter lines from an earlier source: they are quoted by Homer as his own in the *Contest of Homer and Hesiod*, and although that work is possibly as late as the fourth century it incorporates early material.

> ἀλλ᾽ ἄλλῳ κακόν ἐστι, τὸ δ᾽ ἀτρεκὲς ὄλβιος οὐδεὶς
> ἀνθρώπων ὁπόσους ἠέλιος καθορᾷ (167-8).

'One man has one misfortune, another another, and none of all the men on whom the sun looks down is truly happy.'

The character of the collection of poems which has been transmitted under the name of Theognis has been much discussed, and most scholars maintain that it is an anthology of the work of several poets; but it is clear that the poems present a unified picture of man's life, and one forms a clear impression of the personality behind them, sometimes high-spirited, more often despondent and cynical.

The poet Xenophanes wrote some quaint lines at the end of his long life:

> ἤδη δ' ἑπτά τ' ἔασι καὶ ἑξήκοντ' ἐνιαυτοὶ
> βληστρίζοντες ἐμὴν φροντίδ' ἀν' Ἑλλάδα γῆν·
> ἐκ γενετῆς δὲ τότ' ἦσαν ἐείκοσι πέντε τε πρὸς τοῖς,
> εἴπερ ἐγὼ περὶ τῶνδ' οἶδα λέγειν ἐτύμως (8).

'Already there have been sixty-seven years that have sent my wits tossing over the land of Greece; and at that time there had been twenty-five more years from my birth, if indeed I know how to tell the truth about these matters'; prosaic stuff, but the verb *blēstrizo* holds the attention: it is used elsewhere only by medical writers, Hippocrates applying it to an invalid tossing on his bed. Xenophanes made a famous reference to the Pythagorean view of life as a reincarnation:

> καί ποτέ|μιν στυφελιζομένου σκύλακος παριόντα
> φασὶν ἐποικτῖραι καὶ τόδε φάσθαι ἔπος·
> 'παῦσαι, μηδὲ ῥάπιζ', ἐπεὶ ἦ φίλου ἀνέρος ἐστὶν
> ψυχή, τὴν ἔγνων φθεγξαμένης ἀϊών' (7a).

'Why, once they say he [Pythagoras] was passing when a puppy was being beaten and pitied it and said, "Stop, don't thrash it; for it is the soul of a friend of mine, which I recognised when I heard it cry out." ' The impressive epic word *stuphelizo* is used in the *Odyssey* of striking in general and of the maltreatment of guests; *phthengomai*, 'cry out', had been used of human rather than animal cries; both words add to the humour of the passage, as does the combination of conversational language (*rhapizo* is found not in epic but in Hipponax) with epic phraseology.

Phocylides is a gnomologist like Theognis, and many of his topics are the same; but he uses hexameters instead of elegiac couplets, and on the whole his poetry is less exciting.

> χρὴ παῖδ' ἔτ' ἐόντα
> καλὰ διδάσκειν ἔργα (15D.).

'It is children who should be taught fine actions.'

> καὶ τόδε Φωκυλίδου· τί πλέον γένος εὐγενὲς εἶναι
> οἷς οὔτ' ἐν μύθοις ἔπεται χάρις οὔτ' ἐνὶ βουλῇ; (3D.).

'This too belongs to Phocylides: how are men better off for noble birth if their words and advice are not attended by grace?' Several of the maxims carry the author's 'signature' at the beginning. The middle way is commended as by Theognis:

πολλὰ μέσοισιν ἄριστα· μέσος θέλω ἐν πόλει εἶναι (12D.).

'Much turns out best for those in the middle: I wish to be in the middle in city affairs.' Aristotle quotes the line in his *Politics* to support the view that the middle estate, those who are neither rich nor poor, are most secure.

καὶ τόδε Φωκυλίδου· πόλις ἐν σκοπέλῳ κατὰ κόσμον
οἰκεῦσα σμικρὴ κρέσσων Νίνου ἀφραινούσης (4D.).

'This too belongs to Phocylides: a small city on a rock, if it has orderly government, is better than frantic Nineveh.' Phocylides contrasts a small Greek island community with the capital of Assyria which fell to the Medes in 612 B.C. after three centuries of dominance. The lines are quoted by the rhetorician Dio Chrysostom as an example of the brevity of Phocylides.

*   *   *

Simonides and Pindar wrote *thrēnoi*, 'dirges', to be sung by choirs in memory of the dead. None survives complete, unless Simonides' hymn for the warriors who fell at Thermopylae (531) is to be classified as a dirge. What remains in his case is a number of statements about mortality, several of them preserved in the pages of Stobaeus' anthology. They depict man's condition in the gloomiest colours. Since they were presumably intended to comfort the mourners, the songs may have moved, as in Archilochus' poem of consolation (13), from thoughts of the universality of man's wretchedness to the statement that 'our turn has come now' and that we must be strong and endure.

Ancient critics commended the simplicity of his style and attributed to it his ability to stir the emotions:

πάντα γὰρ μίαν ἱκνεῖται δασπλῆτα Χάρυβδιν,
αἱ μεγάλαι τ' ἀρεταὶ καὶ ὁ πλοῦτος (522).

'For all things come to one single horrid Charybdis, great excellences and wealth too.' Charybdis was the terrible whirlpool past which Odysseus had to sail (*Od.* 12.101ff.): Simonides uses it as an image for the pit of Hades, applying to it a rare adjective which Homer had used of the Erinys, the avenging Fury (*Od.* 15. 234); the two words stand out starkly in their surroundings. Similarly one long compound word, not attested elsewhere, creates a memorable line:

ὁ δ' αὖ θάνατος κίχε καὶ τὸν φυγόμαχον (524).

'But death overtakes even the man who runs from the battlefield.' Callinus had expressed the same idea in his elegiacs, and Horace reproduced it in a lapidary alcaic line,

mors et fugacem persequitur virum (*Carm.* 3.2.14).

It would be hard to find a more telling statement of man's feebleness than the following lines, which almost certainly come from a dirge:

ἀνθρώπων ὀλίγον μὲν
κάρτος, ἄπρακτοι δὲ μεληδόνες, αἰ-
ῶνι δ' ἐν παύρῳ πόνος ἀμφὶ πόνῳ ·
ὁ δ' ἄφυκτος ὁμῶς ἐπικρέμαται θάνατος ·
κείνου γὰρ ἴσον λάχον μέρος οἵ τ' ἀγαθοὶ
ὅστις τε κακός (520).

'Slight is the strength of men, impossible their plans, within their brief lifetime toil upon toil; and death hangs inescapable over all alike: an equal portion in death is allotted to good men and bad.' The succession of short statements, none subordinated to another, is effective; the image of death 'hanging over' all men recalls the story of the stone hung above Tantalus (Archilochus 91.14–15) and Mimnermus' words, 'old age hangs over a man's head' (5.6). When Simonides speaks of 'good men and bad' he is likely to be using the terms in their social sense of noblemen and paupers. In another passage from the dirges, the text of which is corrupt, he says that not even the heroes, the half-divine sons of the gods, reached old age without toil, destruction and danger (523).

Man and god are often contrasted:

ῥεῖα θεοὶ κλέπτουσιν ἀνθρώπων νόον (525),

'Easily do the gods cheat men's wits.'

οὐκ ἔστιν κακὸν
ἀνεπιδόκητον ἀνθρώποις · ὀλίγῳ δὲ χρόνῳ
πάντα μεταρρίπτει θεός (527).

'There is no toil which men cannot expect; and in a brief time god turns everything upside down.' Here it is the verb *metarriptei* that makes impact with its connotations of change and overthrow. The theme of change is memorably expressed in lines which were almost certainly written for the Scopads, the wealthy Thessalian family, many of whom were killed by the collapse of their banqueting-hall:

ἄνθρωπος ἐὼν μή ποτε φάσῃς ὅ τι γίνεται αὔριον,
μηδ' ἄνδρα ἰδὼν ὄλβιον ὅσσον χρόνον ἔσσεται ·

ὠκεῖα γὰρ οὐδὲ τανυπτερύγου μυίας
οὕτως ἁ μετάστασις (521).

'You are man. Then never say what will happen tomorrow, nor when you see a prosperous man, how long he will be prosperous. For not even the movement of a long-winged fly is so swift.' The direct address in the second person is arresting: Fraenkel compares the opening of the Old Testament psalms. Again Simonides achieves his effect by an unexpected image: a long-winged fly does not change its position as swiftly as the circumstances of the prosperous man change.

Not only man but his monuments are impermanent:

τίς κεν αἰνήσειε νόῳ πίσυνος Λίνδου ναέταν Κλεόβουλον,
ἀεναοῖς ποταμοῖς ἄνθεσί τ' εἰαρινοῖς
ἀελίου τε φλογὶ χρυσέας τε σελάνας
καὶ θαλασσαίαισι δίναις ἀντιθέντα μένος στάλας;
ἅπαντα γάρ ἐστι θεῶν ἥσσω· λίθον δὲ
καὶ βρότεοι παλάμαι θραύοντι· μωροῦ
φωτὸς ἅδε βουλά (581).

'What man who can trust his wits would commend Cleobulus, dweller in Lindus, who against ever-flowing rivers, spring flowers, the flame of the sun or the golden moon, or the eddies of the sea set the might of a statue? All things are less than the gods. Stone is broken even by mortal hands. That was the judgment of a fool.' This poem is a retort to verses inscribed on the tomb of Midas, which were said to be the work of Cleobulus, tyrant of Lindus *c.* 600 B.C. and regarded by some as one of the Seven Sages:

χαλκῆ παρθένος εἰμί, Μίδεω δ' ἐπὶ σήματι κεῖμαι.
ἔστ' ἂν ὕδωρ τε νάῃ καὶ δένδρεα μακρὰ τεθήλῃ,
ἠέλιός τ' ἀνιὼν λάμπῃ λαμπρά τε σελήνη,
καὶ ποταμοί γε ῥέωσιν ἀνακλύζῃ τε θάλασσα,
αὐτοῦ τῇδε μένουσα πολυκλαύτου ἐπὶ τύμβου
ἀγγελέω παριοῦσι Μίδης ὅτι τῇδε τέθαπται.

'I am a maiden of bronze, and I stand on the tomb of Midas. As long as water flows and tall trees grow, and the rising sun gives light or the bright moon, and rivers flow and the sea boils, here I shall remain on this sad tomb and tell passers-by that Midas is buried here.' Simonides' poem is of the same length as Cleobulus' epitaph. The presentation is direct and forceful with touches of mockery in the epic expressions *noōi pisunos*, 'trusting in his wits', and *menos stalas*, 'the might of a statue', perhaps also in the Doric form *thrauonti* since Cleobulus was a Dorian. The first sentence is rambling in imitation of Cleobulus' long sentence, and it echoes his balanced lines (2–4); the procession of datives places emphasis on the words *antithenta menos stalas*, 'setting against them the might of a statue', as does the sequence of long syllables -*nos stalas*. In contrast the last three sentences are as short as can be, and the asyndeton before the word *mōrou* is expressive.

In spite of all his insistence on man's powerlessness Simonides is emphatic that man has his *aretē*, 'excellence', even if its attainment is difficult:

> ἐστί τις λόγος
> τὰν Ἀρετὰν ναίειν δυσαμβάτοις ἐπὶ πέτραις,
> †νῦν δέ μιν θοαν† χῶρον ἁγνὸν ἀμφέπειν·
> οὐδὲ πάντων βλεφάροισι θνατῶν
> ἔσοπτος, ᾧ μὴ δακέθυμος ἱδρὼς
> ἔνδοθεν μόλῃ,
> ἵκῃ τ' ἐς ἄκρον ἀνδρείας (579).

'There is a tale that Arete (Excellence) dwells on unclimbable rocks and (close to the gods?) tends her holy place; she can be seen by the eyes of no mortal, unless distressing sweat rises on his skin and he reaches the peak of manliness.' The tale comes from Hesiod's *Works and Days* (289–92): 'in front of Excellence the immortal gods have placed sweat: long and steep is the path to her and rough at first, but when one reaches the top (*eis akron hikētai*), then the road is easy, though before it was hard.' Tyrtaeus too had spoken of 'reaching the peak of excellence' (12.43 *aretēs eis akron hikesthai*), and Pindar followed him (*Nem.* 6.23–4). To reach *aretē* one needs the help of the gods:

> οὔτις ἄνευ θεῶν
> ἀρετὰν λάβεν, οὐ πόλις, οὐ βροτός.
> θεὸς ὁ πάμμητις· ἀπή-
> μαντον οὐδέν ἐστι θνατοῖς (526).

'No one ever attained excellence without the gods, no city, no mortal. God is the all-clever one: for mortals nothing is free from misery.' Here again the single word *pammētis*, found nowhere else, adds the distinctive touch; it reminds us of *polumētis Odusseus*, 'Odysseus of the many wiles': god is the supreme schemer. Hesiod made Metis, Counsel or Wisdom, the consort of Zeus, who swallowed her (*Theog.* 886ff.).

The most interesting and difficult of all Simonides' poems presents the view that something more modest and attainable than the Homeric and aristocratic ideal of goodness is acceptable (542). He begins,

> ἄνδρ' ἀγαθὸν μὲν ἀλαθέως γενέσθαι
> χαλεπὸν χερσίν τε καὶ ποσὶ καὶ νόῳ
> τετράγωνον ἄνευ ψόγου τετυγμένον (1-3).

'It is difficult for a man to be truly good, four-square in hands, in feet and in mind, fashioned without flaw.' The words in which the impossible paragon is described are strongly reminiscent of Homer, who spoke of 'all manner of excellence, of foot, in fighting, of mind' (*Il*. 15. 642–3), but Simonides uses the Pythagorean symbol of the square to express the concept of perfection. After some lines, now missing, in which he must have addressed his patron, the noble Scopas of Thessaly, he continues,

> οὐδέ μοι ἐμμελέως τὸ Πιττάκειον
> νέμεται, καίτοι σοφοῦ παρὰ φωτὸς εἰ-
>   ρημένον · χαλεπὸν φάτ' ἐσθλὸν ἔμμεναι.
> θεὸς ἂν μόνος τοῦτ' ἔχοι γέρας, ἄνδρα δ' οὐκ
>   ἔστι μὴ οὐ κακὸν ἔμμεναι,   15
> ὃν ἀμήχανος συμφορὰ καθέλῃ ·
> πράξας γὰρ εὖ πᾶς ἀνὴρ ἀγαθός,
> κακὸς δ' εἰ κακῶς (11-18).

'Nor does the saying of Pittacus ring true to me, although it was spoken by a wise man: he said that it was difficult to be good. Only a god could have that privilege: a man cannot avoid being evil, when he is in the grip of irresistible misfortune. When his luck is good, any man is good; when it is bad, he is bad; (and for the most part they are best whom the gods love).' By 'good' and 'bad' Simonides means 'noble, successful, great' and the opposite, and since man is at the mercy of circumstances, perfect 'goodness' is impossible for him. He continues in somewhat lighter vein:

> τοὔνεκεν οὔ ποτ' ἐγὼ τὸ μὴ γενέσθαι
> δυνατὸν διζήμενος κενεὰν ἐς ἄ-
>   πρακτον ἐλπίδα μοῖραν αἰῶνος βαλέω,
> πανάμωμον ἄνθρωπον, εὐρυεδέος ὅσοι
>   καρπὸν αἰνύμεθα χθονός ·   25
> ἐπὶ δ' ὑμὶν εὑρὼν ἀπαγγελέω.
> πάντας δ' ἐπαίνημι καὶ φιλέω,
> ἑκὼν ὅστις ἔρδῃ
> μηδὲν αἰσχρόν · ἀνάγκᾳ
> δ' οὐδὲ θεοὶ μάχονται (21-30).

'And so I shall never throw away my span of life on an empty, vain hope in quest of the impossible, the completely blameless man among all of us who win the fruit of the wide earth. When I find one I shall tell you. No, I commend and love any man who of his own will does nothing shameful: against necessity not even the gods fight.' Simonides emphasises what man does 'of his own will'; he cannot be blamed for what comes on him by 'necessity'.

In the last stanza Simonides says that he is not a fault-finder: he is satisfied with the man who is not *kakos* ('bad'; but the text is not fully preserved here, and a word like *noon* should perhaps be supplied: 'not weak in understanding'),

μηδ᾽ ἄγαν ἀπάλαμνος εἰ-
δώς γ᾽ ὀνησίπολιν δίκαν,　　　　　35
ὑγιὴς ἀνήρ· οὐδὲ μή μιν ἐγὼ
μωμήσομαι· τῶν γὰρ ἠλιθίων
ἀπείρων γενέθλα.
πάντα τοι καλά, τοῖσίν
τ᾽ αἰσχρὰ μὴ μέμεικται (34-40).

'. . . nor too shiftless, and understands the justice that helps his city, a sound man. I shall not find fault with him; for the generation of fools is numberless. All things are fair in which the base is not mingled.' Simonides lists the standards by which he will award praise to a man: he must be intelligent and competent and must understand the meaning of civic justice; he must be 'sound, healthy', an unusual term by way of summary. 'Goodness' and 'badness' have nothing to do with social standing and external circumstances; Simonides has left behind the world of Theognis.

A papyrus fragment which carries a similar message has been variously attributed to Simonides and Bacchylides (541); part of the text runs,

ἀλλ᾽] ὀλίγοις ἀρετὰν ἔδωκεν ἔχειν
ἐς τ]έλος, οὐ γὰρ ἐλαφρὸν ἐσθλ[ὸν ἔμμεν·
ἢ γ]ὰρ ἀέκοντά νιν βιᾶται
κέ]ρδος ἀμάχητον ἢ δολοπλ[όκου
με]γασθενὴς οἶστρος Ἀφροδίτ[ας
ἀρ]τίθαλοί τε φιλονικίαι (6-11).

'But to few men only has he [god?] granted that they have excellence to the end; for it is not easy to be good: either irresistible greed for profit or the powerful gadfly of guileful Aphrodite or vigorous ambitions coerce a man against his will.' Here the poet spells out the forces that prevent a man from leading a good life: greed for money, sexual desire, political ambition.

Simonides was famous for his epitaphs as well as his choral lyric poems, but in almost all cases it is impossible to tell whether lines attributed to him are in fact his work. He was known to have composed fine epitaphs at the time of the Persian Wars, and many were later ascribed to him, sometimes with no regard for chronology. The name of the composer of an epitaph was not recorded on the stone till the end of the fifth century, and unless there is strong external evidence for authorship it is best to regard the poem as anonymous; Simonides was not the only distinguished composer of epitaphs.

The poem about which there is least doubt of Simonidean authorship is the epitaph for his friend Megistias who died at Thermopylae:

μνῆμα τόδε κλεινοῖο Μεγιστία, ὅν ποτε Μῆδοι
Σπερχειὸν ποταμὸν κτεῖναν ἀμειψάμενοι,

μάντιος, ὃς τότε Κῆρας ἐπερχομένας σάφα εἰδὼς
οὐκ ἔτλη Σπάρτης ἡγεμόνας προλιπεῖν (83D.).

'This is the tomb of glorious Megistias, whom once the Medes killed when they crossed the river Sperchius: he was a seer, who recognised clearly that the Spirits of Death were approaching then, but could not bring himself to desert Sparta's leaders.' Herodotus tells us about Megistias: he was a seer from Acarnania who on the day before the battle warned the Greeks of their approaching death: Leonidas gave him permission to leave, but he chose to stay and die, and sent away his only son instead. The poem turns on the word *mantios*, 'seer', placed at the beginning of the second couplet: it was the fact that he could foresee the future that made his death so poignant. Simonides uses the word *pote*, 'once', with posterity in mind: future generations would read, as it were, 'Once upon a time Megistias was slain by the Persians.'

Simonides was almost but not quite certainly the composer of the most famous epitaph of all:

ὦ ξεῖν', ἀγγέλλειν Λακεδαιμονίοις ὅτι τῇδε
κείμεθα τοῖς κείνων ῥήμασι πειθόμενοι (92D.).

'Stranger, report to the Spartans that we lie here, obedient to their words.' The lines are austere and reticent: there is no mention of numbers or even of valour ('the gallant three hundred'), only of obedience, the virtue so characteristic of Spartan youth. The dead appeal to the 'stranger', the unknown passer-by who will see their tomb. The device was common: a fine example is

ἄνθρωπε, ὃς στείχεις καθ' ὁδὸν φρασὶν ἄλλα μενοινῶν,
στῆθι καὶ οἴκτιρον σῆμα Θράσωνος ἰδών.

'Fellow, you who walk along the road with your mind on other things, stop and pity, now that you have seen Thrason's tomb.'

An impressive epitaph, thought by Bergk to have been composed for the Spartans who fell at Plataea, depends on paradox for its effect:

ἄσβεστον κλέος οἵδε φίλῃ περὶ πατρίδι θέντες
κυάνεον θανάτου ἀμφεβάλοντο νέφος·
οὐδὲ τεθνᾶσι θανόντες, ἐπεὶ σφ' ἀρετὴ καθύπερθεν
κυδαίνουσ' ἀνάγει δώματος ἐξ Ἀίδεω |(121D.).

'These men set imperishable fame about their dear country, and threw around themselves the dark cloud of death. They died but are not dead: their valour gives them glory above and brings them up from the house of Hades.' It is difficult to assess whether the rhetoric of *oude tethnasi thanontes*, 'they died but are not dead', is too bold for Simonides.

Poems of consolation could be written in the concise, reticent manner of epitaphs:

σῆμα καταφθιμένοιο Μεγακλέος εὖτ' ἂν ἴδωμαι,
οἰκτίρω σε, τάλαν Καλλία, οἷ' ἔπαθες (84D.).

'Whenever I see the tomb of dead Megacles, I pity you, poor Callias, for your great loss.' The author begins as if to write an epitaph: *sēma kataphthimenoio Megakleous*, 'the tomb of dead Megacles', can be paralleled from gravestones; but the author moves to the personal relationships involved, Callias' loss of Megacles, 'my' pity for Callias.

Pindar vividly expressed many of the views of the human condition that we have met in earlier poetry. His outlook was essentially as pessimistic as his predecessors', and many of his victory-odes, although their occasion was festive, contain warnings of the impermanence of man's fortunes and his total dependence on the gods. He tells Hieron, tyrant of Syracuse and one of the most powerful rulers in the Greek world,

χρὴ
δὲ πρὸς θεὸν οὐκ ἐρίζειν,
ὃς ἀνέχει τοτὲ μὲν τὰ κείνων, τότ' αὖθ' ἑτέροις
ἔδωκεν μέγα κῦδος (*Pyth.* 2.88-9).

'But one must not strive against god, who at one moment raises aloft the fortunes of these men, at the next gives great glory to others.'

κρίνεται δ' ἀλκὰ διὰ δαίμονας ἀνδρῶν.
δύο δέ τοι ζωᾶς ἄωτον μοῦνα ποιμαί-
νοντι τὸν ἄλπνιστον, εὐανθεῖ σὺν ὄλβῳ
εἴ τις εὖ πάσχων λόγον ἐσλὸν ἀκούῃ.
μὴ μάτευε Ζεὺς γενέσθαι· πάντ' ἔχεις,
εἴ σε τούτων μοῖρ' ἐφίκοιτο καλῶν.　　　　　15
θνατὰ θνατοῖσι πρέπει (*Isthm.* 5.11-16).

'The valour of men is judged by the agency of the gods. Two things only tend the sweetest blossom of life: if a man enjoys success with flourishing prosperity and if he has fine words spoken of him. Do not seek to become Zeus: you have everything if a portion of these two blessings comes to you. Mortal aims befit mortal men.' The words of course suit the victor whose praises Pindar is singing: he has reached the summit of human endeavour: he has fared well and belongs to a prosperous family, and fine words have been spoken of him at the time of his victory and now by Pindar himself; but he must remember that he is mortal and recognise the limits of mortality. The thought is common in Pindar and variously expressed: in the third *Nemean* he writes,

οὐκέτι πρόσω
ἀβάταν ἅλα κιόνων ὕπερ Ἡρακλέος περᾶν εὐμαρές (20-1).

'It is not easy to go further and cross the trackless sea beyond the pillars of Heracles', that is, west of the straits of Gibraltar.

Pindar's most famous statement of the powerlessness of man comes near the end of the eighth *Pythian*, just after he has listed the victories of a young wrestler and spoken of the victor 'flying on the wings of his manly achievements':

ἐν δ᾽ ὀλίγῳ βροτῶν
τὸ τερπνὸν αὔξεται · οὕτω δὲ καὶ πίτνει χαμαί,
ἀποτρόπῳ γνώμᾳ σεσεισμένον.

ἐπάμεροι · τί δέ τις; τί δ᾽ οὔ τις; σκιᾶς ὄναρ
ἄνθρωπος. ἀλλ᾽ ὅταν αἴγλα διόσδοτος ἔλθῃ,
λαμπρὸν φέγγος ἔπεστιν ἀνδρῶν καὶ μείλιχος αἰών (92-7).

'But within a short time the pleasure of mortals grows up, within a short time also it falls to the ground, shaken by the turning away of their purpose.

Creatures of a day! What is anyone? What is he not? Man is the dream of a shadow. But when radiance comes, the gift from Zeus, a bright light rests on men and a gentle existence.' The cry *epameroi* fills the role of a full sentence: men are 'creatures of a day'; and the placing of the word at the beginning of the final epode gives it the greatest possible emphasis. It is followed by a sequence of tiny units, the two questions and the further statement about man: in this he recalls Homer's description of the underworld, where the ghost of Odysseus' mother eluded his embrace 'like a shadow or a dream' (*Od.* 11.207); Pindar combines the images and transfers them from the dead to the living. Yet on this occasion he refuses to end the poem in gloom; he speaks of the 'Zeus-sent gleam' which has come upon the victor now, as though to say that athletic success alone is illuminated in the murk of human existence. Elsewhere Pindar quotes with approval an ancient saying,

ἓν παρ᾽ ἐσλὸν πήματα σύνδυο δαίονται βροτοῖς
ἀθάνατοι (*Pyth.* 3.81-2).

'For every one blessing the immortals apportion two troubles to men.'

The sixth *Nemean* begins by stating that in spite of man's powerlessness he may sometimes have a resemblance to the gods:

ἓν ἀνδρῶν, ἓν θεῶν γένος · ἐκ μιᾶς δὲ πνέομεν
ματρὸς ἀμφότεροι · διείργει δὲ πᾶσα κεκριμένα
δύναμις, ὡς τὸ μὲν οὐδέν, ὁ δὲ
χάλκεος ἀσφαλὲς αἰὲν ἕδος

μένει οὐρανός. ἀλλά τι προσφέρομεν ἔμπαν ἢ μέγαν
νόον ἤτοι φύσιν ἀθανάτοις,   5
καίπερ ἐφαμερίαν οὐκ εἰδότες οὐδὲ μετὰ νύκτας
ἄμμε πότμος
ἄντιν' ἔγραψε δραμεῖν ποτὶ στάθμαν (1-7).

'One and the same is the race of men and of gods; from one and the same
mother [Earth] do we both draw our breath; but we are separated completely
by our allotted power: what we are is nothing, while the bronze heaven
remains for ever as an unshakeable dwelling. And yet to some degree we
resemble the immortals, either in great wisdom or in physical nature, although
we do not know to what finishing-line, whether by day or in the course of the
night, fate has decreed that we should run.' Pindar goes on immediately with
the words

τεκμαίρει καί νυν Ἀλκιμίδας,

'and so now Alcimidas bears witness . . .': again the successful athlete is the
example of a mortal who can raise himself towards immortality, although the
man of intellect may also succeed.

In some of his poems Pindar puts forward a picture of life after death
which contradicts the traditional Homeric view that the dead have no true
existence but are ghosts 'like a shadow or a dream'. The fullest statement of
these beliefs is in the second *Olympian*, which was commissioned by Theron,
tyrant of the Sicilian city of Acragas, and it is likely that they were inserted at
Theron's request. Pindar begins the passage with a long sentence in which he
breaks the syntactical thread:

εἰ δέ νιν ἔχων τις οἶδεν τὸ μέλλον,
ὅτι θανόντων μὲν ἐν-
θάδ' αὐτίκ' ἀπάλαμνοι φρένες
ποινὰς ἔτεισαν – τὰ δ' ἐν τᾷδε Διὸς ἀρχᾷ
ἀλιτρὰ κατὰ γᾶς δικάζει τις ἐχθρᾷ
λόγον φράσαις ἀνάγκᾳ (56-60).

'But if a man who has it [wealth] knows the future, that when men die on this
earth it is the violent spirits among them that undergo punishment; and wrongs
committed in this kingdom of Zeus are judged under the earth by one who
declares his sentence with hostile necessity.' The idea of a judgment is
mentioned also by Pindar's contemporary, Aeschylus, and is said to have been
taught by Pythagoras; and punishment for wrongdoing is mentioned even by
Homer, who says twice that perjurers are punished under the earth (*Il.*
3.278f., 19.259ff.). The sentence continues with the other side of the picture,
the reward enjoyed by the good:

ἴσαις δὲ νύκτεσσιν αἰεί,
ἴσαις δ' ἀμέραις ἅλιον ἔχοντες, ἀπονέστερον
ἐσλοὶ δέκονται βίοτον, οὐ χθόνα τα-
    ράσσοντες ἐν χερὸς ἀκμᾷ
οὐδὲ πόντιον ὕδωρ
κεινὰν παρὰ δίαιταν, ἀλλὰ παρὰ μὲν τιμίοις   65
θεῶν οἵτινες ἔχαιρον εὐορκίαις
    ἄδακρυν νέμονται
αἰῶνα, τοὶ δ' ἀπροσόρατον ὀκχέοντι πόνον (61-7):

'whereas the good receive a trouble-free existence, with sunshine equally by day and by night, disturbing neither the earth nor the water of the sea with the strength of their hands for an empty livelihood; no, those who rejoiced in keeping their oaths lead a life without tears in the presence of the honoured gods [Hades and Persephone], while the others endure suffering that is too grim to behold.' It may have been Homer's mention of punished perjury that leads Pindar to choose 'those who kept their oaths' as the example of 'the good'. He concentrates on their reward, putting it in negative form—no ploughing, no fishing, no tears; and he sums up the punishment of the wicked in the word *aprosoraton*: no one can look at it. Then he adds a new dimension:

ὅσοι δ' ἐτόλμασαν ἐστρὶς
ἑκατέρωθι μείναντες ἀπὸ πάμπαν ἀδίκων ἔχειν
ψυχάν, ἔτειλαν Διὸς ὁδὸν παρὰ Κρό-   70
    νου τύρσιν· ἔνθα μακάρων
νᾶσον ὠκεανίδες
αὖραι περιπνέοισιν· ἄνθεμα δὲ χρυσοῦ φλέγει,
τὰ μὲν χερσόθεν ἀπ' ἀγλαῶν δενδρέων,
    ὕδωρ δ' ἄλλα φέρβει,
ὅρμοισι τῶν χέρας ἀναπλέκοντι καὶ στεφάνους
βουλαῖς ἐν ὀρθαῖσι Ῥαδαμάνθυος,   75
ὃν πατὴρ ἔχει μέγας ἑτοῖμον αὐτῷ πάρεδρον,
πόσις ὁ πάντων Ῥέας
    ὑπέρτατον ἐχοίσας θρόνον (68-77).

'All those who have been brave enough to keep their lives completely clear of injustice during three sojourns in each world complete the journey along the highway of Zeus to the tower of Cronus: there ocean breezes blow round the island of the blessed, and flowers of gold are ablaze, some on dry land from splendid trees, others fed by the water; with chains of these flowers they entwine their arms and weave garlands in keeping with the upright counsels of Rhadamanthys, whom the mighty father [Cronus], husband of Rhea who has her throne above all others, has as his ready partner.' Pindar's examples of those who reached the island of the blessed are Peleus, Cadmus and Achilles.

What is surprising is the mention of three lives in this world, three below it: Pindar is talking of a theory of reincarnation according to which men's souls go to and fro between this world and the next before they can earn their place in the island paradise. Cronus, father of Zeus, now reconciled with his son, has the honour of presiding there, as in Hesiod's version (*Works and Days* 169); Rhadamanthys was brother of king Minos of Crete and was known on earth for his justice. Man then has something to hope for after all; if he is virtuous, he will have a life free from tears, and he may even be one of the chosen few in the isles of the blessed. One of the Attic drinking-songs sets Harmodius, killer of the tyrant Hipparchus, in the islands in company with Achilles and Diomedes (894).

Beliefs of this kind are mentioned also in the few extracts from Pindar's dirges which have been preserved. We do not know whether they too were for Sicilian patrons. In one he gives a famous description of 'the place of the pious':

> τοῖσι λάμπει μὲν μένος ἀελίου
> τὰν ἐνθάδε νύκτα κάτω,
> φοινικορόδοις <δ'> ἐνὶ λειμώνεσσι προάστιον αὐτῶν
> καὶ λιβάνων σκιαρᾶν <   >
> καὶ χρυσοκάρποισιν βέβριθε <δενδρέοις>   5
> καὶ τοὶ μὲν ἵπποις γυμνασίοισι <τε   >
>   τοὶ δὲ πεσσοῖς
> τοὶ δὲ φορμίγγεσσι τέρπονται, παρὰ δέ σφισιν
>   εὐανθὴς ἅπας τέθαλεν ὄλβος·
> ὀδμὰ δ' ἐρατὸν κατὰ χῶρον κίδναται
> †αἰεὶ . . θύματα μειγνύντων πυρὶ τηλεφανεῖ
> <παντοῖα θεῶν ἐπὶ βωμοῖς> (fr. 129.1-10).

'For them the sun's strength shines below while it is night here, and the park in front of their city is among meadows with red roses and . . . of shady frankincense-trees . . . and is heavy with trees that bear golden fruit; and some take their pleasure in horses and bodily exercises . . ., others in draughts, others in lyres; and among them prosperity blossoms in full rich flower; a delightful perfume spreads over the place as they constantly bring sacrifices of all kinds to the far-shining fire on the altar of the gods . . .' The criminals inhabit a pit

> ἔνθεν τὸν ἄπειρον ἐρεύγονται σκότον
> βληχροὶ δνοφερᾶς νυκτὸς ποταμοί (fr. 130),

'from which feeble rivers of murky night belch forth their limitless darkness'. The pleasures of Pindar's Elysium are remarkable, and the mention of horses and physical exercises suggests that the dirge was for a young man. Plutarch, who quotes the passage, says that the blessed enjoy recalling the past, and closes by saying that their happiness is due to 'the rites that free men from toil' (fr. 131a), the rites of initiation into the Mysteries.

Another passage uses distinctive language of the soul:

σῶμα μὲν πάντων ἕπεται θανάτῳ περισθενεῖ,
ζωὸν δ' ἔτι λείπεται αἰῶνος εἴδω-
λον· τὸ γάρ ἐστι μόνον
ἐκ θεῶν· εὕδει δὲ πρασσόντων μελέων, ἀτὰρ εὑ-
δόντεσσιν ἐν πολλοῖς ὀνείροις
δείκνυσι τερπνῶν ἐφέρποισαν χαλεπῶν τε κρίσιν (fr. 131b).

'The body of all men submits to mighty death, but there remains alive an image of their life, for it alone comes from the gods. While the limbs are active it is asleep, but in many dreams it reveals to sleepers an approaching adjudication of things delightful or harsh.' For Pindar, at least in this passage, the image or reflection (*eidōlon*, Homer's term) of the living man, is immortal since it is derived from the gods, and it gives advance warning that man will be judged and rewarded or punished.

Atonement followed by reincarnation appears in another fragment:

οισι δὲ Φερσεφόνα ποινὰν παλαιοῦ πένθεος
δέξεται, ἐς τὸν ὕπερθεν ἅλιον κείνων ἐνάτῳ ἔτεϊ
ἀνδιδοῖ ψυχὰς πάλιν, ἐκ τᾶν βασιλῆες ἀγαυοὶ
καὶ σθένει κραιπνοὶ σοφίᾳ τε μέγιστοι
ἄνδρες αὔξοντ'· ἐς δὲ τὸν λοιπὸν χρόνον ἥροες ἁ-
γνοὶ πρὸς ἀνθρώπων καλέονται (fr. 133).

'As for those from whom Persephone accepts recompense for her ancient grief, she sends their souls back again to the sun above in the ninth year; and from these souls arise august kings and men swift in strength and greatest in wisdom; and for all time to come men call them holy heroes.' It is not certain that we should try to combine this material with the doctrines of the second *Olympian*, in which Pindar spoke of three sojourns in each world and told how some heroes finally reach the island of the blessed, although such combination is often attempted. We are told here that Persephone, whom Homer probably regarded as a judge of perjurers along with Hades (*Il.* 3.278f.), accepts from some an eight-year atonement for her ancient sorrow, by which is probably meant the death of her son, Dionysus-Zagreus: he was killed by the Titans, whose wickedness was inherited by men. Presumably Pindar stated also the fate of those from whom Persephone does not accept recompense: a judgment on her part is implied. The atonement is perhaps to be thought of as a period of purgatory: purgation, like reincarnation, was a Pythagorean doctrine.

In a dirge for an Athenian, Hippocrates, Pindar mentioned specifically the Eleusinian mysteries, presumably because Hippocrates had been initiated:

ὄλβιος ὅστις ἰδὼν κεῖν' εἶσ' ὑπὸ χθόν'·
οἶδε μὲν βίου τελευτάν,
οἶδεν δὲ διόσδοτον ἀρχάν (fr. 137).

'Blessed the man who looks upon these things before he goes below the earth:
he knows the end of life and the Zeus-given beginning.' The culmination of the
rites at Eleusis was the revelation of a holy object which may have been an ear
of corn; that explains Pindar's emphasis on 'looking upon these things'. The
initiate understands the mystery of the death and rebirth of the corn and,
symbolically, the death which for the initiate is followed by a new beginning
in the afterlife.

Bacchylides makes no mention of the mystery religions and indeed has little
to say about death. Unlike Simonides and Pindar he seems to have composed
no dirges. He imagined the underworld as Homer represents it: when Heracles
goes down to fetch Cerberus he sees the souls of wretched mortals by the
waters of Cocytus,

οἷά τε φύλλ' ἄνεμος
Ἴδας ἀνὰ μηλοβότους
πρῶνας ἀργηστὰς δονεῖ (5.65-7),

'like the leaves shaken by the wind on the gleaming headlands of Ida where
sheep graze'. When Heracles threatens to send an arrow through the ghost of
Meleager, the hero assures him that he has nothing to fear from the dead.

For Bacchylides, as for Pindar, the fame won by an athlete lives on after his
death:

καὶ ὅταν θανάτοιο
κυάνεον νέφος καλύψῃ, λείπεται
ἀθάνατον κλέος εὖ ἐρ-
χθέντος ἀσφαλεῖ σὺν αἴσᾳ (13.63-6).

'And when the dark-blue cloud of death covers them, there remains the
immortal glory of a deed well done, with a fortune that is secure.' Another
victory-ode ends with similar thoughts:

τὸ μέλλον
δ' ἀκρίτους τίκτει τελευτάς,
πᾶ τύχα βρίσει. τὸ μὲν κάλλιστον, ἐσθλὸν
ἄνδρα πολλῶν ὑπ' ἀνθρώπων πολυζήλωτον εἶμεν·
οἶδα καὶ πλούτου μεγάλαν δύνασιν,
ἃ καὶ τὸν ἀχρεῖον τί[θησ]ι   50
χρηστόν. τί μακρὰν γ[λ]ῶ[σ]σαν ἰθύσας ἐλαύνω
ἐκτὸς ὁδοῦ; (10.45-52).

'The future gives birth to outcomes which no one can predict so as to tell how fortune will tip the scales. The finest thing is to be a good man much envied by many of his fellows; I know too wealth's great power, which can make even the useless man noble. But why in steering my tongue do I drive far off the course?' With this self-conscious reminder Bacchylides breaks off his generalisations and closes the poem with mention of festivity and music. In speaking of the 'good man much envied' he must have the successful athlete in mind; wealth is often commended in victory-odes, but more often when the victory was won in a chariot-race, the prerequisite for which was great wealth; Bacchylides claims that it can make the useless man *khrēston*, 'noble', but *khrēston* will keep something of its basic meaning of 'useful' also.

Bacchylides' longest gnomic passage occurs at the end of his ode for a boy from his own island who won the boxing contest at the Isthmian games:

φαμὶ καὶ φάσω μέγιστον
κῦδος ἔχειν ἀρετάν· πλοῦ-   160
τός δὲ καὶ δειλοῖσιν ἀνθρώπων ὁμιλεῖ,

ἐθέλει δ᾽ αὔξειν φρένας ἀν-
δρός· ὁ δ᾽ εὖ ἔρδων θεοὺς
ἐλπίδι κυδροτέρᾳ
σαίνει κέαρ. εἰ δ᾽ ὑγιείας   165
θνατὸς ἐὼν ἔλαχεν
ζώειν τ᾽ ἀπ᾽ οἰκείων ἔχει,
πρώτοις ἐρίζει· παντί τοι
τέρψις ἀνθρώπων βίῳ

ἕπεται νόσφιν γε νόσων   170
πενίας τ᾽ ἀμαχάνου.
ἴσον ὅ τ᾽ ἀφνεὸς ἱ-
μείρει μεγάλων ὅ τε μείων
παυροτέρων· τὸ δὲ πάν-
των εὐμαρεῖν οὐδὲν γλυκὺ   175
θνατοῖσιν, ἀλλ᾽ αἰεὶ τὰ φεύ-
γοντα δίζηνται κιχεῖν.

ὅντινα κουφόταται
θυμὸν δονέουσι μέριμναι,
ὅσσον ἂν ζώῃ †χρόνον, τόνδε λάχεν† τι-   180
μάν. ἀρετὰ δ᾽ ἐπίμοχθος
μέν, τ]ελευταθεῖσα δ᾽ ὀρθῶς
ἀνδρὶ κ]αὶ εὖτε θάνῃ λεί-
π[ει πολυ]ζήλωτον εὐκλείας ἄ[γαλ]μα (1.159-84).

'I declare and shall declare that excellence holds the greatest glory: for wealth attends even worthless men and commonly exalts a man's spirit; but he who

treats the gods well comforts his heart with more glorious hope. And if a
mortal has good health and can live off his own resources, he rivals the foremost. Happiness attends men's lives at all levels of society if there is no sickness
and no helpless poverty. The rich man and the less rich have equally strong
desires, the one for great things, the other for less; but to have abundance of
everything brings no pleasure to mortals: they are always trying to catch what
eludes them. The man whose heart is shaken by lightweight ambitions has
honour for such time as he lives; but excellence, although it involves toil, when
rightly achieved leaves a man even after he has died the enviable adornment of
glory.' Bacchylides has moved into this passage from mention of the Isthmian
victory, and the *aretē*, 'excellence', is clearly that displayed by the athlete. In
our last extract Bacchylides seemed to praise wealth, but here he clearly
represents it as inferior to excellence, piety and health. He begins and ends
the passage with *aretē*, 'excellence', holding together the loose assemblage of
maxims by this ring-composition.

Like Pindar, then, he endeavours to show the unmatchable glory that the
victorious athlete can win; but like Pindar also he often reverts to the basic
helplessness and misery of mankind:

> παύροισι δὲ θνατῶν τὸν ἄπαντα χρόνον δαίμων ἔδωκεν
> πράσσοντας ἐν καιρῷ πολιοκρόταφον
> γῆρας ἱκνεῖσθαι, πρὶν ἐγκύρσαι δύᾳ (fr. 25).

'To few mortals only has the god granted that they fare prosperously all their
lives and reach grey-templed old age before meeting with grief.' Man cannot
influence his fortunes:

> θνατοῖσι δ' οὐκ αὐθαίρετοι
> οὔτ' ὄλβος οὔτ' ἄκναμπτος Ἄρης
>   οὔτε πάμφθερσις στάσις,
> ἀλλ' ἐπιχρίμπτει νέφος ἄλλοτ' ἐπ' ἄλλαν
> γαῖαν ἁ πάνδωρος Αἶσα (fr. 24).

'Not by mortals' own choice do they have prosperity or stubborn war or civil
strife that destroys all: no, Destiny, the giver of all, moves the cloud now over
this land, now over that.' Destiny may be 'the giver of all things'—the
adjective recalls Pandora's name—but it is on her evil gifts that Bacchylides
focusses his attention with his image of the cloud.

The long ode for Hieron, tyrant of Syracuse, is the vehicle for Bacchylides'
gloomiest thoughts. The splendid praise of the ruler and his victory leads into
a gnomic bridge passage before the myth:

> ὄλβιος ᾧτινι θεὸς
> μοῖράν τε καλῶν ἔπορεν

σύν τ' ἐπιζήλῳ τύχᾳ
ἀφνεὸν βιοτὰν διάγειν· οὐ
γάρ τις ἐπιχθονίων
πάντα γ' εὐδαίμων ἔφυ (5.50-5).

'Happy the man to whom the god has granted a portion of good things and a life passed in wealth along with an envied fortune; for no mortal is blessed in all things.' The story of Heracles' meeting in Hades with Meleager provides two examples of heroes who had mixed fortunes: the young Meleager, whose run of success ended when his mother brought about his death, and Heracles himself, whose terrible end is hinted at in the last words of the myth. When Heracles has heard the young man's story, he sheds tears for the only time in his life and utters the gloomiest of all thoughts:

'θνατοῖσι μὴ φῦναι φέριστον
μηδ' ἀελίου προσιδεῖν
φέγγος' (160-2).

'Best for mortals not to have been born, not to have looked on the light of the sun.'

Bacchylides emphasised the blessing of health in one of his poems (1.165ff.): a drinking-song, which Plato liked to quote, gave it the same priority:

ὑγιαίνειν μὲν ἄριστον ἀνδρὶ θνητῷ,
δεύτερον δὲ καλὸν φυὰν γενέσθαι,
τὸ τρίτον δὲ πλουτεῖν ἀδόλως
καὶ τὸ τέταρτον ἡβᾶν μετὰ τῶν φίλων (890).

'To be healthy is the best thing for a mortal man; second is to be handsome in appearance; third is to be wealthy without trickery; fourth, to be young with one's friends.'

CHAPTER EIGHT

Poetry and Music

In this chapter I propose to draw attention to passages in which the lyric poets sing of poetry and music, especially those passages in which they refer to their own performance. Their invocation of the Muse is an important aspect of this topic, and so I shall begin by noting what the Muses meant to the earlier poets, Homer, Hesiod and the writers of the Homeric hymns.

In both *Iliad* and *Odyssey* the poet begins with an appeal to the Muse: 'Sing, goddess, of the anger . . .' and 'Tell for me, Muse, of the man . . .' At crucial points in the *Iliad* he again calls on the Muse or Muses, asking them to tell who was 'the first' to perform some action (11.218ff., 14.508ff.), how something 'first' happened (16. 112f.), or which of the Greek warriors was 'best' (2.761f.). In his introduction to the long catalogue of Greeks in Book 2 he explains why divine help is necessary: 'Tell for me now, you Muses who have your homes on Olympus—for you are goddesses and are present and know all things, while we hear the report only and do not in any way know—tell who were the commanders and chieftains of the Greeks. I could not tell their great number nor mention them by name, even if I had ten tongues, ten mouths, an untiring voice and a heart of bronze, unless the Olympian Muses, the daughters of aegis-bearing Zeus, told me of all the Greeks who came to Troy' (484–92). He emphasises the divinity of the Muses, dwellers on Olympus and daughters of Zeus; when he says they 'are present', he means that as immortals they are witnesses of all that happens and so have knowledge of everything, unlike the bard who can only rely on hearsay; so they must prompt him now if his chronicle is to be accurate. It is obvious that the needs of the epic poet and the lyric poet will be different and that the lyric poet will not usually request information; we have seen, however, that Bacchylides in the dithyramb, *Sons of Antenor*, echoed Homer's questions: 'Muse, who was the first to make the claim for justice?' (15.47), and Pindar's question at *Pythian* 4.70 is similar. Pindar uses Homer's words in the sixth Paean,

ἀλλὰ παρθένοι γάρ, ἴσθ᾽ ὅτ[ι], Μο[ῖ]σαι,
πάντα. . .
κλῦτε νῦν (54-8).

'But, maiden Muses, since you know all things, . . . hear me now'; in another paean he says that if anyone tries to find the road to wisdom (or 'poetic skill', *sophia*) without the Muses, his wits are blind (fr. 52h.18–20).

Homer draws an attractive picture of Demodocus, the bard of the Phaeacian court, calling him 'divine' and 'much loved by the Muse', and telling how the Muse 'set him going' on his song (*Od.* 8.43, 63, 73); indeed the Muse in her love has taught all bards the 'paths' of song (479–81). He speaks elsewhere of the Muses' various activities: they sing with beautiful voice at feasts on Olympus (*Il.* 1.604) and, 'nine in all', sang a dirge at the funeral celebrations for Achilles (*Od.* 24.60–1). On one occasion they came face to face with a mortal on earth, the bard Thamyris, who had boasted that his singing was finer than theirs: with typical vindictiveness the goddesses maimed him, presumably with blindness, 'deprived him of his divine song and made him forget his lyre-playing' (*Il.* 2.594–600).

Hesiod begins his *Theogony* with a long hymn to the Muses, in which he recounts their activities on Mount Helicon, including their appearance to Hesiod himself; their song on Olympus; their birth in Pieria and their names; and their care for princes and singers. Homer speaks of them only as daughters of Zeus, but Hesiod tells that their mother was Mnemosyne (Memory), thus associating them with the older gods, since she was daughter of Uranus and Gaia, Heaven and Earth (53–62, 135). At a time before the art of writing was in common use the singer's powers of memory were of the greatest importance, especially if his theme was extensive, as in Homer's case, or his subject factual, as with the genealogies of Hesiod's *Theogony*. Memory also transmitted traditional knowledge from one generation to the next. Homer did not distinguish one Muse from another, but Hesiod gives the nine names, Clio, Euterpe, Thalia, Melpomene, Terpsichore, Erato, Polymnia, Urania and Calliope, the most important among them (77–9). There may originally have been only three, but nine became the canonical figure.

Hesiod presents his encounter with the Muses as a real experience which occurred while he tended his lambs on Mount Helicon: 'once they taught Hesiod beautiful song'—but only after insult and discouragement: 'Shepherds living in the wilderness, miserable disgraces, nothing but bellies, we know how to say many false things that seem like the truth, we know also how to speak the truth when we wish.' The Muses, that is, can deliberately mislead a poet by presenting him with a false version which he transmits in the belief that it is true. But in Hesiod's case their actions were kindly: they gave him a rod of laurel, the bush associated with Apollo who often keeps company with them, breathed into him a divine voice so that he might sing of the future and the past—as he could not without divine help—and told him to sing of the gods and of themselves in particular, first and last (22–34). The 'breath' of poetic inspiration was not adopted as a figure of speech by the lyric poets, but they often used two other expressions of Hesiod: the singer is *Mousaōn therapōn* (100), the 'servant' or 'attendant' of the Muses; and his skill is their 'gift' (103; cf. 93): Hesiod passes to his main theme with the words,

χαίρετε, τέκνα Διός, δότε δ' ἱμερόεσσαν ἀοιδήν (104).

'Greetings, children of Zeus, and give me lovely song.' The thought that the singer banishes sorrow by his song (98–103) was often repeated.

Of the longer, earlier Homeric hymns those to Hermes and Aphrodite begin with an invocation of the Muse; so do some of the shorter hymns, where she is most commonly *Mousa ligeia*, 'clear-voiced Muse', as in the *Odyssey* (24.62).

* * *

Archilochus, like Hesiod, was said to have met the Muses: the encounter is described on a stone set up in the third century B.C. to honour his memory in his native island of Paros. The story may have been told in his poetry, but it is supported on the stone by no quotations from his poems, and it is more likely to have been a local tradition. The young Archilochus, we are told, was sent to town by his father to sell a cow; on his way he met a group of merry women, who teased him and asked if the cow was for sale; told that it was, they said they would give him a good price, whereupon they and the cow disappeared and Archilochus found a lyre at his feet. Shortly afterwards his father was told by Apollo at Delphi that his son would be immortal and famous. There are resemblances with Hesiod's story in the pastoral setting, the Muses' mockery, less harsh in Archilochus' case, and the symbolic gift which marked him out as a lyric poet.

In a famous couplet he says that he has combined the activities of soldier and poet:

εἰμὶ δ' ἐγὼ θεράπων μὲν Ἐνυαλίοιο ἄνακτος
καὶ Μουσέων ἐρατὸν δῶρον ἐπιστάμενος (1).

'I am the servant of lord Enyalius and of the Muses also, having knowledge of their lovely gift.' In Homer Enyalius is an epithet of Ares, god of war, and sometimes as here an alternative name for him; Homer does not have the expression 'servant of Enyalius', but he often calls the Greek warriors *therapontes Arēos*, 'servants' or 'squires' of Ares. We have seen that Hesiod called a singer *Mousaōn therapōn*, 'servant of the Muses', and that he too spoke of his poetic skill as the gift of the Muses. Archilochus' point is that he is both soldier and poet; Achilles in the *Iliad* might sing in his hut of the glorious deeds of men, accompanying himself on his lyre, but Archilochus can claim to be an original poet with understanding of the Muses' gift.

We have seen that he speaks twice of 'leading off' a choral song for the gods:

αὐτὸς ἐξάρχων πρὸς αὐλὸν Λέσβιον παιήονα (121),

'myself leading off the Lesbian paean to the accompaniment of the pipe'; and

ὡς Διωνύσου ἄνακτος καλὸν ἐξάρξαι μέλος
οἶδα διθύραμβον οἴνῳ συγκεραυνωθεὶς φρένας (120),

'since I know how to lead off the beautiful song of Dionysus, the dithyramb, when my mind is blitzed by the wine'. Archilochus is fond of claiming knowledge or ability: 'having knowledge of the Muses' lovely gift' (1), 'I know a remedy' (67), 'I know how to love my friend' (23), 'I know one big thing' (126), and of course 'the fox knows many things, the hedgehog (Archilochus?) one big thing' (201). Here he claims expertise as choral leader of the dithyramb; we have already noted the scraps of his ribald hymn to Dionysus (p. 151 above).

A damaged text seems to speak of the soothing effect of music: West, building on the suggestions of earlier scholars, proposes the reading

κηλεῖται δέ τις
χορ]ῶν ἀοιδαῖς (253),

'Men are enchanted by the songs of choruses'. But when he was mourning for the drowning of his brother-in-law he said,

καί μ' οὔτ' ἰάμβων οὔτε τερπωλέων μέλει (215),

'and I do not care for iambics or (other) pleasures'. Tzetzes, who quotes the line, took him to mean that he was unable to compose, and most scholars have followed him, assuming that Archilochus used 'iambics' as a general term for his compositions, iambic or trochaic lines or epodes; but West has suggested that the iambi were a form of public entertainment, an interpretation which makes it easier to see why iambi should be paired with *terpōlai*, 'pleasures'.

The glee with which he begins one of his epodes no doubt anticipates mockery of some individual:

Ἐρασμονίδη Χαρίλαε,
χρῆμά τοι γελοῖον
ἐρέω, πολὺ φίλταθ' ἑταίρων,
τέρψεαι δ' ἀκούων (168).

'Charilaus, son of Erasmon, I shall tell you a funny story, you who are by far the dearest of my friends, and you will enjoy hearing it.' In another he claims to be bearer of bad news:

ἐρέω τιν' ὕμιν αἶνον, ὦ Κηρυκίδη,
ἀχνυμένη σκυτάλη (185),

'I shall tell you a fable, Cerycides, I, a sad message-stick', and he continues with the story of the ape and the fox. In both passages he envisages the response of his audience, laughter and delight in the first, grief, no doubt unreal, in the second.

If the other earliest writers of elegy and iambus spoke of their poetry, the lines have not survived; but Mimnermus mentioned the Muses in the prelude to his elegiac poem on the battle between the Smyrnaeans and Lydians, distinguishing between two generations, the earlier Muses who were daughters of Uranus and Gaia, Heaven and Earth, and others who were daughters of Zeus (13). The poem was probably a long one, and that may be why he thought an invocation appropriate; it is interesting that he varies the account of Hesiod, according to whom it was Mnemosyne, the Muses' mother, who was daughter of Uranus and Gaia.

We have seen that Solon began his long poem on wealth with an elaborate address to the Muses: 'Glorious children of Mnemosyne and Olympian Zeus, Pierian Muses, hear my prayer' (13.1–2); but the content of his prayer, which is for prosperity from the gods and a good reputation from among men, is quite unexpected, although of course it leads directly into his theme. In the course of his poem he lists various methods of money-making and speaks in traditional language of the poet:

ἄλλος Ὀλυμπιάδων Μουσέων πάρα δῶρα διδαχθείς,
ἱμερτῆς σοφίης μέτρον ἐπιστάμενος (51-2).

'Another (makes his living) since the Olympian Muses have taught him their gifts, and he has skill in the measure of lovely poetry.' We see that the image of the Muses' 'gifts' is already fading, since they 'teach' the poet their gifts. Solon adopts the word *sophia*, 'wisdom, skill', to refer to the poet's skill, and later writers, especially Theognis and Pindar, were fond of the usage. In the Homeric hymn to Hermes the word referred to musical skill (483, 511), and Hesiod called Linus (son of the Muse Urania) 'skilled in all manner of *sophia* (fr. 306). Solon applies to it the adjective *himertos*, 'lovely, desirable', difficult to render in English but possibly stronger and certainly less common than *eratos*, the adjective which Archilochus used of the Muses' gift. The word *metron*, 'measure', suggests 'metre' in this context, but it does not have that sense until the time of Aristophanes, a century and a half later. It is probably less colourful, 'the measure of skill' being simply the skill that has been allotted to him. Solon uses the participle *epistamenos*, as Archilochus did: the poet 'knows, understands' his craft.

In his early poem *Salamis* Solon presented his advice to the Athenians in the guise of a messenger,

κόσμον ἐπέων ᾠδὴν ἀντ' ἀγορῆς θέμενος (1.2),

'having composed a song, an ornament of verses, instead of a speech'. The word *kosmos* suggests both 'order' and 'ornament': Solon may mean not only that he has used decorative words, creating poetry rather than a prose speech, but that he has marshalled his words in metrical order; and the term *epē* may itself suggest elegiac couplets as in Theognis (20, 22).

Solon is said to have used the expression

πολλὰ ψεύδονται ἀοιδοί (29),

'Singers utter many falsehoods', in his elegiac verse. This is not likely to be straightforward abuse, implying deliberate deceit; perhaps it should be related to what the Muses told Hesiod: 'We know how to say many false things that seem like the truth'; perhaps Solon is thinking of alternative versions of legends that were transmitted by the poets, not all of which could be true.

Alcman began many, perhaps all, of his partheneia with an appropriate address to the Muse:

Μῶσ' ἄγε Μῶσα λίγηα πολυμμελὲς
αἰὲν ἀοιδὲ μέλος
νεοχμὸν ἄρχε παρσένοις ἀείδην (14a).

'Muse, come, clear-voiced Muse of many songs, always a singer, begin a new song for maidens to sing.' In this elaborate prelude the word 'new' is given emphasis: the Greeks loved novelty in song as in other spheres, and poets like Pindar were fond of drawing attention to the newness of their creations; as Homer put it, 'For men praise more highly that song which comes newest to their ears' (*Od.* 1.351–2).

Μῶσ' ἄγε Καλλιόπα θύγατερ Διὸς
ἄρχ' ἐρατῶν Ϝεπέων, ἐπὶ δ' ἵμερον
ὕμνῳ καὶ χαρίεντα τίθη χορόν (27).

'Muse, come, Calliope, daughter of Zeus, begin lovely words, set desire on our song and make our dance graceful.' Calliope, to whom Hesiod had given prominence, is the only Muse whom Alcman mentions by name. The invocation is very unlike Homer's request for knowledge: the choral poet has already composed his song and planned the dance-steps, but he still needs divine help: it is the Muse, not the singers, whom he asks to begin, and it is she who can make the performance desirable and successful. In the middle or at the end of another song he again identifies the activity of Muse and singers:

ἁ Μῶσα κέκλαγ' ἁ λίγηα Σηρήν (30).

'The Muse cries out, that clear-voiced Siren.' We are told that he began this poem with the usual invocation, asking the Muse to make him active. Here he equates the Muse with the enchantress Siren, who assumes the Muse's customary epithet. Elsewhere it is his choir that sings:

Μῶσα Διὸς θύγατερ λίγ' ἀείσομαι ὠρανίαφι (28).

'Heavenly Muse, daughter of Zeus, I shall sing in clear tones.'

In these songs he appealed to one Muse (so also in 5 fr. 2 i 22 and in 43), but he began another partheneion by calling on the 'Olympian Muses' (3 fr.1); a badly damaged papyrus seems to say, 'They revealed marvellous new soft utterances to mankind' (4 fr.1)—again the epithet 'new'; and an attractive ionic line runs

Ϝέκατον μὲν Διὸς υἱὸν τάδε Μώσαι κροκόπεπλοι (46),

'The saffron-robed Muses (taught?) the far-shooting son of Zeus [Apollo] these things': Alcman gives them the epithet which Homer applied to Dawn; Hesiod had spoken of their gold headbands (*Theog.* 916). In a puzzling fragment he says of one Megalostrata that she has displayed 'this gift of the sweet Muses' (59b).

So far the Muse has been 'daughter of Zeus' for Alcman as for Homer and Hesiod; one fragment (8.9) has the words 'Muses' and 'Mnemosyne' side by side, so that he probably followed Hesiod in making Mnemosyne their mother. But in the poem in which he sang of the creation of the world he put them two generations earlier as Mimnermus did, making them the daughters of Uranus and Gaia, Heaven and Earth (5 fr. 2 i 28; 67). Fraenkel is likely to be correct when he suggests that his purpose was to give greater authority to his account by putting the Muses close to the beginning of the world, older even than Zeus.

Alcman prays elsewhere for the favour of other gods, mentioning in particular Apollo, the associate of the Muses:

Ϝάδοι Διὸς δόμῳ χορὸς ἁμὸς καὶ τοί, Ϝάναξ (45).

'May our choir please the house of Zeus and you, lord.' He liked to mention the musicians who were associated with the performance, and named three Phrygian pipe-players, Sambas, Adon and Telus (109): perhaps it was one of them who 'piped a Phrygian tune, the Cerbesian' (126). He has his choir commend the lyre-player who accompanied them, most probably Alcman himself:

ὅσσαι δὲ παίδες ἁμέων
ἐντί, τὸν κιθαριστὰν
αἰνέοντι (38).

'We girls praise the lyre-player, every one of us.' His choir several times sings of 'Alcman' in the third person, and it is usually thought that the following lines refer to him:

οὐκ ἦς ἀνὴρ ἀγρεῖος οὐ-
δε σκαιὸς οὐδὲ †παρὰ σοφοῖ-
σιν† οὐδὲ Θεσσαλὸς γένος
Ἐρυσιχαῖος οὐδὲ ποιμήν,
ἀλλὰ Σαρδίων ἀπ' ἀκρᾶν (16).

'He was not a rustic nor clumsy nor . . . a Thessalian by birth, nor a shepherd from Erysiche: he was from lofty Sardis.' In later antiquity there was debate about Alcman's birthplace, and if these lines had referred unequivocally to him, it is difficult to see how the debate arose. The Doric form *ēs*, 'he was', may have caused difficulty, and the past tense is surprising. If the reference was to Alcman, he was probably defending himself against mockery of his foreign origin by an elaborate piece of self-advertisement. Erysiche was a hamlet in Acarnania in north-west Greece. He was certainly concerned with his reputation and named many obscure tribes to which he says his fame had spread from Sparta (148). One striking line was quoted as proof that the Spartans themselves for all their military prowess were a musical people:

ἕρπει γὰρ ἄντα τῶ σιδάρω τὸ καλῶς κιθαρίσδην (41).

'For fine lyre-playing balances the steel.'

A difficult fragment suggests that Alcman composed one of his songs by listening to the song of partridges:

Ϝέπη τάδε καὶ μέλος Ἀλκμὰν
εὗρε γεγλωσσαμέναν
κακκαβίδων ὄπα συνθέμενος (39).

'Alcman discovered these words and the melody by observing the tongued note of partridges.' The words are sometimes taken to mean that Alcman learned his music from bird-song, and another line runs

Ϝοῖδα δ' ὀρνίχων νόμως
παντῶν (40),

'and I know the tunes of all birds'. But if the text is correctly emended and he spoke of 'these words', he may have been talking only of special sound effects created in the lines which preceded or followed the quotation.

Stesichorus was fond of invoking the Muse at the opening of his long epic songs. One began

δεῦρ' ἄγε Καλλιόπεια λίγεια (240),

'Come hither, clear-voiced Calliopeia'. Stesichorus, like Alcman, names no other Muse, at least in the surviving fragments. He gives her the traditional adjective; but he was famous for the number and excellence of his epithets and he could call the Muse *arkhesimolpos* (250), 'beginner of song'; Chamaeleon, the fourth-century scholar who credits him with two palinodes (193), says that one began

δεῦρ' αὖτε θεὰ φιλόμολπε,

'Hither again, goddess, lover of song'. The formations with *molpē*, which may denote song or the combined activity of song and dance, point to the Muse's new role in choral poetry. The beginning of the other palinode, we are told, was *khrusoptere parthene*, 'Maiden of the golden feathers': this is certainly adventurous, and it caught the attention of Bacchylides, who speaks of a poem as 'a golden feather of the Muses' (fr. 20B.4), and of Pindar, who sings of 'the glorious wings of the melodious Pierians' (*Isthm.* 1.64f.). Theognis tells Cyrnus that by celebrating him in his verses he has given him wings, and Pindar has similar images, but no other early poet imagines the Muse herself as winged. The tendency to equate Muses and Sirens, who are usually winged, may be responsible.

Aristophanes in the parabasis of the *Peace* twice adapts lines of Stesichorus: the scholiast there tells us that the second passage is from the *Oresteia* and quotes the original:

τοιάδε χρὴ Χαρίτων δαμώματα καλλικόμων
ὑμνεῖν Φρύγιον μέλος ἐξευρόντας ἁβρῶς
ἦρος ἐπερχομένου (212).

'These public songs of the fair-tressed Graces we must sing, delicately devising a Phrygian song, as spring approaches.' The unique term *damōmata* presumably means 'songs for public performance'; Pindar must have had the word in mind when he wrote

γλυκύ τι δαμωσόμεθα (*Isthm.* 8.8),

'let us make public a sweet song'. The scholiast does not allocate the earlier lines to any named work of Stesichorus, but since they correspond metrically with the second passage they too are likely to be from the *Oresteia* and may be its opening words:

Μοῖσα σὺ μὲν πολέμους ἀπωσαμένα πεδ' ἐμοῦ
κλείοισα θεῶν τε γάμους ἀνδρῶν τε δαίτας
καὶ θαλίας μακάρων (210).

'Muse, thrusting away wars and singing with me of the marriage of gods and the banquets of men and the festivity of the blessed . . .' There is no need to try to identify the wars, since the expression probably means, 'My theme is not war, as it often is, but marriage festivity.' It must be admitted that this makes a strange beginning to an *Oresteia*; one might have expected the subject to be something like the marriage of Peleus and Thetis.

Stesichorus speaks self-consciously of the contents and antecedents of his poetry, notably in the Palinode, where he abandoned the Homeric version of the story of Helen for another more favourable to her reputation: 'That tale is not true' (192.1). Elsewhere he talks of seeking another *prooimion*, 'prelude' (241), but the context is lost. He mentions an earlier lyric poet, Xanthus (229), whose *Oresteia* he was said to have used, and he found fault with Hesiod as well as with Homer (193.1–7). He found room in his poems, presumably in his preludes, for praise of his city, Himera (270). Alcman's mention of 'lofty Sardis' comes to mind.

In Sappho's solo-songs the Muses are no less prominent than in epic or choral song. Despite the fragmentary character of the surviving poetry we can point to several invocations of the Muses and to other passages in which she spoke of them. Unfortunately every invocation is detached from its sequel:

δεῦρο δηὖτε Μοῖσαι χρύσιον λίποισαι . . . (127),

'Hither again, Muses, leaving the golden (house of your father Zeus?)';

δεῦτέ νυν ἄβραι Χάριτες καλλίκομοί τε Μοῖσαι (128),

'Hither now, delicate Graces and lovely-haired Muses';

δεῦτέ ν]υν ἄγναι Χάριτες Πιέριδέ[ς τε] Μοῖ[σαι (103.8),

'Hither now, holy Graces and Pierian Muses'. The Graces alone are summoned in similar language:

βροδοπάχεες ἄγναι Χάριτες δεῦτε Δίος κόραι (53),

'Rosy-armed, holy Graces, hither, daughters of Zeus'. It seems very likely that Sappho asked Muses and Graces to shed grace on her songs. Calliope, Hesiod's senior Muse, is the only one to be mentioned by name in the fragments (124); we have seen that the same is true of Alcman and Stesichorus. Sappho may have spoken of 'the glorious gifts of the Muses' (44A b 5) and made the Muses and Graces dance with Apollo, Leader of the Muses (208). She called her own house 'the house of the *moisopoloi*, 'those who serve the Muse' (150.1), perhaps creating a term that would suggest worship at a shrine.

Sappho links the Muses to the theme of her fame, which she develops more fully than any of her predecessors. Hesiod spoke with pride of the tripod he won in a singing contest (*Works and Days* 656–9); the poet, not certainly earlier than Sappho, who composed the Homeric hymn to Apollo requested that in time to come his songs be called the best of all (166–73); and Alcman claimed that his renown had reached obscure races (148). Sappho declared that the Muses had made her truly blessed and enviable, and that she would not be forgotten after death (193). The words,

αἴ με τιμίαν ἐπόησαν ἔργα
τὰ σφὰ δοῖσαι (32),

'who made me honoured by the gift of their works', must refer to the Muses. We have seen that she spoke harshly of a woman who had 'no share in the roses from Pieria':

κατθάνοισα δὲ κείσῃ οὐδέ ποτα μναμοσύνα σέθεν
ἔσσετ(αι) (55.1-2).

'But when you die you will lie there, and there will never be any recollection of you.' Of herself she said,

μνάσεσθαί τινα φαῖμι †καὶ ἕτερον† ἀμμέων (147).

'Someone, I declare, will remember us (in time to come?).' She may well be speaking of herself again when she says,

οὐδ' ἴαν δοκίμωμι προσίδοισαν φάος ἀλίω
ἔσσεσθαι σοφίαν πάρθενον εἰς οὐδένα πω χρόνον
τεαύταν (56).

'I do not suppose that any maiden who has looked on the light of the sun will have such skill at any time in the future': she almost certainly uses *sophia* to refer to poetic skill. A very tattered papyrus fragment seems to make Aphrodite declare her love for Sappho and promise her glory wherever the sun shines and fame after her death (65).

She speaks of the performance of her song in an isolated line:

τάδε νῦν ἐταίραις ταῖς ἔμαις τέρπνα κάλως ἀείσω (160).

'I shall now sing these songs beautifully to delight my companions'; the gender of the word 'companions' shows that they were women or girls. She addresses the lyre with which she accompanied her song:

ἄγι δὴ χέλυ δῖα †μοι λέγε†
φωνάεσσα †δὲ γίνεο† (118).

'Come, divine lyre, speak to me and find yourself a voice'; the text is uncertain, but we are told that she questioned her lyre and made it answer her. The epithet 'divine' should not be overlooked: the lyre was divine, not simply because it was the invention of Hermes, but because the Muses and Graces were present with her as she made her music.

Horace tells us that Alcaeus sang of the Muses (*Carm.* 1.32.9), but no invocation survives, and we have only one possible reference to them:

τὸ γὰρ θέων ἰότατι ὔμμε λαχόντων †αφυτον θήσει γέρας† (309).

The text is very uncertain, but the meaning may be, 'For the privilege of those who obtained you [the Muses?] shall by the will of the gods flower imperishable.' In a poem about Pittacus he says

ἀθύρει πεδέχων συμποσίω. [
βάρμος (70.3-4),

'the lyre, sharing in the banquet, makes merry'. The symposium must have been the occasion of most of his poems, political, convivial or amatory.

Ibycus wrote a puzzling choral song of some length on the heroes of the Trojan wars (282a). Most of the surviving lines are occupied by the fate of Troy and a catalogue of Trojans and Greeks of whom he will not or cannot speak: his purpose may be to present a sample of his wares to Polycrates, tyrant of Samos, and to declare his intention of abandoning epic themes for love poetry. At one point in his catalogue he sings,

καὶ τὰ μὲ[ν ἂν] Μοίσαι σεσοφ[ισμ]έναι
εὖ Ἑλικωνίδ[ες] ἐμβαίεν λόγ[ῳ·
θνατὸς δ᾽ οὔ κ[ε]ν ἀνὴρ
διερὸ[ς] τὰ ἕκαστα εἴποι
ναῶν. . . (23-7).

'And the skilled Muses of Helicon could finely embark on these themes in story; but no living mortal man could tell each detail of the ships . . .' The contrast between the powers of singer and Muse recalls that drawn by Homer in the *Iliad* (2.484–92); but while Homer invokes the Muses to give authority to his catalogue of ships, appealing to them for the knowledge he needs, Ibycus rejects that theme by comparing his knowledge unfavourably with theirs. He calls them *sesophismenai*, 'practised' in *sophia*, the craft of poetry.

Ibycus moves from the great warriors, Achilles and Ajax (33-4), to the handsome youths at Troy, the Greek Zeuxippus and the Trojan Troilus, a theme doubtless introduced to suit the tastes of Polycrates, and he ends his song as follows:

τοῖς μὲν πέδα κάλλεος αἰέν,
καὶ σύ, Πολύκρατες, κλέος ἄφθιτον ἑξεῖς
ὡς κατ᾽ ἀοιδὰν καὶ ἐμὸν κλέος (46-8).

'They share in beauty for ever; and you too, Polycrates, shall have undying fame as song and my fame can give it.' Zeuxippus and Troilus are beautiful for ever, since the poets made them so; and Polycrates also will have everlasting fame thanks to the present song and the fame of the poet. Ibycus ends by mentioning his patron and himself in the same breath and by declaring that his glory will be responsible for the glory of the great ruler. Pindar and Bacchylides later ended poems with the same confident boast.

Anacreon's surviving poems and fragments have no invocations of the Muse. This may be no more than coincidence, since he speaks of them in conventional terms: one of our few papyrus texts has the words

ἐρόεντα . . . δῶρα πάρεστ[ι]. . . Πιερίδων (346 fr. 3.7-9),

'the lovely gifts of the Pierians are here'; mention of the Graces follows. Grace was the characteristic of his songs in which he took pride:

ἐμὲ γὰρ †λόγων† εἵνεκα παῖδες ἂν φιλέοιεν·
χαρίεντα μὲν γὰρ ᾄδω, χαρίεντα δ᾽ οἶδα λέξαι (402c).

'Since boys might love me for my words: for I sing graceful songs, and I know how to speak graceful words.' The repeated *kharienta* gives balance to his elegant line. For Athenaeus he is *ho kharieis Anakreōn*, 'graceful Anacreon'.

He twice refers to his lyre-playing, each time setting it against a background of revelry:

ψάλλω δ᾽ εἴκοσι
†χορδαῖσι μάγαδιν† ἔχων,
ὦ Λεύκασπι, σὺ δ᾽ ἡβᾷς (374).

'Holding the magadis I strike its twenty strings, while you, Leucaspis, enjoy the fun of youth.'

νῦν δ᾽ ἁβρῶς ἐρόεσσαν
ψάλλω πηκτίδα τῇ φίλῃ κωμάζων †παιδὶ ἁβρῇ† (373.2-3).

'Now [i.e. after my dinner] I tenderly strike my lovely lyre, serenading (my dear girl?).' When he speaks of the symposium he prescribes the topics for the singers:

οὐ φιλέω ὃς κρητῆρι παρὰ πλέῳ οἰνοποτάζων
νείκεα καὶ πόλεμον δακρυόεντα λέγει,
ἀλλ᾽ ὅστις Μουσέων τε καὶ ἀγλαὰ δῶρ᾽ Ἀφροδίτης
συμμίσγων ἐρατῆς μνήσκεται εὐφροσύνης (eleg. 2).

'I do not love the man who while drinking his wine beside the full mixing-bowl talks of strife and tearful war: I love him who by mingling the glorious gifts of the Muses and Aphrodite remembers the loveliness of the feast'. Anacreon uses Homeric language to outlaw the epic theme of war; Alcaeus' songs of strife may also have been in his mind.

Xenophanes expresses the same thought (1.21ff.): in the well-ordered symposium the fighting of Titans or Giants or Centaurs is not fit material for singer or story-teller. He perhaps has in mind the epic poems called *Titanomachia* and *Gigantomachia*. In the following phrase he proscribes the theme of 'violent factions', probably thinking here of Alcaeus' political drinking-songs. In these, he says, there is nothing that is *khrēston*, 'good, useful': better always to show due consideration for the gods. We have seen that in his view Homer and Hesiod did not measure up to this standard (10D.).

The value of the poet to the community is bravely stated in his poem about the rewards lavished on the successful athlete:

ταῦτά κε πάντα λάχοι,
οὐκ ἐὼν ἄξιος ὥσπερ ἐγώ· ῥώμης γὰρ ἀμείνων
ἀνδρῶν ἠδ᾽ ἵππων ἡμετέρη σοφίη (2.10-12).

'All these he would get, although not deserving them as I do: better than the strength of man or of horses is our skill.' The term *sophiē* distinguishes clearly between his poetic skill, together with the wisdom it teaches, and the physical strength of the athlete. How is the city better governed, he asks, for the prowess of its boxers or pentathletes or wrestlers or runners?

οὐ γὰρ πιαίνει ταῦτα μυχοὺς πόλεως (22).

'For these things do not enrich a city's chambers.' This can be taken both literally and figuratively: the rewards given to athletes are a drain on the city's resources; and the poet by his wise advice can enrich the city as the athlete cannot.

Theognis has much to say about his verses and about poetry in general. His invocation to the Muses and Graces (15–18: p. 175f. above) consists simply in an address to the goddesses and a reminder of the song they sang at the wedding of Cadmus and Harmonia:

ὅττι καλὸν φίλον ἐστί, τὸ δ᾽ οὐ καλὸν οὐ φίλον ἐστί (17).

'What is beautiful is dear, what is not beautiful is not dear.' He clearly intends his words to have relevance to his own song, in which he will aim to express noble thoughts in beautiful poetry.

In famous lines he speaks of the seal he affixes to his verses:

Κύρνε, σοφιζομένῳ μὲν ἐμοὶ σφρηγὶς ἐπικείσθω
τοῖσδ᾽ ἔπεσιν, λήσει δ᾽ οὔποτε κλεπτόμενα,   20
οὐδέ τις ἀλλάξει κάκιον τοὐσθλοῦ παρεόντος·
ὧδε δὲ πᾶς τις ἐρεῖ· Θεύγνιδός ἐστιν ἔπη
τοῦ Μεγαρέως· πάντας δὲ κατ᾽ ἀνθρώπους ὀνομαστός.'
ἀστοῖσιν δ᾽ οὔπω πᾶσιν ἁδεῖν δύναμαι·

οὐδὲν θαυμαστόν, Πολυπαΐδη· οὐδὲ γὰρ ὁ Ζεὺς   25
οὔθ' ὕων πάντεσσ' ἁνδάνει οὔτ' ἀνέχων (19-26).

'Cyrnus, let me, a poet practising my craft, set a seal on these lines, and they will never be stolen unnoticed nor will anyone substitute worse for the good that is there, but everyone will say, "They are the lines of Theognis the Megarian, and his name is known throughout the whole world." But I can in no way please all the citizens; no wonder, son of Polypaus, since not even Zeus pleases everyone either by raining or by stopping.' Interpretation is not easy, and the identity of the seal has been much debated. It seems best to take it as a reference to Theognis' name, introduced in this prefatory poem as proof of the collection's authenticity. The seal is intended as a precaution against the theft of his poetry and the substitution of inferior work, and also as a means of identifying the author. The boast, 'and his name is known throughout the whole world', forms part of the guarantee, a deterrent to any would-be pilferer. The fear of possible plagiarism can be linked with the fondness shown by poets for claiming that theirs is 'new' poetry, not verses taken over from another. Theognis may be the first to express this anxiety: perhaps he saw the danger as greater in the case of a collection of poems. His strong individuality comes out in the contrast between the proud words of the first five lines and the bitter realism of the sixth. Perhaps the strongly aristocratic sentiments he expressed had left him unpopular in the new Megara. He makes a similar complaint elsewhere:

οὐ δύναμαι γνῶναι νόον ἀστῶν ὅντιν' ἔχουσιν·
οὔτε γὰρ εὖ ἕρδων ἁνδάνω οὔτε κακῶς·
μωμεῦνται δέ με πολλοί, ὁμῶς κακοὶ ἠδὲ καὶ ἐσθλοί·
μιμεῖσθαι δ' οὐδεὶς τῶν ἀσόφων δύναται (367-70).

'I cannot understand the mind of the citizens; for I do not please them either by good deeds or by bad. Many find fault with me, the good and the bad alike; but none of those boors can imitate me.' 'Either by good deeds or by bad' is an example of the 'polar' construction, common in Greek, whereby the extremes are mentioned to cover all cases: 'I fail to please them, no matter what I do.' Theognis creates a fine antithesis with the assonance of *mōmeuntai* and *mimeisthai*: many cavil at me, no one can copy me. 'The good and the bad' will as usual be the aristocrats and the others; the 'boors', *asophoi*, are those with no poetic skill, no *sophia*.

A short poem of great interest and, unhappily, of great difficulty also, sets out the public duty of the poet:

χρὴ Μουσῶν θεράποντα καὶ ἄγγελον, εἴ τι περισσὸν
εἰδείη, σοφίης μὴ φθονερὸν τελέθειν,
ἀλλὰ τὰ μὲν μῶσθαι, τὰ δὲ δεικνύναι, ἄλλα δὲ ποιεῖν·
τί σφιν χρήσηται μοῦνος ἐπιστάμενος; (769-72).

'The servant and messenger of the Muses, if he has greater knowledge than others, must not be miserly with his skill: he must seek out some things, reveal others, create others. What use can he make of his knowledge if he keeps it to himself?' Theognis combines the now conventional description *Mousōn theraponta*, 'servant of the Muses', with the novel *angelon*: the poet is the Muses' messenger, carrying their words to his audience. The conditional form, 'if he has greater knowledge', does not imply doubt: one might replace 'if' by 'since'. The noun *sophiē* clearly means poetic skill, and the 'knowledge' referred to by the verbs *eideiē* and *epistamenos* is another way of referring to it. The poet's first activity is *mōsthai*, an uncommon word; ancient authorities use the term *zētein*, 'to seek', in their explanations of it, and Theognis must mean that the poet ought to investigate or enquire, perhaps into questions of morality and politics. The second activity is clear enough: he must 'reveal' his findings, make them public. The third verb is the most difficult: 'he must make, create, other things.' Perhaps the strong contrast suggested by the translation 'some things . . . others . . . others' is misleading, and Theognis is simply listing the poet's duties as investigating, revealing, creating. The last line gives unity to the poem by reinforcing the image of the hoarder suggested earlier by the word *phthoneron*, 'miserly, grudging'.

One of Theognis' longest poems is an elaborate statement of the poet's ability to confer immortality. The theme goes back to Homer, who in the *Iliad* made Helen predict that she and Paris would be *aoidimoi*, 'famous in song' (6.357–8), and there are many Homeric expressions and echoes in the poem:

σοὶ μὲν ἐγὼ πτέρ' ἔδωκα, σὺν οἷς ἐπ' ἀπείρονα πόντον
  πωτήσῃ καὶ γῆν πᾶσαν ἀειρόμενος
ῥηϊδίως· θοίνῃς δὲ καὶ εἰλαπίνῃσι παρέσσῃ
  ἐν πάσαις, πολλῶν κείμενος ἐν στόμασιν,   240
καί σε σὺν αὐλίσκοισι λιγυφθόγγοις νέοι ἄνδρες
  εὐκόσμως ἐρατοὶ καλά τε καὶ λιγέα
ᾄσονται. καὶ ὅταν δνοφερῆς ὑπὸ κεύθεσι γαίης
  βῇς πολυκωκύτους εἰς Ἀίδαο δόμους,
οὐδέποτ' οὐδὲ θανὼν ἀπολεῖς κλέος, ἀλλὰ μελήσεις   245
  ἄφθιτον ἀνθρώποις αἰὲν ἔχων ὄνομα,
Κύρνε, καθ' Ἑλλάδα γῆν στρωφώμενος, ἠδ' ἀνὰ νήσους
  ἰχθυόεντα περῶν πόντον ἐπ' ἀτρύγετον,
οὐχ ἵππων νώτοισιν ἐφήμενος· ἀλλά σε πέμψει
  ἀγλαὰ Μουσάων δῶρα ἰοστεφάνων.   250
πᾶσι δ', ὅσοισι μέμηλε, καὶ ἐσσομένοισιν ἀοιδὴ
  ἔσσῃ ὁμῶς, ὄφρ' ἂν γῆ τε καὶ ἠέλιος.
αὐτὰρ ἐγὼν ὀλίγης παρὰ σεῦ οὐ τυγχάνω αἰδοῦς,
  ἀλλ' ὥσπερ μικρὸν παῖδα λόγοις μ' ἀπατᾷς (237-54).

'To you I have given wings, on which you shall fly over the boundless sea and the whole earth, soaring easily; you shall be present at all dinners and banquets, couched on the lips of many; and of you, to the accompaniment of clear-voiced pipes, lovely youths shall sing in orderly fashion with fine, clear voice. And when in the recesses of the gloomy earth you go to the sorrowful home of Hades, never, not even when you are dead, shall you lose your fame; no, you shall be the concern of mankind, with an imperishable name for ever, Cyrnus, ranging through the land of Greece and over the islands, crossing the fishy, unharvestable sea, not riding on horseback; no, the glorious gifts of the violet-crowned Muses shall send you on your way. For all men who are concerned with these gifts and equally for men still unborn you shall be their song, so long as earth and sun remain. But I meet with not the slightest respect from you: you deceive me with your words as though I were a little child.' Stesichorus had mentioned the Muses' golden wings; Theognis makes distinctive use of the image: it is he himself who has sent the youth winging over land and sea, although 'the gifts of the Muses' are ultimately responsible. 'Lovely youths' will sing of Cyrnus, and we should doubtless regard the words as applicable to Cyrnus himself, the word *eratoi*, 'lovely', carrying strongly erotic overtones. The vaunt extends over eight full couplets, then, very much as in the 'seal' poem, a complaint is made in the final couplet, all the more telling because of the lopsidedness of the structure. Theognis begins with 'I have given you' (*soi men egō*), and the antithesis, long postponed, is 'but I get from you' (*autar egōn . . . para seu*); the sequence of future tenses yields to present tenses, and the verb *apatāis* ('you deceive') gives a strong ending to the poem. Deception is one of Theognis' favourite topics. The use of enjambment in the second and fourth couplets adds interest and holds the structure together, and the long, unique adjective *polukōkutous* (244, 'sorrowful, where much wailing is heard') is effective when so much of the language is Homeric.

Theognis was merry when he heard the sound of sweet music:

> αἰεί μοι φίλον ἦτορ ἰαίνεται, ὁππότ' ἀκούσω
> αὐλῶν φθεγγομένων ἱμερόεσσαν ὄπα.
> χαίρω δ' εὖ πίνων καὶ ὑπ' αὐλητῆρος ἀείδων,
> χαίρω δ' εὔφθογγον χερσὶ λύρην ὀχέων (531-4).

'My heart is always cheered when I hear the delightful sound of the pipes' voice. I enjoy drinking well and singing to the piper's accompaniment, I enjoy holding the sweet-voiced lyre in my hands.' Elsewhere he speaks of making libation to the gods while lyre and pipe make 'holy' music (761–62). Once he addresses the piper:

> ἀλλὰ λόγον μὲν τοῦτον ἐάσομεν, αὐτὰρ ἐμοὶ σὺ
> αὔλει, καὶ Μουσῶν μνησόμεθ' ἀμφότεροι·
> αὗται γὰρ τάδ' ἔδωκαν ἔχειν κεχαρισμένα δῶρα
> σοὶ καὶ ἐμοί, <μέλο>μεν δ' ἀμφιπερικτίοσιν (1055-8).

'But let us put an end to this talk: you pipe to me, rather, and let us both remember the Muses: for it was they who gave these delightful gifts to you and me, and our neighbours pay attention to us.' The text of the last phrase is uncertain. The words 'let us remember the Muses' can be paraphrased, 'let us play and sing', but the following sentence reminds us that the Muses are not a mere abstraction but divinities who give gifts.

Music and morality are closely linked in one poem:

> μήποτέ μοι μελέδημα νεώτερον ἄλλο φανείη
> ἀντ' ἀρετῆς σοφίης τ', ἀλλὰ τόδ' αἰὲν ἔχων   790
> τερποίμην φόρμιγγι καὶ ὀρχηθμῷ καὶ ἀοιδῇ,
> καὶ μετὰ τῶν ἀγαθῶν ἐσθλὸν ἔχοιμι νόον,
> μήτε τινὰ ξείνων δηλεύμενος ἔργμασι λυγροῖς
> μήτε τιν' ἐνδήμων, ἀλλὰ δίκαιος ἐών (789-94).

'Never may any new concern appear for me in place of excellence and skill: with this concern always, may I enjoy the lyre and dance and song, and may I think noble thoughts in the company of the good, harming neither stranger nor citizen with hurtful acts, but being a just man.' Text and meaning are disputed; Theognis seems to state his concern with *aretē*, 'excellence', and *sophiē*, 'poetic skill'; then, reversing the order, speaks first of lyre, song and dance and secondly, in traditional terms, of morality; if this interpretation is correct, *aretē* is 'excellence' or 'goodness' in an ethical sense.

Hipponax amused his listeners by flouting traditional poetic standards: his subject-matter was low life, his vocabulary colloquial, his usual metre a jerky version of the iambic line. Parody was said to be his invention, and there is rather poor evidence for a comic version of the *Odyssey*. It comes as no surprise to find that his only surviving invocation of the Muse is in Homeric parody:

> Μοῦσά μοι Εὐρυμεδοντιάδεα τὴν ποντοχάρυβδιν,
> τὴν ἐγγαστριμάχαιραν, ὃς ἐσθίει οὐ κατὰ κόσμον,
> ἔννεφ', ὅπως ψηφῖδι <κακὸς>κακὸν οἶτον ὀλεῖται
> βουλῇ δημοσίῃ παρὰ θῖν' ἁλὸς ἀτρυγέτοιο (128).

'Muse, tell for me of the son of Eurymedon, the sea-swallower, the knife-in-belly, who eats in no orderly manner: tell how the wretch will die a wretched death by stoning on the shore of the unharvestable sea by a decree of the people.' Hipponax recalls the opening of the *Odyssey*, *andra moi ennepe, Mousa*, 'Tell for me, Muse, of the man', the first line of the *Iliad* with its long patronymic *Pēlēiadeō*, 'son of Peleus', and the first words of the Homeric hymn to Aphrodite, *Mousa moi ennepe*, 'Tell for me, Muse'. His line-endings are all Homeric, and most of line 4 is occupied by a Homeric formula. He characterises the glutton by grotesque compound forms of his own creation, neither of them particularly successful: 'the sea-Charybdis', who could drain the sea dry, 'knife-in-belly', who did not chop his food before bolting it. Death by stoning is the fate of the *pharmakos* or community scapegoat, mentioned several times by Hipponax.

If Simonides composed invocations to the gods, they have not survived. He is sometimes regarded as a rationalist with no deeply religious feelings; but at any rate he is ready to speak conventionally of the Muses when he describes them as fond of dancing and singing, especially when Apollo leads the dance on Helicon (578). A papyrus fragment mentions them along with the Peneus, the Thessalian river south of Pieria and Mount Olympus (519 fr. 22). He talks of Cassiotis, the spring at Delphi from which 'the holy water of the lovely-haired Muses is drawn for purifications', and calls Clio its overseer (577).

In one or two fragments he speaks of the poet's activity, comparing it to that of the bee as she 'contrives her yellow honey' (593). An anonymous fragment, not certainly by him, uses a similar image:

ἁ Μοῦσα γὰρ οὐκ ἀπόρως γεύει τὸ παρὸν μόνον ἀλλ' ἐπέρχεται
πάντα θεριζομένα (947a).

'For the Muse does not helplessly taste only what is to hand but goes forward harvesting all things.' Theognis said that one of the poet's tasks is *mōsthai*, 'to seek things out', and these lines may mean that the poet should be adventurous in his choice of subject-matter.

Various saying of Simonides on the subject of poetry are preserved, the most famous being, 'Painting is silent poetry, poetry is painting that speaks.' Some of his work, for example the lines on Danae and her infant son Perseus adrift on stormy seas, has a strongly pictorial appeal, and he may be saying that such poetry makes us visualise the scene as vividly as if we were looking at a painting of it. Another saying, 'The word is the image (*eikōn*) of the thing', may express the same idea: an *eikōn* is a likeness, often a picture. He called Hesiod a gardener, Homer a garland-maker, perhaps to contrast the methods of the poets: Homer composed connected narratives, whereas Hesiod simply put his stories side-by-side like plants in rows. When he said that wine and music have the same origin (647) he may have meant that the musician, maybe the poet too, performs or composes when in the grip of an outside force; we badly miss the context of the words.

Simonides had the reputation of being a skinflint, and it is likely that he owed it to his practice of charging fees for his commissioned work. He was not the first to make a livelihood from his poetry, however: Arion of Corinth travelled professionally to Italy and Sicily, and Ibycus and Anacreon lived in the courts of tyrants. Perhaps he was the first to be paid in cash.

Pratinas, the writer of satyr-plays, composed a song of splendid vigour in protest against the increased importance of the aulos-player: the choruses, says Athenaeus, were now singing an accompaniment to the pipers. Pratinas' song was probably performed in the theatre by a chorus of satyrs: in other words it was dramatic rather than lyric poetry; but it makes fine reading as a self-contained choral song:

> τίς ὁ θόρυβος ὅδε; τί τάδε τὰ χορεύματα;
> τίς ὕβρις ἔμολεν ἐπὶ Διονυσιάδα πολυπάταγα θυμέλαν;
> ἐμὸς ἐμὸς ὁ Βρόμιος, ἐμὲ δεῖ κελαδεῖν, ἐμὲ δεῖ παταγεῖν
> ἀν' ὄρεα σύμενον μετὰ Ναϊάδων
> οἷά τε κύκνον ἄγοντα ποικιλόπτερον μέλος.
> τὰν ἀοιδὰν κατέστασε Πιερὶς βασίλειαν· ὁ δ' αὐλὸς   5
> ὕστερον χορευέτω· καὶ γάρ ἐσθ' ὑπηρέτας.
> κώμῳ μόνον θυραμάχοις τε πυγμαχίαισι νέων θέλοι παροίνων
> ἔμμεναι στρατηλάτας.
> παῖε τὸν φρυνεοῦ ποικίλαν πνοὰν ἔχοντα,   10
> φλέγε τὸν ὀλεσισιαλοκάλαμον
> λαλοβαρύοπα παραμελορυθμοβάταν
> ὑπαὶ τρυπάνῳ δέμας πεπλασμένον.
> ἢν ἰδού· ἅδε σοι δεξιᾶς καὶ ποδὸς διαρριφά·
> θρίαμβε διθύραμβε κισσόχαιτ' ἄναξ,   15
> <ἄκου'> ἄκουε τὰν ἐμὰν Δώριον χορείαν (708).

'What is this din? What are these dance-steps? What outrage has come to the noisy altar of Dionysus? Mine, mine is Bromius [Dionysus]: it is for me to shout and stamp, rushing over the mountains with the Naiads, bearing a song of flashing wings like the swan. Song was made queen by the Pierian [the Muse]: so let the pipe dance in second place: he is the servant! May he wish only to be commander-in-chief of revels and the street-brawling boxing-matches of drunken youths. Beat the one with the mottled toad-breath, burn the spittle-wasting reed with its prattling growl, striding across tune and rhythm, its body the product of the carpenter's auger! Look this way! Here is how to fling out hand and foot! Thriambus, dithyrambus, lord with ivy in your hair, hear, hear my Dorian dance-song.'

The song must have been preceded by a dance with noisy pipe accompaniment in parody of Lasus or one of the other poets who increased the importance of instrumental music in choral performance. Pratinas begins with a breathless, alliterative outburst of short syllables; the rhythm is calmer in the central passage of the poem (6–9), where the poet's view of the matter is given; but the sequence of short syllables recurs when the abuse of the pipe reaches its height (11–12), and there is strong alliteration in line 10. Dionysus is both god of the theatre, where he has his altar in the orchestra (2), and god of the ecstatic mountain rites (3–5). The dance-song in his honour is 'Dorian' either because the music was in the Dorian mode or because Pratinas was a Dorian from the Peloponnese.

He mentions the Aeolian mode in another poem, perhaps because of its novelty:

μήτε σύντονον δίωκε
μήτε τὰν ἀνειμέναν
μοῦσαν, ἀλλὰ τὰν μέσαν
νεῶν ἄρουραν αἰόλιζε τῷ μέλει (712a).

'Do not pursue the tight-strung Muse nor the relaxed Muse either: plough the middle of the field and Aeolise in your song.'

πρέπει τοι
πᾶσιν ἀοιδολαβράκταις
Αἰολὶς ἁρμονία (712b).

'The Aeolian tuning is appropriate for all singer-braggarts.' By 'tight-strung' and 'relaxed' Pratinas refers to high and low pitch: the Aeolian was between the extremes. 'Singer-braggarts' sounds like a comic term for professional musicians who took pride in their performance.

A savage attack by Timocreon on the exiled politician Themistocles begins with the words

Μοῦσα, τοῦδε τοῦ μέλεος
κλέος ἀν' Ἑλλανας τίθει,
ὡς ἐοικὸς καὶ δίκαιον (728).

'Muse, carry the fame of this song throughout Greece, as is fit and just.' He does not request that the Muse give him information or confer any quality on his song, simply that she ensure that it reaches the ears of all Greeks.

Corinna of Tanagra in Boeotia may or may not belong in this company: there are strong reasons for setting her in the third century B.C. But since various anecdotes connected her with Pindar, as we have seen, she deserves to be mentioned here. Her best-known lines are those in which she refers to another obscure Boeotian poetess:

μέμφομη δὲ κὴ λιγουρὰν
Μουρτίδ' ἰώνγ' ὅτι βανὰ φοῦ-
σ' ἔβα Πινδάροι πὸτ ἔριν (664a).

'I for my part blame the clear-voiced Myrtis because she, a woman, entered into competition with Pindar.' It would be good to know something about the background of this judgment, which was presumably expressed at the beginning or end of one of her poems on mythological subjects. She steps outside her heroic theme in the opening of another poem:

ἐπί με Τερψιχόρα [Ϝίδοι
καλὰ Ϝεροῖ' ἀισομ[έναν
Ταναγρίδεσσι λε[υκοπέπλυς ·
μέγα δ' ἐμῆς γέγ[αθε πόλις

λιγουροκω[τί]λυ[ς ἐνοπῆς (655.1-5).

'May Terpsichore (look?) on me as I prepare to sing beautiful heroic songs (?) for the white-robed women of Tanagra; greatly has the city rejoiced in the clear prattling of my voice.' The word (w)*eroia* is difficult, and 'heroic songs' is no more than a guess which fits the contents of her poetry. The tone of the word *liguro-kōtilos* is hard to assess: *liguro-* is straightforward and indicates that her singing, like that of Myrtis, was clear and penetrating; *kōtilos* seems disparaging, 'prattling' or perhaps 'coaxing'. She may have felt inhibited by her sex, as her remarks on Myrtis suggest, and may be contrasting her slight, unpretentious verses with those of a Pindar.

The theme of one of her longer poems (654.i) was a singing contest between the mountains Cithaeron and Helicon; when the songs had been performed, the gods, organised by the presiding Muses, gave the verdict to Cithaeron. It is not difficult to see literary significance in the choice of mountains: Helicon is always associated with Hesiod, and Cithaeron may represent the Theban song of Corinna herself.

*   *   *

Scarcely one of Pindar's victory-odes does not contain some statement about his craft, and the fragments of the other genres reveal the theme there also. He took an exalted view of his role. As the professional praise-singer he maintains that the feats of the athletes which he celebrates would be forgotten but for him, and as composer of commissioned poems for the most powerful and wealthy men of the Greek world he not only claims to move as honoured guest among them but speaks of himself as their equal: the first *Olympian*, his most important commission, ends with these words addressed to Hieron, prince of Syracuse:

> εἴη σέ τε τοῦτον ὑψοῦ χρόνον πατεῖν,
> ἐμέ τε τοσσάδε νικαφόροις
> ὁμιλεῖν πρόφαντον σοφίᾳ καθ᾽ Ἑλ-
> λανας ἐόντα παντᾷ (115-16).

'May it be yours to walk on high throughout your lifetime, mine to consort with victors for the length of my days, conspicuous for my skill among Greeks everywhere.' The pronouns *se* and *eme*, translated 'yours' and 'mine', are tightly bracketed, and it is with the prayer for poet, not ruler, that the poem ends: his preeminence rather than Hieron's reverberates when the music dies away.

He speaks of his function in terms which have strongly religious associations. Just as the famous Theban seer of mythology is

Διὸς . . . προφάταν . . . , ὀρθόμαντιν Τειρεσίαν (*Nem.* 1.60-1),

'the spokesman of Zeus, the true seer Teiresias', so Pindar calls himself

ἀοίδιμον Πιερίδων προφάταν (fr. 52f.6),

'spokesman of the Pierians in song', and uses the words *mantis . . . hierapolos*, 'seer . . . high priest', of himself (fr. 94a.5–6: cf. 75.13). He stands in close relation to the Muse:

μαντεύεο, Μοῖσα, προφατεύσω δ᾽ ἐγώ (fr. 150).

'Give your oracle, Muse, and I shall be your spokesman.' His role is analogous to that of the priests at Delphi. In one of his dithyrambs he uses different terminology:

ἐμὲ δ᾽ ἐξαίρετο[ν
κάρυκα σοφῶν ἐπέων
Μοῖσ᾽ ἀνέστασ᾽ Ἑλλάδι κα[λ]λ[ιχόρῳ (fr. 70b. 23-5).

'Me the Muse has appointed as chosen herald of wise words for Greece with its fair dancing-places.' Whether as spokesman or as herald he occupies ground of his own between Muses and men, and the traditional words 'servant of the Muse' are discarded as unworthy of his status.

His invocations of the Muse also carry the stamp of individuality. He is seldom content simply to call on her in the opening lines of an ode, since he prefers more startling preludes; even when he does invoke her, his language is unexpected:

ὦ πότνια Μοῖσα, μᾶτερ ἀμετέρα, λίσσομαι, . . .
ἵκεο Δωρίδα νᾶσον Αἴγιναν· ὕδατι γὰρ
μένοντ᾽ ἐπ᾽ Ἀσωπίῳ μελιγαρύων τέκτονες
κώμων νεανίαι, σέθεν ὄπα μαιόμενοι (*Nem.* 3.1-5).

'Lady Muse, our mother, I beseech you, . . . come to the Dorian island of Aegina; for by Asopus' water young carpenters of honey-voiced triumph-songs await you, seeking your voice.' Whether we take Pindar to mean 'my mother' or 'mother of us poets', his language is bold. He begins the ninth *Nemean* with *kōmasomen . . .*, *Moisai*, 'Let us go in triumphal procession . . ., Muses,' and the fourth *Pythian* by bidding the Muse stand by the side of the victor, king Arcesilas of Cyrene. The Muses are givers of fame (e.g. *Ol.* 10.95–6) and of poetic skill (e.g. fr. 198a). As Homer had put it, they have knowledge and prompt the mortal poet (fr. 52f. 51–8). They are associated with their mother Memory, as in these lines from a paean:

ἐ]πεύχο[μαι] δ' Οὐρανοῦ τ' εὐπέπλῳ θυγατρὶ
Μναμ[ο]σύ[ν]ᾳ κόραισί τ' εὐ-
μαχανίαν διδόμεν.
τ]υφλα[ὶ γὰ]ρ ἀνδρῶν φρένες,
ὅ]στις ἄνευθ' Ἑλικωνιάδων
βαθεῖαν . . . ἐρευνᾷ σοφίας ὁδόν (fr. 52h. 15-20).

'I pray to Mnemosyne, the fair-robed daughter of Uranus, and to her daughters to grant me rich resource. Blind are the wits of any man who searches for the rich path of wisdom without the Heliconians [the Muses].' By *sophia*, 'wisdom', Pindar refers to the skill of the poet, a usage which he was ready to take over from his predecessors since it matched his concept of his art; whether we translate by 'wisdom' or by 'poetic skill', the word connotes both.

The poet, especially if he has to compose dozens of poems on a single topic, the victory of the successful athlete, must be inventive, and here too the Muse lends her aid:

Μοῖσα δ' οὕτω ποι παρέ-
στα μοι νεοσίγαλον εὑρόντι τρόπον
Δωρίῳ φωνὰν ἐναρμόξαι πεδίλῳ
ἀγλαόκωμον (*Ol.* 3.4-6).

'For this purpose the Muse somehow stood by me when I found a bright new fashion of fitting the voice of the glorious triumph-song to the Dorian rhythm.' Pindar like earlier poets emphasises the newness of his product:

αἴνει δὲ παλαιὸν μὲν οἶνον, ἄνθεα δ' ὕμνων
νεωτέρων (*Ol.* 9.48-9).

'Praise an old wine but the flowers of new hymns.' 'New' gates have been thrown wide for the dithyramb (70b. 4–5 as supplemented by Grenfell and Hunt). He prays for powers of invention:

εἴην εὑρησιεπὴς ἀναγεῖσθαι
πρόσφορος ἐν Μοισᾶν δίφρῳ·
τόλμα δὲ καὶ ἀμφιλαφὴς δύναμις
ἕσποιτο (*Ol.* 9.80-3).

'May I be a finder of words so as to ride forward aptly in the Muses' chariot; and may daring and wide-embracing power attend me.' Here as in the third *Olympian* the verb 'find' will not denote chance discovery but painstaking invention; Aristophanes expressed the concept well when he made Dionysus pine for something *parakekinduneumenon* (*Frogs* 99), something over which a risk has been taken.

Like Sappho, Pindar felt that the goodwill of the Graces was also of importance (*Nem.* 4.6–8, 9.54). His fourteenth *Olympian* takes the form of a short hymn to them, since Orchomenus, the home of the victor, was a centre of their worship:

ὦ λιπαρᾶς ἀοίδιμοι βασίλειαι
Χάριτες Ἐρχομενοῦ. . .
κλῦτ᾽, ἐπεὶ εὔχομαι · σὺν γὰρ ὑμῖν τά <τε> τερπνὰ καὶ
τὰ γλυκέ᾽ ἄνεται πάντα βροτοῖς,
εἰ σοφός, εἰ καλός, εἴ τις ἀγλαὸς ἀνήρ (3-7).

'Graces of gleaming Orchomenus, queens of song, . . . hear me, since I pray to you: for with your help all that is pleasant and sweet is accomplished for mortals, whether a man be skilled in song or handsome or glorious.'

A theme to which he often reverts is inborn ability. We have seen that in his view successful athletes have it (above, p. 65), and the poet needs it no less:

σοφὸς ὁ πολλὰ εἰδὼς φυᾷ ·
μαθόντες δὲ λάβροι
παγγλωσσίᾳ κόρακες ὡς ἄκραντα γαρύετον
Διὸς πρὸς ὄρνιχα θεῖον (*Ol.* 2.86-8).

'The poet is he who knows many things by nature; those who have had to learn are wild in their babbling and like a pair of crows chatter idly against the holy bird of Zeus.' Here the contrast is between the one who is *sophos*, 'wise, a skilled poet, a true poet', and the unfortunates labelled *mathontes*, 'the learners', crows as against the Theban eagle. In the first *Pythian* Pindar says simply that poets (*sophoi*), warriors and orators have their powers *ek theōn*, 'from the gods' (41–2: cf. *Ol.* 9.28–9).

Some of Pindar's most attractive poetry is devoted to the praise of choral song. The best-known example is his address to 'the golden lyre', which forms the prelude of his first *Pythian*:

χρυσέα φόρμιγξ, Ἀπόλλωνος καὶ ἰοπλοκάμων
σύνδικον Μοισᾶν κτέανον · τᾶς ἀκούει
　μὲν βάσις ἀγλαΐας ἀρχά,
πείθονται δ᾽ ἀοιδοὶ σάμασιν
ἁγησιχόρων ὁπόταν προοιμίων
　ἀμβολὰς τεύχῃς ἐλελιζομένα.
καὶ τὸν αἰχματὰν κεραυνὸν σβεννύεις　　　5
αἰενάου πυρός. εὕδει δ᾽ ἀνὰ σκάπτῳ Διὸς αἰετός, ὠκεῖ-
αν πτέρυγ᾽ ἀμφοτέρωθεν χαλάξαις,

ἀρχὸς οἰωνῶν, κελαινῶπιν δ᾽ ἐπί οἱ νεφέλαν
ἀγκύλῳ κρατί, γλεφάρων ἁδὺ κλάϊ-

θρον, κατέχευας· ὁ δὲ κνώσσων
ὑγρὸν νῶτον αἰωρεῖ, τεαῖς
ῥιπαῖσι κατασχόμενος (1-10).

'Golden lyre, rightful possession of Apollo and the violet-haired Muses, you are heeded by the dancer's step, that commencement of celebration, and your notes are obeyed by singers when with your throbbing you fashion the opening for the preludes that lead off the choral dance. You quench even the everflowing fire of the warrior thunderbolt; and on the sceptre of Zeus the eagle sleeps, drooping his swift wings on both sides, lord of birds, when you pour a dark cloud over his curving head, a sweet closing of his eyelids; and as he slumbers he heaves his supple back, captivated by your rhythms.' Even Ares and the other gods are soothed, thanks to the *sophia*, the musical skill, of Apollo and the Muses. The lyre is Pindar's symbol for all the arts over which the Muses preside:

ὅσσα δὲ μὴ πεφίληκε Ζεύς, ἀτύζονται βοὰν
Πιερίδων ἀΐοντα (13-14);

'and everything that Zeus does not love is alarmed to hear the voice of the Pierians'. Pindar is composing celebratory choral song, and its three important elements are those which he mentions, the playing of the lyre, the dancing of the choir and their singing voices. He subordinates the last two to the first: the lyre indeed is 'golden', as being the possession of gods; Sappho had called it 'divine'.

Pindar speaks in his third *Pythian* of the magic spell cast by song, wishing that Chiron the centaur were still alive, so that the poet's honey-voiced hymns might put a *philtron*, a charm, on his heart and persuade him to send a healer to cure Hieron; elsewhere he uses the verb *thelgō*, 'enchant', of the effect of song. His tongue can be heard even by the dead relatives of the victor (e.g. *Nem.* 4. 85–6).

If song has magic power it is also dangerous in that it can mislead by its very attractiveness. In the first *Olympian*, talking of the false version of the myth of Tantalus, he says

δεδαιδαλμένοι ψεύδεσι ποικίλοις
ἐξαπατῶντι μῦθοι (29).

'Tales decked out with elaborate lies are deceptive.' The words which follow immediately show that he is thinking of poetry:

Χάρις δ', ἅπερ ἅπαντα τεύχει τὰ μείλιχα θνατοῖς,
ἐπιφέροισα τιμὰν καὶ ἄπιστον ἐμήσατο πιστὸν
ἔμμεναι τὸ πολλάκις·

ἁμέραι δ' ἐπίλοιποι
μάρτυρες σοφώτατοι (30-4).

'The Grace, who fashions all gentle things for mortals, confers honour and so contrives that often what is beyond belief is believable; but the days that are to come are the wisest witnesses.' In the seventh *Nemean* he mentions Homer in this connection: Odysseus, he says, would not have been awarded the armour of Achilles if he had been seen in his true colours:

ἐγὼ δὲ πλέον' ἔλπομαι
λόγον 'Οδυσσέος ἢ πάθαν
διὰ τὸν ἁδυεπῆ γενέσθ' "Ομηρον·
ἐπεὶ ψεύδεσί οἱ ποτανᾷ <τε> μαχανᾷ
σεμνὸν ἔπεστί τι· σοφία
δὲ κλέπτει παράγοισα μύθοις. τυφλὸν δ' ἔχει
ἦτορ ὅμιλος ἀνδρῶν ὁ πλεῖστος (20-4).

'But I think that the praise of Odysseus was greater than his sufferings, thanks to sweet-voiced Homer. For there is a majesty on his [Homer's] lies and his winged skill: poetic craft deceives, leading men astray with its tales, and the great mass of men is blind at heart.' The *Odyssey*, in other words, has an august, almost sacred, quality that blinds its hearers to the truth. Truth was a theme to which Pindar often turned. He personifies her, making her daughter of Zeus (*Ol.* 10.3–4), and he prays to her as to a goddess:

ἀρχὰ μεγάλας ἀρετᾶς,
ὤνασσ' 'Αλάθεια, μὴ πταίσῃς ἐμὰν
σύνθεσιν τραχεῖ ποτὶ ψεύδει (fr. 205).

'Lady Truth, commencement of great excellence, do not make my good faith stumble against a rough falsehood.' One of his favourite images, his wish to hit the target, refers to his desire for accuracy, whether in the recounting of an athlete's exploits or in the telling of a myth (e.g. *Nem.* 6.26–8). Time is the final judge in the matter (*Ol.* 1.33–4, 10.53–5).

Pindar uses a dazzling array of images when talking of his art, and he sometimes moves disconcertingly from one to another: in the ninth *Olympian*, having stated that the victor is from the Locrian city of Opus, he continues,

ἐγὼ δέ τοι φίλαν πόλιν
μαλεραῖς ἐπιφλέγων ἀοιδαῖς
καὶ ἀγάνορος ἵππου
θᾶσσον καὶ ναὸς ὑποπτέρου παντᾷ
ἀγγελίαν πέμψω ταύταν,
εἰ σύν τινι μοιριδίῳ παλάμᾳ
ἐξαίρετον Χαρίτων νέμομαι κᾶπον (21-7).

'And I, setting aflame that dear city with fiery songs, shall more swiftly than proud horse or winged ship send this message everywhere, if fate has given me the skill with which I cultivate the choice garden of the Graces.'

One group of images reaches back to a time before Homer, who uses the word *oimē*, 'way' or 'path', as a straightforward equivalent for 'song': the Muse, for example, has taught singers *oimas*, the paths of song (*Od.* 8.481). Pindar can talk of

ἐπέων . . . οἶμον λιγύν (*Ol.* 9.47),

literally 'a clear-sounding path of words'; when speaking of the many themes that the island of Aegina offers the poet, he refers to 'wide avenues for the chroniclers' (*Nem.* 6.45; cf. *Isthm.* 3/4.19); a moment later he alludes to Achilles' killing of Memnon and says that singers of old discovered this 'carriageway' (*Nem.* 6.53).

Pindar develops the metaphor by various devices. He elaborates it, as when he says in effect that he has lost his way in the ode:

ἦρ', ὦ φίλοι, κατ' ἀμευσίπορον τρίοδον ἐδινάθην,
ὀρθὰν κέλευθον ἰὼν
τὸ πρίν· ἤ με τις ἄνεμος ἔξω πλόου
ἔβαλεν, ὡς ὅτ' ἄκατον ἐνναλίαν; (*Pyth.* 11.38-40).

'My friends, I have been whirled around at the interchange of roads, although I was going along the correct path before; or did a wind thrust me off course like a boat at sea?' The path of song may indeed be a sea-voyage: in the tenth *Pythian* he tells the story of Perseus and then returns to his praise of the victor as follows:

κώπαν σχάσον, ταχὺ δ' ἄγκυραν ἔρεισον χθονὶ
πρῴραθε, χοιράδος ἄλκαρ πέτρας (*Pyth.* 10.51-2).

'Check your oar, and from the prow swiftly thrust your anchor into the ground, protection against the hog's-back rock.' In the third *Nemean* he breaks off a digression by asking to what foreign headland he has diverted his voyage (26–7). Place-names may even be introduced: in the fourth *Nemean* he ends his myth with the words

Γαδείρων τὸ πρὸς ζόφον οὐ περατόν· ἀπότρεπε
αὖτις Εὐρώπαν ποτὶ χέρσον ἔντεα ναός (69-70).

'One may not pass to the western darkness beyond Cadiz: turn back your ship's sails towards Europe and dry land'; the straits of Gibraltar symbolised the furthest limit of endeavour (*Ol.* 3.44, *Isthm.* 3/4.30).

In the eleventh *Pythian* Pindar wondered if a wind had pushed him off course (39–40). The Muse can herself make 'the breeze of hymns' blow more strongly

(*Pyth.* 4.3) or direct 'a glorious breeze of words' on the victor (*Nem.* 6.29). His sending of a poem to his patron can be 'a flowing wave' washing along the rolling pebbles (*Ol.* 10.9–10). Conversely the songs of his girls' choir can bring calm after storm (fr. 94b. 14–19).

The metaphorical paths may be through the air no less than on land and sea. Pindar can speak of the victor as 'soaring on the splendid wings of the tuneful Pierians' (*Isthm.* 1.64–5); we noted a winged Muse in an invocation of Stesichorus. He is fond of the word *potanos*, 'winged': a young victor is 'winged among the Muses' (*Pyth.* 5.114); his own song is 'winged', thanks to his skill (*Pyth.* 8.34), and Homer's is a 'winged skill' (*Nem.* 7.22).

The eagle is 'lord of birds' (*Pyth.* 1.7, *Isthm.* 6.50) and a suitable symbol for Pindar himself. We have seen that he, true poet, is an eagle as against crows (*Ol.* 2.86–8). There is a similar passage at the end of the third *Nemean*:

> ἔστι δ᾽ αἰετὸς ὠκὺς ἐν ποτανοῖς,
> ὃς ἔλαβεν αἶψα, τηλόθε μεταμαιόμενος,
> δαφοινὸν ἄγραν ποσίν·
> κραγέται δὲ κολοιοὶ ταπεινὰ νέμονται (3.80-2).

'The eagle is swift among winged creatures: searching from afar, it suddenly seizes the bloody prey with its talons. Cawing jackdaws inhabit lower levels.' Pindar's manner, in other words, is elevated, and his aim is unerring, whereas rival poets are pedestrian, noisy and ineffectual. 'Eagles swoop even beyond the sea' (*Nem.* 5.21, with reference to himself).

A further development of the 'path' of song is the image of the Muses' chariot. It rushes to celebrate a boxer's victory (*Isthm.* 8.61); or the Thessalian nobleman who has commissioned an ode 'has yoked this four-horse chariot of the Muses' (*Pyth.* 10.65). Poets climbed on board in time past (*Isthm.* 2.1–2), and Pindar may himself ride in it (*Ol.* 9.81); in a paean he bids his singers 'Shout hymns, not travelling along Homer's well-trodden path but (riding in) the winged chariot of the Muses' (fr. 52h. 10–14). In a curious blend of realism and metaphor he asks the victorious charioteer, Phintis, to yoke the mules so that Pindar may set his chariot racing along the open road to his theme (*Ol.* 6.22–4). The image can be varied still further as when the poetry itself becomes a mulecart:

> ὦ Θρασύβουλ᾽, ἐρατᾶν ὄχημ᾽ ἀοιδᾶν
> τοῦτό <τοι> πέμπω μεταδόρπιον (fr. 124a).

'Thrasybulus, I send you this cart of lovely songs as dessert for your supper.' If the poet can ride in a chariot, he can also be an athlete:

> εἰ δ᾽ ὄλβον ἢ χειρῶν βίαν ἢ σιδαρίταν ἐπαινῆ-
> σαι πόλεμον δεδόκηται, μακρά μοι

αὐτόθεν ἄλμαθ' ὑποσκά-
πτοι τις · ἔχω γονάτων ὁρμὰν ἐλαφράν (*Nem.* 5.19-20).

'But if the decision is taken to praise prosperity or the strength of hands or iron-clad war, then let someone dig me a long jumping-pit from here: I have a light spring in my knees.'

Metaphors based on archery and javelin-throwing are among Pindar's favourites. He can use them as a way of describing poetic achievement: the poets of old shot forth (*etoxeuon*) hymns about boys (*Isthm.* 2.3); the Muse is keeping a strong shaft (*belos*) for him (*Ol.* 1.111–12): his tongue has many arrows (*toxeumata*) for the praise of the heroes of Aegina (*Isthm.* 5.46–7); the golden lyre has shafts (*kēla*) which enchant even the gods (*Pyth.* 1.12). The metaphor is more extensive in famous lines from the end of the second *Olympian*:

πολλά μοι ὑπ'
ἀγκῶνος ὠκέα βέλη
ἔνδον ἐντὶ φαρέτρας
φωνάεντα συνετοῖσιν (83-5).

'I have many swift arrows within my quiver under my arm, arrows that speak to the intelligent.' A moment later he says,

ἔπεχε νῦν σκοπῷ τόξον, ἄγε θυμέ · τίνα βάλλομεν
ἐκ μαλθακᾶς αὖτε φρενὸς εὐκλέας ὀ-
ϊστοὺς ἱέντες; ἐπί τοι
Ἀκράγαντι τανύσαις
αὐδάσομαι ἐνόρκιον λόγον ἀλαθεῖ νόῳ... (89-92).

'Come, my soul, turn your bow on the target now. At whom do we shoot, sending glorious arrows from gentle heart? Aiming at Acragas I shall utter words on oath with true intent . . .' So the hitting of the target becomes an image for the telling of the truth in his victory-songs (cf. *Nem.* 6.26–8, *Ol.* 13.93). Another elaborate passage occurs near the beginning of the ninth *Olympian*, when he tells himself to shoot from the Muses' bow at Zeus and Olympia:

πτερόεντα δ' ἵει γλυκὺν
Πυθῶνάδ' ὀϊστόν · οὔτοι χαμαιπετέων λόγων ἐφάψεαι... (11-12).

'And let fly a sweet winged arrow at Pytho: you will not be handling words that fall to the ground (if you sing of the wrestler Epharmostus).' The arrows are here assimilated to Homer's winged words.

The image of the javelin-throw is more often used to express Pindar's superiority over his rivals: the ninth *Nemean* ends with the words

εὔχομαι ταύταν ἀρετὰν κελαδῆσαι
σὺν Χαρίτεσσιν, ὑπὲρ πολλῶν τε τιμαλφεῖν λόγοις
νίκαν, ἀκοντίζων σκοποῖ' ἄγχιστα Μοισᾶν (54-5).

'I pray that with the help of the Graces I sing this feat of excellence, and beyond many others honour the victory with my words, throwing my javelin closest to the target of the Muses.' So in the first *Pythian* (42–5) and second *Isthmian* (35) he prays to throw further than his opponents (cf. *Nem.* 7.70–2).

The crafts of building, masonry, metal-working and weaving supplied other metaphors, although Pindar uses the word *tekhnē*, 'craft', of poetry only once and that in a highly figurative passage of a paean where he speaks of 'dedicating the oracle [of Tenerus] to the crafts of the Muses' (fr. 52k. 39–40). We have noted that he aimed for an impressive opening to his odes; he mentions this aim in what is itself a fine example:

χρυσέας ὑποστάσαντες εὐ-
τειχεῖ προθύρῳ θαλάμου
κίονας ὡς ὅτε θαητὸν μέγαρον
πάξομεν· ἀρχομένου δ' ἔργου πρόσωπον
χρὴ θέμεν τηλαυγές (*Ol.* 6.1-4).

'Setting columns of gold beneath the finely-built porch of the chamber we shall build, as it were, a marvellous hall; for when the work is beginning the façade must be made to shine afar.' As in the first *Pythian* 'gold' is the first word of the poem and connotes a divine grandeur; in Bowra's words, 'This is no building to be seen on earth.' In another striking opening Pindar declares that at Delphi there has been built *Puthionikos . . . humnōn thēsauros*, 'a Pythian victor's treasure-house of hymns', which shall defy the elements: its façade (*prosōpon*) shall with its pure brightness proclaim the victory (*Pyth.* 6.5ff.). Pindar is thinking here of the treasuries built by Greek cities on the Sacred Way at Delphi as show-pieces of their architectural prowess and storehouses for their dedications. In the third *Pythian* he speaks of poetry 'constructed by skilled architects' (113–14), and we have seen that he claims to have thrown wide 'new gates' for the dithyramb (fr. 70b. 4–5).

Pindar can be mason, building a *stēlē*, a memorial stone, whiter than Parian marble for the victor's deceased uncle, himself a victor in his day (*Nem.* 4.79–81), or setting up *lithon Moisaion*, 'a stone of the Muses', for the victor and his family (*Nem.* 8.46–7). But he can also boast of the superiority of his poetic creation to the work of a sculptor who might glorify an athlete by representing him in stone or bronze:

οὐκ ἀνδριαντοποιός εἰμ', ὥστ' ἐλινύσοντα ἐργά-
ζεσθαι ἀγάλματ' ἐπ' αὐτᾶς βαθμίδος
ἑσταότ' (*Nem.* 5.1-2).

'I am no sculptor, making statues that will stand motionless there on their pedestals.' My song, he says, will cross the seas from Aegina, spreading the news of the victory.

Weaving as a metaphor for devising goes back to Homer, but the 'weaving' of poems is first clearly attested in Pindar and Bacchylides. Pindar can weave 'a varied hymn' (*Ol.* 6.86–7) or 'a varied head-band' (fr. 179): the adjective *poikilos*, 'varied', suggests the different strands or themes that must be worked into the victory-ode. So a song sung in the Lydian mode is an embroidered (*pepoikilmenan*) Lydian head-dress (*Nem.* 8.15), and Pindar can say, 'I shall sing a sweet-tuned adornment to go with your wreath of golden olive' (*Ol.* 11.13). The Muse makes a garland of gold, ivory and coral for the victor (*Nem.* 7.77–9).

Adjectives compounded with *meli*, 'honey', are among Pindar's favourites: he often uses *meligarus*, which is Homeric, and *meliphthongos*, both 'honey-voiced', and his creations include *meligdoupos*, 'honey-sounding', and *melikompos*, 'honey-vaunting', both used of celebratory songs. His voice, he says, is sweeter than 'bee-fashioned honeycombs' (fr. 152). More surprisingly, his poetry may itself be spoken of as honey: in one of the paeans he says, 'My tongue loves (to pour forth) the choicest sweet honey' (fr. 52f. 58–9); he 'sprinkles with honey the noble city of the Locrians' in praising a victor from the city (*Ol.* 10.98–9); the praise-poem is 'this honey mixed with white milk . . ., a drink of song' (*Nem.* 3.76–9: cf. *Isthm.* 5.53–4, fr. 97). The image of the bee is differently used: it illustrates the progress of the epinician ode from one topic to the next: 'the choice song of triumph-hymns flits like a bee now to one theme, now to another' (*Pyth.* 10.53f.).

Other liquids appear: in the rich opening of the seventh *Olympian* the poet sends the victors

νέκταρ χυτόν, Μοισᾶν δόσιν, . . . γλυκὺν καρπὸν φρενός (7–8),

'liquid nectar, gift of the Muses, sweet harvest of my mind': nectar, as the drink of the gods, could appropriately be given to the poet by the Muses, so that the traditional phrase for poetry, 'gift of the Muses', is given new application (cf. fr. 74b. 76–8). Pindar ends the sixth *Isthmian* with the words, 'I shall give the victor a drink of the pure water of Dirce [the Theban spring], which the deep-girdled daughters of golden-robed Memory made to gush by the fine walls of Cadmus' (74–5). So a victor offers sweet cause for the streams of the Muses to flow (*Nem.* 7.11–12), and his excellence can be 'sprinkled with soft dew under the outpourings of revel-songs' (*Pyth.* 5.98–100). Likewise Pindar's own thirst for song may be quenched by the composition of the poem (*Pyth.* 9.103–4).

The tale is not yet told: images of fire and light are common; or the poet can hold up a mirror for the victor's exploits (*Nem.* 7.14). The images do more than add richness and excitement to the songs: they constantly draw attention to the lofty view which Pindar takes of his god-given art. Yet he is ready to talk also of the mercenary aspect of commissioned poetry: in the eleventh *Pythian* he recalls his Muse to the theme of praise,

εἰ μισθοῖο συνέθευ παρέχειν
φωνὰν ὑπάργυρον (41-2),

'since you made a bargain to provide your voice for a fee of silver'. Talking of the love-songs of earlier poets, he says,

ἁ Μοῖσα γὰρ οὐ φιλοκερδής
πω τότ' ἦν οὐδ' ἐργάτις ·
οὐδ' ἐπέρναντο γλυκεῖ-
αι μελιφθόγγου ποτὶ Τερψιχόρας
ἀργυρωθεῖσαι πρόσωπα μαλθακόφωνοι ἀοιδαί (*Isthm.* 2.6-8).

'For in those days the Muse was not yet greedy for gain nor a hired worker; sweet soft-voiced songs were not sold abroad by honey-voiced Terpsichore, their faces silvered over.' Now, he continues, poets must pay attention to the saying of Aristodemus of Argos, 'Money is man.' Terpsichore is represented as a madam exporting prostitutes, whose faces are artificially whitened to make them more saleable. The harshness of the image is relieved by the epithets given to songs and to Terpsichore.

Bacchylides invokes or mentions the Muses in most of his epinicians and dithyrambs, usually at the beginning. The fragmentary first epinician opens with the words

κλυτοφόρμιγγες Δ[ιὸς ὑ-
ψιμέδοντος παρθένοι,
Πι]ερίδες,

'Maidens, famous lyre-players, daughters of high-ruling Zeus, Pierians', and continues by requesting them to weave hymns. The fine poem for Hieron's Olympic chariot-victory begins by requesting 'Clio of the sweet gifts' to sing of Demeter, Persephone and the successful horses of Hieron (3.1–4), while the twelfth epinician uses a striking simile in the appeal:

ὡσεὶ κυβερνήτας σοφός, ὑμνοάνασ-
σ' εὔθυνε Κλειοῖ
νῦν φρένας ἁμετέρας,
εἰ δή ποτε καὶ πάρος.

'Like a skilled helmsman, Clio, queen of hymns, guide my thoughts now if ever you did before.' One of the dithyrambs begins by saying, 'Urania of the fine throne has sent me a golden cargo-boat from Pieria, laden with renowned hymns' (16.1–4). We notice that Bacchylides is more ready than Pindar to name a single Muse: Clio, Urania and Calliope all appear more than once in the fragments.

The reference to the Muses which opens the fifth epinician shows a subtlety of technique: Bacchylides tells his patron Hieron that he if anyone will be a good judge of 'the sweet gift of the violet-crowned Muses which glorifies him' (*iostephanōn Moisan glukudōron agalma*). The expression is resplendent in its compound adjectives: 'violet-crowned' is traditional, but *glukudōros*, 'of sweet gifts', is Bacchylides' own: he applies it to the Muse Clio and to Victory, here more boldly to *agalma*, 'glory': the sweet gift may be either the traditional gift of Muses to poet or the poet's gift of the poem to Hieron. The noun *agalma* is one of Bacchylides' favourite terms for a poem: it denotes an object which confers glory, honour or delight, and can be used of a gift given to the gods or of a statue.

The Graces may as in Pindar be linked with the Muses; they are asked to give glory (9.1–2), and they bestow honour on hymns (19.5–8).

The functions of the Muses for Bacchylides are the granting of immortality to mortal achievements (3.90–2, 9.82–7), the giving of delight by their sweet gifts (e.g. 10.11–13, 13.228–31) and, as in Homer, the supplying of exact information (15.47, 'Muse, who first began . . .?'). Bacchylides as praise-singer is concerned with the accuracy of his account and speaks several times of truth: a fragment doubtfully attributed to him calls Truth 'fellow-citizen of gods, sole sharer of their life' (fr. 57); the Muses confer immortality with the help of truth on mortals' part (9.85–7); truth loves to be victorious (13.204–5). He is concerned too with the newness of his poetry: it is difficult, he says, to find 'the gates of words unuttered before' (fr. 5.3–4); he must 'weave something new' for Athens (19.8–10). When he addresses himself as *euainete Kēia merimna*, 'much-praised genius of Ceos' (19.11), he probably alludes to the intellectual effort involved in composition; Fagles' 'genius' is a more apt translation than Jebb's 'fantasy'; Bacchylides' contemporary, the philosopher Empedocles, used the word of his own thinking.

In speaking of his relationship to the Muses Bacchylides can use the same proud term as Pindar, calling himself

Μουσᾶν . . . ἰοβλεφάρων θεῖος προφάτας (9.3),

'the divine spokesman of the violet-eyed Muses'. The poet is set apart from other men, according to lines doubtfully ascribed to him:

οὐ γὰρ ἐν μέσοισι κεῖται
δῶρα δυσμάχητα Μοισᾶν
τὠπιτυχόντι φέρειν (fr. 55 = *PMG* 959).

'For the keenly-contested gifts of the Muses are not available to all, for anyone to carry off.' He also uses a traditional term which Pindar seems to have avoided, describing himself to Hieron as

χρυσάμπυκος Οὐρανίας
κλεινὸς θεράπων (5.13-14),

'glorious servant of Urania with her gold headband'. If proof were needed that *therapōn*, 'servant', does not signify a humble position, the adjective 'glorious' supplies it. The words 'servant of the Pierians' appear in fragment 63, which may be by Bacchylides. He certainly calls Hesiod the *propolos*, 'attendant', of the sweet Muses (5.191–3); the word, like *prophatas*, has religious associations.

Bacchylides' images for the poet and his craft have a strong resemblance to Pindar's, and it must be emphasised that we can rarely say which of the two is indebted to the other. We have met some of his images already: the poem is a voyage with Clio at the helm (12.1–4), apt choice for an Aeginetan victor, since Aegina was famous for its naval power; Urania sends 'a cargo-boat full of hymns' (16.1–4); song is the 'gift' of the Muses (3.3, 5.4, fr. 55.2); they 'weave' hymns (5.9, 19.8). The poet searches for 'gates of words' (fr. 5.3); but even if we take *agalma*, 'glory', to suggest also a statue, images from the crafts are less common than in Pindar.

He makes impressive use of the 'paths' of song: a dithyramb for the Athenians begins,

πάρεστι μυρία κέλευθος
ἀμβροσίων μελέων,
ὅς ἂν παρὰ Πιερίδων λά-
χησι δῶρα Μουσᾶν (19.1-4).

'A thousand paths of ambrosial songs lie open for the man who gets gifts from the Pierian Muses.' In the fifth epinician a splendid passage on the flight of the eagle, for whom mountains and sea form no barrier, leads into the words,

τὼς νῦν καὶ <ἐ>μοὶ μυρία πάντᾳ κέλευθος
ὑμετέραν ἀρετὰν
ὑμνεῖν (31-3).

'Even so I too now have a thousand paths in all directions to sing of your excellence.' The opening of Pindar's fourth *Isthmian* is very similar, but we cannot say who is the debtor. The Muse is charioteer in the fifth epinician, where after the long myth Bacchylides reverts to praise of the victor:

λευκώλενε Καλλιόπα,
στᾶσον εὐποίητον ἅρμα
αὐτοῦ (176-8).

'White-armed Calliope, stop your well-made chariot here.' Bacchylides is himself the charioteer in the tenth epinician, in which the image is again used to change the direction of a poem:

τί μακρὰν γ[λ]ῶ[σ]σαν ἰθύσας ἐλαύνω
ἐκτὸς ὁδοῦ; (51-2).

'Why in guiding my utterance do I drive far off course?'

If Pindar regarded himself as the Theban eagle, Bacchylides spoke of his own grace as that of 'the honey-tongued nightingale of Ceos', *meliglōssou . . . Kēias aēdonos* (3.97–8). These are the final words of his most important commission, and they form a perfect answer to Pindar's boast. If the nightingale is less imposing to the eye than the eagle, it is incomparably the finer singer. 'Honey-tongued' is used twice by Bacchylides, who elsewhere is himself 'the clear-voiced bee' (10.10). A poem can be 'the flower of the Muses' (fr. 20C. 3) or 'a golden feather of the Muses' (fr. 20B. 4): he is as fond as Pindar of exploiting the divine associations of gold.

Speaking of the poet's ability to confer immortality he says,

κάλλιστον, εἴπ[ερ καὶ θάνῃ τις,
λε[ί]πεται Μουσ[ᾶν. . . ἄθ]υρμα (9.86-7).

'Even if a man die, there remains in all its beauty the plaything of the Muses.' The poem is something that gives delight to Muses and so to sensitive men also.

Questions of borrowing, common sources and literary tradition have arisen in these last pages. Simonides, who was a generation older than Bacchylides (his nephew) and Pindar, may have influenced them both strongly, as the first poet to compose victory-odes. Although so little of his work remains, we can point to similarities in language: Bacchylides, for example, speaks of 'the dark blue cloud of death' and uses the striking adjective *khlōraukhēn*, 'with youth's bloom on her neck', both of which expressions are in Simonides. Pindar's *moira khronou* is like Simonides' *moira aiōnos*, 'the allotted span of life'. All three use *doru* in the unusual sense of 'ship'; *thalassaios*, 'of the sea', is common to Simonides and Pindar. Simonides has figurative terms of the type which the two later poets use commonly: the poet is a bee (593), the Muse a harvester (947a). His sayings on the subject of poetry suggest a readiness to think about the art which may have been equally apparent in his poetry. Pindar and Bacchylides may also have borrowed from each other, even although they were competitors for commissions: we should not forget Pindar's tribute to the poets of Ceos (fr. 52d. 23–4). Bacchylides may refer to the borrowing process in the lines,

ἕτερος ἐξ ἑτέρου σοφὸς
τό τε πάλαι τό τε νῦν (fr. 5.1-2).

'Poet from poet, both in days of old and now.'

*   *   *

σπένδωμεν ταῖς Μνάμας παισὶν Μούσαις
καὶ τῷ μουσάρχῳ <τῷ> Λατοῦς υἱεῖ (*PMG* 941).

'Let us pour libation to the Muses, the daughters of Memory, and to Leto's son, leader of the Muses.'

Note on Metre

The Greekless reader may wish to know how Greek metrical practice differs from English. Those who know Greek are referred for fuller accounts to D. S. Raven, *Greek Metre* or James Halporn, Martin Ostwald, Thomas Rosenmeyer, *The Metres of Greek and Latin Poetry*, both suitable for beginners, or to Paul Maas, *Greek Metre* (tr. Lloyd-Jones) and the works of A. M. Dale.

1.   English verse depends on stress. A Shakespearean iambic line will have five stressed syllables:

For this relief much thanks: 'tis bitter cold.

Greek verse depends not on a stress accent but on the 'quantity', i.e. the length or shortness, of syllables. Syllables which contain long vowels (η, ω) or diphthongs ($\alpha\iota$, $\alpha\upsilon$ and so on) are long; so in general are syllables in which a short vowel ($\bar{\epsilon}$ or o, short α, ι or υ) is followed by a double consonant (ζ, ξ, ψ) or by two or more consonants. A line such as Sappho's

ἔλθε μοι καὶ νῦν, χαλέπαν δὲ λῦσον,

elthe moi kai nun, khalepan de luson,

allows only one scansion, namely

— ∪ — — — ∪ ∪ — ∪ — — .

2:   Our earliest surviving poetry, that of Homer and Hesiod, is composed in the 'dactylic hexameter'. The name implies a line of six dactyls; but since the convention was that two short syllables were the equivalent of one long, the dactyl (— ∪ ∪) might be replaced, and in the sixth foot always was replaced, by a spondee (— —). The pattern then is

— ∪ ∪ | — ∪ ∪ | — ∪ ∪ | — ∪ ∪ | — ∪ ∪ | — — ,

and the line is repeated (a a a a . . .). Monotony was avoided by the regular use of a caesura, a break between words in the middle of the third or fourth foot, and by variation between the extremes of the entirely spondaic line and the line which begins with a run of five dactyls.

3.   An early variation of the dactylic hexameter was the 'elegiac couplet', in which a dactylic hexameter was followed by a shorter line labelled the 'pentameter':

$$- \underset{\smile\smile}{\smile} \,|\, - \underset{\smile\smile}{\smile} \,|\, - \,\|\, - \,\smile\,\smile\,|\, - \,\smile\,\smile\,|\, - \,.$$

This line opens like a hexameter, but at the caesura after two-and-a-half feet the listener's expectation is cheated, since the two-and-a-half foot pattern is repeated, so that the couplet has an internal pattern approximating to ab/aa. The creation of the couplet was an important step in the direction of lyric poetry: instead of the repeated line of epic (a a a a . . .) the couplet offered a line-pattern ab ab ab . . . : early elegiac poets felt no need to enclose the sense within the couplet, and enjambment, in which the sentence flows from one couplet to the next, is frequent; but the couplet had a long history as the medium for inscriptions on dedications or monuments and for gnomic utterances which relied on concision and the air of finality imparted by the form of the single couplet. The most important composers of elegiac verse were Archilochus (who used many other metres also), Tyrtaeus, Mimnermus, Solon, Xenophanes and Theognis. Simonides perfected the art of the epitaph: the most famous example, composed for the Spartans who died at Thermopylae, is scanned as follows:

− −	− −	− ‖ ⏑ ⏑	− ⏑ ⏑	− ⏑ ⏑	− −
o xein'	angel	lein	Lake	daimoni	ois hoti	teide

− ⏑ ⏑	− −	− ‖ − ⏑ ⏑	− ⏑ ⏑	−
keimetha	tois kei	non	rhemasi	peithome	noi.

4.   Next to the dactylic hexameter iambic verse is the commonest metrical form in Greek: it was used for most of the dialogue of Greek tragedy and comedy, but it too has a long history since from early times it was a medium for cult ritual and for proverbial expressions. According to Aristotle (*Poet.* 1449a. 24), iambics were closer than any other metre to the rhythms of conversation.

The commonest form is the iambic trimeter:

$$\underset{\smile}{\smile} \;-\; \smile \;-\; |\; \underset{\smile}{\smile} \;-\; \smile \;-\; |\; \underset{\smile}{\smile} \;-\; \smile \;-$$

with caesura after the fifth or seventh syllable:

⏑ − ⏑ −	− ‖ − ⏑ −	⏑ − ⏑ −
ekhousa thal	lon	mursines	eterpeto.

The trochaic tetrameter (classed by the ancients with iambic verse, since in both the short syllables come singly and not in pairs) gives a longer, weightier line:

— ∪ — ∪ | — ∪ — ∪ ‖ — ∪ — ∪ | — ∪ — :

— ∪ — ∪ | — ∪ — ∪ ‖ — ∪ — ∪ | — ∪ —
thume, thum' a | mekhanoisi ‖ kedesin ku | komene.

These examples are from Archilochus, who also used a couplet built of iambic trimeter and iambic dimeter for poems of personal abuse:

∪ — ∪ — | ∪ ‖ — ∪ — | ∪ — ∪ —
pater Lycam | ba, ‖ poion eph | raso tode?

— — ∪ — | — — ∪ —
tis sas pare | eire phrenas?

In time iambic came to be regarded as the appropriate metre for invective of this type, although Archilochus sometimes mixes his iambics and trochaics with dactylic lengths. Other iambic poets were Semonides (e.g. in his long satire on women), Solon (whose iambics and trochaics may have influenced their use in Attic drama) and Anacreon.

Hipponax gave a twist to this type of line by dislocating its distinctive ending: his 'limping' iambic takes the form

∪ — ∪ — | ∪ — ∪ — | ∪ — — — —,

as in

— — ∪ — | — — ∪ ‖ — | ∪ — — —
dos khlainan Hip | ponakti, ‖ kar | ta gar rhigo,

where the unexpected long first syllable of *rhigo* creates a bumping effect. His trochaics were marked by a similar limp:

— ∪ — ∪ | — ∪ — ∪ ‖ — ∪ — ∪ | — — — —
amphidexi | os gar eimi ‖ kouk hamarta | no kopton.

5. The composers of personal lyric favoured a short stanza form, usually of four lines. The earliest, Sappho and Alcaeus, living on the Aeolian island of Lesbos, use what are known as the Aeolic metres, the distinguishing feature of which is the choriamb (— ∪∪ —). Their favourite stanza forms were the Sapphic and Alcaic: the Sapphic has three eleven-syllable lines followed by a five-syllable, as follows:

1, 2, 3   — ∪ — ∪ ⦙ — ∪ ∪ — ⦙ ∪ — — —

4   — ∪ ∪ — —.

The first stanza of Sappho's prayer to Aphrodite runs

— ᴗ— ᴗ — ᴗ ᴗ — ᴗ — —
poikilothron athanat' Aphrodita

— ᴗ— ᴗ— ᴗ ᴗ — ᴗ — —
pai Dios doloploke, lissomai se,

— ᴗ —ᴗ — ᴗ ᴗ—ᴗ — —
me m' asaisi med' oniaisi damna,

— ᴗᴗ — —
potnia, thumon.

The Alcaic stanza has two eleven-syllable lines, one nine-syllable and one ten-syllable:

1, 2 $\overset{ᴗ}{—}$ — ᴗ — $\overset{ᴗ}{—}$ ⋮ — ᴗ ᴗ — ⋮ ᴗ —

3 $\overset{ᴗ}{—}$ — ᴗ — $\overset{ᴗ}{—}$ ⋮ — ᴗ — —

4 — ᴗ ᴗ — ᴗ ᴗ — ⋮ ᴗ — — ,

e.g.
ᴗ — ᴗ — ᴗ — ᴗ ᴗ — ᴗ —
asunnetemi ton anemon stasin:

ᴗ — ᴗ — — — ᴗ ᴗ— ᴗ—
to men gar enthen kuma kulindetai,

ᴗ — ᴗ — — — ᴗ — —
to d' enthen, ammes d' on to messon

—ᴗ ᴗ — ᴗ ᴗ — ᴗ — —
nai phoremmetha sun melainai.

Sappho and Alcaeus used a wide variety of Aeolic rhythms, e.g. the greater asclepiad, an extended glyconic: $\overset{ᴗ}{—}$ $\overset{ᴗ}{—}$ ⋮ — ᴗ ᴗ — ⋮ — ᴗᴗ— ⋮ — ᴗ ᴗ — ⋮ ᴗ — .

Anacreon preferred stanzas in which two, three or four eight-syllable lines (glyconic) were rounded off by a seven-syllable (pherecratean);

— — ⋮ — ᴗ ᴗ — ⋮ ᴗ —

— $\overset{ᴗ}{—}$ ⋮ — ᴗ ᴗ — ⋮ — :

— — — ᴗ ᴗ — ᴗ —
sphairei deute me porphurei

— — — ᴗ ᴗ — ᴗ —
ballon khrusokomes Eros

— — — ᴗ ᴗ— ᴗ —
neni poikilosambaloi

‑ ‑‑ ᴜ ᴜ‑ ‑
sumpaizein prokaleitai.

6.   The Ionian Anacreon also used stanzas in 'Ionic' metres. The basic Ionic unit (ᴜ ᴜ ‑ ‑) is less common than a unit labelled 'anacreontic', which is created by inverting the fourth and fifth syllables of an Ionic dimeter:

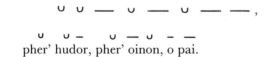

e.g.   pher' hudor, pher' oinon, o pai.

7.   The metrical systems of choral poetry are far more complex than those of personal lyric. The longest fragment of Alcman has a fourteen-line stanza, predominantly trochaic with dactylic elements. It is possible to see in the line pattern (ab ab ab ab cc dd ef) the triadic structure familiar from later choral poetry, the scheme of which depends on three stanzas, strophe, antistrophe, epode, strophe and antistrophe having the same metrical pattern. In Alcman's poem lines 1–4 would form the strophe, 5–8 the antistrophe, 9–14 the epode, the entire fourteen-line scheme being repeated for a possible total of 140 lines.

8.   Stesichorus and Ibycus certainly used this triadic structure, preferring a variety of dactylic lengths, which allowed them to incorporate Homeric phrases in epic-type narrative poetry.

9.   Simonides, Pindar and Bacchylides elaborated dactylic lengths (especially the hemiepes, — ᴜᴜ — ᴜᴜ —) by linking them with cretics (— ᴜ —) in the 'dactylo-epitrite' rhythm. Much variety is possible in the length and pattern of lines: a common type is

$$— \ ᴜ \ — \ \vdots \ — \ \vdots \ — \ ᴜ \ ᴜ \ — \ ᴜ \ ᴜ \ — \ \vdots \ —,$$

i.e. a cretic + a linking syllable + the dactylic unit + a final linking syllable.

10.   Most complex of all is the choral poetry written by Simonides, Pindar and Bacchylides in free Aeolic rhythm with a strong iambic admixture. Analysis is often difficult; indeed the Latin poet Horace, lauding Pindar's achievements, could say *numerisque fertur lege solutis* (*Carm.* 4.2.11–12), 'he rushes along in measures that are absolved from law'. But these 'lawless' rhythms are repeated precisely within the triadic structure, and the audience was helped to sense the rhythms by the melody and dance-steps of the choir which was performing the poetry. We must make do with only the bare text.

Biographical Notes on the Poets in chronological order

Eumelus: active *c.* 730, i.e. a contemporary of Homer and Hesiod; of noble Corinthian family. Composed epic poetry, e.g. history of Corinthian kings, and processional-song for Messenians for performance at Delos.

Archilochus: b. on Paros *c.* 680; father Telesicles a prominent citizen, mother said to have been slave. Went to Thasos, Parian colony, and fought against Thracians; cenotaph of Glaucus, to whom he addressed poems, found on Thasos (erected *c.* 600). Lycambes promised him his daughter Neobule in marriage but changed his mind: A.'s verses said to have driven them to suicide. Refers to eclipse of sun, probably that of 6 April 648. Died fighting in war between Paros and Naxos *c.* 640. Sanctuary of A. established on Paros: damaged stones of 3rd and 1st cc. give details of his life and quotations from his poetry. Composed iambic and trochaic verses, epodes and elegiacs. Considerable papyrus finds.

Callinus: from Ephesus; mid-seventh c. at the time of Cimmerian attacks on Ionia and Ephesian destruction of Magnesia; composed elegiac verse.

Tyrtaeus: composed elegiac poetry to spur on Spartans during second Messenian war (dated between 670 and 630); also verses about Sparta's history and constitution, e.g. *Eunomia* (Lawfulness). Some papyrus scraps.

Semonides: b. on Samos, led Samian colony to Amorgos; dates perhaps 650–600. Composed elegiacs, including history of Samos, and iambics, notably the long tirade on women.

Alcman: composer of hymns and lyrics for Spartan girls' choirs, perhaps between 660 and 590. Some ancient scholars said he was Lydian from Sardis, but evidence inconclusive; there was a tradition that he was a slave. Poems collected in 6 books. Extensive papyrus fragments of two maiden-songs.

Mimnermus: perhaps from Smyrna, though some ancient authorities said Colophon; born *c.* 670, died some time after the Lydian sack of Smyrna *c.* 600.

Composer of elegiacs: fragments cited from *Nanno*, named after a girl he loved, and *Smyrneis*. Famous for short love-poems and praise of youth, but dealt also with mythological subjects and history of Smyrna, e.g. wars with the Lydians.

Solon: famous Athenian statesman, archon in 594/3; first important Athenian poet. Composed elegiacs to urge capture of Salamis, to defend his political reforms and to present reflections on money-making and wider topics, and iambics and trochaics on political matters. Death later than Pisistratus' seizure of power in 561.

Stesichorus: b. probably in Mataurus in S. Italy *c.* 630, lived in Sicily at Himera, died at Catana *c.* 556. Said to have opposed Phalaris, tyrant of Acragas. Acc. to *Suda* his name was Teisias, S. being a nickname, 'organiser of choruses'. Composed long narrative poems on epic themes in predominantly dactylic rhythms, probably for choral rather than solo performance. Works collected in 26 books. Important papyrus fragments of *Geryoneis*, *Sack of Troy* and other poems.

Sappho: b. at Eresus or Mytilene on Lesbos *c.* 630. Names of her parents, three brothers, husband (Cercolas, a wealthy trader from Andros) and daughter (Cleis) are known. Said to have been an orphan at the age of 6, short, dark and ugly. Exiled in Sicily (date between 604/3 and 596/5). Perhaps speaks of her old age (fr. 58). May have taught poetry and music to local girls and others. Poems collected in 9 books. Important papyrus finds, but only one complete poem survives.

Alcaeus: contemporary of Sappho, b. at Mytilene *c.* 620 or 630. Fought against the Athenians for Sigeum before 600. Belonged to a noble family which competed unsuccessfully for political power against the tyrants Melanchrus, Myrsilus and Pittacus. Attacked them in poems, exiled three times, finally forgiven by Pittacus (590–580). Other themes were wine and love; wrote short hymns, e.g. to Apollo. Speaks of his 'grey chest' (50), so did not die young. Poems probably collected in 10 books. Important papyrus finds.

Ibycus: b. at Rhegium in S. Italy; went to court of Polycrates, tyrant of Samos (*c.* 535–*c.* 522). Said to have refused to become tyrant of Rhegium; buried there. Wrote narrative poetry, presumably choral, on epic themes, like that of Stesichorus, and love-poetry. Poems arranged in 7 books. Little survives.

Anacreon: b. at Teos in Asia Minor *c.* 570; when Persians attacked Greek coastal cities, sailed with fellow-Teians to Thrace, where they founded Abdera *c.* 540. Like Ibycus, invited to Polycrates' court in Samos; after P.'s murder, taken to Athens by Hipparchus, brother of tyrant Hippias. May have gone to Thessaly after Hipparchus' assassination in 514; statue on acropolis. Wrote personal lyric on love and wine and some elegiacs and satire; may have composed partheneia. Poems probably arranged in 5 books. Few papyrus finds.

Xenophanes: b. at Colophon in Asia Minor *c.* 570. When aged 25, began 67 years of travel in Greek world (fr. 8). Lived in Zancle, Catana and perhaps Syracuse in Sicily, perhaps also in Elea in S. W. Italy; d. in 478 or later. Critic of morals and religion. Wrote *Silloi* (Lampoons) in at least 5 books, *Parodiai*, *Foundation of Colophon*, *Colonisation of Elea*, probably all in hexameters like his philosophical writing, also elegiacs and iambics.

Phocylides: from Miletus, probably mid-sixth c. Wrote *Gnomai* (Maxims) in short hexameter poems and perhaps epigrams in elegiac couplets.

Demodocus: from island of Leros, probably also mid-sixth c. One or two epigrams and a trochaic line survive.

Theognis: of Megara, perhaps *c.* 550 to *c.* 480 (but West dates his poems *c.* 640–600). Almost 1400 lines of elegiacs (300–400 poems) survive in mss. under his name: some critics regard them as anthology from various poets of seventh to fifth cc., finding genuine T. for certain only in poems addressed to Cyrnus; according to others, T. deliberately quoted earlier poets, sometimes to revise them; or the compilers of T.'s poems mistakenly included the work of others. Writes from viewpoint of aristocrat appalled at rise to power of merchants and peasants, indignant at loss of farmlands. Composed paederastic poetry (1231–1389), maxims, exhortations and elegy *The Siege of Syracuse*. Text in some 50 mss., complemented by one papyrus and two ostraca.

Hipponax: b. in Ephesus; after banishment lived in Clazomenae in second half of sixth c. Famous for invectives against Chian sculptor, Bupalus. Fragments mostly colloquial verses in 'limping' iambics, with scraps of epodes, trochaics and hexameters. Works collected in 2 or 3 books. Papyrus finds doubled the amount surviving in quotation.

Simonides: b. on Ceos in 556; like Anacreon, summoned to Athens by Hipparchus (527–514) to grace the tyranny; lived in Thessaly at courts of Aleuadae and Scopadae. Probably back in Athens during Persian Wars, for which he composed famous epitaphs and commemorative poems. Moved to Sicily: friend of Hieron of Syracuse; said to have prevented war between him and Theron of Acragas; d. in 468, buried in Acragas. Noted for his choral poetry (victory-odes, dirges, paeans, dithyrambs above all—56 victories in contests are recorded) as well as epitaphs and epigrams. Some papyrus finds, mostly very tattered. (Mary Renault reconstructs the first half of his career in *The Praise Singer*.)

Lasus: b. at Hermione in Argolid soon after 550; rival of Simonides, with whom he was at Hipparchus' court in Athens. Wrote hymns and dithyrambs with musical innovations, helped to introduce dithyrambic contests at Athens. Hardly anything survives.

Tynnichus: from Chalcis; *c.* 500 wrote highly praised paean, now lost.

Pratinas: Peloponnesian dramatist from Phlius, famous for satyr-plays, lyre-playing and musical compositions. Competed in Athens in 500/497, perhaps d. before 467.

Timocreon: pentathlete from Ialysus in Rhodes. Medized in Persian Wars and wrote invective against Themistocles after 479. Unfriendly exchange in elegiacs with Simonides. Wrote convivial songs.

Myrtis: Boeotian poetess, said to have taught Corinna and Pindar. Criticised by Corinna for competing with Pindar. Wrote poem on the Boeotian hero Eunostus: Plutarch's summary survives.

Corinna: Boeotian poetess from Tanagra. Late anecdotes make her an elder contemporary of Pindar; but no one mentions her before first c. B.C., and orthography of papyrus fragments shows that our text was not written till *c.* 200 B.C.: West argues for date between 250 and 200. Wrote narrative lyric poems on Boeotian themes, e.g. *Seven against Thebes*.

Pindar: b. in 518 at Cynoscephalae in Boeotia of noble family; learned poetic craft in Thebes and Athens. Commissioned to write choral poetry of all kinds by many cities and individuals from Macedonia to Cyrene and Sicily, notably by Aeginetans and by Hieron of Syracuse; earliest and last dated poems 498 and 446; d. in 438 at Argos. Poems arranged in 17 books: 4 books of victory-odes survive. Large amounts of paeans and dithyrambs discovered on papyrus.

Bacchylides: b. on Ceos *c.* 517 or a few years earlier or later; nephew of Simonides. Wrote choral poetry of all types except the dirge for patrons from Macedonia to Sicily and S. Italy: important commissions from Hieron of Syracuse 476–468. Exiled from Ceos for a time, lived in Peloponnese. Earliest datable poem possibly before 485, last 452. Works collected in 9 books. Extensive papyrus finds of victory-odes and dithyrambs.

Telesilla: lyric poetess from Argos; famous for leading resistance of old and young men, slaves and women of Argos against Cleomenes of Sparta after his destruction of Argive army *c.* 494. Composed hymns, mentioning Argive cults of Apollo and Artemis.

Lamprocles: Athenian, probably early fifth c.; composed famous hymn to Athena (2 lines survive) and dithyrambs; noted musician.

Ion: b. in Chios *c.* 480, lived in Athens also. Successful tragic and dithyrambic poet; composed elegiacs, various types of choral poetry, *Epidemiai* (probably on visitors to Chios) and memoirs. D. before 421.

Praxilla: poetess from Sicyon, mid-fifth c.; composer of hymns, a dithyramb and drinking-songs. Little survives.

Euenus: sophist from Paros, b. before 470, d. after 399; composer of elegiacs, hexameter and iambic verse.

Select Bibliography

Texts

The numbers of the poems and fragments are those used in the following editions:

M. L. West, *Iambi et Elegi Graeci* (2 vols., Oxford 1971, 1972), supplemented where necessary by E. Diehl, *Anthologia Lyrica Graeca* (rev. R. Beutler, Leipzig 1949, 1952)

D. Page, *Poetae Melici Graeci* (Oxford 1962)

E. Lobel et D. Page, *Poetarum Lesbiorum Fragmenta* (Oxford 1955, repr. 1963)

D. Page, *Supplementum Lyricis Graecis* (Oxford 1974)

B. Snell—H. Maehler, *Pindarus* (2 vols., Leipzig 1971⁵, 1975⁵)

B. Snell—H. Maehler, *Bacchylides*¹⁰ (Leipzig 1970)

Other important editions are:

I. Tarditi, *Archilochus* (Rome 1968)

C. Prato, *Tyrtaeus* (with commentary, Rome 1968)

A. Garzya, *Alcmane, I Frammenti* (with commentary, Naples 1954)

E.-M. Voigt, *Sappho et Alcaeus* (Amsterdam 1971)

B. Gentili, *Anacreon* (Rome 1958)

M. Untersteiner, *Senofane* (with commentary, Florence 1955)

D. Young, *Theognis*² (Leipzig 1971)

O. Masson, *Les fragments du poète Hipponax* (with commentary, Paris 1962)

A. Turyn, *Pindari carmina* (Oxford 1952)

C. M. Bowra, *Pindari carmina*² (Oxford 1947)

D. L. Page, *Epigrammata Graeca* (Oxford 1975)

Commentaries (in English)

D. A. Campbell, *Greek Lyric Poetry* (London 1967, repr. 1976)

D. E. Gerber, *Euterpe* (Amsterdam 1970)

H. Lloyd-Jones, *Females of the Species: Semonides on Women* (London 1975)

D. L. Page, *Alcman: the Partheneion* (Oxford 1951)

D. Page, *Sappho and Alcaeus* (Oxford 1955)

B. L. Gildersleve, *Pindar: the Olympian and Pythian Odes*² (New York 1890, republ. 1970)

J. B. Bury, *The Nemean Odes of Pindar* (London 1890, repr. 1965), *The Isthmian Odes of Pindar* (London 1892, repr. 1965)

L. R. Farnell, *Critical Commentary to the Works of Pindar* (London 1932, repr. 1961)

R. C. Jebb, *Bacchylides* (Cambridge 1905)

D. L. Page, *Corinna* (London 1953)

English translations

J. M. Edmonds, *Lyra Graeca* (3 vols., Loeb, London 1922–7), *Elegy and Iambus* (2 vols., Loeb, London 1931)

R. Lattimore, *Greek Lyrics*[2] (Chicago 1960), *The Odes of Pindar* (Chicago 1947)

W. Barnstone, *Greek Lyric Poetry* (Bloomington 1961, repr. 1967)

G. Davenport, *Carmina Archilochi* (Berkeley 1964)

M. Barnard, *Sappho* (Berkeley 1958)

S. Q. Groden, *The Poems of Sappho* (Indianapolis 1966)

R. Fagles, *Bacchylides* (with introd. and notes by A. M. Parry, New Haven 1961)

Criticism (in English)

C. M. Bowra, *Early Greek Elegists* (Cambridge, Mass. 1938), *Greek Lyric Poetry*[2] (Oxford 1961), *Pindar* (Oxford 1964)

A. R. Burn, *The Lyric Age of Greece* (London 1960)

R. W. B. Burton, *Pindar's Pythian Odes* (Oxford 1962)

H. Fränkel (tr. Hadas and Willis), *Early Greek Poetry and Philosophy* (Oxford 1975)

G. M. Kirkwood, *Early Greek Monody* (Ithaca 1974)

M. R. Lefkowitz, *The Victory Ode* (Park Ridge 1976)

H. D. Rankin, *Archilochus of Paros* (Park Ridge 1977)

B. Snell (tr. T. G. Rosenmeyer) *The Discovery of the Mind* (Harvard 1953), ch. 3–4

M. West, *Studies in Greek Elegy and Iambus* (Berlin 1974)

Surveys of publications

G. M. Kirkwood, *C.W.* 47 (1953) 33–42, 49–54 (1936–52)

D. E. Gerber, *C.W.* 61 (1967–8) 265–79, 317–30, 378–85 (1952–67), *C.W.* 70 (1976) 66–157 (1967–75)

Chapter 1 (Love)

K. J. Dover, *Greek Homosexuality* (London 1978)

S. B. Pomeroy, *Goddesses, Whores, Wives and Slaves: Women in Classical Antiquity* (New York 1975)

J. Boardman and E. La Rocca, *Eros in Greece* (London 1978)

Chapter 2 (Wine)

C. Seltman, *Wine in the Ancient World* (London 1957)
R. J. Forbes, *Studies in Ancient Technology* (Leiden 1965) iii 72ff., 111ff.
Page, *Sappho and Alcaeus* 299–310

Chapter 3 (Athletics)

E. N. Gardiner, *Greek Athletic Sports and Festivals* (London 1910, repr. 1970);
    Athletics of the Ancient World (Oxford 1930, repr. 1955)
H. A. Harris, *Greek Athletes and Athletics* (London 1964); *Sport in Greece and Rome*
    (London 1972)
M. I. Finley and H. W. Pleket, *The Olympic Games: the first thousand years*
    (Toronto 1976)
C. A. P. Ruck and W. H. Matheson, *Pindar, Selected Odes*, tr. with interpretive
    essays (Ann Arbor 1968) 52ff. on *Ol.* 7
D. C. Young, *Three Odes of Pindar* (Leiden 1968) 69ff. on *Ol.* 7
Lefkowitz 125ff. on Bacch. 3

Chapter 4 (Politics)

A. Andrewes, *The Greek Tyrants* (London 1956)
W. G. Forrest, *A History of Sparta 950–192 B.C.* (London 1968)
A. W. H. Adkins, *Moral Values and Political Behaviour in Ancient Greece* (London
    1972)
Page, *Sappho and Alcaeus*, 149–243
I. M. Linforth, *Solon the Athenian* (Berkeley 1919, repr. 1971)

Chapter 5 (Friends and Enemies)

J. Ferguson, *Moral Values in the Ancient World* (London 1958) ch. 4, 'Friendship'
L. Pearson, *Popular Ethics in Ancient Greece* (Stanford 1962) ch. 5, 'Justice,
    Friendship and Loyalty'
West, *Studies* ch. II, 'Iambus'
Lloyd-Jones 11–33
G. Nagy, *The Best of the Achaeans* (Baltimore 1979) part 3, 'Praise, Blame and
    the Hero'

Chapter 6 (Gods and Heroes)

W. K. C. Guthrie, *The Greeks and their Gods* (London 1950)
E. R. Dodds, 'The Religion of the Ordinary Man in Classical Greece' in *The
    Ancient Concept of Progress* (Oxford 1973)

D. G. Rice and J. E. Stambaugh, *Sources for the Study of Greek Religion* (Missoula 1979)
Bowra, *Pindar* ch. 2, 'Gods, Heroes and Men'

Chapter 7 (Life and Death)
Guthrie, ch. 11, 'The Orphics'
Rice and Stambaugh, ch. 5, 'Mystery Cults', ch. 6, 'Death and Afterlife'
P. Friedländer (with H. B. Hoffleit), *Epigrammata: Greek Inscriptions in Verse* (Berkeley and Los Angeles 1948)
E. Vermeule, *Aspects of Death in Early Greek Art and Poetry* (Berkeley 1979)

Chapter 8 (Poetry and Music)

R. Harriott, *Poetry and Criticism before Plato* (London 1969)
Bowra, *Pindar* ch. 1, 'The Theory of Poetry'
W. D. Anderson, *Ethos and Education in Greek Music* (Harvard 1966) ch. 1, 'Introduction', ch. 2 'From Pindar to Aristophanes'

Index of passages

General index

Abdera, 182
Acarnania, 241, 259
Achaeia, 150
Achelous, 151
Acheron, 33, 226
Achilles, 44f., 54f., 89, 113, 117, 119, 128f., 134, 148, 172, 173, 183, 191, 196, 201, 202–4, 217, 245f., 253, 254, 263, 278, 279
Acragas, 244, 281
Acrisius, 179
Admetus, 71f.
Adonis, 166, 200f.
Adrastus, 57
Aeacus, 182f., 196
Aegaeon, 201
Aegeus, 196
Aegina, 81, 182f., 196, 198, 274, 279, 281, 283, 286
Aelian, 152
Aenesimbrota, 159
Aenus, 172, 178
Aeschylus, 33f., 66, 196, 199, 244
Aesop, 109, 126, 130, 140f.
Agamemnon, 100, 104, 119, 128f., 175, 203
Agasicles, 187
Agesilaidas, 103f.
Agido, 157f., 160
Aisa (portion, destiny), 214, 250
Ajax of Locris, 55, 86, 105f., 172f.
Ajax of Salamis, 87, 173, 196, 263
Alcaeus: choice of consonants, 11, 171; heroes, 172f.; hymns, 149, 169–72, 175; imagery, 101–4, 170f.; love poetry, 10; Muses, 263; on poverty, 227; political poems, 39, 84, 99–107, 113, 122, 134, 264f.; symposium, 30, 226f.; use of myth, 32f., 106, 172f.; water and wine, 29; wine, 30–4, 39
Alcaic stanza, 31, 101, 170
Alcibiades, 82
Alcimidas, 244
Alcinous, 28, 119f., 122
Alcmaeonidae, 117
Alcman, 153, 184, 214f., 258f., 261; gods, 153–61, 214; imagery, 9f.; man's condition, 214; Muses and music, 257–9; partheneia, 9f., 21, 153, 155–61, 186, 187f., 200, 215, 257f.; personal lyric, 9; wine, 35f.
Alcmena, 75f.
Alexander, 52f.

allegory, 86, 100–2, 171
Alpheus, 67, 74, 191, 200
Althaea, 196
Alyattes, 70, 118
Amalthea, 227
Amarynceus, 55
Ammon, 181
Amorgos, 84, 140
Amphidamas, 55
Amphitrite, 195, 201
Amyntor, 75f.
Anacreon: appeals to gods, 173f.; choral poetry, 174; few political themes, 108; imagery, 21–3, 228; love poetry, 20–4; Muses and music, 264; on death, 227–9; Polycrates, 20, 108, 263f., 270; preaches moderation, 227; satire, 134f.; symposium, 30, 36–9, 264; water and wine, 29, 38f.; wine, 36–9
Anactoria, 15, 26
Anaximander, 99
Anchises, 4
Andromache, 168f., 203
Andromeda, rival of Sappho, 132f.
Antenor, 193, 252
Antigone, 201
Antilochus, 54
Antimenidas, 105
Antissa, 172
Aotis, 159f.
Aphrodite, 1f., 3f., 9, 11–13, 15, 16f., 18, 20, 24, 25, 26, 27, 36, 39, 52, 74, 148, 149, 154, 157, 164–7, 185, 194, 195, 202, 215, 240, 264
Apollo, 28, 55, 57, 66f., 69–72, 75f., 88, 149, 150, 152, 153, 163, 166, 168f., 170, 175, 176, 181–3, 187, 189, 191–3, 194, 196, 197, 198, 200, 201, 224, 253, 254, 258, 261, 270, 277, 287
Apollodorus, 162
Arcadia, 81, 169, 201
Arcesilas, 274
Archeanassa, 133
Archenactides, 207
Archestratus, son of, 25
Archilochus: coarseness, 6–8, 151; gods, 150f., 206f., 227; imagery, 5f., 8, 32, 93, 211, 236; love poetry, 5–9; man's condition, 205–12, 225, 235; metres, 4; Muses, 254f.; new approach to poetry, 4; personal relationships, 120, 127; political poems, 84–6, 144;